C0-AJQ-629

ESSENTIAL STATISTICAL METHODS FOR BUSINESS

ESSENTIAL STATISTICAL METHODS FOR BUSINESS

Edward N. Dubois

University of Northern Colorado

McGraw-Hill Book Company

New York   St. Louis   San Francisco   Auckland   Bogotá   Düsseldorf
Johannesburg   London   Madrid   Mexico   Montreal   New Delhi
Panama   Paris   São Paulo   Singapore   Sydney   Tokyo   Toronto

191574

519.5
D 815

This book was set in Times Roman by Automated Composition Service, Inc.
The editors were Donald E. Chatham, Jr., Charles E. Stewart, and
Madelaine Eichberg; the cover was designed by Scott Chelius; the production
supervisor was Leroy A. Young. The drawings were done by J & R Services, Inc.
Fairfield Graphics was printer and binder.

ESSENTIAL STATISTICAL METHODS FOR BUSINESS

Copyright © 1979 by McGraw-Hill, Inc. All rights reserved.
A major revision of ESSENTIAL METHODS IN BUSINESS STATISTICS, copyright
© 1964 by McGraw-Hill, Inc. All rights reserved.
Printed in the United States of America. No part of this publication may be reproduced,
stored in a retrieval system, or transmitted, in any form or by any means, electronic,
mechanical, photocopying, recording, or otherwise, without the prior written permission
of the publisher.

1234567890   FGRFGR   7832109

Library of Congress Cataloging in Publication Data

Dubois, Edward N
  Essential statistical methods for business.

  Edition of 1964 published under title: Essential
methods in business statistics.
  Includes index.
  1. Statistics.   2. Commercial statistics.
I. Title.
HA29.D8   1979   519.5   78-23241
ISBN 0-07-017889-5

To
Jean Hall Dubois

CONTENTS

Part 2 Statistical Description of Quantitative Data

Part 3   Statistical Inference

Part 5   The Analysis of Data Classified Through Time

PREFACE

The title of this book explains its basic objective. The book is conceived and designed to be a clear, concise discussion of the *essential statistical methods* in use today in business and economics. The emphasis is on the methods themselves and their proper use. Theoretical background is included only to the extent needed for the proper understanding and application of the methods. The approach is nonmathematical, although some familiarity with the use of symbolic notation and elementary algebra is helpful in mastering the material presented.

The book covers all the basic statistical techniques used in business and economics. It begins with a brief introduction to data collection and to tabular and graphic presentation of statistical data. This is followed by a section on averages and measures of variability—the basic techniques of statistical description. Next comes a comprehensive section on probability and statistical inference (sampling), techniques essential to modern statistical applications. This section includes extensive material on hypothesis testing, as well as an introduction to such techniques as the analysis of variance and statistical quality control. Bayesian decision-making techniques are also introduced and illustrated. The sampling section is followed by one on regression and correlation, including an introduction to multiple techniques. The final section contains a discussion of the methods used in time series analysis and index numbers, areas unique to business and economics.

Although the book is written primarily for undergraduates, it would be useful to other individuals, particularly graduate students who need an introduction to statistical methods and to business managers unfamiliar with the field who need a clear basic introduction to business statistics. The text is set up to serve either as a terminal discussion or as an introduction to advanced statistics. The importance of statistical methods to the making of wise decisions in business has been stressed throughout.

A distinctive feature of the text is the inclusion of the Study Guide as an integral part of the text. Each chapter closes with its own study guide, consisting of sections on Concepts Worth Remembering, Self-Test, Questions to Think About, Problems, and Student Projects. This enables students to check immediately their understanding and mastery of the material covered in that chapter and is itself a learning experience. A glossary of terms is also included, at the end of the text.

The author is indebted to the Literary Executor of the late Sir Ronald A. Fisher, F.R.S., to Dr. Frank Yates, F.R.S., and to the Longman Group Ltd., London, for permission to adapt and reprint Tables III, IV, and V from their book, *Statistical Tables for Biological, Agricultural, and Medical Research*, 6th ed., 1974.

Edward N. Dubois

ESSENTIAL STATISTICAL
METHODS FOR BUSINESS

ONE

WHY STATISTICS?
AN INTRODUCTION

Let us begin our answer to the question, "Why statistics?" by first asking another question, "What is or are statistics?" The importance of statistics and of a study of the subject will be easier to appreciate if we begin by clarifying the meaning of the term. The word "statistics" may be used in either a singular or a plural sense, so that here we encounter our first confusion. In the plural sense the term is used to indicate a group of numbers or collections of numerical data. (The old cry "Get the facts" might well be rephrased "Get the statistics.") In the singular sense the term is used to represent a subject field in its own right. It differs from subject fields like history or chemistry in that it is a methodological field. In this respect it resembles fields like accounting and mathematics. Actually, statistics in the singular is the term used to describe the methods of handling statistics in the plural. Statistics is composed of both methods and the theory underlying and guiding the application of these methods. The theory of statistics is in many cases highly complex and mathematical; therefore, in this book, no attempt will be made to present it formally, only to include as much of the underlying theory as is necessary to the understanding of the methods and their application. For our purposes we shall define statistics as a body of methods for *obtaining* and *analyzing* numerical data in order to make better decisions in an uncertain world.

This definition calls for more explanation since it introduces several new aspects of statistics. The definition contains the phrase "obtaining and analyzing." Statistics deals with both these aspects of numerical data. Ingenious methods can do little to overcome the obstacles presented when the data are improperly collected, and properly collected data deserve the best possible tools of analysis. The statistician should be included in any study or survey involving numbers, from its very beginning, to make certain that proper information is obtained to answer the questions of the study fully

1

and completely. Too often statisticians are called in after the data have been collected, at a fairly large expenditure of time and money, and find they can do little to answer the questions of the survey with the data available. Even though the greater portion of this book is devoted to a discussion of statistical tools and their uses, the importance of having statistical advice in the planning stages of a statistical study cannot be emphasized too strongly. Methods of analysis, although technical in character, are general in application, and the same or similar methods are used for many kinds of problems. Techniques for collecting data are more general in nature but vary greatly in specific applications. It is this general character that leads many to feel that statistical advice is not needed in their application. Just the reverse is true; they must be adapted most skillfully to specific situations. If the proper kinds and amounts of data are collected, the application of the methods of analysis generally become quite straight-forward and mechanical. Good statistical advice prior to collecting data is a must to make this latter condition hold. This book will begin with a discussion of some of the problems of data collection. It is the natural starting point of a statistical investigation, once it is defined.

Our definition also states that the purpose of statistics is "to make better decisions in an uncertain world." Statistical results are not an end in themselves. The basic objective of modern statistics is to identify the variables which make this world un-certain and provide as much control as possible over them. Making a decision resolves itself into a choice among alternative courses of action. The consequences of choosing a particular alternative (making a decision) depend upon an unknown knowledge of what constitutes the real (true) state of the world. Statistics helps to identify the possible courses of action that are available and often to find or predict the true state of the world, and hence to judge the consequences of making a particular decision. Therefore, statistics helps one to choose which of several alternative courses of action is best to follow and in many cases indicates the risks of making a wrong choice in following a particular course of action.

One can now return to the question, "Why statistics?" and attempt to answer it. We study statistics because we live in a world which is uncertain and at the same time numerically oriented. We have a diversity of individuals and agencies that compile and publish numbers, the subject matter of statistics. Business and government are both great producers of numbers. Statistics is an instrument whereby more people (including government and business) become consumers of numbers. Although the future is always unpredictable and uncertain, statistics aids greatly in reducing the degree of this uncertainty where numbers are involved.

PART
ONE

GATHERING AND PRESENTING
NUMERICAL DATA

TWO

OBTAINING NUMERICAL DATA

LEARNING OBJECTIVES

The basic learning objective is to investigate the data-collecting phase of a statistical study. Specifically, you will become familiar with the following:

1. The phases of a statistical investigation.
2. The ways in which statistical data are classified.
3. The difference between:
    (*a*) Statistical description and statistical inference.
    (*b*) Primary data and secondary data.
    (*c*) Primary sources and secondary sources.
    (*d*) A census and a sample.
    (*e*) Personal enumeration and mail questionnaires.
4. The types of errors which can occur during a statistical study and how they are controlled.

INTRODUCTION

As stated in Chapter 1, obtaining the numerical data is as much a part of a statistical investigation as the analysis itself. Chapter 2 will discuss briefly the problems involved in this phase of statistics. Each new investigation presents its own unique collection problems, of course, so the discussion here will be of a general character.

For purposes of studying statistical methods it will be helpful to divide a statistical investigation into four interrelated phases. These are, in their normal order of occurrence: (1) collection (the statistician's word for obtaining data), (2) classification, (3) analysis, and (4) presentation. It will also be helpful to distinguish between "statistical description" and "statistical inference." The former term refers to the process of and techniques for summarizing the essential characteristics of a limited set of data, usually a sample. The latter term refers to the process of and techniques for generalizing on the basis of sampling about the statistical universe from which that sample was drawn. In the first case we analyze only the data of the specific set (sample), while in the second case we make statements (inferences) about the larger set (universe) from which the sample was chosen. Collection is the subject of this chapter, but a word of explanation of the other phases is needed first.

CLASSIFICATION OF STATISTICAL DATA

Classification represents in a sense a preliminary step in analysis; the appropriate form of analysis depends largely on how the data were classified. Several types of classifications are commonly used in statistics. These types need not be mutually exclusive, in that a given set of data is often classified in several ways. The basic types of classifications and the several terms used to refer to each are given in the following outline:

1. At a point in time
   (*a*) Numeric, quantitative
   (*b*) Nonnumeric, qualitative
      (i) Kind
      (ii) Area, geographic
2. Through time, chronological

Quantitative Classifications

If data are classified numerically according to their size, or magnitude (e.g., from smallest to largest), the classification may be described as quantitative or numeric. If one made a survey of the rents of three-room apartments in a given city and then classified these rent figures by five-dollar groupings from the smallest rent up, he would be setting up the commonest form of a quantitative classification, known as a "frequency distribution." Quantitatively classified data are probably of greater interest to the statistician than data classified in any other way. The descriptive tools of analysis for this type of data are among the most highly developed in statistics and deal with such interesting problems as the general magnitude of the data and the amount they vary in magnitude.

Qualitative Classifications

If data are classified by some nonnumerical, unmeasurable attribute, the classification is referred to as qualitative. If the attribute in question is a geographic area, the classification is referred to as geographical, or area. We shall illustrate briefly, again using rent data, to emphasize the point that a given type of data (information) may be classified in several different ways. Rental figures classified according to the city from which they were collected (e.g., New York, St. Louis, or Los Angeles) would be an example of a geographic classification. Rental figures classified by the type of structure they represent (e.g., house, duplex, or apartment building) illustrate a more general qualitative, or kind, classification. Generally speaking, the statistician has somewhat less interest in these types of data than in quantitative data since their descriptive analysis consists largely of counting the number in each class or computing the percentage in each class. However, some very ingenious types of analysis have been developed for certain types of problems involving qualitative classifications.

Chronological Classifications

Data are classified chronologically when the numbers involved are associated uniquely with a consecutive set of actual historical dates. For example, we might collect data on the annual rental income of an apartment building over a period of years. Such a series would represent a chronological classification of rental income, or what is more commonly called a "time series." Time series are of major importance in the field of economic and business statistics. The philosophy of analyzing a time series is essentially the same as for any other class of statistical data, but the methods used are unique and largely descriptive and therefore will be dealt with separately in Chaps. 17 through 19 (Part V).

ANALYSIS: A PREVIEW

Part II (Chaps. 4 through 6) of the text deals with the descriptive techniques of analysis and appropriate interpretations for quantitative data. Part III (Chaps. 7 through 14) deals with inferences made on the basis of quantitative and qualitative data. Part IV (Chaps. 15 and 16) gives an introduction to analytical techniques for problems dealing with several quantitative series simultaneously. As mentioned above, descriptive techniques for chronological data are discussed in Part V (Chaps. 17 through 19).

PRESENTATION: A PREVIEW

In Chap. 3 we shall attempt to show how the way data are classified affects the way they are presented. Formal presentation of the results of a statistical study may employ tables, graphs, or words, or any combination of these. The general form, or layout, of tables and graphs depends on how the data they present were classified. This will be illustrated in Chap. 3.

PRIMARY VS. SECONDARY DATA

Data used in a statistical study are termed "primary" or "secondary" according to whether they were collected specifically for the study in question. When the data used in a statistical study were collected under the control and supervision of the person making the particular study, they are termed "primary data." When the data were not collected under the supervision of the statistical investigator doing the study, they are termed "secondary data." The data from a sample taken to study what portions of delivery times for telephone directories are spent walking vs. riding or the data from the Decimal Population Census would be examples of primary data. Data on wage rates collected by the U.S. Bureau of Labor Statistics but used by the Personnel Director of the La Plata Pancake Mix Company would be secondary data to him or her. Actual large-scale studies may well involve the use of some data of each kind.

Primary Data

The chief advantage of primary data is their appropriateness. Since their collection is under the control of the investigator, he or she should be able to see that the information collected is exactly what is needed for the problem at hand. The investigator is in a position to define terms, to word questions, to select samples, and to direct the collection procedures in ways that will produce the desired information in detail. Good control over the collection procedures comes only at definite costs in both time and money, and therefore the chief drawback of primary data is the expense.

Secondary Data

Since secondary data do not involve the costs of collection, only the costs of obtaining them from a library or similar source, their use will save the investigator substantial sums when they are pertinent. Many good secondary data are available to the investigator doing a statistical study, but there are definite limitations to their use. Typical problems facing the investigator using secondary data include the timeliness of the data (i.e., whether they are sufficiently up to date), definitions of terms, conflicting purposes for collecting data (data on housing collected by insurance companies may be of debatable value to sociologists), and the basic reliability of the source.

Collecting Primary Data

Primary data may be obtained by personal investigation or through the use of mail questionnaires. The former method, while generally more costly, is in most cases far more satisfactory. The latter tends to give poor results because of the low number of questionnaires returned. Good use of mail questionnaires does occur in some situations, by the federal government, for example, in certain census taking, where completion of the questionnaire is required by law. Even in such cases, follow-up by personal interviewers is necessary to get total coverage. The fact still remains, however, that in general mail questionnaires give poor results. On the other hand, although the hiring and training of enumerators for personal investigation is somewhat expensive, it is usually money well spent, since the employment of well-trained enumerators ensures better coverage and allows for the collection of more complete and detailed information.

Secondary-data Sources

Secondary data may be obtained from two kinds of sources, primary and secondary. A source is considered to be primary if the source was its own collection agency. For example, if the Personnel Director of the La Plata, Pancake Mix Company got necessary wage data from the *Monthly Labor Review* published by the Bureau of Labor Statistics, he or she would be using a primary source. However, if the source does not do its own collection but is merely a compiling agency, it is a secondary source. Almanacs and the *Statistical Abstract of the United States* are examples of secondary sources. For most statistical work, primary sources are to be preferred. These generally give more detailed information, provide information on definitions and collection procedures helpful in evaluating the usability and reliability of the secondary data, and avoid possible errors of transcription. Secondary sources are often more general in character than primary sources and are therefore of greater value for general reference purposes and in making preliminary investigations as to kinds of data available in a given field.

CENSUS VS. SAMPLE

In theory, in a collection problem the investigator has a choice between making a complete enumeration (census) or taking a sample. In actual practice, few investigators have sufficient resources for taking a census. Experience has shown that the use of properly chosen samples (discussed in Chap. 9) is not only cheaper but yields completely satisfactory results with respect to the accuracy needed to make sound decisions. A major preliminary step in any scientific study, statistical or otherwise, is to define the problem carefully. In doing this for a statistical study one will almost automatically define a concept known as the "statistical universe," or "statistical population." This term is defined as all items (not necessarily people) that might be surveyed in a particular problem if a complete enumeration were made. As stated previously, the surveying of all items is unlikely, but a clear knowledge of the composition of the statistical universe is an essential prerequisite to collecting any information by a census or a sample, to make certain that the proper items for the study are collected and that time and money are not wasted in gathering unwanted information and that it is clear to what group (universe) inferences properly apply.

TYPES OF ERRORS IN A STATISTICAL STUDY

We shall close this chapter with a discussion of the types of errors to which a statistical study is subject: (1) sampling error and (2) nonsampling error. The latter type of error may be further subdivided into (1) unsystematic error and (2) systematic error, or bias. The latter two will be discussed here since their control is best exercised during the collection process. Sampling error, which is the error of the difference that may exist between a sample result and the true universe result and which is caused by chance factors in sample selection, will be discussed in detail in Chap. 10. Here it will be sufficient to state that random sampling error is measurable and controllable and may be made as small as is economically feasible.

Unsystematic Error

"Unsystematic error" is the term applied to human or mechanical errors which have no set pattern of occurrence. Examples would include such errors as the misanswering of a question or the incorrect addition of a column of numbers. Such errors are generally few and, as they have no pattern, will often cancel themselves out in a large survey. They will seldom have any major effect on the survey results. Many of them can be eliminated by careful checking of returned questionnaires or schedules (a process known as "editing") and the wise use of machine tabulation and other mechanical processing with built-in checking procedures, which can do much to prevent their occurrence.

Systematic Error, or Bias

"Systematic error," or "bias," is a much more serious type of error. Bias results when there is a persistent error in one direction (overestimation or underestimation) during the collection process so that the survey result is unrepresentative of the true result. Bias may result in sampling when the sample includes an overrepresentation of one segment of the population (the classic example of this case is the *Literary Digest* poll of 1936, which predicted a landslide victory for Landon in the presidential elections of that year, because it had an overrepresentation of upper economic groups, and thereby predicted itself out of business) or during a census, when people consistently overstate or understate some characteristic, such as income or age. Bias obviously has a definite effect on the final results of a survey, but unfortunately, the amount of its effect is generally unmeasurable. Therefore, bias cannot be controlled as sampling error is (i.e., by measurement), but must be controlled during the collection process itself, by measures designed to eliminate it.

Specific control measures must be applied for specific studies, but in general there are certain points during a survey where one needs to exercise particular caution. The first of these is in making up and wording the questions to be used. If a question reads, "You are in favor of the proposed sewer bond issue, aren't you?" one should hardly be surprised to receive a positive response. Certain topics involving taboos, such as asking a respondent his income, must be handled with extreme caution if the final results are not to be biased.

The selection of the items to be surveyed represents a second item calling for the exercise of caution. One must not fall into the trap of using a convenient list such as the telephone directory or automobile registrations to obtain names to interview since such lists may not be representative of the statistical universe one wishes to learn about. (Again, this is essentially the mistake made by the *Literary Digest*.)

As a final point of caution, one must check to see that a representative set of completed schedules of questions results from the collection process. This precaution is most important when dealing with mail questionnaires, where the rate of non-response is often very high.

A well-conducted survey should be reasonably free of bias, and as careful planning is the only way of controlling and eliminating bias, time and money spent at this stage represent a very worthwhile investment.

STUDY GUIDE

Concepts Worth Remembering

Define:

1. Statistical description
2. Statistical inference
3. Collection
4. Classification
5. Quantitative (numeric) classification
6. Qualitative (nonnumeric) classification
7. Kind classification
8. Area (geographic) classification
9. Chronological (time series) classification
10. Analysis
11. Presentation
12. Primary data
13. Secondary data
14. Mail questionnaire
15. Personal investigation
16. Primary source
17. Secondary source
18. Census

19. Sample
20. Statistical universe (population)
21. Unsystematic error
22. Systematic error (bias)
23. Nonsampling error
24. Sampling error
25. Editing

Self-Test

Multiple-choice questions. Circle the *letters* of the statements which correctly complete the questions. There may be from one to four correct answers.

1 The classification of statistical data termed "quantitative":
   (*a*) Represents data classified at a point in time.
   (*b*) Is also referred to as "numeric."
   (*c*) May be subdivided into "kind" and "area" classifications.
   (*d*) Is analyzed chiefly by counting the number in each class.

2 A "chronological" classification of statistical data:
   (*a*) Contains data classified through time.
   (*b*) Is also referred to as "quantitative."
   (*c*) Is analyzed by a body of techniques different from those used for other statistical data.
   (*d*) Is a special subdivision of qualitatively classified data.

3 The classification of statistical data referred to as "nonnumeric":
   (*a*) Is subject to statistical description only.
   (*b*) Has the subclassification "geographic" as a special case.
   (*c*) Is data classified on the basis of some unmeasurable attribute.
   (*d*) Is descriptively analyzed by counting the number in each class.

4 Primary data are:
   (*a*) Data from a primary source.
   (*b*) Data collected for a particular study under the control and supervision of the person making that study.
   (*c*) Generally less expensive to collect than secondary data.
   (*d*) Generally more appropriate than secondary data.

5 Secondary data are:
   (*a*) Data from a secondary source.
   (*b*) Generally less expensive to collect than primary data.
   (*c*) Data from a mail questionnaire.
   (*d*) Data collected by agencies other than the federal government.

6 A primary source is:
   (*a*) A source of secondary data.
   (*b*) Illustrated by the *Decimal Census Reports*.
   (*c*) A source which was its own collection agency.
   (*d*) More complete than a secondary source.

7 The term "sampling error" describes a type of error which:
   (*a*) Can be measured and thereby controlled.

(b) May be eliminated by taking a complete count.

(c) Is the result of chance factors in sample selection.

(d) Results mostly from using mail questionnaires.

8 The term "bias" refers to a type of error which:

(a) Results from the use of a sample.

(b) Can be measured by mathematical methods.

(c) Has a systematic pattern of overestimation or underestimation.

(d) Is particularly common when using mail questionnaires.

Questions to Think About

1. Distinguish clearly the difference between statistical description and statistical inference.
2. List and illustrate the ways in which statistical data may be classified.
3. What is the difference between primary data and secondary data?
4. Give an example of a primary source and of a secondary source and explain the difference between them.
5. List the possible types of errors in a statistical study, and explain what procedures are used to control each type.

Problem

1 You have been hired by the Alliance for Progress as a special consultant to help plan a survey of the agriculture of a small Central American country. Most available statistics for the country are out of date, and a new study must be made. Only a limited amount of funds is available for the study, but it is sufficient to hire a small competent staff to conduct the survey.

The agriculture of the country is quite varied. The eastern portion of the country along the Gulf of Mexico is, in its natural state, a tropical rain forest. Some of the land has been cleared and is farmed as banana and cocoa plantations. Mahogany and chicle are also commercial crops in this region. The uplands at the middle of the country raise a large variety of crops. The chief commercial crop is coffee. Small farmers also raise corn, beans, and cattle, some of which is for sale. The chief crop of the Pacific Coast is sugar, but corn, cotton, beans, and cattle are also raised, as well as bananas on irrigated plantations.

The country is relatively progressive, with above-average social equality for the general area. Even so, illiteracy is fairly high in sections of the country. Roads are only fair, but there is railroad service to all major sections of the country.

The purpose of the survey is to obtain reliable estimates of the quantities of the country's crops grown for both commercial and subsistence purposes, of the number of cattle in the country, and of the size and ownership status of the various farms and plantations.

(a) What is the statistical universe of the survey?

(b) Since data must be collected on a variety of items, design one or several schedules of questions to be used for the survey. Try to keep questions relatively simple so that they may be answered numerically or by checking the appropriate answer.

(c) Make a list of the basic terms that must be defined before the survey can be undertaken.

(d) Since primary data must be collected and limited funds prevent a complete census, should the data be collected by mailed questionnaire or by personal interview? Explain your choice.

(e) Illustrate with information that would be collected during the survey the various types of data classifications used in statistics.

(f) Indicate where the three types of errors that can occur in a statistical study might occur in this one and how they could be controlled.

Student Project

Assume that your college is planning to build additional resident facilities for the students and that you have been hired to do an opinion survey of what the students would like in these facilities. Define the appropriate universe, decide on the methods to be used in collecting data, design the necessary questionnaires, and indicate what procedures you plan to use to control possible errors.

Answers to Self-Test

The following letters should have been circled:
1 (a), (b); 2 (a), (c); 3 (b), (c), (d); 4 (b), (d); 5 (b); 6 (a), (b), (c), (d);
7 (a), (b), (c); 8 (c), (d).

THREE
THE ART OF PRESENTING
STATISTICAL DATA

LEARNING OBJECTIVES

The basic learning objective is to understand how statistical data are presented in the form of tables and graphs. Specifically, you will learn:

1. To identify a table and its parts.
2. To identify a graph and its parts.
3. The effect of how data are classified on tables and graphs.
4. The difference between:
    (*a*) Special-purpose and general-purpose tables.
    (*b*) Bar charts and line graphs.
5. The differences in use and emphasis of tables and graphs.

INTRODUCTION

The final phase of any statistical survey is the drawing up of a report to those parties interested in the survey on the results of the collection and analysis procedures employed during the survey. While certain aspects of statistical presentation have become quite standardized with time, there remains a large segment of the presentation problem in which great latitude exists as to the specific methods to be used, and the choice among these will determine how effective a particular presentation is. As this choice is not automatic, but rests primarily on "artistic" considerations, we have chosen to entitle this chapter "The Art of Presenting Statistical Data." However, we do not set ourselves artistic aims. As a matter of fact, our discussion will be confined to those aspects of presentation which have become relatively standardized. The illustrations included in this chapter are meant to illustrate *good* form, but might all be subject to arts of improvement.

Three basic methods are employed separately or in combination to present statistical information: (1) tables, (2) graphs, and (3) words. Our discussion will be confined to the more technical aspects of the first two.

TABULAR FORM

The basic form of a table or graph depends upon the way in which the data in question are classified. Tables and graphs appropriate to kind, geographic, and chronological classifications of data will be illustrated in this chapter. Tables and graphs used for quantitative data present special problems and will be discussed in Chap. 4.

Table 3-1 illustrates the basic parts of a table as follows. A table may be defined as an arrangement of numerical data in columns and rows. The column headings (see Table 3-1) are called the "caption," and the row headings are the "stub." The table

Table 3-1 Installment credit held by commercial banks in the United States, May 1977

Type of credit	Amount, millions	Percentage of total
Automobile	$37,910	42.7
Personal loans	16,180	18.2
Revolving	14,025	15.8
Mobile homes	8,123	9.2
Other bank loans	7,000	7.9
Home improvement	5,531	6.2
Total	$88,769	100.0

Caption ⟶ Type of credit

Stub ⟶

Body ⟵

Source: Federal Reserve Bulletin, July 1977, p. A42.

Table 3-2 Value of United States foreign trade by geographic regions, 1975 and 1976 (billions)

Geographic region	1975		1976	
	Merchandise exports	General imports	Merchandise exports	General imports
Africa	$ 4.9	$ 8.3	$ 5.2	$12.6
Asia	28.2	27.1	29.7	39.4
Australia and Oceania	2.3	1.5	2.7	1.7
Europe	32.7	21.5	35.9	23.6
Northern North America	21.8	21.8	24.1	26.2
Southern North America	8.3	8.8	8.4	9.3
South America	8.8	7.2	8.6	7.8

Source: Survey of Current Business.

title customarily gives the subject, place, and date of the data in the table. A source note, if one is required, is located below the table. The stub of the table illustrated shows that the data have been classified qualitatively. This table may be further classified as a special-purpose table since the arrangement in the stub (by magnitude) is designed to emphasize the importance of automobile credit in installment credit. General-purpose, or reference, tables are designed to be used just as their name implies and would have a stub arranged in a manner (e.g., alphabetically) which would allow quick discovery of a particular item.

Table 3-2 illustrates a general-purpose table and also a much more complex table. The stub shows a geographic classification of data, while the complex caption contains a chronological classification and a qualitative classification.

A table with a chronological classification in the stub is illustrated by Table 3-3.

Table 3-3 United States Consumer Price Index, annual averages, 1961–1976 (1967 = 100)

Year	Index	Year	Index
1961	89.6	1969	109.8
1962	90.6	1970	116.3
1963	91.7	1971	121.3
1964	92.9	1972	125.3
1965	94.5	1973	133.1
1966	97.2	1974	147.7
1967	100.0	1975	161.2
1968	104.2	1976	170.5

Source: Monthly Labor Review.

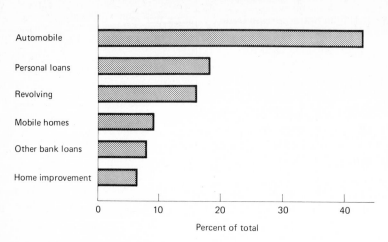

Figure 3-1 Percentage distribution of installment credit held by commercial banks in the United States, May 1977. (*Source:* Table 3-1.)

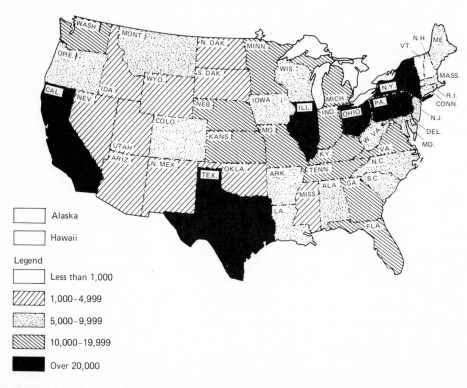

Figure 3-2 Railroad employment in the United States by states, 1976. (*Source:* Association of American Railroads.)

GRAPHIC FORM

Graphs and charts (the terms are used somewhat interchangeably) are pictorial representations of data. Each classification of data has its own typical form of graph. Kind data are generally presented in the form of horizontal-bar charts. Geographic data use maps for presentation, and chronological data may be presented either in a line graph or by vertical bars. Each of these is illustrated below.

Figure 3-1 shows the data from Table 3-1 presented as a horizontal-bar chart.

Like tables, graphs should have complete titles and source notes. In addition, one must be careful to label all scales on a graph. An essential on a bar chart is a complete scale, starting from a zero base, since the comparison is one-dimensional on the basis of the length of the bars and thus must start at zero to avoid distortion.

Figure 3-2 illustrates the use of an outline map to present geographically classified information.

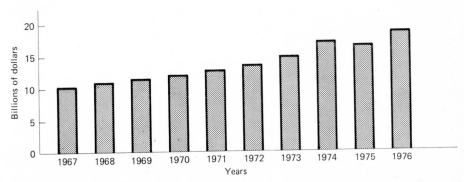

Figure 3-3 Railroad operating revenues in the United States, 1967–1976. (*Source:* Association of American Railroads.)

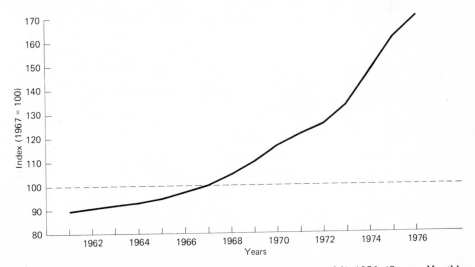

Figure 3-4 United States Consumer Price Index, annual averages, 1961–1976. (*Source:* Monthly Labor Review.)

The use of vertical bars to present time series data is shown in Fig. 3-3, and Fig. 3-4 shows the use of a line graph for the same purpose, with the data from Table 3-3. Vertical bars are generally used for more popular presentations and for shorter periods of time, while the line graph is used in analysis and for longer periods of time.

To be effective, graphs should emphasize simplicity and clarity. In tables, although these properties are desirable, they need not be emphasized to so great an extent. Tables are the proper place for presenting detailed information; the graph should be kept simple, so that it can most effectively make its basic point.

STUDY GUIDE

Concepts Worth Remembering

Define:

1. Table
2. Caption
3. Stub
4. Special-purpose table
5. General-purpose table
6. Graph (chart)
7. Bar chart
8. Line graph

Self-Test

Circle the proper letter to indicate whether the following statements are true or false.

T F 1 A table is a pictorial method of presenting statistical data.

T F 2 A table may be classified as "general-purpose" or "special-purpose."

T F 3 A table is an arrangement of numerical data in columns and rows.

T F 4 To be effective, a table should emphasize simplicity and clarity.

T F 5 A graph is composed of a stub, a caption, and a body.

T F 6 A graph is used for presenting detailed statistical information.

T F 7 "Kind" data are graphed in the form of a horizontal-bar chart.

T F 8 A bar chart must have a zero base and a complete scale.

T F 9 A line graph is used in the plotting of qualitative data.

T F 10 "Chronological" data are graphed as a line graph or in the form of vertical bars.

Questions to Think About

1. Explain and illustrate how the ways in which statistical data may be classified affect the form of tables and graphs.
2. Explain the basic differences in use and emphasis between a table and a graph.

Problems

1 The Federal Reserve Bulletin for July 1977 gives data on page A24 on the commercial and industrial loans outstanding held by large weekly reporting commercial banks. As of June 29, 1977, these banks held $15,246 million of loans to companies classified as durable goods manufacturing. Of this amount $2,416 million was to companies in the primary metals field; $4,804 million to machinery companies; $2,398 million to transportation equipment firms; $1,961 million to firms classified as other fabricated metal products; and the balance to firms classified just as other durable goods. Present this information in the form of a special-purpose table designed to show the relative importance of the various classifications of companies.

2 (*a*) Present in table form the following data derived from the *Life Insurance Fact Book '77*, American Council of Life Insurance, Washington, D.C., p. 21. The data are on the amounts of ordinary, group, industrial, and credit life insurance in force for the year 1976. All figures are in millions of dollars. The figures for the New England region are 69,322 of ordinary insurance, 59,319 of group insurance, 1,020 of industrial insurance, and 5,434 of credit insurance. For the Middle Atlantic region the data are 211,221 of ordinary, 192,525 of group, 5,229 of industrial, and 18,825 of credit insurance. Corresponding figures for the East North Central region are 235,683, 218,632, 6,734, and 23,378. For the West North Central region they are 100,676, 74,113, 1,324, and 10,078. Data for the South Atlantic region are 179,428, 147,214, 12,448, and 21,343. For the East South Central region the figures are 62,170, 50,642, 5,606, and 9,723. For the West South Central region they are 112,815, 84,479, 4,837, and 13,934. For the Mountain states the data are 56,033, 38,887, 400, and 7,858. Finally, for the Pacific states they are 150,324, 136,836, 1,577, and 12,996.

(*b*) What types of classifications have you used in presenting the data?

3 Present in table form the following data, taken from the *Life Insurance Fact Book '77*, p. 13.

In 1966 life insurance purchases in the United States totaled 23,950 thousand policies and amounted to $121,990 million, of which 10,131 thousand were ordinary policies amounting to $88,693 million, 4,055 thousand were group certificates amounting to $26,219 million, and the remaining were industrial life insurance purchases.

In 1971 total life insurance purchases in the United States had increased to 25,010 thousand policies, amounting to $188,811 million, of which ordinary policies were 11,281 thousand amounting to $132,130 million; 5,403 thousand were group certificates amounting to $49,407 million; and the balance were industrial purchases.

By 1976 total life insurance purchases in the United States had risen to 27,193 thousand policies, amounting to $321,167 million, of which 12,925 thousand ordinary policies amounted to $212,003 million; 8,168 thousand group certificates amounted to $102,791 million; and the remaining were industrial policies.

4 Present the data of Prob. 1 in the form of an appropriate graph.

5 Present the data of Prob. 2 on an outline map of the United States.

6 (*a*) Plot a divided bar chart of the data on the dollar *amount* of life insurance purchases given in Prob. 3.

(*b*) Plot a percentage divided bar chart of the data on the dollar *amount* of life insurance purchases.

(*c*) What conclusion can you draw from a comparison of the two bar charts?

7

Credit life insurance in force in the United States, 1957–1976

Year	Amount, billions	Year	Amount, billions
1957	$19.4	1967	$ 61.5
1958	20.5	1968	68.4
1959	25.0	1969	74.6
1960	29.1	1970	77.4
1961	31.1	1971	81.9
1962	35.3	1972	93.4
1963	40.7	1973	101.2
1964	46.5	1974	109.6
1965	53.0	1975	112.0
1966	58.1	1976	123.6

Source: *Life Insurance Fact Book '77*, p. 18.

Plot a graph of the data in the table above.

Student Project

Continue the project of Study Guide of Chap. 2 by laying out the possible tables and graphs which you might use in presenting the results of your opinion survey.

Answers to Self-Test

1 F; 2 T; 3 T; 4 F; 5 F; 6 F; 7 T; 8 T; 9 F; 10 T.

PART

TWO

STATISTICAL DESCRIPTION OF QUANTITATIVE DATA

FOUR

ORGANIZING QUANTITATIVE DATA

LEARNING OBJECTIVES

The basic learning objective is to study the special tables and graphs used to present quantitatively (numerically) classified statistical data. Specifically, you will become familiar with the following:

1. The array.
2. The frequency table and how it is constructed.
3. Class intervals, their correct writing, and their size determination.
4. Column diagrams and frequency polygons.
5. Frequency curves.
6. The properties of bell-shaped frequency curves.

INTRODUCTION

The analysis of quantitative data is of great interest in statistical work. The organization of these data in proper table form is the beginning point of such an analysis. The statistician is particularly interested in the general magnitude and spread of this type of data, and tables are designed to aid in evaluating these properties.

THE ARRAY

The simplest tabular arrangement of quantitative data is an array. This is merely an arrangement of the data in order of magnitude. Arrays may be in ascending or descending order, but for statistical purposes an arrangement in ascending order (small to large) is most common. Table 4-1 illustrates an array of this type.

The spread of the data from $74 to $108 can be seen at a glance in this array, but locating a single value to represent the general magnitude of the values of the series is more difficult. Such a value would appear to be in the low 90s. The tabulated illustration contains about the maximum number of items that can be effectively arrayed. A larger number of items would become very unwieldy and difficult to work with. For

Table 4-1 Monthly installment payments for 42 used automobiles (dollars)

74	83	88	92	95	100
75	85	88	92	95	100
78	86	90	93	96	101
79	86	90	93	96	102
79	87	91	94	98	105
82	87	91	95	98	105
82	88	92	95	99	108

Table 4-2 Monthly installment payments for 42 used automobiles

Monthly payment	Number of automobiles (frequency)
$ 71–75	2
76–80	3
81–85	4
86–90	9
91–95	12
96–100	7
101–105	4
106–110	1
Total	42

this reason, when the number of items becomes large, an alternative form of table, known as a "frequency table," is used. Table 4-2 illustrates such a table.

THE FREQUENCY TABLE

A frequency table consists, basically, of two parts. The possible numerical values of the items in the series are arranged in order of magnitude in what are known as "class intervals" and appear as the stub of the table. The number of items having a value within each class interval is indicated in the first column of the table as frequencies. In a frequency table the actual identity (value) of each individual item is lost. This loss is more than offset by the gains of increased compactness of presentation and new knowledge of the pattern of how the items distribute themselves. The general magnitude of the items, with a concentration in the low 90s, and their spread from about $71 to $110 may be seen quite readily.

Class Intervals

Since frequency tables are widely used in statistical work, an understanding of their construction is important. We shall begin this discussion with a consideration of the proper way to write a class interval. The main object is to make clear exactly where each item in the ungrouped (nonfrequency distribution) data was classified when the data were grouped or arranged as a frequency distribution. The following arrangement is one form of interval writing which should never be used:

$$10-20$$
$$20-30$$
$$30-40$$
$$40-50$$
$$50-60$$

Here the intervals overlap, and one could not be certain where the value 30, for instance, was classified, i.e., in the second or third interval. This problem is overcome by writing the intervals as follows:

$$10-19$$
$$20-29$$
$$30-39$$
$$40-49$$
$$50-59$$

It is obvious that the value 30 is classified in the third interval. Suppose that we now consider the problem of classifying the number 29.7 in the last set of intervals. One might argue that, since this number is less than 30 (the beginning of the third interval), it must be classified in the second interval. However, if the number is rounded to the nearest whole number, it will be rounded to 30 and placed in the third interval, with the result that we are again not sure where this number should be classified. An extension in writing the class intervals follows:

10.0–19.9
20.0–29.9
30.0–39.9
40.0–49.9
50.0–59.9

This order eliminates the problem, for it is now obvious that the number belongs in the second interval. A workable and widely adopted rule of thumb is to write the class intervals to as many decimal places as the data being classified, thus eliminating ambiguity and providing an indication of the precision of the data.

An alternative approach to the problem through the use of words is illustrated below:

10 and under 20
20 and under 30
30 and under 40
40 and under 50
50 and under 60

Such a system of interval writing is quite general and allows classification without ambiguity in all cases. However, it may fail to give an indication of the precision of measurement existing in the ungrouped data.

Determining Interval Size

A separate problem when dealing with intervals is determining the size of a class interval. Most people would consider all the intervals listed above to be of size 10. This result is obtained by taking the size of a class interval to be the distance between its lower limit and the lower limit of the next class interval. Whether this procedure is actually correct depends on whether the data being classified are for a discrete or continuous variable. A discrete variable is one which takes on value only at certain points along its possible range of values. Discrete data result from the process of counting and are subject to gaps or breaks. For example, a count of people in a room would be in whole numbers. A continuous variable, on the other hand, has value at all points along its possible range of values. Continuous data result from the process of measurement and have a complete set of values within the range being measured. The number of these actually observed depends on the precision of the measuring process. If the intervals listed above represent continuous data, they do truly run from the lower limit of one interval to the lower limit of the next (which is also the upper limit of the first) and are of size 10. If the data being classified are discrete but are counted in values very small relative to the total range of values involved (e.g., money, where the basic unit of count is the cent), they are usually treated as if they were continuous. Most distributions of truly discrete data do not involve intervals at all, but appear as follows:

Number of children per family	Number of families
0	
1	
2	
3	
4	
5	
6	
7	
8 and over	

CONSTRUCTING A FREQUENCY DISTRIBUTION

To actually set up a frequency distribution from ungrouped data generally involves a certain amount of trial and error since it may be that several acceptable frequency distributions can be constructed from a given set of data. To illustrate the procedure, we shall use the data given in Table 4-3, from which our earlier array (Table 4-1) and frequency distribution (Table 4-2) were derived. The order of Table 4-3 is some form of file order by code number or perhaps alphabetical.

Table 4-3 Monthly installment payments for 42 used automobiles (dollars)

Automobile number	Payment	Automobile number	Payment	Automobile number	Payment
1	82	15	86	29	88
2	87	16	79	30	79
3	91	17	88	31	98
4	93	18	88	32	92
5	96	19	92	33	91
6	100	20	95	34	78
7	100	21	108	35	102
8	95	22	105	36	96
9	90	23	99	37	85
10	93	24	98	38	94
11	87	25	101	39	75
12	82	26	95	40	83
13	74	27	90	41	95
14	86	28	92	42	105

Choosing the Size of Class Interval

The first decision necessary in constructing a frequency distribution is to choose a size of class interval. The following rule of Sturges, while not foolproof, often gives a good approximation to a workable size of class interval. The rule states that

$$i \cong \frac{R}{1 + 3.3 \log n}$$

where i = size of class interval

R = range (merely the difference between the lowest and highest values to be grouped)

n = number of items to be grouped

For our illustration we obtain the following:

$$i \cong \frac{108 - 74}{1 + 3.3 \log 42} \cong 5.4$$

This indicates that an interval of either 5 or 6 can be experimented with to find a satisfactory distribution. We shall try 5, because of its repetitive pattern in our decimal-number system.

Trial Distributions

The second choice to be made is the starting number. We can begin with 74 or any of the four numbers prior to it. All five possibilities are illustrated in Table 4-4. This is not to suggest that one needs to make as many trial distributions as the size of the interval since a satisfactory one may well be found on the first trial. They are included here to indicate some of the criteria for choosing among trial distributions.

Of the five distributions tabulated, examples (1) and (5) are not acceptable. Example (5) fails to show a single interval with more frequencies than any other interval (important in determining the mode of the data, as discussed in Chap. 5) since the maximum of 9 appears in two intervals. The peak need not be in the middle of the data, but should be single and distinct. The objection to example (1) is less important.

Table 4-4 Trial distributions of monthly automobile payments

(1)		(2)		(3)		(4)		(5)	
i	f	i	f	i	f	i	f	i	f
70–74	1	71–75	2	72–76	2	73–77	2	74–78	3
75–79	4	76–80	3	77–81	3	78–82	5	79–83	5
80–84	3	81–85	4	82–86	6	83–87	6	84–88	8
85–89	8	86–90	9	87–91	9	88–92	10	89–93	9
90–94	10	91–95	12	92–96	12	93–97	9	94–98	9
95–99	9	96–100	7	97–101	6	98–102	7	99–103	5
100–104	4	101–105	4	102–106	3	103–107	2	104–108	3
105–109	3	106–110	1	107–111	1	108–112	1		
Totals	42		42		42		42		42

If possible, distributions whose successive frequencies increase to the peak and decrease consistently thereafter are preferred, but example (1) increases from 1 to 4, going from the first to the second interval, but decreases to 3 in the third interval before continuing to rise. More serious, but not illustrated, would be the appearance of two peaks of almost equal magnitude several intervals apart. If this occurs, one should investigate the data for a heterogeneous classification. Such a result might occur, for instance, if the weights of both men and women were placed in one distribution. There would be a peak at the average weight of each sex. All the tabulated distributions were constructed with equal class intervals throughout. This is desirable, but not always possible if the data are not symmetrical, i.e., if the peak is either at the low end or high end of the scale. Income data provide an example of the former. Once a satisfactory trial distribution has been found, it can be drawn up in good tabular form, as has been done for example (2), as illustrated in Table 4-2.

GRAPHING FREQUENCY TABLES

Graphs of frequency tables are of two types: (1) column diagrams (histograms) and (2) frequency polygons. Both are illustrated in Fig. 4-1a and b for Table 4-2.

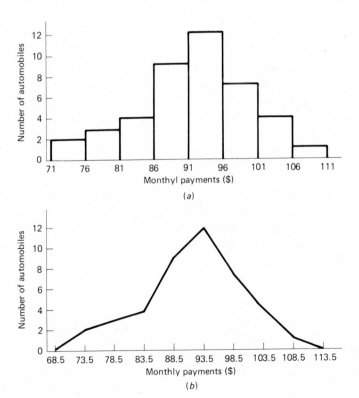

Figure 4-1 Monthly installment payments for 42 used automobiles. (a) Column diagram. (b) Frequency polygon.

For the column diagram, note the use of the continuous scale for the payments and indication of the common limit only. For the frequency polygon, the payments scale value is the midpoint of the interval, and the graph is closed by extending it to the zero base line at the midpoint of the interval which precedes the first interval actually having frequencies and the midpoint of the interval following the last actually containing data. This gives to both forms of graphing a frequency table the same area, which is quite important in theoretical statistics.

FREQUENCY CURVES

The term "frequency curve" is used to describe a smooth curve presentation of a conceptual frequency distribution. Such a distribution might be either a simplified picture of the universe or population from which a sample has been drawn (e.g., a smoothed-out version of the frequency polygon of installment payments for used automobiles) or one of several theoretical distributions important to statistical work. These curves may be of several types, as shown in Fig. 4-2.

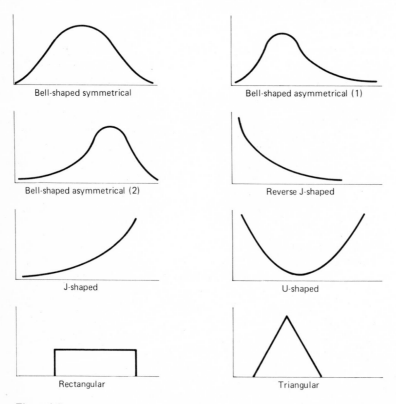

Figure 4-2

Most distributions encountered in economics and business (in most fields, for that matter) are of the bell-shaped type. A J-shaped curve is illustrated by the incidence of disease with age, while the classic example of a U-shaped curve is the death rate as plotted against age. The rectangular and triangular distributions are mostly of theoretical interest.

PROPERTIES OF BELL-SHAPED CURVES

Several properties of a bell-shaped frequency curve, or distribution, are of interest for purposes of analysis. Because of the wide existence of these curves, standard methods of analysis have been developed to summarize and describe their basic properties.

Location

The first of these basic properties is to determine where the curve (distribution) is located or centered on the scale of values. Curves A and B in Fig. 4-3 are the same, except that B is located farther to the right on the horizontal axis, or among the higher values. X_A is a point showing where curve A is located, and X_B does the same for curve B. Such points are variously termed "points of central tendency," "clustering points," "measures of location," or most commonly, "averages." Chapter 5 deals with the methods of calculating such points from actual data.

Figure 4-3

Variability

In Fig. 4-4 curves A and B have the same point of central tendency (X_{AB}) but differ chiefly in that the values of B differ more from that point and cover a larger interval of the horizontal axis. This property is termed "dispersion," or "variability," and is

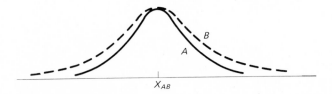

Figure 4-4

Figure 4-5

measured as an interval. Chapter 6 will deal with methods for computing measures of variability for actual data.

Skewness

The third property of a bell-shaped curve is its symmetry or asymmetry. This lack of symmetry is termed "skewness." In Fig. 4-5 curve A is said to be right, or positively, skewed, and curve B is left, or negatively, skewed. Ordinarily, it is not necessary to measure the amount of skewness, merely to note its absence or presence and, if present, its direction.

Kurtosis

The last property of a bell-shaped curve is its peakedness. Statistically, this is measured as relative peakedness and is called "kurtosis." In Fig. 4-6 curve A has greater kurtosis than curve B because it is more peaked relative to its dispersion. Little attention is paid to kurtosis in ordinary statistical analysis.

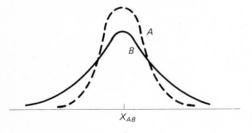

Figure 4-6

STUDY GUIDE

Concepts Worth Remembering

Define:

1. Array
2. Frequency table (distribution)

 3. Class intervals
 4. Discrete variable
 5. Continuous variable
 6. Sturges' rule
 7. Column diagram
 8. Frequency polygon
 9. Frequency curve
10. Bell-shaped curve
11. Averages (measures of location, points of central tendency, clustering points)
12. Dispersion (variability)
13. Skewness
14. Kurtosis

Self-Test

Circle the proper letter to indicate whether the following statements are true or false.

T F   **1** A frequency distribution is the common way of tabulating quantitatively classified data.

T F   **2** An array is an arrangement of numerical data in order of magnitude.

T F   **3** Discrete data result when the data are obtained by the process of measurement.

T F   **4** Good or acceptable frequency distributions have a single and distinct peak and a gradually increasing number of frequencies up to the peak and a gradually decreasing number after the peak.

T F   **5** The frequency values of a frequency polygon are plotted at the lower limit of the interval in question.

T F   **6** When plotting a frequency distribution, the variable of the problem is plotted on the horizontal axis.

T F   **7** The term "variability" refers to the relative peakedness of a frequency curve.

T F   **8** The term "skewness" refers to the lack of symmetry in a frequency curve.

T F   **9** Skewness is said to be to the left or negative if the shorter tail of a frequency curve is on the left side of the curve's peak.

T F   **10** The property of a frequency curve known as variability or dispersion is measured as an interval.

Questions to Think About

1. Describe the procedure used to write unambiguous class intervals.
2. Explain the criteria used for deciding whether a frequency distribution constructed from ungrouped data is an "acceptable" one.
3. Compare and contrast a column diagram with a frequency polygon.
4. List and define the properties of bell-shaped frequency curves.

Problems

The accompanying table gives third-quarter profit margins (percentage of sales) of major companies for 1976 and 1977. The data are from the October 31, 1977, issue of *Business Week,* page 30.

| Company | 3rd-quarter margin | | Company | 3rd-quarter margin | |
	1977	1976		1977	1976
A	9.0	8.1	AB	5.0	5.9
B	3.3	3.8	AC	4.6	4.7
C	3.0	2.6	AD	7.0	6.2
D	13.0	12.2	AE	5.1	5.2
E	8.9	8.3	AF	10.0	9.7
F	8.8	8.4	AG	6.1	6.0
G	6.7	7.8	AH	5.5	4.4
H	4.2	5.6	AI	2.8	3.1
I	7.9	6.3	AJ	8.1	7.1
J	4.7	4.9	AK	3.3	4.2
K	4.7	4.3	AL	6.2	6.8
L	3.5	3.0	AM	6.2	6.0
M	4.7	5.3	AN	9.8	6.9
N	10.5	10.4	AO	4.3	2.5
O	12.2	12.4	AP	4.3	3.8
P	5.1	4.0	AQ	3.2	4.2
Q	3.2	3.1	AR	6.2	6.9
R	11.5	11.4	AS	0.6	1.0
S	6.2	6.0	AT	5.3	5.4
T	12.5	10.4	AU	4.5	5.0
U	1.8	2.9	AV	9.6	7.1
V	8.2	8.4	AW	6.4	4.9
W	15.1	14.8	AX	4.6	4.8
X	6.7	6.7	AY	4.8	4.0
Y	3.7	5.0	AZ	5.2	5.7
Z	0.1	1.1	BA	5.6	5.8
AA	3.1	2.8	BB	7.1	7.2

1 (*a*) Construct a frequency table for the 1977 third-quarter profit margins, observing all rules of good tabular form.

    (*b*) Explain why you think you have a satisfactory distribution.

    (*c*) Present a graph of the distribution constructed in (*a*).

2 (*a*) Construct a frequency table for the 1976 third-quarter profit margins, observing all rules of good tabular form.

    (*b*) Explain why you think you have a satisfactory distribution.

    (*c*) Present a graph of the distribution constructed in (*a*).

3 Characterize and compare the patterns of the two distributions you have constructed in Probs. 1 and 2.

Student Project

Having studied Chap. 4, what additional tables and graphs might you like to add to those you suggested in answering the Student Project section of the Study Guide for Chap. 3 for presenting the results of your survey of student opinions of new college resident facilities?

Answers to Self-Test

1 T; 2 T; 3 F; 4 T; 5 F; 6 T; 7 F; 8 T; 9 F; 10 T.

FIVE
MEASURES OF LOCATION
FOR QUANTITATIVE DATA

LEARNING OBJECTIVES

The basic learning objective is to discover how the several measures of location (averages) are used in summarizing and describing numeric data. Specifically, you will learn:

1. The classes of averages.
2. For the arithmetic mean:
    (a) What it is and how to interpret it.
    (b) How to calculate it for ungrouped and grouped data.
    (c) Its advantages and disadvantages in use.
3. For the median:
    (a) What it is and how to interpret it.
    (b) How to calculate it for ungrouped and grouped data.
    (c) Its advantages and disadvantages in use.
4. For the mode:
    (a) What it is and how to interpret it.
    (b) How to calculate it for ungrouped and grouped data.
    (c) Its advantages and disadvantages in use.
5. The mathematical properties of each of the averages.
6. The effect of skewness on each of the averages.
7. What average or averages, if any, to use in given situations.

INTRODUCTION

With this chapter we begin our formal discussion of the statistical methods for summarizing and describing numerical data. The methods described in this chapter and in Chap. 6 will be discussed in their application to a specific set of data. If the specific set of data proves to be a properly chosen sample, inferences may be made from it about the universe from which it was drawn. Methods for making such inferences will be described in Part III, Chaps. 7 through 14. The specific methods to be described in this chapter are those for determining the location of a distribution on the scale of values. As noted in Chap. 4, these measures are also variously termed "measures of central tendency," "measures of the clustering point," or simply "averages." The object here is to find one value (point) which can be used to locate and summarize the entire set of varying values making up the distribution. This one value then can be used to make many decisions concerning the entire set. For example, a decision as to what type of light bulb to purchase might be based on the average burning length of the types of bulbs under consideration.

CLASSES OF AVERAGES

Two general approaches may be taken to compute a measure of location, and these two approaches lead to two different classes of averages. The first approach is to define a mathematical operation which might yield a useful summary value. This approach is very old and gives us what are known as "calculated averages," or "means." These means are all defined in terms of some arithmetic operation and include as their best-known members the arithmetic mean and the geometric mean.

The second approach is to describe a specific place or location in the data and then try to find methods giving a value for this location. Such averages are called "positionary averages." There are two such averages, the median and the mode.

THE ARITHMETIC MEAN

The arithmetic mean is the best known of all the averages, being what most people have referred to from their youth as the "arithmetic average," or just "average." In statistics the term "average" is used (often misused) to refer to any of the measures of location, but to avoid confusion one should use the average's more correct name.

The arithmetic mean is a calculated average; i.e., it is defined in terms of an arithmetic operation. Specifically, the arithmetic mean is defined as being equal to the sum of the numerical values of a series of items or numbers divided by the number of items or numbers. For example, if we wish to determine the arithmetic mean length of fish in our day's catch, we note that we caught 10 fish whose lengths to the nearest inch were 7, 8, 9, 10, 10, 10, 11, 11, 12, and 13 in, respectively. The arithmetic mean length of fish, then, is 7 + 8 + 9 + 10 + 10 + 10 + 11 + 11 + 12 + 13 divided by 10, or 101 divided by 10; therefore, the arithmetic mean length equals 10.1 in. It is customary in statistical work to express such a calculation in terms of shorthand notation employing symbols. X is the symbol for an item. X_1 is the symbol for the first item, X_2 for the second, X_i for the ith, or general, item, and X_n for the nth item. The sum of the values of the items can be expressed as $X_1 + X_2 + \cdots + X_i + \cdots + X_n$, or even more concisely, as $\sum_{i=1}^{n} X_i$, where Σ (the capital Greek sigma) is read "sum of," or "total of;" the notation $i = 1$ and n indicate the range of the summation, in this case from the first to the nth item. Since most of our sums in statistical work are, as above, over the entire set of items, it will suffice merely to write ΣX to indicate a totaling of the values of the items. No completely standard symbol exists for the arithmetic mean, but a widely used convention is merely to use the symbol of the items being averaged with a bar over it. Here, then, $\overline{X}$ (X-bar) would be our symbol for the arithmetic mean. If we use n to stand for the number of items, our complete shorthand notation, or formula, for the arithmetic mean becomes

$$\overline{X} = \frac{\Sigma X}{n}$$

Applied to our fish data, we obtain, as before,

$$\overline{X} = \frac{101}{10} = 10.1 \text{ in}$$

Although several interpretations are possible, one unique and useful interpretation is to note that the 10.1 in represents a length that all 10 fish would have to be if they were all of an equal length and were still to total 101 in in length for all 10. In other words, the arithmetic mean is that value all items would have if all the items of a set were of equal value.

The Arithmetic Mean of a Frequency Distribution

We have seen how to compute the arithmetic mean for ungrouped data. Now let us consider what modifications of our procedure are necessary for grouped data. The problem is that when the items are classified into a frequency distribution, we no longer know their exact values, which are needed to obtain their sum. There is a simple solution to this problem. We merely assume that the items in any one interval have an average value equal to the midpoint of the interval. If this is so, we may multiply the midpoint of each interval by the number of items (frequencies) in the interval to obtain a total for the items in the interval. This can be done for each interval, and when these products are totaled for all the intervals, we have an estimate of the total of all the items. If we then divide this last total by the sum of the frequencies, which is the same as n, we shall have an arithmetic mean for the distribution. This approach is illustrated in Table 5-1. The intervals are assumed to be continuous, so the midpoints are halfway between any two consecutive lower limits. The result would be interpreted as before, indicating that, if all the employees had had the same weekly commission, that value would have been $30.05.

Table 5-1 Calculation of arithmetic mean of a frequency distribution

Weekly commission	Number of employees (f)	Midpoint (m)	fm
$10.00–14.99	1	12.5	12.5
15.00–19.99	5	17.5	87.5
20.00–24.99	9	22.5	202.5
25.00–29.99	14	27.5	385.0
30.00–34.99	11	32.5	357.5
35.00–39.99	8	37.5	300.0
40.00–44.99	5	42.5	212.5
45.00–49.99	2	47.5	95.0
Total	55		1,652.5

$$\overline{X} = \frac{\Sigma fm}{\Sigma f} = \frac{1,652.5}{55} = \$30.05$$

Mathematical Properties of the Arithmetic Mean

Because the arithmetic mean is defined operationally, it has several useful mathematical properties. One of these is that the arithmetic means of several sets of numbers may be combined into a single arithmetic mean for the combined sets of data without going back to the original data. As a simple illustration of this, consider the situation of a professor, with three sections of beginning statistics, for each of which he has computed the arithmetic mean grade on the last hourly examination. The problem is to find the arithmetic mean for all three sections combined. The procedure is illustrated as follows:

Section	(1) $\overline{X}$	(2) Number of students	(3) r (1) × (2)
1	72	30	2,160
2	75	20	1,500
3	70	25	1,750
Total		75	5,410

$\overline{\overline{X}}$ (mean of the means) = 5,410/75 = 72.1

The foregoing illustration is a special case of a calculation known as the "weighted mean." In this case the weights (number of students in each section) were internal to the problem since they were the denominators used to compute the original section means. A familiar example with external weights would be the calculation of a student's grade average where the weights (credit hours) are determined independently of the grade. The formula for the weighted mean may be written

$$\text{wt. } \overline{X} = \frac{\Sigma wX}{\Sigma w}$$

where w is the symbol for the weights, and X, for the items being averaged (the $\overline{X}$'s in our illustration).

Two more useful mathematical properties of the arithmetic mean are in terms of the deviations of the items from the arithmetic mean. If we let x equal a deviation of an item from the arithmetic mean, i.e., $x = X - \overline{X}$, these properties are that (1) $\Sigma x = 0$ and (2) $\Sigma x^2 = $ a minimum. The fact that the total of the deviations from the mean equals zero is of value in developing certain shortcut procedures for calculations involving the arithmetic mean. We shall meet an example of this when we study correlation in Chap. 15. The second property, that the total of the squares of the deviation equals a minimum, i.e., the total of the squares of the deviations from any other value than the mean value will be greater than the total from the mean, is of importance in measuring dispersion, and will be discussed further in Chap. 6.

Advantages of the Arithmetic Mean in Use

A great advantage of the arithmetic mean in actual use is that it is the most familiar of the averages and does not require long accompanying explanations of its nature. A specific interpretation of the result may be of value, however, to avoid misconceptions arising out of overfamiliarity with the arithmetic mean.

If the distribution from which the mean is computed is bell-shaped and symmetrical, or nearly symmetrical, the arithmetic mean will have the further advantage of being a representative measure for the data since it will fall under, or almost under, the peak of the curve. If the distribution is skewed, the arithmetic mean, as will be discussed below, loses its representative quality.

One final advantage of the arithmetic mean: it is the most reliable average when using samples to make inferences about the universe. This means either that it is less subject to error for a given sample size than the other averages or that, if a given amount of precision is desired, this may be obtained with a smaller sample (at less cost) if the average being used is the arithmetic mean.

Disadvantages of the Arithmetic Mean in Use

The major disadvantage one faces in using the arithmetic mean is that its value as a representative figure may be distorted by the presence of extreme values among the items. For example, let us assume that an eleventh fish was caught and added to our original 10. Let us further assume that we were fortunate and our new addition was 25 in long. The arithmetic mean of the 11 fish is 11.6 in, whereas the mean of the original 10 fish was 10.1 in. The addition of the one large value (the 25-in fish) has very definitely distorted our mean as a representative value. Originally, 3 fish had lengths almost identical with the mean, while 3 were shorter and 4 were longer. Now

8 fish are shorter and only 3 longer than the mean. The effect of one-sided extremes in a distribution (skewness) is to distort the mean in the direction of the skewness. We shall illustrate this later when we discuss the mode.

A minor disadvantage in using the arithmetic mean sometimes occurs with secondary data. Often the distributions given for such data have, for requirements of "confidentiality," open-end intervals; e.g., the final interval reads $10,000 and over. The arithmetic mean cannot be computed for such distributions, since it is impossible to assign a midpoint value to the open-end interval.

THE MEDIAN

The median is defined as that value which exceeds the values of no more than one-half of the items or is itself exceeded in value by no more than one-half of the items. This may be stated somewhat differently (but less rigorously): the median is the value of the middle item when the series is arranged in order of size or magnitude. The median length of fish caught in our earlier illustration would be 10 in. The lengths of the 10 fish in order of magnitude were 7, 8, 9, 10, 10, 10, 11, 11, 12, and 13 in. There is no middle item in an even number of items, so by convention we take the mean of the two middle items, which in this case are both 10 in, and our median length is then 10 in. Only three fish (less than half the fish) are shorter than 10 in and only four fish (less than half the fish) are longer than 10 in, so we again confirm that the median is 10 in, by our original definition. Suppose that we had caught an odd number of fish, say, the first five with lengths of 7, 8, 9, 10, and 10 in; what would the median length of this group be? In a group of five items the middle item is the third item, which here has a value of 9 in, so our median would be 9 in. This is exceeded in value and exceeds in value less than one-half of the items (two-fifths in each case). The median of a series of numbers is obtained by a counting process rather than a calculation process as was done for the arithmetic mean. The abbreviation for the median is usually Md.

An Interesting Contrast

We can easily illustrate at this point an interesting contrast between the median and the arithmetic mean. Consider again the five fish mentioned above, with lengths of 7, 8, 9, 10, and 10 in. The median length equals 9 in, while the arithmetic mean length equals 8.8 in. Now suppose that we change the length of the last fish from 10 to 15 in and observe the effect of this on the values just determined. The median would remain 9 in, but the arithmetic mean becomes 9.8 in. The median remains unchanged because its value depends upon the number of items in the series, which has remained five. The value of the arithmetic mean changes because it depends on the values of the items, one of which has been changed.

The Median of a Frequency Distribution

The calculation of the median of a frequency distribution is illustrated in Table 5-2. The objective is the same as before, namely, to find a value that divides the distribu-

Table 5-2 Calculation of the median of a frequency distribution

Miles per hour	Number of cars (f)	Less than cumulative frequencies (cf)
25.0–29.9	2	2 < 22
30.0–34.9	8	10 < 22
35.0–39.9	20	30 > 22
40.0–44.9	9	39
45.0–49.9	3	42
50.0 and over	2	44
Total	44	

$$\frac{\Sigma f}{2} = \frac{44}{2} = 22 \qquad 22 - 10 = 12 \qquad \frac{12}{20} \times 5 = 3 \qquad Md = 35 + 3 = 38 \text{ mph}$$

tion into two equal groups of items, one group having values smaller than the median and one group having values greater than the median.

The first step in calculating the median is to total the frequencies and divide by 2. Here we have $\frac{44}{2}$ = 22. This will establish the number of items on either side of the median. When the total is an odd number of items, half an item is carried in each group.

The second step is to determine the "less than cumulative frequencies;" i.e., add up the number of frequencies that are less than the upper limit of each interval. This is illustrated in Table 5-2 in column cf.

The third step is to compare the cumulative frequency figure for each interval, starting at the first interval, with the $\Sigma f/2$ figure computed in step 1. As long as the cf number is less than the $\Sigma f/2$ number, proceed to the next interval, since the number of frequencies accumulated so far is less than half the frequencies. However, as soon as the first interval where the cf number is greater than the $\Sigma f/2$ number is reached, stop, for we have now accumulated over half the frequencies. This last interval will be the one which contains the median. Some place in this interval the value dividing the items into two equal groups has been passed. The median of the above distribution falls in the interval 35.0–39.9.

In order to get a single value for the median we must make an assumption as to the unknown distribution of the items in the median interval. We shall assume that they are distributed equally throughout the interval so that we may make a simple straight line interpolation for the median. For the distribution above we note from the cf column that we have 10 frequencies in the intervals prior to the median interval. Since the $\Sigma f/2$ = 22, this means that we need 12 additional items (22 – 10) in the median interval. From the f column there are 20 items in the median interval. If we assume that these are spread equally, we need $\frac{12}{20}$, or $\frac{3}{5}$, of the interval to determine the median value. The interval is of size 5, so we need $\frac{3}{5}$ of 5, or 3 more than the lower limit of the median interval, to have the median. The median, therefore, is 35 + 3, or 38 mph.

We may interpret this value as showing that 22 cars had a speed of over 38 mph, while the other 22 cars had a speed of less than 38 mph.

Mathematical Properties of the Median

The median has only one interesting mathematical property. If one sums deviations from the median $(X - Md)$ without regard to sign, i.e., treats them all as plus values, the resulting sum is a minimum value for the operation in question. We shall refer to this property again in Chap. 6 when we study variability.

As the median is a positionary average, it cannot be combined with other medians to obtain the median of the medians as was the case for the arithmetic mean. One must always work from the original data to obtain the median.

Advantages of the Median in Use

Although the median is not as well known as the arithmetic mean, it does have the advantages of being both easy to determine and easy to explain when it is chosen as the average to use. A single statement interpreting it precisely will often suffice.

Because, as illustrated earlier, the median is affected by the number of items rather than the values of the items, it will be less distorted as a representative value by skewness in a distribution than the arithmetic mean. To a degree it will be pulled in the direction of the skewness, however.

An additional advantage of the median in use is that it may be computed for an open-end distribution as was done above. The only interval for which we make any assumption in the median's calculation is the one containing the median, and this will not usually be the open-end one.

Disadvantages of the Median in Use

Although simple to explain and use, the median in actual use has the disadvantage that it is a less familiar measure than the arithmetic mean. Therefore, it must be used either with an accompanying explanation or exclusively with a more sophisticated audience.

Another disadvantage is that the median is generally a poorer (less reliable) measure than the arithmetic mean in sampling problems. To have the same level of error, larger samples must be used when sampling for the median than when sampling for the mean. Unfortunately, larger samples are generally had only at increased monetary cost.

THE MODE

The mode is the second of our positionary averages. It is defined as the value which occurs most often and around which the values of the other items tend to cluster provided there is sufficient clustering to establish it. One must be careful not to confuse the mode (the value which occurs most often or with the greatest frequency) with the item having the largest value, which generally occurs with a frequency of only 1. By now it has undoubtedly occurred to the reader that the term "mode" is essentially synonymous with the concept of clustering point, or point of central tendency, discussed earlier. Unfortunately, giving a new name to our concept does not solve the problem of how to quantify it for a specific set of data. The arithmetic mean was obtained by calculation, and the median by counting; the mode will be obtained by inspection.

Estimating the Mode

The word "estimating" here indicates what is basically true about the mode, that except for certain theoretical curves, it cannot be calculated. In contrast to the median, which was obtained by a counting process, and to the mean, which was obtained by a calculation, we merely inspect the data to find out which value occurs most frequently and designate that as the mode. If we consider our fish data once again, we observe that the fish lengths were 7, 8, 9, 10, 10, 10, 11, 11, 12, and 13 in. The value 10 in occurs three times, which is more often than any other length, so the modal fish length is 10 in. The interpretation is fairly obvious. We caught more fish of length 10 in than of any other length. The abbreviation Mo is generally used to indicate the mode. Where a small number of items is involved, it may be difficult, and even impossible, to estimate the mode. Suppose that our fish lengths had been 7, 8, 8, 10, 11, 12, 12, and 13 in. What would the modal value of this set be? One could say either 8 or 12 in, since both occur with the largest frequency (two). However, here it is probably best not to designate one.

The Mode of a Frequency Distribution

There are several ways of estimating the mode of a frequency distribution. For most purposes it will suffice to designate what is commonly called the "crude mode." This procedure merely uses the value of the midpoint of the interval containing the mode as the value for the mode. There are, then, in this approach, two simple steps for estimating the mode:

1. Locate the modal interval (the interval containing the mode). This is usually the interval with the greatest number of frequencies, but one must exercise caution if the intervals are not all of the same size.
2. Determine the midpoint of the interval and use this value for the mode. Thus, if we refer back to our median illustration, Table 5-2, we find that the modal interval is 35.0-39.9. The midpoint of this interval is 37.5, so the mode is 37.5 mph. In the example presented by the table, our interpretation would be that more cars were traveling at 37.5 mph than at any other speed.

Advantages of the Mode in Use

The chief advantage of the mode is that it is, by definition, the most representative value of the distribution. It is completely unaffected by skewness. It is used, there-

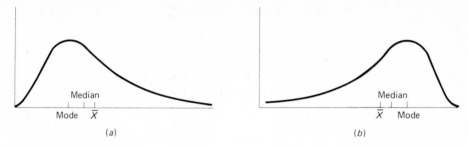

Figure 5-1 Locations of the three averages in a skewed distribution. (*a*) Right-skewed distribution. (*b*) Left-skewed distribution.

fore, when it is very important to have a representative or typical value or when one wishes to determine how representative the median or arithmetic mean is in a given situation. It serves as a standard by which to judge the representative character of other averages. The locations of the three averages in a skewed distribution are illustrated in Fig. 5-1.

Disadvantages of the Mode in Use

The main disadvantage of the mode is that it is an indeterminate value; i.e., we cannot calculate its value precisely in a frequency distribution, but merely estimate it. Several other disadvantages flow from this main one: the mode has no useful mathematical properties; the mode is the least reliable average under sampling conditions. Because of these disadvantages, in actual practice the mode is more important as a conceptual idea than as a working average.

WHAT AVERAGE OR AVERAGES, IF ANY?

The popular conception of averages has often led to the conclusion that such a measure is always the appropriate one for making a decision, but such is not the case. The classic (counter) illustration makes this point well. It is the story of the man who could not swim who drowned while trying to wade the river. He had heard that, on the average, the river was only 3 ft deep. Some knowledge of the dispersion of depths (to be discussed in Chap. 6) would have been of great value to him.

Assuming that an average is an appropriate measure as an aid in reaching a decision in a given problem, which average should be used? The answer to this question depends on several factors, which can be considered under two headings: (1) the concept desired and (2) mechanical considerations.

The Concept Desired

The nature of a particular problem will often dictate the average to be used. If, for example, one desires to know the *typical* annual expenditure for gasoline for private automobiles, the mode is suggested, because we are sure it will give a typical result.

Or one may desire an average which divides a group of people into two equal parts, so that it may be determined who is in the upper half and who is in the lower half. Here the measure needed is obviously the median. If the problem is one of averaging certain time ratios in the construction of index numbers, the appropriate average, as we shall show in Chap. 19, is the geometric mean. Obviously, then, in many cases there is no choice; the nature of the problem will determine the concept desired, and hence the appropriate average to use.

Mechanical Considerations

Often special consideration of the data or mechanical limitations of the average will be influential in the choice of average. If the only data available are the total of the values and the number of items, the arithmetic mean must be used. (A mean calculated from just these two values is usually termed an "isolated mean.") On the other hand, if the data are in the form of an open-end distribution, the arithmetic mean cannot be used. If the data are skewed, the mode and median will be more representative than the arithmetic mean. However, if the data are a sample, the arithmetic mean is more reliable than the median or mode.

Considerations of the type just discussed are important in the choice of average in many problems and are related to knowledge both of the properties of averages and of the nature of the data in a given problem.

It should be noted in closing that when all factors are considered, the arithmetic mean is the most important and widely used of the averages. This stems from its familiarity, its mathematical properties, and its importance in sampling. The median and mode (particularly the former) are regularly used in certain specific applications, but do not have the wide general application of the arithmetic mean.

STUDY GUIDE

Concepts Worth Remembering

Define:

1. Calculated averages (means)
2. Positionary averages
3. Arithmetic mean
4. Ungrouped data
5. Grouped data
6. Weighted mean
7. Open-end interval
8. Median
9. Less than cumulative frequencies
10. Mode
11. Crude mode

Self-Test

Matching questions. Listed in Group 1 below are the averages studied in Chap. 5. In Group 2 are listed some definitions or properties of the measures in Group 1. In the blanks provided, indicate the number of the measure in Group 1 referred to by the Group 2 description.

Group 1

1. Arithmetic mean
2. Median
3. Mode

Group 2

_____ 1 A calculated average.

_____ 2 A positionary average obtained by counting.

_____ 3 An average whose value is affected by the number of items rather than by their values.

_____ 4 The value all items in a set would be equal to if all the items were to have the same value.

_____ 5 The average whose value is most affected by the skewness of a distribution.

_____ 6 The sum of the absolute deviations from this average equals a minimum.

_____ 7 The average whose value is least affected by the skewness of a distribution.

_____ 8 The most reliable average when sampling.

_____ 9 Linear interpolation is used when computing this measure for a frequency distribution.

_____ 10 The value of this average is determined by inspection.

_____ 11 The sum of the deviations from this average equals zero.

_____ 12 This average is defined as the value which occurs with the greatest frequency.

_____ 13 The sum of the squared deviations from this average equals a minimum.

_____ 14 No more than one-half of the items in a set are greater in value, and no more than one-half the items are less in value than this average.

_____ 15 This average is equal to the sum of the values of a series of items divided by the number of items in the series.

Questions to Think About

1. List the classes of averages studied in this chapter and explain the difference between them. Tell to which class the averages studied in this chapter belong.
2. Discuss the mathematical properties of each of the averages studied.
3. Explain the effect of skewness on the representative character of each of the averages.
4. Review for each of the averages their advantages and disadvantages in use.
5. Explain how one decides which average to use in a particular problem.

Problems

1

Percentage distribution of standard academic-year salaries of assistant and associate professors, 1976–1977

Academic-year salaries	Assistant professor	Associate professor
$8,000 and under 10,000	1.2	0.3
10,000 and under 12,000	9.1	1.7
12,000 and under 14,000	28.6	6.3
14,000 and under 16,000	34.8	16.0
16,000 and under 18,000	18.9	29.0
18,000 and under 20,000	5.0	24.3
20,000 and under 22,000	1.4	14.7
22,000 and under 24,000	1.0	4.7
24,000 and under 26,000	–	1.9
26,000 and under 28,000	–	1.1
Total	100.0	100.0

Source: American Association of University Professors.

(*a*) Compute the arithmetic means of the distributions above.

(*b*) What is true of the mean salaries of assistant professors relative to associate professors?

(*c*) Using a weighted mean, determine the arithmetic mean salary for both types of professors combined.

(*d*) Of what use might this information be to college administrators?

(*e*) Of what use might this information be to college professors?

2

Age of the husband of married couples with wife of age 35 to 44 years for husbands of black and Spanish origin, March 1976

Age of husband, years	Number, thousands	
	Black	Spanish origin
25–34	26	24
35–44	453	269
45–54	200	164
55–64	38	17
65–74	6	2
Total	723	476

Source: Household and Family Characteristics, March 1976, Current Population Reports, Series P-20, No. 311, August 1977.

(*a*) Compute the arithmetic means of the distributions above.

(*b*) What conclusions can you draw from your calculations in (*a*)?

(*c*) What is the nature of the skewness in the distributions above, and how has it affected your answers?

3

Payments to life insurance beneficiaries, number and amount, by type of insurance, United States, 1976

Type of insurance	Payments	
	Number, thousands	Amount, millions
Ordinary	1,110	$4,665
Group	882	4,453
Industrial	933	475

Source: Life Insurance Fact Book '77, p. 46.

(*a*) Compute the average payment for each type of insurance.

(*b*) What type of average did you use for your calculations in (*a*)?

(*c*) Show how the average payment for all types of insurance combined can be determined in *two* different ways.

4

Percentage distributions of baseball salaries, 1973 and 1975

Salaries	Percent of players	
	1973	1975
$20,000 and under[†]	38.1	19.1
20,001–30,000	17.7	20.2
30,001–40,000	13.9	16.6
40,001–50,000	10.0	10.8
50,001–60,000	5.1	7.2
60,001–70,000	4.9	6.5
70,001–80,000	4.1	6.1
80,001–90,000	1.1	2.8
90,001–100,000	1.3	3.1
100,001–120,000	1.3	3.1
Over 120,000	2.5	4.5
Total	100.0	100.0

[†]1973 minimum salary was $14,000; 1975 minimum salary was $16,000.

Source: Baseball Players' Association.

(*a*) Determine the median salary for both 1973 and 1975. Interpret in terms of these data the values you have computed.

(*b*) Estimate the modal salary for both 1973 and 1975. Interpret in terms of these data the values you have obtained.

(c) Discuss briefly the nature and effects of the skewness in the distributions above.

(d) Discuss briefly what happened to the salaries of baseball players in the 2-year period.

5

United States labor force projections for 1980 and 1990 by sex and age

| Age, years | Projection, millions | | | |
| | 1980 | | 1990 | |
	Male	Female	Male	Female
16–19	5.2	4.2	4.3	3.7
20–24	8.9	7.0	7.5	6.7
25–34	16.9	10.6	19.1	13.6
35–44	11.9	7.6	16.9	11.8
45–54	9.9	6.6	10.9	7.8
55–64	7.3	4.6	6.7	4.5
65 and over	1.9	1.1	1.9	1.3
Total	62.0	41.7	67.3	49.4

Source: *Special Labor Force Report, December 1976,* U.S. Bureau of Labor Statistics.

These distributions may be used for additional practice in determining the median and the mode.

6

Number of mothers ever married with one or two children ever born by age of mother, June 1976

| Age of mother, years | Number of mothers (thousands) with: | |
	One child ever born	Two children ever born
15–19	407	87
20–24	1,856	1,024
25–29	2,114	2,431
30–34	1,118	2,289
35–39	611	1,591
40–44	523	1,222
45–49	570	1,381
50–54	846	1,451
55–59	819	1,345

Source: *Fertility of American Women: June 1976,* Current Population Reports, Series P-20, No. 308, June 1977.

These distributions may be used for additional practice in determining any of the averages.

Answers to Self-Test

$\underline{1}$ 1

$\underline{2}$ 2

$\underline{2}$ 3

$\underline{1}$ 4

$\underline{1}$ 5

$\underline{2}$ 6

$\underline{3}$ 7

$\underline{1}$ 8

$\underline{2}$ 9

$\underline{3}$ 10

$\underline{1}$ 11

$\underline{3}$ 12

$\underline{1}$ 13

$\underline{2}$ 14

$\underline{1}$ 15

SIX
MEASURES OF VARIABILITY FOR QUANTITATIVE DATA

LEARNING OBJECTIVES

The basic learning objective is to discover how the several measures of variability (dispersion) are used in summarizing and describing numeric data. Specifically, you will learn:

1. The importance of measuring variability.
2. The two approaches to measuring variability.
3. For the range:
   (*a*) What it is.
   (*b*) How to calculate it.
   (*c*) Its advantages, disadvantages, and uses.
4. For the quartile deviation:
   (*a*) What it is.
   (*b*) How to calculate it for ungrouped and grouped data.
   (*c*) Its advantages, disadvantages, and uses.
5. For the mean deviation:
   (*a*) What it is.
   (*b*) How to calculate it for ungrouped and grouped data.
   (*c*) Its advantages, disadvantages, and uses.
6. For the standard deviation:
   (*a*) What it is.
   (*b*) How to calculate it for ungrouped and grouped data.
   (*c*) Its advantages, disadvantages, uses, and importance.
7. The concept of relative dispersion and its uses.

INTRODUCTION

In this chapter we continue our formal discussion of the statistical methods for summarizing and describing numerical data. In the previous chapter we dealt with the problem of locating a distribution on a scale of values; here our attention will be confined to studying the ways of measuring the variability, or dispersion, of a specific set of data (e.g., a single sample). As our discussion of the properties of frequency curves in Chap. 4 indicated, variability, or dispersion, deals with the concentration or spread of the items on the horizontal axis. In general, the greater the spread, the greater the variability, or dispersion, while the greater the concentration, the less the variability, or dispersion. In Fig. 4-3 curve *B* has greater spread, or variability, while curve *A* has less variability, because of the concentration (or clustering) of its values.

IMPORTANCE OF MEASURING VARIABILITY

Measuring variability is important both to managerial decision making and to (advanced) statistical analysis. Our poor friend in Chap. 5 would not have drowned in the river, i.e., would not have made the wrong decision to wade the river, if he had known the river was 10 ft deep at its deepest point. Management may have to choose between two sources of raw material which have the same average level of quality but differ with respect to variability. Assuming that both are available for the same price, the source with the lesser variability, i.e., having greater uniformity of the material, would probably be chosen. In some cases uniformity of raw material (low variability) may be more important in making a choice than the average level of quality. Yarn of high strength but uneven quality (high variability) causes more difficulty in weaving because of unexpected and perhaps frequent breakages than yarn of a lower strength but of a uniform quality. Variability is important, therefore, in decision making, both in evaluating averages and for its own sake.

Measuring variability is of great importance to advanced statistical analysis. Sampling, or statistical inference, our next subject, beginning with Chap. 7, is essentially a problem in measuring variability. Correlation is a problem in explaining variability. However, before we can consider these interesting subjects, we must have tools with which to work. This chapter will develop the necessary tools, or measures of variability.

APPROACHES TO MEASURING VARIABILITY

In contrast to the measures of location, which were points, the measures of dispersion are intervals. The larger the interval, the greater the variability, and the smaller the interval, the less the variability. Larger and smaller imply comparisons, and problems in variability usually take the form of comparing the results of calculating similar measures for several sets of data to determine which set has the greater numerical interval and hence the greater variability. Isolated results of measuring dispersion are generally of little interest by themselves and take on meaning only when compared with similar results from other data or with some standard or norm.

Two general approaches exist for measuring variability: (1) the distance approach and (2) the deviation approach. The distance approach uses the difference (interval) between two points as the measure of dispersion. The two points may be the extremes of the data, as in the case of the "range" itself, or between two other points, usually one high value and one low value. We shall consider the quartile deviation as an example of the latter type. Distance-type measures of dispersion are in general easy to compute and understand; however, because they are not comprehensive in character but based on only two points, they may give misleading results.

The deviation approach is comprehensive in character, involving every item in the set of data in the calculation. Deviation-type measures are therefore better measures of variability, even though somewhat more complicated to compute. The two measures of this type are called the "mean (average) deviation" and the "standard deviation." Both are computed by (1) determining an average for the data, (2) finding by how much each item in the data differs from this average (i.e., computing the deviations of the items from the average), and (3) computing an average of the deviations, some of which will be large and others small, or even zero, as the measure of variability. The two methods differ as to the choice of average in step 1 and the method used to average the deviations in step 3.

We shall now consider in turn each of four commonly used measures of dispersion.

THE RANGE

The range is defined as the difference between the highest (numerically largest) value in a set of data and the lowest (numerically smallest) value of the set. In terms of symbols this may be indicated as

$$R = H - L$$

where R = range

H = highest value

L = lowest value

As an example, consider the following weights of nine packaged T-bone steaks displayed at a supermarket: 0.9, 1.0, 1.1, 1.2, 1.3, 1.5, 1.7, 1.8, and 2.1 lb, respectively. The range of the weights of the steak is

$$R = 2.1 - 0.9 = 1.2 \text{ lb}$$

The interpretation of this result is fairly obvious. It merely shows that there is a difference of 1.2 lb between the weights of the heaviest and lightest steaks. As suggested earlier, such a result would be more meaningful if one had another range with which to compare it. If one were to check nine porterhouse steaks and find that their range was 1.9 lb, one might (tentatively) conclude that there was more variety of choice among porterhouse steaks than among T-bone steaks.

Advantages of the Range

The foregoing example well illustrates the chief advantage of the range. It is the easiest measure of variability to compute. Its calculation involves only one subtraction.

A second advantage of the range, which can only be stated but not illustrated at this time, is that it is a good measure of dispersion to use with small samples, particularly those of less than 10 items. We shall discuss this in more detail in Chap. 14.

Disadvantages of the Range

One disadvantage of the range is that it emphasizes the extremes and not the typical items. It may therefore give a distorted picture of the amount of dispersion involved.

A second disadvantage is that the same value for the range may result for several distributions which in fact have quite different amounts and patterns of variability. This is illustrated in Fig. 6-1. The bell-shaped curve (A) and the rectangular distribution (B) have the same range ($H - L$), but the rectangular distribution (B) has the greater dispersion.

A final disadvantage of the range is that its value will depend in part upon the number of items in the set for which it was computed. The range will tend to be larger when more items are involved, because the more items one includes, the greater the chance of having extremes. This was our reason for comparing the same number of steaks in each case above.

Some Uses of the Range

The range is used as a measure of variability only in certain special cases where its advantages far outweigh its disadvantages. The most important example of this is in statistical quality control in industry. In the type of control known as "process control," use is made of a large number of small samples (e.g., five items) taken at frequent intervals. For this work the range is often used to compute the variability in each of the samples. It is easier to compute than the standard deviation (and the computation is repeated many times) and almost as efficient for the size of sample being used. Furthermore, emphasis on extremes may even be desirable here, since these indicate poor quality, which is what is being watched for.

Information for computing the range is supplied for most organized market quotations, as, for example, those of the New York Stock Exchange, which gives daily

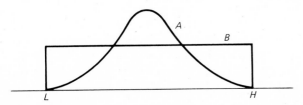

Figure 6-1 Two different distributions with the same range.

highs and lows. The number and frequency of stock transactions preclude the furnishing of sufficient data for any other calculation.

These examples are typical of the specialized uses to which the range is put.

THE QUARTILE DEVIATION

We shall consider the quartile deviation as our second example of distance-type measures of variability, although it is just one of a very large number of similar measures. The quartile deviation is designed to overcome one disadvantage of the range, that of emphasis on the extremes. The quartile deviation uses for its calculation points one-fourth of the way in from the ends of the distribution. These points are called quartiles and are similar in character to the median. The first quartile (Q_1) is a point at which no more than one-fourth of the values are smaller and no more than three-fourths are larger. The third quartile (Q_3) is a point at which no more than three-fourths of the values are smaller and no more than one-fourth are larger. The second quartile (Q_2) corresponds to the median. The quartile deviation (QD) is defined as one-half the distance between the first and third quartiles. In symbols, we have

$$QD = \frac{Q_3 - Q_1}{2}$$

The division by 2 is a holdover from early statistics, when most work was with symmetrical distributions. In such a distribution the quartile deviation as defined would be equal to the distance from the median to either quartile.

Example: Ungrouped data To illustrate the computation of the quartile deviation, let us look again at our nine T-bone steaks, for which we computed the range. These weighed 0.9, 1.0, 1.1, 1.2, 1.3, 1.5, 1.7, 1.8, and 2.1 lb, respectively. The first step in obtaining the quartile deviation is to determine the quartiles. The first quartile will have the value of the weight of the third steak; that is, $Q_1 = 1.1$ lb. Two steaks or two-ninths (less than one-fourth) weigh less than this amount, while six steaks or six-ninths (less than three-fourths) weigh more. Similarly, the third quartile has the value of the seventh steak; that is, $Q_3 = 1.7$ lb. From these values we may compute the quartile deviation for T-bone-steak weights as

$$QD = \frac{Q_3 - Q_1}{2} = \frac{1.7 - 1.1}{2} = 0.3 \text{ lb}$$

This answer, like all dispersion answers, is best interpreted in relation to another similar measure from other data.

Example: Grouped data The computation of the quartile deviation itself does not differ if the data are in the form of a frequency distribution, but a procedure similar to the calculation of the median of grouped data must be adopted to find the quartiles themselves. The necessary steps are illustrated in Table 6-1.

The first step in locating the first quartile is to determine one-fourth of the total

Table 6-1 Calculation of the quartile deviation of a frequency distribution

Weight of turkeys, lb	Number of turkeys (f)	Less than cf
0.0– 4.9	1	$1 < 8$
5.0– 9.9	3	$4 < 8$
10.0–14.9	5	$9 > 8$
15.0–19.9	10	$19 < 24$
20.0–24.9	6	$25 > 24$
25.0–29.9	4	29
30.0 and over	3	32
Total	32	

$$\frac{\Sigma f}{4} = \frac{32}{4} = 8 \qquad \begin{array}{r} 8 \\ -4 \\ \hline 4 \end{array} \qquad \frac{4}{5} \times 5.0 = 4.0$$

$$Q_1 = 10.0 + 4.0 = 14.0 \text{ lb}$$

$$\frac{3\Sigma f}{4} = 24 \qquad \begin{array}{r} 24 \\ -19 \\ \hline 5 \end{array} \qquad \frac{5}{6} \times 5 = \frac{25}{6} = 4.2$$

$$Q_3 = 20.0 + 4.2 = 24.2 \text{ lb}$$

$$\text{QD} = \frac{Q_3 - Q_1}{2} = \frac{24.2 - 14.0}{2} = \frac{10.2}{2} = 5.1 \text{ lb}$$

frequencies ($\frac{32}{4} = 8$). Next, the "less than cumulative frequencies" are added up. Then one-fourth of the frequencies is compared with the cf column to locate the interval containing the first quartile. In this case it is the interval 10.0–14.9 lb. By straight line interpolation in this interval we find the first quartile to be 14 lb. By using three-fourths of the total frequencies ($\frac{3}{4} \times 32 = 24$) in step 1, and proceeding in the same fashion, we find the third quartile to be 24.2 lb. From these two values we can easily determine the quartile deviation to be 5.1 lb. Whether or not this represents a large variability depends on how it compares with other quartile deviations for comparable data.

Advantages of the Quartile Deviation

The quartile deviation is superior to the range in that it removes the emphasis from the extremes. Although somewhat more complicated, it is still an easy measure to compute.

The major advantage of the quartile deviation, however, is that it is the only measure of variability to be studied which can be computed for distributions whose final interval is open, as in our grouped illustration, where the last interval is 30.0 lb and over.

Disadvantages of the Quartile Deviation

The disadvantages of the quartile deviation lie basically in the fact that it is a distance-type measure of dispersion. Such measures are not comprehensive in their coverage. Different patterns of variability might conceivably yield the same quartile deviation since the patterns in the tails or between the quartiles affect the results only indirectly.

Use of the Quartile Deviation

The chief use of the quartile deviation is for that case where it has its unique advantage, i.e., with distributions which have an open-end interval. Many such distributions occur in secondary data because of the need to keep certain information confidential. For these, only the quartile deviation can be used to measure variability.

THE MEAN DEVIATION

As our first example of a deviation-type measure of dispersion, we shall consider the mean (or average, as it is sometimes called) deviation. This type of measure, it will be recalled, is computed as the average of a set of deviations which are themselves deviations from some average of the original data. For the mean deviation the measure used to average the deviations (thereby giving the measure its name) is the arithmetic mean; the average of the original data used to compute the deviations is the median. Again letting X equal the items and MD the mean deviation, we can summarize the preceding steps in one expression as follows:

$$MD = \frac{\Sigma |X - Md|}{n}$$

The vertical bars ($|\ |$) around $X - Md$ indicate that the deviations are all to be treated as if they were positive; that is, they are to be summed without regard to sign. For purposes of measuring variability, this may be done safely since an item five units below the median represents the same amount of variability as an item five units above the median. Although the arithmetic mean is sometimes used as the basis for computing the deviations in the calculation of the mean deviation, this is not theoretically sound. It will be recalled from Chap. 5 that the sum of the absolute deviations (deviations without regard to sign) is a minimum only when these deviations are computed from the median. Such minimum sums are important in measuring variability to ensure that differences in the results obtained by comparing two mean deviations represent differences in variability only. Differences in minimums can represent differences in variability only.

Example: Ungrouped data The calculation of the mean deviation for ungrouped data is illustrated in Table 6-2, again making use of our T-bone-steak data.

The first step is to determine the median of the data. For these data the median is the value of the middle item (1.3 lb). The second step is to determine by how much

Table 6-2 Calculation of the mean deviation for ungrouped data

Steak number	Weight (X), lb	$|X - \text{Md}|$, lb
1	0.9	0.4
2	1.0	0.3
3	1.1	0.2
4	1.2	0.1
5	1.3	0.0
6	1.5	0.2
7	1.7	0.4
8	1.8	0.5
9	2.1	0.8
Total	. . .	2.9

Md = 1.3 lb

$$\text{MD} = \frac{\Sigma|X - \text{Md}|}{n} = \frac{2.9}{9} = 0.32 \text{ lb}$$

each item differs from the median, by subtracting the value of the median from the value of the item. This is illustrated in column $|X - \text{Md}|$. The third step is to take an arithmetic mean of the deviations, ignoring their signs; i.e., total the deviations (2.9) and divide by the number of items (9) to obtain the mean deviation (0.32 lb). This may be interpreted as any arithmetic mean. Specifically, we could note that if each steak had differed from the median by the same amount, it would have differed by 0.32 lb. The amount of variability this actually represents can be determined only by comparing this mean deviation with other similar mean deviations.

Example: Grouped data We shall again use our data on the weights of turkeys to illustrate the computation of the mean deviation for a frequency distribution, but we must modify our distribution by closing the last interval so that the calculation may be made. This is illustrated in Table 6-3.

The same three basic steps as before are used in calculating the mean deviation of a frequency distribution, but with a few modifications to take account of the fact that the data are in the form of a frequency distribution. Again the first step is to determine the median. This is done for the frequency distribution as explained in Chap. 5 and here works out to be 18.5 lb. The major modification is in the second step, determining the deviations. We no longer know the values of the individual items, and to overcome this difficulty we use the solution adopted in calculating the arithmetic mean of a frequency distribution; i.e., we substitute the midpoint of each interval for the unknown values. The calculation of deviations using these midpoints is illustrated in column $|m - \text{Md}|$. Since these deviations represent varying numbers of items as shown in the frequency (f) column, it is necessary to weight each deviation by the number of times it occurs. The results of doing this are shown in the last column of the table. The last step is the same as for ungrouped data: an arithmetic mean is taken

Table 6-3 Computation of the mean deviation for a frequency distribution

Weight of turkeys, lb	Number of turkeys (f)	Less than cf (cf)	Midpoint (m)	Deviation (|m − Md|)	Weighted deviation (f|m − Md|)
0.0– 4.9	1	1	2.5	16.0	16
5.0– 9.9	3	4	7.5	11.0	33
10.0–14.9	5	9	12.5	6.0	30
15.0–19.9	10	19	17.5	1.0	10
20.0–24.9	6	25	22.5	4.0	24
25.0–29.9	4	29	27.5	9.0	36
30.0–34.9	3	32	32.5	14.0	42
Total	32	. . .	. . . .	. . . .	191

$$\frac{\Sigma f}{2} = \frac{32}{2} = 16 \qquad \frac{\begin{array}{c}16\\-9\\\hline 7\end{array}}{10} \times 5 = 3.5$$

$$Md = 15.0 + 3.5 = 18.5 \text{ lb}$$

$$MD = \frac{\Sigma f |m - Md|}{\Sigma f} = \frac{191}{32} = 5.97 = 6.0 \text{ lb}$$

of the (weighted) deviations. These total to 191 lb for 32 items; we therefore have a mean deviation of $\frac{191}{32}$ = 6.0 lb for the data.

Advantages of the Mean Deviation

The mean deviation has the advantage of any deviation-type measure of variability compared with distance-type measures of being more comprehensive and thereby giving a better picture of the amount of variability.

It has the further advantage of being an easily understood measure. This is not as true of its companion measure, the standard deviation.

Disadvantages of the Mean Deviation

The major disadvantage of the mean deviation is its lack of mathematical properties that might make it useful for advanced statistical analysis. This lack stems from the ignoring of signs in its calculation, which is an algebraically inconsistent thing to do.

A minor disadvantage is illustrated by our need to close the turkey distribution before illustrating the calculation of the mean deviation from a frequency distribution. The closing was necessary to make it possible to determine a midpoint for the last interval.

Use of the Mean Deviation

Although the mean deviation is an excellent measure of variability, its use is limited by the fact that it is nothing more and cannot be used in advanced work. If one desires only to measure and compare variability among several sets of data, the mean deviation may be used quite satisfactorily. It is used in this way in some problems studying variability over time in chronologically classified data.

THE STANDARD DEVIATION

As our last measure of variability we shall study the standard deviation, the second of the deviation-type measures of dispersion. For this measure (1) an arithmetic mean of the data is computed to serve as the average of the data from which the deviations will be determined and (2) the arithmetic mean is subtracted from the value of each item to obtain a complete set of deviations. It will be recalled from Chap. 5 that such a set of deviations, when totaled, sums out to zero. If nothing were done to prevent this canceling out of positive and negative values, it would imply no variation where variation obviously existed. Rather than ignoring signs to overcome this difficulty, as was done in the case of the mean deviation, the calculation of the standard deviation involves squaring the deviations during the averaging procedure. The deviations are squared, averaged by dividing through by the number of items (deviations), and restored to their original units by taking the square root of the average. Such an averaging procedure is called the "quadratic mean," or "root mean square," and serves as the third step in the calculation of the standard deviation, namely, that of averaging the deviations determined in step 2. Symbolically, the calculation of the standard deviation may be represented as

$$s = \sqrt{\frac{\Sigma(X - \overline{X})^2}{n}}$$

where s is the symbol for the standard deviation.[1] We again have a measure which is theoretically sound in that it is based on a minimum total. It was pointed out in Chap. 5 that $\Sigma(X - \overline{X})^2$ would yield a minimum.

Example: Ungrouped data Table 6-4 illustrates the calculation of the standard deviation for our T-bone-steak data.

The arithmetic mean was first calculated to be 1.4 lb by totaling the values of the nine items and dividing by 9 (12.6/9 = 1.4 lb). Deviations for each item are shown in column $X - \overline{X}$ and are obtained by subtracting the value of the mean from the value of each item. These deviations are squared in column $(X - \overline{X})^2$ and totaled to 1.30. Division of this total by the number of items gives an average of 0.1444. The square root of this figure gives a standard deviation of 0.4 lb.

Example: An alternative An alternative method for calculating the standard deviation for ungrouped data is illustrated in Table 6-5. This alternative method is not necessarily shorter than the method illustrated above, although it may very often

---

[1] The lower case Greek sigma (σ) is often used as the symbol for standard deviation, but we shall reserve it to refer to a universe standard deviation. The use of s implies, therefore, a sample standard deviation.

Table 6-4 Calculation of the standard deviation for ungrouped data

Steak number	Weight (X), lb	$X - \overline{X}$	$(X - \overline{X})^2$
1	0.9	-0.5	0.25
2	1.0	-0.4	0.16
3	1.1	-0.3	0.09
4	1.2	-0.2	0.04
5	1.3	-0.1	0.01
6	1.5	0.1	0.01
7	1.7	0.3	0.09
8	1.8	0.4	0.16
9	2.1	0.7	0.49
Total	12.6	0.0	1.30

$$\overline{X} = \frac{\Sigma X}{n} = \frac{12.6}{9} = 1.4 \text{ lb}$$

$$s = \sqrt{\frac{\Sigma (X - \overline{X})^2}{n}} = \sqrt{\frac{1.30}{9}} = \sqrt{0.1444} = 0.38 = 0.4 \text{ lb}$$

Table 6-5 Computation of the standard deviation for ungrouped data (alternative method)

Steak number	Weight (X), lb	X^2
1	0.9	0.81
2	1.0	1.00
3	1.1	1.21
4	1.2	1.44
5	1.3	1.69
6	1.5	2.25
7	1.7	2.89
8	1.8	3.24
9	2.1	4.41
Total	12.6	18.94

$$\overline{X} = \frac{\Sigma X}{n} = \frac{12.6}{9} = 1.4 \text{ lb}$$

$$s = \sqrt{\frac{\Sigma X^2}{n} - (\overline{X})^2} = \sqrt{\frac{18.94}{9} - (1.4)^2}$$

$$= \sqrt{2.1044 - 1.9600} = \sqrt{0.1444}$$

$$= 0.38 = 0.4 \text{ lb}$$

be faster, since it eliminates the need for computing deviations. Actual speed and ease of calculation will depend on the size of the numbers involved and the mechanical aids available, such as tables of squares and pocket calculators.

Step 1 in this alternative method, as before, computes the arithmetic mean. However, step 2 of the first method of computing the deviations is replaced by a direct squaring of each item, as shown in column X^2. These squares are then totaled (18.94), and the total is divided by the number of items (9) to obtain an average: $18.94/9 = 2.1044$. Since items, rather than deviations from the mean, were squared, the last figure of 2.1044 is next adjusted by subtracting from it the square of the mean $[(1.4)^2 = 1.96]$ to obtain a figure of $0.1444 = 2.1044 - 1.9600$. The standard deviation is the square root of 0.1444 and again equals 0.4 lb. This is the same result as was obtained by the original method, which should not be too surprising, since the standard deviation is a mathematically defined measure, and there can be only one standard deviation for any set of data. The following relation must therefore hold:

$$s = \sqrt{\frac{\Sigma(X - \overline{X})^2}{n}} = \sqrt{\frac{\Sigma X^2}{n} - (\overline{X})^2}$$

The standard deviation is a bit difficult to interpret precisely because it involves computing a quadratic mean. It does, however, represent an average or net amount of variability for the data in question. More important, it is readily comparable with other standard deviations, and the greater the standard deviation, the greater the variability.

Example: Grouped data The calculation of the standard deviation for a frequency distribution will be illustrated in Table 6-6. The method is a straightforward modifi-

Table 6-6 Calculation of the standard deviation for a frequency distribution

Value of accounts receivable— shoestore	Number of accounts (f)	Midpoint (m)	fm	$m - \overline{X}$	$(m - \overline{X})^2$	$f(m - \overline{X})^2$
$10–19	1	15	15	−31	961	961
20–29	3	25	75	−21	441	1,323
30–39	6	35	210	−11	121	726
40–49	10	45	450	−1	1	10
50–59	5	55	275	+9	81	405
60–69	3	65	195	+19	361	1,083
70–79	2	75	150	+29	841	1,682
Total	30	...	1,370	....	...	6,190

$$\overline{X} = \frac{\Sigma fm}{\Sigma f} = \frac{1,370}{30} = 45.6 = \$46$$

$$s = \sqrt{\frac{\Sigma f(m - \overline{X})^2}{\Sigma f}} = \sqrt{\frac{6,190}{30}} = \sqrt{206} = 14.4 = \$14$$

cation of the method given above, involving the use of deviations. Frequency distribution methods similar to the second method discussed above do exist, but will not be illustrated here.

The calculation of the standard deviation again begins with the calculation of the arithmetic mean of the data. This is done as was explained in Chap. 5, and has a value of $46. The computation of deviations from this mean, the next step, is illustrated in column $m - \overline{X}$. We again substitute the midpoint value m for our unknown item values. These deviations are squared to eliminate signs in column $(m - \overline{X})^2$. These squared deviations represent varying numbers of items (f column), so they are next multiplied by the number of times each occurs. This is done in column $f(m - \overline{X})^2$. The total of this column (6,190) is now averaged by dividing through by the number of items (30), giving a figure of 206. The square root of this last number (206) is our standard deviation of $14.

Advantages of the Standard Deviation

The standard deviation is a good comprehensive measure of variability, having a value based on every item in the series. More important, the standard deviation has useful mathematical properties. These exist because, in the calculation of the standard deviation, the deviations were squared to prevent canceling, rather than being ignored, as in the case of the mean deviation. Some of the properties exist for the square of the standard deviation rather than for the standard deviation itself. The square of the standard deviation is itself a measure of variability and is termed the "variance." $s^2 = 206$ is the variance of our accounts receivable distribution, for example. We shall refer again to variances in Chaps. 14, 15, and 16.

Disadvantages of the Standard Deviation

The disadvantages of the standard deviation are of a fairly minor character. At first the measure seems to be abstract and a bit difficult to understand. However, one need only realize that it represents an average of the individual amounts of variability, and the greater the average, the greater the variability in the series.

There is again the mechanical disadvantage that the standard deviation cannot be computed for an open-end distribution because of the lack of a midpoint for the open-end interval.

Uses of the Standard Deviation

The uses of the standard deviation, the most commonly used of the measures of variability, are many. Of most interest is the fact that it is the measure of variability used with a great deal of advanced statistical work. We shall use it in Chap. 8 in connection with the normal curve, in the chapters on sampling which follow Chap. 8, and in Chaps. 15 and 16 on regression and correlation.

Importance of the Standard Deviation

It cannot be emphasized too strongly that the standard deviation is the most important measure of variability. It is commonly used to measure variability, while all the other measures, as indicated when they were discussed, have rather special uses. In addition, it is the measure possessing the necessary mathematical properties to make it useful for advanced work, where it is so widely used.

RELATIVE DISPERSION

We have frequently indicated above that dispersion problems generally involve comparisons of the results of measuring the variability in several different sets of data. Usually these comparisons can be made directly between the two standard deviations, the two ranges, or whatever measures were used. However, two kinds of comparisons cause difficulty, and for these, relative measures of dispersion have been developed.

Comparisons in Different Units

The first type of comparison causing difficulty is between two (or more) sets of data which are in different units. It is impossible to compare an inch with a pound directly; one cannot say either is larger, since they measure different things. As an example of the error of such comparisons, let us consider the data in Table 6-7, representing times and distances for salespersons' trips.

Table 6-7 Salespersons' travel data

	Distance, mi	Time, min
Mean	100	120
Standard deviation	20	30

It would be a false conclusion that because 30 (min) is greater than 20 (miles), there was greater variability in time traveled than in distance traveled. The error can be shown by changing the units involved: the miles to feet and the minutes to hours.

Following the data of Table 6-8, one should now conclude there was greater variability in distances because 105,600 (ft) is greater than $\frac{1}{2}$ (h). However, only one, distance or time, can show greater variability. No direct comparison of data in different units can be made.

Table 6-8 Revised salespersons' travel data

	Distance, ft	Time, h
Mean	528,000	2
Standard deviation	105,600	$\frac{1}{2}$

The solution lies in the use of relative measures. These compute the absolute amount of variability (i.e., variability measured in units of the data) as a percentage of an appropriate average. In the case of the standard deviation, the relative standard deviation, called the "coefficient of variation," is the standard deviation divided by the mean. In symbols,

$$V = 100 \, \frac{s}{\overline{X}}$$

using V to stand for the coefficient of variation and multiplying by 100 to obtain a percentage answer. The answers may be left as decimals if one prefers. For our travel data we have

$$V_{\text{distance}} = 100 \times \frac{20 \text{ mi}}{100 \text{ mi}} = 100 \times \frac{105{,}600 \text{ ft}}{528{,}000 \text{ ft}} = 20\%$$

$$V_{\text{time}} = 100 \times \frac{30 \text{ min}}{120 \text{ min}} = 100 \times \frac{\frac{1}{2} \text{ h}}{2 \text{ h}} = 25\%$$

On the basis of these calculations we may properly conclude that there is greater (relative) variability in the times traveled.

Comparisons of Different Magnitudes

The second type of comparison for which relative measures are used involves the comparison of measures in the same units but computed from data of differing magnitudes. Here direct comparisons can be made, but relative comparisons are often of value in determining the significant relationships in the data. Consider a comparison between our T-bone-steak data, which had a mean of 1.4 lb and a standard deviation of 0.4 lb, and some rib-roast data, which had a mean of 6.0 lb and a standard deviation of 1.0 lb. Based on a comparison of the absolute data, the roasts showed greater variability, for 1.0 lb is greater than 0.4 lb. However, the explanation may lie in the fact that roasts in general are heavier than steaks. A comparison of coefficients of variation shows greater relative dispersion in steak weights:

$$V_{\text{steaks}} = 100 \times \frac{0.4 \text{ lb}}{1.4 \text{ lb}} = 28\tfrac{4}{7}\%$$

which is greater than

$$V_{\text{roasts}} = 100 \times \frac{1.0 \text{ lb}}{6.0 \text{ lb}} = 16\tfrac{2}{3}\%$$

This may indicate a greater variety of choice in steaks than in roasts, which is not indicated by the first comparison.

Table 6-9 Absolute and relative forms of measures of variability

Measure	Absolute form	Relative form
Range	$R = H - L$	$\text{Rel. } R = 100 \dfrac{H - L}{\overline{X}}, \text{ or } 100 \dfrac{H - L}{(H + L)/2}$
Quartile deviation	$QD = \dfrac{Q_3 - Q_1}{2}$	$\text{Rel. } QD = 100 \dfrac{Q_3 - Q_1}{2 \, Md}, \text{ or } 100 \dfrac{Q_3 - Q_1}{Q_3 + Q_1}$
Mean deviation	$MD = \dfrac{\Sigma \lvert X - Md \rvert}{n}$	$\text{Rel. } MD = 100 \dfrac{MD}{Md}$
Standard deviation	$s = \sqrt{\dfrac{\Sigma(X - \overline{X})^2}{n}}$	$V = 100 \dfrac{s}{\overline{X}}$

Relative Measures

All four measures of variability discussed earlier have a relative form. These are shown in Table 6-9. All are used either for comparisons involving series in different units or series in the same units but of differing magnitudes.

STUDY GUIDE

Concepts Worth Remembering

Define:

1. Distance measures
2. Deviation measures
3. Range
4. Quartile deviation
5. Quartiles
6. Mean (average) deviation
7. Standard deviation
8. Variance
9. Relative measures of variability
10. Coefficient of variation

Self-Test

Matching questions. Listed in Group 1 below are the measures of variability studied in Chap. 6. In Group 2 are listed some definitions or properties of the measures in Group 1. In the blanks provided, indicate the number of the measure in Group 1 referred to by the Group 2 description.

Group 1

1. Range
2. Quartile deviation
3. Mean deviation
4. Standard deviation

Group 2

_____ 1 A measure of variability used in "process control."

_____ 2 A distance-type measure of variability despite its name.

_____ 3 The square of this measure is called the "variance."

_____ 4 A deviation-type measure of variability with valuable mathematical properties.

_____ 5 Signs are ignored to calculate this measure of variability.

_____ 6 The easiest measure of variability to calculate.

_____ 7 The relative form of this measure is called the "coefficient of variation."

_____ 8 The only measure of variability studied that can be determined for an open-end distribution.

_____ 9 A deviation-type measure of variability with no mathematical properties.

_____ 10 The most widely used measure of variability.

_____ 11 Signs are eliminated by squaring in the calculation of this measure.

_____ 12 The calculation of this measure uses deviations from the median of the data.

_____ 13 The calculation of this measure emphasizes the extremes of the data.

_____ 14 This measure of variability is one of a very large family of similar measures.

_____ 15 The calculation of this measure uses deviations from the arithmetic mean of the data.

Questions to Think About

1. Discuss the importance to managerial decision making and to statistical analysis of measuring variability.
2. List the approaches to measuring variability studied in this chapter and explain the difference between them. Tell to which approach each measure of variability studied in this chapter belongs.
3. Review the advantages and disadvantages of each of the measures of variability studied.
4. List the measures of variability studied in this chapter and explain when each is used in statistical work.
5. What is the concept of relative dispersion? What problem situations call for the use of relative dispersion in their solution?

Problems

1

Ordinary life insurance purchases in the United States by age of the insured, 1976

Age of insured	Percent of total policies	Percent of total amount
Under 15	15	4
15–24	29	22
25–34	31	41
35–44	14	20
45 or over	11	13
Total	100	100

Source: *Life Insurance Fact Book* '77, p. 14.

(*a*) Determine by using the quartile deviation whether there is greater variability among ages of insured based on number of policies purchased or on dollar amount of insurance purchased.

(*b*) Why was the quartile deviation used to measure variability in these distributions?

2

Life insurance in force in the United States by regions, 1976 (billions of dollars)

Region	Ordinary	Industrial
New England	69.3	1.0
Middle Atlantic	211.2	5.2
East North Central	235.7	6.7
West North Central	100.7	1.3
South Atlantic	179.4	12.4
East South Central	62.2	5.6
West South Central	112.8	4.8
Mountain	56.0	0.4
Pacific	150.3	1.6

Source: *Life Insurance Fact Book* '77, p. 21.

(*a*) Compute the range and relative range for each type of insurance. Which type of insurance shows greater variability among regions?

(*b*) Compute the quartile deviation and relative quartile deviation for each type of insurance. Which type of insurance shows greater variability among regions?

(*c*) Compute the mean deviation and relative mean deviation for each type of insurance. Which type of insurance shows greater variability among regions?

3

Credit life insurance in force in the United States by regions, 1976

Region	Amount (billions of dollars)
New England	5.4
Middle Atlantic	18.8
East North Central	23.4
West North Central	10.1
South Atlantic	21.3
East South Central	9.7
West South Central	13.9
Mountain	7.9
Pacific	13.0

Source: *Life Insurance Fact Book '77*, p. 21.

Compute the standard deviation of the data above by *two* different methods.

4

Percentage distribution of standard academic-year salaries of assistant and associate professors, 1976–1977

Academic-year salaries	Assistant professor	Associate professor
$8,000 and under 10,000	1.2	0.3
10,000 and under 12,000	9.1	1.7
12,000 and under 14,000	28.6	6.3
14,000 and under 16,000	34.8	16.0
16,000 and under 18,000	18.9	29.0
18,000 and under 20,000	5.0	24.3
20,000 and under 22,000	1.4	14.7
22,000 and under 24,000	1.0	4.7
24,000 and under 26,000	–	1.9
26,000 and under 28,000	–	1.1
Total	100.0	100.0

Source: American Association of University Professors.

(*a*) Compute the mean deviation of the salaries for both ranks.
(*b*) Compute the standard deviation of the salaries for both ranks.
(*c*) Which rank showed greater uniformity in its salaries?

5

Age of the husband of married couples with wife of age 35 to 44 years for husbands of black and Spanish origin, March 1976

Age of husband, years	Number, thousands	
	Black	Spanish origin
25–34	26	24
35–44	453	269
45–54	200	164
55–64	38	17
65–74	6	2
Total	723	476

Source: Household and Family Characteristics, March 1976, Current Population Reports, Series P-20, No. 311, August 1977.

(*a*) Compute the mean deviation of the ages for both classifications of husbands.

(*b*) Compute the standard deviation of the ages for both classifications of husbands.

(*c*) What conclusion can you draw about the variability of the two distributions?

6 The distributions of Prob. 5 of the Study Guide for Chap. 5 may be used for additional drill in computing any of the measures of variability.

Answers to Self-Test

1	1	1	6	4	11
2	2	4	7	3	12
4	3	2	8	1	13
4	4	3	9	2	14
3	5	4	10	4	15

PART
THREE

STATISTICAL INFERENCE

SEVEN
PROBABILITY

LEARNING OBJECTIVES

The basic learning objective is to become familiar with probability, the tool used by statisticians to measure the uncertainties surrounding business decisions. Specifically, you will learn:

1. To distinguish between:
   (*a*) Objective and subjective probabilities.
   (*b*) Discrete and continuous probabilities.
   (*c*) A priori (prior) and a posterori (posterior) probabilities.
2. To measure probability.
3. The techniques of sophisticated counting, including:
   (*a*) Multiple choices.
   (*b*) Permutations.
   (*c*) Combinations.
4. The rules for combining probabilities, including:
   (*a*) The addition rule for both ordinary and mutually exclusive events.
   (*b*) The multiplication rule for both dependent and independent events.
5. Bayes' theorem—its derivation and use.

INTRODUCTION TO STATISTICAL INFERENCE

In Part II we learned the techniques used to describe and summarize a particular set of numeric data. The measures thus calculated are strictly true only for the set itself. However, if the set is a "properly chosen" sample from a statistical universe, it is possible to make generalizations (inferences) about that universe from the sample results. Here in Part III we shall learn the fascinating ways in which samples can be used to make inferences (decisions) about populations.

Chapters 7 and 8 deal with the topics of probability and probability distributions, the basic tools essential to measuring uncertainties in decision making. Chapter 9 discusses how that "properly chosen" sample can actually be obtained. The theory base for making inferences is covered in Chap. 10, on sampling distributions. The balance of Part III (Chaps. 11 through 14) covers various applications, including estimation (Chaps. 11 and 14), classical hypothesis testing (Chaps. 12 and 14), and modern (bayesian) decision procedures (Chap. 13).

INTRODUCTION TO PROBABILITY

In Chap. 1 the point was made that statistical methods are particularly useful in analyzing the uncertainties which surround us all, and which surround business managers in particular. In large part these uncertainties are ignored in everyday living, but business managers need ways of measuring and evaluating uncertainties to make the best decisions for their firms. Probability, the subject of this chapter, is the formal tool for measuring and expressing degrees of certainty or uncertainty. As such, it lies at the very heart of the statistical tools that make up Part III.

PROBLEMS OF DEFINITION

Whole books have been written and heated controversy has developed over the way to best define probability. Much of this discussion is essentially philosophical and need not concern us. Regardless of what definition of probability is adopted, methods of measuring probability are essentially the same. Most persons have a strong intuitive feeling for the notion of probability, similar to the feeling they have for the notion of time, which is also hard to define except by measurement.

Strength of Belief

A common thread which underlies most formal definitions of probability and which agrees with common intuition is that probability statements represent statements of the strength or degrees of belief that one has that the event about which the statement is made will actually occur. To state that the probability of obtaining a head when tossing a penny is one-half is to indicate that one believes that the event (head) is about as likely to occur as not. When the probability of rain is given as 20 percent, it indicates (if one believes weather forecasters) that there is only a small likelihood of a shower and that leaving one's umbrella home should be a relatively safe course of action. For our purposes we will treat probability statements as indicating the degree or strength of belief that we may have that a specified event will occur.

Sources of Belief

Sources or bases of belief may be objective or subjective, leading to probabilities of the same name. Objective probabilities have as their source of belief either complete advance knowledge of the process in question (called "a priori probabilities") or are based on experimental evidence (called "empirical probabilities"). A priori probabilities are those of coin tossing or other games of chance where all possible outcomes and their method of occurrence are known before a coin is tossed or a die is rolled. An example of an empirical probability would be the examination of a production run of 10,000 bolts to discover the number of defective bolts as the basis for determining the probability of finding a defective bolt in the future.

Both of the cases above are objective, in that anyone knowing the rules of the game of chance or the outcome of the experiment would assign the same probability to a future event (tossing a head or getting a defective bolt).

Subjective probabilities are sometimes called "personal probabilities" because they are just that. They are based on an individual's personal assessment of his or her strength of belief that an event will occur. These beliefs will be based on evidence both quantitative and qualitative and will differ from one individual to another and from one time to another for the same individual as more evidence becomes available. For example, if required to assign a probability value to the sales success of a new product, a company's president and its vice-president for sales would be likely to assign differing values based on their different personal evaluations of the product's chance for success. Both evaluations could change with time and would become closer together if the results of a market research study were to become available. In many complex business situations these may, in effect, be the only probabilities available, although one job of statistical methods is to help with added evidence to make them more objective.

MEASUREMENT OF PROBABILITY

Regardless of one's philosophical approach to defining probability, the techniques of measuring (quantifying) probability statements and combining them for more complex situations are essentially the same.

Definition

For our purposes we shall define the measure of the probability of the event A occurring as

$$P(A) = \frac{M(A)}{M(S)}$$

where the symbol $P(A)$ is read "the probability of the event A occurring"; the symbol $M(A)$ represents a measure of the set A; and the symbol $M(S)$ represents a measure of the set S of which A is typically a subset.

In statistical work measurement either takes the form of counting, in which case we have what are termed "discrete probabilities," or the measurement uses calculus to determine areas, as in the case of continuous probabilities.

Discrete Probabilities

Tossing a coin is the simplest and commonest example illustrating the computation of discrete probabilities. Here our measurement takes the form of counting the ways various outcomes can occur. Using the conventional wisdom that tossed coins do not land on their edges, we have $M(S) = N(S) = 2$; i.e., the coin will show either a head or a tail when tossed. [We may use the symbol $N(S)$, indicating the number of elements in the set S when working with discrete probabilities.]

If we define the desired event (A) to be the occurrence of a head (H), we get $M(A) = N(A) = N(H) = 1$. Formally, then, we determine the probability of getting a head (H) on a single coin toss as

$$P(A) = P(H) = \frac{N(A)}{N(S)} = \frac{N(H)}{N(S)} = \frac{1}{2}$$

For an additional illustration, we shall consider the game of roulette. The conventional American roulette wheel has slots for 38 numbers [the digits 1 through 36 plus 0 and 00 (double zero)]. Hence, $N(S) = 38$. Assume that we are betting on the digit 17; it is then the probability of the appearance of the number 17 that we wish to know. Defining this probability as A, there is only one slot numbered 17, so $N(A) = 1$. The probability of our digit appearing therefore is

$$P(A) = P(17) = \frac{N(A)}{N(S)} = \frac{1}{38}$$

This is not necessarily a good bet. If we bet on all 38 digits, we would be certain to win, as one number must occur. Formally,

$$N(A) = 38 \quad \text{and} \quad P(A) = \frac{N(A)}{N(S)} = \frac{38}{38} = 1$$

The value 1 in probability indicates certain success; the value zero indicates certain failure. If we do not bet, we cannot win:

$$N(A) = 0 \quad \text{and} \quad P(A) = \frac{N(A)}{N(S)} = \frac{0}{38} = 0$$

All probabilities are proper fractions; i.e., $0 \leqslant P(A) \leqslant 1$. The reason that betting in roulette is not favorable is that even if one does bet on all 38 numbers, ensuring success $[P(A) = 1]$, the house payoff is only 35:1, leaving the bettor two chips in the hole.

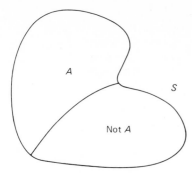

Figure 7-1 Hypothetical set for determining probabilities by areas.

Continuous Probabilities

Consider the set S illustrated in Fig. 7-1 and made up of the subsets A and not-A. All three sets have an infinite number of points, so it would be impossible to determine $P(A)$ by counting. However, if one could measure the area of subset A and divide it by the area of S, one could use the result as $P(A)$. We shall look at many situations in later chapters where our probabilities are based on the ratio of a specified area to the total area, usually for some type of frequency curve in the form of one of the continuous probability distributions to be discussed in Chap. 8.

SOPHISTICATED COUNTING

Before considering how to determine probabilities for more complex situations, a review of some of the methods of sophisticated counting will be helpful. Without these methods the task of counting the number of possible outcomes in more complex situations would prove tedious if not impossible. We shall begin our discussion by considering the fundamental principle of counting.

Fundamental Principle

If a desired outcome is the result of several individual events occurring simultaneously or in sequence, the total number of such possible outcomes can be determined by using the fundamental principle of counting. In its simplest form, the principle states that if a first event can be performed in h different ways and a second can be performed in k different ways, the total number of possible outcomes is given by the product hk. For example, if one were flipping a nickel and a dime, there are two ways the nickel may come up (heads or tails) and two ways the dime may come up (again, heads or tails). According to the principle, there are $2 \times 2 = 4$ ways or outcomes which can occur when both are flipped simultaneously or successively. These are, of course, *HH*, *HT*, *TH*, or *TT*, where the first letter represents the result on the nickel and the second the result on the dime.

The principle extends to more than two events. If there are three ways to ship a product from the factory to the warehouse, five ways to ship it from there to a wholesaler, and two ways of shipping it from the wholesaler to the retailer, there are $3 \times 5 \times 2 = 30$ ways to move the product from the factory to the retailer.

We shall now discuss briefly three special cases of this principle: (1) multiple choices, (2) permutations, and (3) combinations.

Multiple Choices

The method of multiple choices is used to count the total number of possible outcomes in situations where order is important, i.e., $HT \neq TH$, and repetition of elements is permitted, i.e., HH or TT are possible outcomes.

The basic formula for multiple choices is

$$_nM_r = n^r$$

where $_nM_r$ is read "the number of multiple choices of n events or things taken r at a time."

A coin when flipped may land either of two ways (H or T). If we flip twice we have $r = 2$, and once more get four possible outcomes, i.e.,

$$_2M_2 = 2^2 = 4$$

Consider the three letters X, Y, and Z. How many multiple choices can we obtain of these three letters in sets of two? We have $_3M_2 = 3^2 = 9$, or

$$
\begin{array}{ccc}
XX & YX & ZX \\
XY & YY & ZY \\
XZ & YZ & ZZ
\end{array}
$$

The multiple-choice formula may be used to count the number of possible outcomes in an ordinary dice game. Each die has six ways of appearing and there are two dice. Therefore, we get $_6M_2 = 6^2 = 36$ possible outcomes for each roll of a pair of dice.

How many two-letter prefixes can a state have for its license plates if it does not wish to use I or O? Again, multiple choices will give us the answer. It is $_{24}M_2 = 24^2 = 576$ such prefixes.

If plates were issued at random, what would be the probability of obtaining a plate with a prefix beginning with A? By fundamental counting, there are $1 \times 24 = 24$ ways this may occur. We have shown that there are 576 total possible outcomes. Therefore,

$$P(A) = \frac{N(A)}{N(S)} = \frac{24}{576} = \frac{1}{24}$$

Permutations

If we modify our outcomes to exclude repetition but still specify order as important, we are dealing in permutations. These arrangements can be counted by direct application of the counting principle. However, certain standard formulas are easier to work with. These are

$$_nP_r = \frac{n!}{(n-r)!} \quad \text{and} \quad _nP_n = n!^1$$

where $_nP_r$ is read "the number of permutations of n things taken r at a time" and $_nP_n$ is "the number of permutations of n things taken all together."

For our first example consider again the letters X, Y, and Z. How many permutations of these three letters can be obtained taking them two at a time? We have

$$_nP_r = \frac{n!}{(n-r)!} = _3P_2 = \frac{3!}{(3-2)!} = \frac{3!}{1!} = \frac{3 \cdot 2 \cdot 1}{1} = 6$$

These are as follows:

$$
\begin{array}{ccc}
XY & YX & ZX \\
XZ & YZ & ZY
\end{array}
$$

Note that XX, YY, and ZZ are no longer possible outcomes. How many permutations of the three letters can we get using all three?

$$_nP_n = n! = _3P_3 = 3! = 3 \cdot 2 \cdot 1 = 6$$

These would be

$$
\begin{array}{ccc}
XYZ & YXZ & ZXY \\
XZY & YZX & ZYX
\end{array}
$$

A three-man subcommittee is to be chosen at random from a 10-member board of directors. The first person chosen is to be its chairman, the second its vice-chairman, and the third its secretary. What is the probability that this subcommittee will be composed of committee members X, Y, and Z? Because order of choice is important, this problem is solved using permutations. We have already seen that there are six permutations of three individuals taken three at a time. We must also determine the total possible number of ordered subcommittees. This would be

$$_{10}P_3 = \frac{10!}{(10-3)!} = \frac{10 \cdot 9 \cdot 8 \cdot 7!}{7!} = 720$$

Therefore, the probability is

$$P(A) = \frac{N(A)}{N(S)} = \frac{6}{720} = \frac{1}{120}$$

Combinations

For our final form of sophisticated counting, we shall look at combinations. For combinations we relax our requirement that order is important; i.e., HT and TH are the

---

[1] $n!$ is called "n factorial" and is the product of the integers from 1 to n, e.g., $5! = 5 \times 4 \times 3 \times 2 \times 1$. $10! = 10 \times 9 \times 8 \times 7 \times 6 \times 5 \times 4 \times 3 \times 2 \times 1$. It may be convenient to write $10!$ in a form such as $10! = 10 \times 9 \times 8 \times 7 \times 6 \times 5!$ or $10! = 10 \times 9 \times 8 \times 7!$.

same combination. A combination is merely a grouping of things the order of which is unimportant. As for every combination of r things there are $r!$ permutations, we may write $_nP_r = r! \, _nC_r$, where $_nC_r$ is read "the combination of n things taken r at a time." Therefore,

$$_nC_r = \frac{_nP_r}{r!} = \frac{n!}{r!(n-r)!}$$

which is our basic formula for counting the number of possible combinations.

Considering X, Y, and Z one last time, how many combinations can we have of these three letters taken two at a time?

$$_nC_r = \frac{n!}{r!(n-r)!} = \, _3C_2 = \frac{3!}{2!(3-2)!} = \frac{3 \cdot 2!}{2!} = 3$$

These are XY, XZ, and YZ.

How many combinations can we have taking them three at a time?

$$_3C_3 = \frac{3!}{3!(3-3)!} = 1 \quad (0! = 1)$$

Note that the $_nC_n$ always equals 1.

How many combinations can we have taking them one at a time?

$$_3C_1 = \frac{3!}{1!(3-1)!} = \frac{3 \cdot 2!}{1! \, 2!} = 3$$

The $_nC_1$ always equals n.

What is the probability that X and Y will be chosen to represent (speak for) the board at the annual meeting if the choice is to be made by lot? Here we shall use combinations, as two are to be chosen, but order is immaterial. The total possible combinations are

$$_{10}C_2 = \frac{10!}{2!(10-2)!} = \frac{10 \cdot 9 \cdot 8!}{2! \cdot 8!} = 45$$

XY or YX represents one of these combinations; therefore, the probability of their being chosen (A) is

$$P(A) = \frac{N(A)}{N(S)} = \frac{1}{45}$$

RULES FOR COMBINING ELEMENTARY PROBABILITIES

The solution to many probability problems involves combining elementary (simple) probabilities by either addition or multiplication. If the problem is to find the probability of *either* one event (A) *or* a second event (B) occurring, the solution involves adding elementary probabilities. If the problem is to find the probability of two (or more) events occurring simultaneously or in succession, i.e., *both* a first *and* a second event occurring, the solution involves multiplying probabilities.

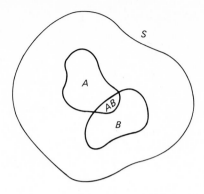

Figure 7-2 Addition rule illustration.

Addition Rule

The addition rule states that $P(A$ or $B) = P(A) + P(B) - P(AB)$. $P(A$ or $B)$ refers to the probability of A or B or both occurring. $P(AB)$ refers to the joint probability of A and B occurring together. Figure 7-2 illustrates the logic of the rule and the subtraction of $P(AB)$ to prevent the double counting of elements A and B where they overlap.

As an example of how this rule operates, consider an ordinary deck of cards. What is the probability of drawing a single card and having it be either a king (K) or a heart (H)?

$P(K) = \frac{4}{52}$, $P(H) = \frac{13}{52}$, and $P(KH) = \frac{1}{52}$. Therefore,

$$P(K \text{ or } H) = P(K) + P(H) - P(KH) = \frac{4}{52} + \frac{13}{52} - \frac{1}{52} = \frac{16}{52}$$

This may be checked very easily against our original definition. $N(S) = 52$ cards. There are 13 hearts and three additional kings, so

$$N(A) = 16 \quad \text{and} \quad P(A) = \frac{N(A)}{N(S)} = \frac{16}{52}$$

As an additional example, consider a secretarial pool composed of three men and seven women. Two of the men and three of the women are under 30 years of age. What would be the probability that one member of the pool, if picked at random would be a man, or under 30, or both? It would be

$$P(M \text{ or} <30) = P(M) + P(<30) - P(M \text{ and} <30)$$

$$= \frac{3}{10} + \frac{5}{10} - \frac{2}{10} = \frac{6}{10}$$

Special Case: Mutually Exclusive Events

Figure 7-3 illustrates the nature of mutually exclusive events. An event may be either A or B but not both A and B. A coin when flipped will land either heads or tails but not both. Only one number can occur in a single spin of a roulette wheel, because the ball can fall into only one slot. These are examples of mutually exclusive events.

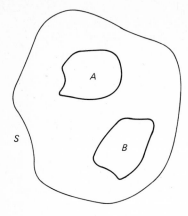

Figure 7-3 Addition rule illustration: mutually exclusive events.

Our addition rule for the probability of A or B now becomes $P(A \text{ or } B) = P(A) + P(B)$, as $P(AB) = 0$ for mutually exclusive events.

Again considering an ordinary deck of cards, what is the probability of drawing a single card and having it be a spade (S) or a heart (H)? These are mutually exclusive events, so we would have

$$P(S \text{ or } H) = P(S) + P(H)$$

$$= \tfrac{13}{52} + \tfrac{13}{52} = \tfrac{26}{52} = \tfrac{1}{2}$$

In roulette it is possible to bet on two numbers at the same time by placing one's chip on the line between the numbers. What is the probability of winning if one bets on the numbers 7 and 8?

$$P(7) = \tfrac{1}{38} \quad \text{and} \quad P(8) = \tfrac{1}{38}$$

so

$$P(7 \text{ or } 8) = P(7) + P(8) = \tfrac{1}{38} + \tfrac{1}{38} = \tfrac{2}{38} = \tfrac{1}{19}$$

(This is an even poorer bet than the one discussed earlier, as the payoff is now only $17:1$.)

Multiplication Rule

As noted above, the multiplication rule is used to determine the probability of an outcome which requires the successive or simultaneous occurrence of several events. Again we need to consider two subcases, one for dependent events and one for independent events.

Dependent Events

The multiplication rule for dependent events states that

$$P(AB) = P(A) P(B|A)$$

The new symbol, $P(B|A)$, is that of a conditional probability and is read "the probability of B occurring given that the event A has occurred." Referring back to Fig. 7-2, we see that

$$P(B|A) = \frac{P(AB)}{P(A)}$$

i.e., already being in the subset A [the given condition and represented by $P(A)$] the only B's qualifying are those of the joint area AB, represented by $P(AB)$. When the latter expression is solved for $P(AB)$, we obtain the stated multiplication rule for dependent events. To illustrate this rule, assume that we have a box of 20 identical pieces of candy except that 10 have hard centers and 10 have soft centers. What is the probability of choosing two pieces in a row with soft centers (S)? The probability of the first piece would be $\frac{10}{20}$. However, the probability of drawing a second soft center is a conditional probability and would be $\frac{9}{19}$. For two successive soft-center pieces, we get

$$P(SS) = P(S)\,P(S|S) = \tfrac{10}{20} \times \tfrac{9}{19} = \tfrac{90}{380}$$

A deck of cards may also be used to illustrate this rule. For example, what is the probability of drawing two kings on successive draws of two cards from a well-shuffled deck? The probability of the first king would be $\frac{4}{52}$. The probability of the second king would be a conditional probability and equal to $\frac{3}{51}$ (one king has already been drawn). Applying our rule, we get

$$P(KK) = P(K)\,P(K|K) = \tfrac{4}{52} \times \tfrac{3}{51} = \tfrac{12}{2,652} = \tfrac{1}{663}$$

The rule extends to any number of events. For example, for three kings we get

$$P(KKK) = P(K)\,P(K|K)\,P(K|KK) = \tfrac{4}{52} \times \tfrac{3}{51} \times \tfrac{2}{50}$$

For four kings

$$P(KKKK) = P(K)\,P(K|K)\,P(K|KK)\,P(K|KKK) = \tfrac{4}{52} \times \tfrac{3}{51} \times \tfrac{2}{50} \times \tfrac{1}{49}$$

For five kings

$$P(KKKKK) = P(K)\,P(K|K)\,P(K|KK)\,P(K|KKK)\,P(K|KKKK)$$
$$= \tfrac{4}{52} \times \tfrac{3}{51} \times \tfrac{2}{50} \times \tfrac{1}{49} \times \tfrac{0}{48} = 0$$

This last case shows that the rule will even protect us when we ask foolish questions.

Independent Events

Two events are independent when the probability of one occurring is unaffected by the occurrence of the other event. The probability of tossing a head on our earlier nickel is $\frac{1}{2}$ regardless of what event occurs when tossing the dime. If one of a pair of dice is green and the other red, the appearance of a six on the green die has no effect on the probability of getting a six on the red die.

In symbols, independence may be stated as $P(B|A) = P(B)$ or $P(A|B) = P(A)$. The multiplication rule for independent events obviously becomes

$$P(AB) = P(A)P(B)$$

The probability of a red number in roulette is $P(R) = \frac{18}{38}$, as 18 of the 38 numbers are red (18 are black, with the zero and double zero being green). What is the probability of winning twice in a row when betting on red? As each spin of the wheel is an independent event, we may apply the rule given above and we get

$$P(RR) = P(R)P(R)$$

$$= \tfrac{18}{38} \times \tfrac{18}{38} = \tfrac{324}{1,444}$$

Let us assume that to win at a particular game one must first obtain a head tossing a nickel (A) and then roll a five with a single die (B). In order to bet intelligently, one should compute the probability of winning (AB). This turns out to be

$$P(AB) = P(A)P(B) = \tfrac{1}{2} \times \tfrac{1}{6} = \tfrac{1}{12}$$

The rule extends directly to any number of independent events. For example, what would be the probability of winning if in addition to the events above we need to follow them by drawing an ace from a deck of cards (C). Now we would have

$$P(ABC) = P(A)P(B)P(C) = \tfrac{1}{2} \times \tfrac{1}{6} \times \tfrac{4}{52} = \tfrac{4}{624} = \tfrac{1}{156}$$

BAYES' THEOREM

Bayes' theorem is used to compute what are termed as posterori (or just posterior) probabilities, as contrasted to those which we have been illustrating, which may be termed a priori (or prior) probabilities. Posterior probabilities are ones determined after some event has occurred; i.e., ones computed in light of some evidence or experiment. When using Bayes' theorem they may be treated as a revision of some earlier prior probabilities in light of experimental evidence. Treated this way the theorem becomes very useful in certain decision statistics.

Derivation

Bayes' theorem is a special case of conditional probabilities where the answer (a conditional probability) is a revision of a prior (elementary) probability on the basis of experimental evidence (the condition).

To begin our derivation of Bayes' theorem, we need to define first a partition of the set S. If the set S may be divided into subsets $A_1, A_2, \ldots, A_n$ which are mutually exclusive [i.e., $P(A_i A_j) = 0$ when $i \neq j$] and collectively exhaustive [i.e., $P(A_1) + P(A_2) + \cdots + P(A_n) = P(S)$], such a division is defined as a "partition."

Next let us consider another subset B of set S which may intersect with any of the partitioned subsets A_i (see for example Fig. 7-4). We desire to develop an equation for $P(B)$ in terms of the partitions. We would get $P(B) = P(A_1 B) + P(A_2 B) + \cdots +$

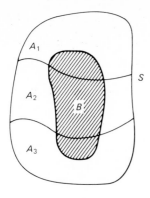

Figure 7-4 Partition of the set S.

$P(A_n B)$. We may rewrite this as:

$$P(B) = \frac{P(A_1)P(A_1 B)}{P(A_1)} + \frac{P(A_2)P(A_2 B)}{P(A_2)} + \cdots + \frac{P(A_n)P(A_n B)}{P(A_n)}$$

Using our conditional probability definition that

$$P(B|A) = \frac{P(AB)}{P(A)}$$

we may further rewrite our expression as

$$P(B) = P(A_1)P(B|A_1) + P(A_2)P(B|A_2) + \cdots + P(A_n)P(B|A_n)$$

This is our desired equation for $P(B)$.

Next consider our expression for the joint probability $P(AB)$, which may be written

$$P(AB) = P(A)P(B|A) \quad \text{or} \quad P(AB) = P(B)P(A|B)$$

and therefore

$$P(B)P(A|B) = P(A)P(B|A) \quad \text{and} \quad P(A|B) = \frac{P(A)P(B|A)}{P(B)}$$

The latter expression is Bayes' theorem, which can be written in more general terms using the equation for $P(B)$ derived earlier. This was

$$P(B) = P(A_1)P(B|A_1) + P(A_2)P(B|A_2) + \cdots + P(A_n)P(B|A_n)$$

$$= \sum_{i=1}^{n} P(A_i)P(B|A_i)$$

and Bayes' theorem becomes

$$P(A_i|B) = \frac{P(A_i)P(B|A_i)}{\displaystyle\sum_{i=1}^{n} P(A_i)P(B|A_i)}$$

The $P(A_i)$ are our prior probabilities, and the conditional probabilities $P(A_i|B)$ are our posterior probabilities for the same events A_i revised in terms of the experimental evidence (condition) B.

Illustration

Suppose that a manufacturer, while assembling a product, discovers a defective part and wishes to know from which of four suppliers of such parts it came. Unfortunately, the parts from all four suppliers appear identical, and all identifying labels have been lost. Designate the four suppliers as A_1, A_2, A_3, and A_4. On an a priori basis, each supplier would be equally likely and $P(A_1) = P(A_2) = P(A_3) = P(A_4) = \frac{1}{4}$. However, if we had some additional evidence, it might be possible to use it to revise the probabilities. Let us assume that past records indicate that supplier A_1 sends 10 percent defectives, supplier A_2 5 percent defectives, supplier A_3 4 percent defectives, and supplier A_4 only 1 percent defectives. Let B be the appearance of a defective part. Table 7-1 shows how this information may be used following Bayes' theorem to determine the probability of each supplier in the light of this evidence. Compare the prior probabilities with the posterior probabilities. We see that in light of the revision supplier A becomes the most likely source of the defective part.

Table 7-1 Bayes' theorem illustration

Supplier	Prior probability $[P(A_i)]$	Likelihood $[P(B\|A_i)]$	Joint probabilities $[P(A_iB)]$	Posterior probabilities $[P(A_i\|B)]$
A_1	0.25	0.10	0.0250	0.50
A_2	0.25	0.05	0.0125	0.25
A_3	0.25	0.04	0.0100	0.20
A_4	0.25	0.01	0.0025	0.05
Total	1.00	$\cdots$	$P(B) = 0.0500$	1.00

Bayes' theorem:

$$P(A_i|B) = \frac{P(A_iB)}{\displaystyle\sum_{i=1}^{n} P(A_iB)} = \frac{P(A_i)\,P(B|A_i)}{\displaystyle\sum_{i=1}^{n} P(A_i)\,P(B|A_i)}$$

Uses

Bayes' theorem is at the heart of a fairly new and controversial set of statistical techniques known as "bayesian statistics." These techniques are used primarily in statistical decision problems and will be discussed in greater detail in Chap. 13. The techniques are somewhat broader than Bayes' theorem itself and often make extensive use of subjective prior probabilities. To the extent that they are controversial, it is in the use of such probabilities and not in the theorem itself, which our derivation showed to be merely a rearrangment of well-established probability relationships.

STUDY GUIDE

Concepts Worth Remembering

Define:

1. Probability
2. Objective probabilities
3. Subjective (personal) probabilities
4. Discrete probabilities
5. Continuous probabilities
6. A priori (prior) probabilities
7. A posterori (posterior) probabilities
8. Empirical probabilities
9. Fundamental principle of counting
10. Multiple choices
11. Permutations
12. Combinations
13. Addition rule
14. Mutually exclusive events
15. Multiplication rule
16. Dependent events
17. Conditional probabilities
18. Independent events
19. Bayes' theorem

Self-Test

Multiple-choice questions. Circle the *letters* of the statements which correctly complete the questions. There may be one to four correct answers.

1 Probability:

(*a*) Is the formal tool for measuring and expressing degrees of certainty or uncertainty.

(*b*) Is easily defined and measured.

(*c*) Is based on the concept of "strength of belief."

(*d*) Must be based on objective evidence.

2 Sources of belief:

(*a*) May be classified as objective or subjective.

(*b*) If objective may be further subclassified as a priori or empirical.

(*c*) If subjective may be further subclassified as a priori or personal.

(*d*) May also be classified as discrete or continuous.

3 The measurement of probability:

(*a*) Depends on one's philosophical approach to defining probability.

(*b*) Takes only the form of counting.

(*c*) If based on counting, leads to "discrete probabilities."

(*d*) May involve the use of calculus.

4 Discrete probabilities:

(*a*) Result from measuring areas.

(b) May be illustrated by gambling games such as roulette.

(c) Are based on the process of counting.

(d) Are a special case of subjective probabilities.

5 Continuous probabilities:

(a) Involve an infinite number of points and cannot be determined.

(b) Are usually presented as probability distributions.

(c) Are generally measured as the ratio of two areas.

(d) Use the form of sophisticated counting known as combinations.

6 Combinations are a form of sophisticated counting:

(a) Where order is important and duplication is permitted.

(b) Used in the hypergeometric distribution.

(c) Helpful in determining discrete probabilities.

(d) Which defines HT and TH as the same combination.

7 Permutations are a form of sophisticated counting:

(a) Where order is important and duplication is not permitted.

(b) Used for the binomial distribution.

(c) Helpful for continuous probabilities.

(d) Which defines HT and TH as the same permutation.

8 The Addition Rule:

(a) Applies to dependent events.

(b) Is used to calculate the probability of A or B or both occurring.

(c) Considers mutually exclusive events as a special case.

(d) Is used to calculate conditional probabilities.

9 The Multiplication Rule:

(a) Is used to calculate the probability of simultaneous or successive events occurring.

(b) Considers independent events as a special case.

(c) May involve the use of conditional probabilities.

(d) Is used to calculate joint probabilities.

10 Bayes' theorem is:

(a) A special case of conditional probabilities.

(b) Used to calculate posterior probabilities.

(c) Used in decision statistics.

(d) A controversial theorem.

Questions to Think About

1. Explain clearly the difference between objective and subjective probabilities. Give examples of each type of probability.

2. Explain clearly the difference between discrete and continuous probabilities. Give an illustration of type of problem for which each might be used.

3. List and define the methods of sophisticated counting.

4. State the addition rule for determining probabilities and explain for what situations it applies.

5. State the multiplication rule for determining probabilities and explain for what situations it applies.

6. State Bayes' theorem. For what kind of problems is it used?

Problems

1 Answer the following questions assuming that you are drawing from a well-shuffled standard bridge deck of cards.

(*a*) What is the probability of drawing the jack of diamonds?

(*b*) What is the probability of drawing an eight?

(*c*) What is the probability of drawing the king or queen of spades?

(*d*) What is the probability of drawing a red six?

(*e*) What is the probability of drawing a black card?

(*f*) How would you classify the probabilities computed in (*a*) through (*e*)?

2 Assume that a state designs its license plates with a three-letter prefix but does not use the letters *I* or *O*.

(*a*) How many such three-letter prefixes are possible?

(*b*) What is the probability that a plate assigned at random will have *BBB* as a prefix?

(*c*) What is the probability that a plate assigned at random will have *BB*- as a prefix? (The symbol - indicates any letter other than *B*.)

(*d*) What is the probability that a plate assigned at random will have *B*-- as a prefix?

(*e*) What methods of counting did you use to solve these problems?

3 The problem is to construct words (real or nonsense) out of the letters of the word "mean."

(*a*) How many one-letter words are there?

(*b*) How many two-letter words are there?

(*c*) How many three-letter words are there?

(*d*) How many four-letter words are there?

(*e*) What method of counting did you use to solve these problems?

4 The Board of Directors of Probability, Inc., is made up of five statisticians and three lawyers.

(*a*) A three-member committee is to be chosen from the board at random. How many possible committees are there?

(*b*) How many committees of three will contain two statisticians and one lawyer?

(*c*) What is the probability that a randomly selected committee will have two statisticians and one lawyer?

(*d*) What methods of counting did you use in these problems?

5 Probability, Inc., employs 500 persons. Of these, 300 are men and 200 are women. Participating in the company-sponsored health insurance plan are 400 employees (including 250 men).

(*a*) What is the probability that an employee chosen at random is male or participates in the health plan (or both)?

(*b*) What is the probability that an employee chosen at random is female or participates in the health plan (or both)?

(*c*) What rule for combining elementary probabilities did you use to solve these problems? Why?

6 The 500 employees of Probability, Inc., are classified as either professional or clerical. The professional employees include 75 computer experts, 25 mathematicians, and 250 statisticians.

(*a*) What is the probability that an employee chosen at random is a professional?

(*b*) What is the probability that an employee chosen at random is a computer expert or a clerical employee?

(*c*) What rule for combining elementary probabilities did you use to solve these problems? Why?

(*d*) How does this problem differ from Prob. 5?

7 A set of 20 parts is known to contain two defective parts.

(*a*) What is the probability that two successive parts chosen at random will be the defective parts?

(*b*) What is the probability that three successive parts chosen at random will all be nondefective?

(*c*) What is the probability that if three parts are chosen at random, the set will contain one defective part?

(*d*) What rules for combining elementary probabilities did you use to solve these problems?

8 A telephone call sales business makes a sale once in every 10 telephone calls.

(*a*) What is the probability that sales will be made on three randomly selected consecutive calls?

(*b*) What is the probability that at least one sale will be made in three randomly selected consecutive calls? [*Hint:* P(success) = 1 - P(failure).]

(*c*) What rule for combining elementary probabilities did you use to solve these problems?

(*d*) How does this problem differ from Prob. 7?

9 The Beau Jardin Nursery has the problem of pricing a package of grass seed mix. The proper price depends upon the amount of bluegrass seed in the mix. The package does contain bluegrass, but it could have come from either of three bins, the first of which contains a mix of one-half bluegrass and the other two of which contain mixtures which are only one-fourth bluegrass. It is not known for certain which bin the package in question came from. Compute the probability that the package came from each of the three bins.

10 Probability, Inc., gets one-half of its supply of a particular electronic part from supplier A, two-tenths each from suppliers B and C, and the balance from supplier D. In the course of using this part during assembly, a part with a serious defect was discovered. It was no longer possible to determine which supplier supplied the particular part, but company records show that in the past supplier A had a record of supplying 6 percent defectives while the past record for the other suppliers is 10 percent each. Calculate for Probability, Inc., the probability that the part came from each of the suppliers.

Answers to Self-Test

The following letter should have been circled:

1 (*a*), (*c*); **2** (*a*), (*b*); **3** (*c*), (*d*); **4** (*b*), (*c*); **5** (*b*), (*c*); **6** (*b*), (*c*), (*d*); **7** (*a*); **8** (*b*), (*c*); **9** (*a*), (*b*), (*c*), (*d*); **10** (*a*), (*b*), (*c*).

EIGHT
PROBABILITY DISTRIBUTIONS

LEARNING OBJECTIVES

The basic learning objective is to study the determination of the probabilities of a complete set of outcomes through the use of a probability distribution. Specifically, you will become familiar with:

1. What a probability distribution is and the ways of presenting one.
2. Several useful discrete probability distributions including the:
   (*a*) Binomial distribution.
   (b) Poisson distribution.
   (*c*) Hypergeometric distribution.
3. The normal curve—its nature and use.

INTRODUCTION

Quite often we wish to know not only the probability of a particular outcome from a set of events but also the probability of each and every outcome in the set. In rolling dice, for example, we would want to know the probability of all the outcomes (all the sums from 2 through 12) to play the game wisely. Probability distributions are the statistician's way of studying the probabilities of all outcomes in a set.

Definition

A probability distribution is a special form of frequency distribution where the frequencies take the form of probabilities and the basic variable is a collectively exhaustive, mutually exclusive list of possible events or outcomes. Probability distributions may be expressed in the form of an equation (usually called the probability function) or presented as a table. Tables of values exist for all the commonly used distributions and greatly simplify the statistician's work. Probability distributions may be either discrete or continuous. Let us consider several simple examples.

For our first example, imagine that we have designed a new type of roulette wheel, which has only 10 slots. One slot is numbered with a 1, two slots with 2s, three slots with 3s, and the final four slots with 4s. What would the probability distribution be like for our hypothetical wheel? In functional form we can write

$$f(x) = p(x) = \frac{x}{10} \quad \text{for } x = 1, 2, 3, 4$$

The equivalent table appears as Table 8-1, which shows the character of a probability distribution as a frequency distribution. Note that, as required, the entire set of probabilities sums to 1.

As a second example, let us look at the probability distribution for runs of pluses or minuses where the appearance of a plus or a minus at any point in the sequence is equally likely, i.e., $p(+) = p(-) = \frac{1}{2}$. The functional form of the distribution is

$$f(x) = P(x) = (\tfrac{1}{2})^x \quad \text{for } x = 1, 2, 3, 4, \ldots$$

Table 8-1 Hypothetical probability distribution

Possible outcomes (x)	Frequencies [P(x)]
1	$\frac{1}{10}$
2	$\frac{2}{10}$
3	$\frac{3}{10}$
4	$\frac{4}{10}$
Total	$\frac{10}{10} = 1$

Table 8-2 Probability distribution for a run of pluses

Possible outcomes number of pluses (x)	Frequencies $[P(x)]$
1	$(\frac{1}{2})^1 = \frac{1}{2}$
2	$(\frac{1}{2})^2 = \frac{1}{4}$
3	$(\frac{1}{2})^3 = \frac{1}{8}$
4	$(\frac{1}{2})^4 = \frac{1}{16}$
5	$(\frac{1}{2})^5 = \frac{1}{32}$
6	$(\frac{1}{2})^6 = \frac{1}{64}$
.	.
.	.
.	.
Total	1

This distribution is shown in tabular form in Table 8-2. Note that the distribution is open-ended.

The examples above are rather simple and somewhat limited in application, although the second example does have some practical uses. More complex distributions, however, may be presented in the same two ways. We shall now take a brief look at a number of useful probability distributions. These will be presented in functional form as mathematical models, but are ones which identify readily with certain real-world situations of great interest to the statistician and for which they may be used to compute the probabilities of the outcomes in those situations. The underlying assumptions or conditions for the proper use of the distribution will be discussed fully. We shall begin with the generally used discrete distributions.

SOME USEFUL DISCRETE PROBABILITY DISTRIBUTIONS

There are three discrete probability distributions that are of sufficient importance to be included here. They are (1) the binomial distribution, (2) the Poisson distribution, and (3) the hypergeometric distribution.

Binomial Distribution

If a random or chance event may take either of two forms, say A or not-A $(\overline{A})$ and $P(A) = p$ and $P(\overline{A}) = q = 1 - p$, on a single trial and we repeat the experiment for n independent trials, recording as x the number of A's appearing in the n trials, the binomial distribution will give the probabilities that various numbers of A will appear. The functional form of the binomial is

$$P(x) = {}_nC_x p^x q^{n-x} \quad \text{for } x = 0, 1, 2, \ldots, n$$

The equation is for the probability of exactly x appearances of A in the n trials. It is the general term of the expansion of binomial $(q + p)^n$, which is a special case of the traditional binomial $(a + b)^n$ that readers may recall from algebra. To apply the equation we need numerical values for n and p, which are termed the "parameters" of the equation.

To illustrate, suppose that in an attempt to control quality we wish to sample a production process thought to produce 10 percent defectives (items are classified as either defective or nondefective). This would give us $p = 0.1$ and, of course, $q = 0.9$. Let us draw a random sample of 10 items ($n = 10$) and determine the probability of observing two defectives ($x = 2$). Using our equation, we get

$$P(2) = {}_{10}C_2 (0.1)^2 (0.9)^8 = \frac{10 \cdot 9 \cdot 8!}{2 \cdot 1 \cdot 8!} (0.01)(0.43)$$

$$= 45(0.01)(0.43) = 0.1935$$

Repeating for other values of x, we would end up eventually with the values of Table 8-3. Note that a binomial has $n + 1$ terms when expanded as x varies from 0 through n.

The values of Table 8-3 may also be (and mostly were) obtained from the general binomial tables found in App. G, which gives the $P(x)$ for selected values of the parameters of p and n, the only values needed to use (enter) the tables. One first finds the subtable corresponding to n and then the column of that table corresponding to p. Listed under p will be the probabilities of various possible x's, as indicated by the row headings.

Table 8-3 Binomial illustration

Number of defectives (x)	$P(x)$
0	0.3487
1	0.3874
2	0.1937†
3	0.0574
4	0.0112
5	0.0015
6	0.0001
7	0.0000
8	0.0000
9	0.0000
10	0.0000
Total	1.0000

†The small difference between the value calculated above and the value here is merely a rounding difference.

The binomial is the correct distribution to use to study our production process. Mathematically, the binomial requires a dichotomous classification and independence. Our production was classified as defective or nondefective; and if the production process is in control, chance will determine the appearance of a defective, i.e., a condition of independence will occur. Thus, we see that our production conditions match our model.

If in drawing a sample of 10 we should actually observe an event of rare probability [e.g., we observe five defectives, an event with $P(5) = 0.0015$], we may wish to question the assumptions on which our binomial is based; i.e., we may wish to reject the assumptions that the process is in control and/or producing 10 percent defectives. This illustrates the way in which the binomial may be of use to management in making decisions (in this case deciding whether the production process is functioning properly).

In summary, the binomial may be used to determine the probabilities of outcomes in situations characterized by independence (i.e., the probability of the appearance of an event remains constant from one trial to the next) and for which the events are classified as one or another of only two categories. The condition of independence can be met by sampling from an infinite universe as with our production process or by sampling with replacement. If the sample is small relative to the size of a finite universe, the condition of independence will be substantially met and the binomial may be used.

Poisson Distribution

If an event can occur repeatedly at random over a large area or long period of time, the Poisson distribution may be used to determine the probability of its occurrence in a small area or short interval of time. Poisson events differ from binomial events in that their appearance is readily identifiable, but a nonappearance is undefined. It is possible to identify a flaw in an enameled surface as on a refrigerator, but how do we count nonflaws? We can count the number of telephone calls through a switching mechanism or the number of airplanes trying to land at an airport, but what constitutes a noncall or a nonplane? We know when an accident occurs in the plant but cannot count the number of nonaccidents. These all illustrate situations in which we may use the Poisson distribution to calculate the probabilities.

The functional form of the distribution is

$$P(x) = \frac{m^x}{x!} e^{-m} \quad \text{for } x = 0, 1, 2, \ldots$$

The equation has only one parameter, m, which equals the expected, or average, number of appearances in a specified space or period of time. Parameter m is usually determined by studying the number of occurrences of our event over a long period of time or in a large area. Tables for the Poisson distribution are to be found in App. H for various values of m, the only value needed to use the tables. One merely finds the subtable corresponding to the desired m and listed thereunder are the probabilities of the relevant outcomes (x's).

Table 8-4 Poisson illustration

Number of defects (x)	$P(x)$
0	0.8187
1	0.1637
2	0.0164
3	0.0011
4	0.0001
5	0.0000
6	0.0000
.	.
.	.
.	.
Sum	1.0000

To illustrate the use of the Poisson distribution, let us assume that a process used to insulate electric wire produces from time to time a pinhole-sized defect and that we wish to study the probabilities of such defects occurring in a foot of wire. The Poisson distribution is appropriate here as a defect can be identified but a nondefect is without meaning. To determine a value for m, a study is made of 1,000 ft of wire wherein 200 defects are discovered. The average or expected number of occurrences per foot of wire (m) then equals 0.2 (200/1,000 ft). Table 8-4 gives the probabilities of observing various numbers of pinpoint defects (x) per foot of wire and was derived from App. H using $m = 0.2$. Although the Poisson is theoretically open-ended, we see there is no practical probability of seeing five, six, or more defects in a foot of wire. This information can be used by management to see if the insulating process remains stable. If in some future randomly selected foot of wire, two or more defects were discovered, management should be suspicious of the process as the probability of such an event is quite small. [Specifically, $P(x \geqslant 2) = P(x = 2) + P(x = 3) + P(x = 4) + P(x = 5) + \cdots = 0.0164 + 0.0011 + 0.0001 + 0.0000 + \cdots = 0.0176.$]

In summary, the Poisson distribution is used to determine the probabilities of observing varying numbers of occurrences of an event of interest (a pinpoint defect) in a small area (a foot of wire) or a small interval of time if the event can occur at random over a large area (many feet of wire) or a long period of time. The occurrences of the event are countable, but nonoccurrences are not countable.

Hypergeometric Distribution

The binomial distribution required a condition of independence which could be obtained by sampling from an infinite universe or by sampling a finite universe *with* replacement. However, if we sample from a finite universe *without* replacement, our condition of independence no longer holds. For this situation we use the hypergeometric distribution to calculate the probabilities of various possible outcomes. We are again considering events which may be identified as either one or another of a twofold classification scheme.

If we are sampling from a finite population N composed of elements of two kinds such that there are A of the first kind and $N - A$ of the second kind and x is the number of occurrences of A in a sample of size n, the probability of x is given by

$$P(x) = \frac{{}_AC_x \; {}_{N-A}C_{N-x}}{{}_NC_n} \qquad \max(0, A - N + n) \leqslant x \leqslant \min(n, A)$$

This is the hypergeometric distribution and is actually based on our elementary definition of probability. The denominator counts the number of total possible samples of size n from N and the numerator counts the number of these with the desired number of x's. The description of the sample space $[\max(0, A - N + n) \leqslant x \leqslant \min(n, A)]$ i.e., the list of the possible outcomes or values for x, appears frightening, but it merely details the obvious facts that we can get no more x's than there are A's $[\min(n, A)]$ or that if we use up all the $N - A$'s, we must get more than zero x's $[\max(0, A - N + n)]$. We shall clarify this further in our illustration.

To illustrate, imagine that we have a bowl of 10 apples ($N = 10$). Of these, five are red Delicious ($A = 5$) and five are yellow Delicious ($N - A = 5$). Let us take a sample of six apples ($n = 6$) and concentrate on the number of red Delicious as x. First, let us determine the possible values for x. We have

$$\max(0, 5 - 10 + 6) \leqslant x \leqslant \min(6, 5)$$

$$\max(0, 1) \leqslant x \leqslant \min(6, 5) \qquad 1 \leqslant x \leqslant 5$$

In a sample of six we must get at least one red Delicious (there are only five yellows) but can do no better than getting all of them (five). We may now make use of the formula to compute the probability of various outcomes. For example, the probability of obtaining one red apple ($x = 1$) is

$$P(1) = \frac{{}_AC_x \; {}_{N-A}C_{n-x}}{{}_NC_n} = \frac{{}_5C_1 \; {}_5C_5}{{}_{10}C_6} = \frac{5 \cdot 1}{210} = \frac{5}{210}$$

Table 8-5 shows our complete probability distribution. The hypergeometric distribution is difficult to tabulate as its values depend on three parameters: n, N, and A. However, limited tables are available. Various tables of factorials and logs of factorials are also available to help in solving hypergeometric problems.

Table 8-5 Hypergeometric illustration

Number of red Delicious (x)	$P(x)$
1	$\frac{5}{210}$
2	$\frac{50}{210}$
3	$\frac{100}{210}$
4	$\frac{50}{210}$
5	$\frac{5}{210}$
Total	$\frac{210}{210} = 1$

Note should also be taken of the fact that the hypergeometric distribution is often approximated by the binomial distribution. As pointed out earlier, if the sample size (n) is small relative to the universe size (N), the binomial condition of independence is substantially met.

A BRIEF INTRODUCTION TO SOME USEFUL CONTINUOUS PROBABILITY DISTRIBUTIONS

We now turn our attention to a look at some continuous probability distributions. For this type of distribution, the probabilities are almost always determined by the use of tables. Our introduction, therefore, will emphasize primarily the nature and use of such tables. The first distribution to be discussed (and by all odds the most important probability distribution) will be the normal curve.

The Normal Curve

The normal curve is a theoretical mathematical curve; i.e., like our discrete distributions discussed earlier it may be written in a functional form. However, the specific nature of the equation of the normal curve need not concern us here, since all values of interest for the curve have been tabulated. When plotted, the curve is bell-shaped and symmetrical, with tails approaching, but not touching, the horizontal axis.

Importance of the Normal Curve in Statistical Work

Of all the various theoretical frequency distributions used in statistical work, the normal curve is the most important. First, it serves as a standard to which other distributions are compared. Others have the same (none) or more skewness than the normal curve or have either more, the same, or less kurtosis. Second, the curve can be used to approximate many kinds of natural phenomena, such as certain IQs, heights of adult males, or tree diameters. Third, the logical and mathematical assumptions underlying the normal curve are well known, making it a useful theoretical model. Finally, the curve is basic to much advanced statistical work. Large portions of sampling theory rest on or make use of the normal curve to determine probability values. Much of correlation also depends on the normal curve.

Working with the Normal Curve

The normal curve is an easy curve with which to work, as it has a standard geometrical shape and depends upon only two constants to describe it: its arithmetic mean (μ) and its standard deviation (σ).[1] It is a standard geometrical shape in the same sense that a square is a standard geometrical shape. The two squares in Fig. 8-1a and b are of differ-

---

[1]Since we are talking about a theoretical distribution, we shall use the Greek letters μ (mu) and σ (sigma) for the mean and standard deviation, respectively.

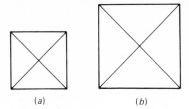

(a)   (b)   **Figure 8-1** Two squares.

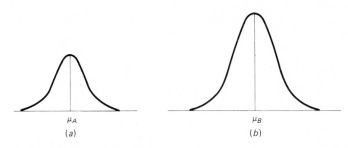

μ_A μ_B
(a)   (b)

Figure 8-2 Two normal curves.

ent size, but each has one-half of its area on either side of a diagonal and one-fourth of its area in each pie-shaped section.

The two normal curves shown in Fig. 8-2a and b have different sizes too, but also have certain relative relationships in common. Each curve has one-half of its area above (or below) a vertical ordinate erected at the arithmetic mean. The irregular shape of each half of the area under a normal curve makes it difficult to divide the total area into quarters by eye, but this can be done easily with the aid of tables.

The Standard Normal Curve

Before one can make use of the tables of normal curve values, one must know how to convert any normal curve into the standard normal curve upon which the tables are based. The standard normal curve is one with a mean of 0 and a standard deviation equal to 1. The conversion is illustrated in Fig. 8-3a and b for two different normal curves.

The item, or X scale, of each curve shows values in the original units of the data. The means of both curves lie right under the curves' peaks, and one additional value is shown for each curve. The second scale, labeled $X - \mu$, is called the "deviation scale." This scale is still in the units of the original data, but it should be noted that, in terms of this scale, both curves now have a mean of 0. The third scale, labeled $Z [Z = (X - \mu)/\sigma]$, is the standard scale. To obtain values for the standard scale, we divide corresponding values of the deviation scale through by the value of the curve's standard deviation. The standard scale has no units since these cancel with the division. The values of Z are called "normal deviates." The scale is standard in that like values of this scale have like relative values in any normal curve. As 12 lb and \$30 both work out to be standard scale values of +1, the vertical ordinates above, 12 lb and \$30, are the same fraction

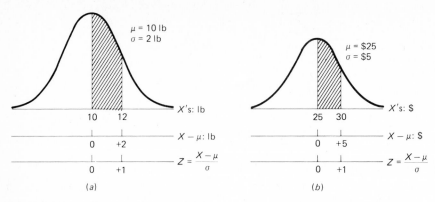

Figure 8-3 Normal curve scale conversion.

(0.6065) of the height of the ordinate at the mean. More important, the same percentage of the area under the curve will lie in an area bounded by an ordinate at the mean and an ordinate at +1 (the shaded areas). This area is 34.13 percent for either curve.

Normal Curve Tables

Normal curve tables are of two general types, tables of ordinates and tables of areas. We are chiefly interested in the latter types, which, as their name implies, give portions of the total area lying between or beyond ordinates erected at various standard scale values. These areas may be interpreted as probabilities directly as the total area is taken as one or as 100 percent. An example of this type of table is given in App. B_1. This particular table gives areas as percentages of the total area of 100 percent. The percentages given are those for the area beyond the standard scale value to plus infinity. The same areas would apply for negative standard scale values, since the curve is symmetrical. The use of this table is illustrated in the discussion that follows.

A variation of the table of areas is also given in App. B_2. In this table we may look up normal deviates (standard scale values) corresponding to certain areas, whereas in the previous table we determined areas corresponding to certain normal deviates. The use of this table is also illustrated in the following discussion.

Normal Curve Tables: Numerical Examples

For our examples of the use of normal curve tables, let us assume we have a lot of 5,000 washers whose diameters may be approximated by a normal curve with a mean of 2.0 in and a standard deviation of 0.3 in. (Whether the diameters of these washers can be fairly approximated by a normal curve can and should be tested before proceeding. However, our objective here is merely to illustrate the use of the table, so we shall assume that the diameters are distributed normally.) We can use our normal curve tables to answer a large variety of questions about these washers. Our choice of questions will primarily illustrate the use of the table rather than a specific problem of management interest.

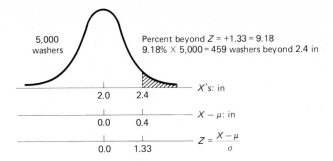

Figure 8-4 Normal curve illustration.

Let us first ask how many of the 5,000 washers are over 2.4 in in diameter. The steps to find this factor are illustrated in Fig. 8-4. The shaded area in the sketch represents washers over 2.4 in in diameter. To make use of the tables, this value (2.4 in) must be converted to a standard-scale (Z) value. Here

$$Z = \frac{2.4 - 2.0}{0.3} = \frac{0.4}{0.3} = 1.33$$

Appendix B_1 gives the percentages beyond a given normal deviate (Z). We may read directly from the table, then, that 9.18 percent of any normal curve lies beyond Z = +1.33. Multiplying by our 5,000 washers, we find 459 washers of over 2.4 in in diameter.

The calculation used here would also give the answer to the related question, "What is the probability that a washer chosen at random will have a diameter greater than 2.4 in?" The probability is 9.18 percent, or the same as the area beyond 2.4 in, since the entire curve represents all washers and those greater than 2.4 in are represented by the area computed for the tail of the curve. Any area under a normal curve may be similarly interpreted as a probability.

Some questions involve areas which may not be read directly from the table. Such problems may be solved by adding and/or subtracting areas read from the table. For example, suppose that our question is, "How many washers have diameters between 2.0 (the mean) and 2.1 in?" The solution is illustrated in Fig. 8-5.

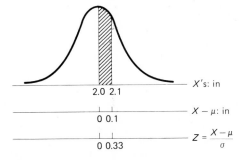

Percent beyond Z = 0.00 = 50.00

Percent beyond Z = 0.33 = 37.07

Percent between Z = 0.0 and
Z = 0.33 = 12.93

12.93 × 5,000 = 646 washers

Figure 8-5 Normal curve illustration.

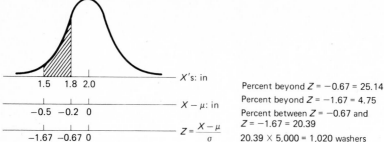

Percent beyond $Z = -0.67 = 25.14$
Percent beyond $Z = -1.67 = 4.75$
Percent between $Z = -0.67$ and
$Z = -1.67 = 20.39$
$20.39 \times 5{,}000 = 1{,}020$ washers

Figure 8-6 Normal curve illustration.

The diameters in question are first converted to Z values and the percent beyond each obtained by reference to App. B_1. The 50.00 percent beyond $Z = 0.00$ includes both the shaded and plain portions of Fig. 8-5 to the right of the mean. The 37.07 percent beyond $Z = 0.33$ is the plain area beyond 2.1 in in the figure. Therefore, to obtain the shaded area only, we substract the plain area (37.07 percent) from that of the shaded and plain combined (50.00 percent). The difference is 12.93 percent, or 646 washers between 2.0 and 2.1 in.

Figure 8-6 indicates another question, which is merely a variation of the above: "How many washers have diameters between 1.5 and 1.8 in?" The solution again involves the subtraction of areas and differs only in that the areas are below the mean. Negative Z values give the same areas as positive Z values since the curve is symmetrical.

One final kind of question will be illustrated, "How many washers lie between 1.7 and 2.6 in?" The answer is shown in Fig. 8-7. This differs from previous questions in that the area desired lies on both sides of the mean. One may obtain the two plain areas, i.e., below 1.7 in and above 2.6 in, directly from the table. If these are added and subtracted from 100 percent, one has the solution to the question, 4,092 washers.

We shall now illustrate several reverse-type problems, making use of App. B_2, which presents a table of the normal deviates corresponding to various one- and two-tailed percentages. As our first question, let us ask, "Above what diameter are the

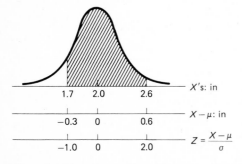

Percent beyond $Z = -1.0 = 15.87$
Percent beyond $Z = +2.0 = \underline{2.28}$
18.15

Percent between $Z = -1.0$ and $Z = +2.0 =$
$= 100.00 - 18.15 = 81.85$

$81.85\% \times 5{,}000 = 4{,}092$ washers

Figure 8-7 Normal curve illustration.

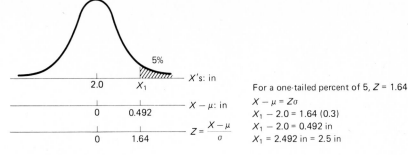

For a one-tailed percent of 5, $Z = 1.64$

$X - \mu = Z\sigma$

$X_1 - 2.0 = 1.64 \, (0.3)$

$X_1 - 2.0 = 0.492$ in

$X_1 = 2.492$ in $= 2.5$ in

Figure 8-8 Normal curve illustration.

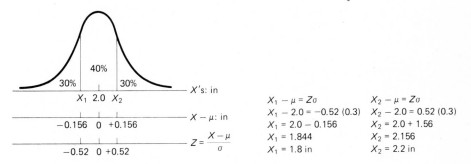

$X_1 - \mu = Z\sigma$	$X_2 - \mu = Z\sigma$
$X_1 - 2.0 = -0.52 \, (0.3)$	$X_2 - 2.0 = 0.52 \, (0.3)$
$X_1 = 2.0 - 0.156$	$X_2 = 2.0 + 1.56$
$X_1 = 1.844$	$X_2 = 2.156$
$X_1 = 1.8$ in	$X_2 = 2.2$ in

Figure 8-9 Normal curve illustration.

largest 5 percent of the diameters to be found?" The solution is sketched in Fig. 8-8. The procedure just reverses those from above in that we work from the Z scale back up to the X scale. Appendix B_2 tells us that 5 percent of any normal curve lies beyond a $Z = 1.64$. In general, however, $Z = (X - \mu)/\sigma$. Therefore $X - \mu = Z\sigma$. Substituting our known values for μ, Z, and σ, we solve and obtain an X of 2.5 in.

As our final illustration, consider the question, "The middle 40 percent of the washers lies between what two diameters?" The solution is shown in Fig. 8-9. The main points here are, first, to realize that, since the table gives curve tails, one must look up 30 percent one-tailed or 60 percent two-tailed to determine the Z's of 0.52 and, second, that the Z below the mean is negative.

Other Useful Distributions

In addition to the normal curve, there are three other continuous probability distributions that are of particular use in statistical work. These are (1) the t distribution, (2) the χ^2 distribution, and (3) the F distribution. The t distribution is useful with small samples, the χ^2 distribution is used in single-sample problems involving variances, and the F distribution finds use in two-sample tests of variances and in analysis of variance problems. All three distributions and their applications are discussed in Chap. 14.

STUDY GUIDE

Concepts Worth Remembering

Define:

1. Probability distribution
2. Binomial distribution
3. Poisson distribution
4. Hypergeometric distribution
5. Normal curve
6. Normal deviates
7. Standard normal curve

Self-Test

Circle the proper letter to indicate whether the following statements are true or false.

T F **1** The binomial distribution is a special case of determining probabilities for a set of dependent events.

T F **2** The binomial distribution has two parameters, n and p.

T F **3** To use the binomial distribution, sampling should be from an infinite universe or from a finite universe with replacement.

T F **4** The binomial distribution is a continuous probability distribution.

T F **5** The Poisson distribution has one parameter, m.

T F **6** The Poisson distribution is a discrete probability distribution.

T F **7** The Poisson distribution is used in problems where the occurrence of an event can be recognized but a nonoccurrence is undefined.

T F **8** The functional form of the Poisson distribution makes use of combinations.

T F **9** The hypergeometric distribution has two parameters, n and A.

T F **10** The formula for the hypergeometric distribution makes use of permutations.

T F **11** The hypergeometric distribution is used for problems where sampling is from a finite universe without replacement.

T F **12** The binomial distribution may be used to approximate the hypergeometric distribution if the sample being drawn is small relative to the size of the universe being sampled.

T F **13** The standard normal curve table is based on a normal curve with a zero mean and a unit standard deviation.

T F **14** The normal curve is tangent to the x axis at ± 3 standard deviations.

T F **15** The normal curve may be used to approximate many kinds of natural phenomena.

T F **16** The normal curve is the most useful of the discrete probability distributions.

Questions to Think About

1. Describe the nature of the binomial distribution, being sure to indicate its parameters and the conditions necessary for its use.
2. Describe the nature of the Poisson distribution and indicate the types of problems for which it may be used.
3. Compare and contrast the hypergeometric distribution with the binomial distribution. Under what conditions may the binomial distribution be used to approximate the hypergeometric distribution?
4. Describe the general nature of the normal curve. How is any normal curve converted to the "standard normal curve"? Explain briefly the importance of the normal curve in statistical methods.

Problems

1 A particular machine process used by Probability, Inc., has been producing 5 percent defectives (production is classified as either defective or nondefective). A random sample of eight items has been drawn to check on the machine process.

   (a) What is the probability of finding no defectives in the sample?
   (b) What is the probability of finding one defective in the sample?
   (c) What is the probability of finding two or more defectives in the sample?
   (d) What might one conclude if one found three defectives in the sample?
   (e) What probability distribution did you use to solve this problem? Why?

2 La Plata Press, a mail-order publisher, has a sales letter which has had a 10 percent response rate. This letter has been mailed to a random sample of 25 individuals on a new mailing list in an effort to test out the list. Assuming the 10 percent rate applies to the new list:

   (a) What is the probability of having no responses to the sample mailing?
   (b) What is the probability of having exactly two responses to the mailing?
   (c) What is the probability of having three or more responses to the mailing?
   (d) What probability distribution did you use to solve this problem? Why?
   (e) What assumption did you make about the size of the new mailing list?

3 Flawless Steel, Inc., makers of fine stainless steel plate, produces stainless steel plate which in fact has an occasional defect. However, these defects occur only once in every 10 m² of steel plate.

   (a) What is the probability that a square meter of stainless steel plate will have no defects?
   (b) What is the probability that a square meter of stainless steel plate will have exactly one defect?
   (c) What is the probability that a square meter of stainless steel plate will have two or more defects?
   (d) What probability distribution did you use to solve this problem? Why?

4 The machine repair department of Flawless Steel receives an average of two calls for service per hour. If calls are randomly distributed:

   (a) What is the probability of receiving no service calls in an hour?
   (b) What is the probability of receiving exactly two service calls in an hour?
   (c) What is the probability of receiving more than three calls in an hour?
   (d) What probability distribution did you use to solve this problem? Why?

5 Probability, Inc., has just received a shipment of a box containing 50 delicate parts, 10 percent of which can be expected to break during shipment. It wishes to determine the probability of various numbers of broken parts in a sample of eight parts if breakage is normal. Calculate for Probability, Inc., the sample space and the probability of each of the possible number of broken parts in the sample.

6 A large public utility maintains a car pool for the use of its employees when traveling on company business. Company records indicate that the cost per mile of operating company cars is normally distributed around a mean of 17.9 cents, with a standard deviation of 0.9 cent.

(a) What portion of the company's cars costs less than 16.5 cents to operate?

(b) What portion of the company's cars costs between 17.5 and 18.5 cents to operate?

(c) What portion of the company's cars costs between 18.0 and 19.0 cents to operate?

(d) The most expensive 5 percent will have an operating cost of at least how many cents?

(e) The middle 80 percent of the cars' operating costs will lie between what two cost figures?

7 An investigation of the burning properties of a particular brand of fluorescent light tubes found that the length of life of the 40-W tubes is normally distributed around a mean life of 9,120 h, with a standard deviation of 215 h.

(a) What percentage of tubes of the type described above has a length of life between 9,120 and 9,400 hr?

(b) What percentage of such tubes has a length of life between 9,000 and 9,300 h?

(c) What percentage of such tubes has a length of life between 9,200 and 9,400 h?

(d) The middle 60 percent of the tubes have lengths of life between what two figures?

(e) At what length of life will only 10 percent of the tubes still be burning?

8 Analysis of past data has shown a manufacturing firm that the hub thickness of a particular type of gear it manufactures is normally distributed around a mean thickness of 5 cm, with a standard deviation of 0.1 cm.

(a) In a production run of 5,000 such gears, how many will have a thickness greater than 5.15 cm?

(b) How many of the production run will have thicknesses between 4.825 and 5.075 cm?

(c) How many will have thicknesses between 4.725 and 4.875 cm?

(d) The thickest 3,400 gears will exceed what thickness?

(e) The thinnest 200 gears will be less than what thickness?

Answers to Self-Test

1 F; 2 T; 3 T; 4 F; 5 T; 6 T; 7 T; 8 F; 9 F; 10 F; 11 T; 12 T; 13 T; 14 F; 15 T; 16 F.

NINE

THE NATURE OF SAMPLES

LEARNING OBJECTIVES

The basic learning objective is to learn about that "properly chosen" sample—what it is and how to obtain it. Specifically, you will study:

1. The advantages of sampling.
2. The concepts of a universe and a frame and their relationship.
3. A classification of samples, including:
   (*a*) Convenience samples.
   (*b*) Judgment samples.
   (*c*) Probability samples.
4. Random selection procedures.
5. The sources of error in probability sampling.

INTRODUCTION

The use of sampling techniques is not new in the applications of statistical methods, but the number of new sampling applications is growing rapidly. Particularly rapid advances have been made in the last few decades in such fields as statistical quality control, survey sampling, and statistical (bayesian) decision theory. These developments exist to such an extent that the term "modern statistics" is sometimes applied to sampling techniques even though many aspects of their theory and application are quite old. Although, for reasons set forth below, sampling techniques are widely used in business and industry to aid management in its decision making, one must not assume that all problems are amenable to sampling techniques. In some cases the universe is so small that it is possible to consider it in its entirety. In others, the expense of taking a sample may be greater than the savings which would result from having the sample information. It would be foolish to spend $500 on a survey when the potential savings are only $100.

ADVANTAGES OF SAMPLING

Money Savings

Samples are used widely as an aid in decision making because of certain general advantages of the techniques. The first of these is the money savings made possible. Interviewing or testing costs are substantially the same per person interviewed or item tested. By use of sampling techniques, only a portion of the universe is interviewed or tested.

Greater Speed of Collection

The second is that a sample's smaller size makes it possible to collect sample data more quickly than census data. Quicker collection and presentation of the results make for more timely decisions. The ability to make decisions quickly, yet correctly, is very important in business. In the introduction of a new product, for example, the first in the market may capture the lion's share.

Greater Overall Accuracy

The third advantage is that it is possible with samples to have greater overall accuracy than with a census. This is true even though the use of samples introduces sampling error. The smaller size of the sample leaves enough funds remaining in the survey budget to exercise tighter control on nonsampling errors (bias and unsystematic errors). It is often possible to reduce these errors to an extent that more than compensates for the extra error introduced by sampling, thus resulting in greater overall accuracy. Numerous experiments with 100 percent inspection of large lots in quality-control work show an inability to determine correctly the percentage defective in the lot as accurately as could be done by sampling. The tedium of 100 percent inspection introduces large nonsampling errors, which exceed the sampling errors of the less tedious sample inspection.

Destructive Testing and Infinite Universes

Finally, for several classes of problems, sampling is the only practicable method. Some testing procedures involve the destruction of the item being tested. Tensile strength is tested by stretching a piece of rope until it breaks. The length of life of a light bulb is determined by burning it until it no longer burns. When testing procedures of a destructive nature are used, one must sample to find the universe properties or have no universe left after testing.

Another class of problems for which sampling is necessary is that having a universe which is conceptually infinite. The universe to a manufacturer of a new measles vaccine would not be only the children or people who might be alive now, but would also include many uncountable children not yet born who would receive the vaccine at some future date. Hence, the universe is conceptually infinite. A manager trying to study absenteeism is most likely more interested in the process or pattern by which people are absent than in past absenteeism itself. The universe of such a study, again, is infinite, because it includes future uncountable absentees. Production of a machine, which turns out goods for an undeterminable period of time, may likewise be thought of as an infinite process. To study such universes one must of necessity sample. All past experience itself is nothing more than a sample of the infinite universe represented by the process.

We have suggested, under the foregoing headings, four reasons for the wide use and popularity of sampling techniques. We shall now continue by discussing several aspects of samples themselves. One must not forget, however, that not all statistical problems are sampling problems.

SEVERAL IMPORTANT CONCEPTS

Statistical Universe

In order to aid our discussion it will be helpful to clarify several important concepts. The first of these is the statistical universe, or population (both terms seem to have wide popular use). The statistical universe was defined in Chap. 2 as a totality consisting of all items that might be surveyed in a particular problem if a complete enumeration were made. The items may be either people or things, and generally have several characteristics of either a quantitative or a qualitative nature which may be of interest in the particular problem. Full identification of a universe consists, then, of specifying both the items to be studied and the characteristics to be observed. The terms "elements" and "elementary units" are also used to refer to the "items" making up a universe. As an example we might consider the item a TV tube. A particular problem would perhaps limit the universe to a particular manufacturer's tubes as of a certain date. Some characteristics which might be studied would include size, color vs. black-and-white, and length of life. Definition of the universe in a statistical study is of great importance, whether the study is to be a census or a sample survey. In either case careful definition is necessary in order to identify the items to be studied and thereby prevent waste motion during the collection process. In a sample study careful definition is also necessary in order to ascertain what the inferences being made apply to.

Frame

In actual practice, in many statistical studies, before any survey work can be done, it is necessary to establish a "frame." A frame is a means of identifying the items to be surveyed. It may consist of a list, a map, or any other definite means of identifying the universe items. Not all studies require a formal frame. If one is testing a lot of fuses, one usually has the whole lot definitely identified and readily available. Alternatively, if one wished to survey housewives' opinions of soap products, one would find it difficult to identify and list all housewives in a given area. For the latter type of problem a frame must definitely be developed, and this is usually done by the use of maps which will identify blocks and even houses. Of course, even a complete list of houses may not give a complete list of housewives, but the difference should not cause insuperable difficulties. In a sample survey, obtaining an adequate frame is often a greater problem than choosing a representative sample. For this type of study the items in the frame may be referred to as "sampling units," because they are the items from which the sample is actually chosen.

TYPES OF SAMPLES

Samples are generally classified on the basis of how the items are chosen from the universe (or frame) to be part of the sample. On this basis we have three broad types of samples: (1) convenience samples, (2) judgment (selective) samples, and (3) probability samples.

Convenience Samples

Convenience samples are identified by the fact that the universe items making up the sample are selected on the basis of taking those items which are most readily available (convenient). The most familiar example of this type of sample is that chosen by the "inquiring reporter," who merely stations himself on a handy street corner and asks his questions of any passerby who will stop long enough to answer. Obviously, samples of this type are not particularly scientific and may be subject to great errors. Even worse, the errors in this type of sample are unmeasurable and unpredictable. This should not imply that there is no place for such samples, but they are of little use in serious statistical work. They are inexpensive and may be of real use if one is interested only in producing ideas.

Judgment (Selective) Samples

In this type of sample the sample items are deliberately chosen from the universe, the basis for the selection resting on the experience and judgment of the selector, who is usually an expert in the subject field involved in the study. While samples of this type may be subject to relatively small errors if the expert's judgment is good (and certainly subject to less errors than convenience sampling), the errors involved still cannot be measured or predicted. Hence, this type of sample is again to be avoided except for certain special situations. Experience has indicated that small judgment samples, particularly if chosen from highly variable universes, have smaller errors than probability samples (defined below) of the same size. An example of a legitimate use of a judgment sample is the use by the U.S. Bureau of Labor Statistics of a list of approximately 400 items to construct the Consumer Price Index. Four hundred items actually constitute a fairly large sample, but it is small in comparison with the large number of varying items composing the universe of consumer prices. Factors of index number construction partly influence the Bureau's choice of method, but it still remains that the sample chosen is a judgment one.

Probability Samples

In contrast to choosing items for the sample by convenience or by deliberate selection, the choice of items in probability sampling is left to some form of chance (random) procedure. Several such procedures are described below. A probability sample is defined as one for which each universe item has a known chance of appearing in the sample. The great advantage of probability samples is that, for samples of this type, the errors of sampling can be measured. Statisticians prefer the use of this type of sample in general, for the ability to measure the sampling errors assures the ability to determine the risks of making incorrect decisions. Although the two previously discussed types of samples are used as indicated for certain special types of problems, most sampling work done in statistics today uses some form of probability sample.

Some Types of Probability Samples

The commonest type of probability sample is the one known as the (simple) random sample. A random sample is one chosen from the universe in such a way that all samples of the same size have an equal chance of being selected. For this type each universe item has an *equal* chance of appearing in the sample. We shall use this type of sample throughout our sampling discussion. An understanding of the theory and use of this type of sample underlies the theory and use of all types of probability samples.

A second type of probability sample is the stratified random sample. Here the universe is first subdivided into relatively homogeneous subuniverses (strata) and a simple random sample drawn from each. If one wished to determine the average age of a group of college students, it would be advantageous first to divide (stratify) the students by class, since each class is more homogeneous with respect to age than the entire universe of students. Such stratification, by taking advantage of what we know about the universe, allows either smaller errors than simple random sampling for the same sample size, the same error for a smaller sample size, or something in between. Making use of known information to stratify reduces total sampling costs relative to the errors involved.

A third form of probability sampling designed to reduce sampling costs and overcome the lack of an adequate frame is multistage sampling. We can illustrate this type of sample by our previously discussed problem of reaching a sample of housewives in a given city. We might begin by listing the blocks in the city and designating these as our first, or primary, stage. We should then draw a certain number of blocks (primaries) at random. For each primary selected we could then make a list (frame) of the houses on the selected block. These houses would be our secondary stage. We should then select as our final sample for interviewing a certain number of houses (secondaries) at random. The procedure may, of course, be extended beyond two stages.

A variation of the previous type of sampling, known as "cluster sampling," would consist of interviewing all houses within a drawn block or cluster. Although this technique may involve a larger sample than other techniques, it may still represent an overall saving by reducing planning and interview costs.

The types of samples above involve the use of a fixed, predetermined sample size. An interesting alternative is the sequential sample, wherein the items are selected one at a time up to the point where a decision can be made or where a cutoff point is reached. This type of sampling is most useful in quality-control work, particularly where destructive testing is involved, since it utilizes minimum sample sizes. The idea underlying the procedure is that a very bad or very good lot can be quickly identified with the use of only a small sample and that larger samples are needed for lots of in-between quality.

Other types of probability samples exist, but those discussed here will give the reader a good general idea of their nature and use.

RANDOM SELECTION PROCEDURES

As all probability samples are based on chance, or random selection procedures, a knowledge of just what is involved in such procedures is important to understanding probability sampling.

Goldfish-bowl Techniques

Random selection may be divided into three types. The first of these we shall designate "goldfish-bowl" techniques, after the goldfish bowl used to select draftees for service in the Armed Forces. This technique is like drawing names from a hat. The idea is simple enough. Each universe item is represented by a slip of paper, capsule, and so on; the slips are well stirred up; and then they are drawn, without looking, to determine the winner (sample item). If the items are in fact well stirred, each should have an equal chance of being selected. Goldfish-bowl techniques are not widely used in practice because of the difficulties of obtaining large enough containers and ensuring adequate stirring.

Random Digits

A second, more widely used technique is the use of a table of random digits. One such table is given in App. C. In this table the digits are arranged so that the probability of any one digit appearing at any position in the table is $\frac{1}{10}$ (10 digits are used, 0 to 9). This probability is the same (equal) for all positions in the table. Conceptually, such a table might be constructed by drawing slips of paper numbered 0 to 9 from a hat, replacing the drawn slip after recording its digit before drawing again; by rolling a 10-sided die and recording the results; or by playing roulette with a 10-digit wheel. In practice, more efficient and more sophisticated methods are used. The important feature of the table is that the appearance of any digit or combination of digits is equally likely, and therefore such a table may be used to draw items, each item having an equal chance of selection.

To use such a table to draw a simple random sample we first begin by numbering the items in our universe (frame) in order. Sometimes we may be lucky and find our items already numbered, as for example with a set of sales slips. We then read numbers consecutively out of our table, thereby identifying the items in our universe which are to become our sample. If a number in our table does not have a number in the universe corresponding to it, we merely skip it and proceed to the next table number. If we draw the same item twice, we usually skip it on the second draw. We proceed in this manner until we have a full set for our sample.

To illustrate, let us assume that the sales slips to be sampled are restaurant checks of a luncheon counter in a hotel and that, on the day for which the study is made, there are 750 checks, numbered from 000 to 749. Also, assume that a sample of 50 checks is to be drawn. Our first random number is 1339. As we need only three digits, here our first sample item would be check 133. Our second number is 4089, giving us check 408. The third three-digit number is 761, which we skip, since no slip corresponds to it. We proceed in this fashion until 50 slips are drawn.

Tables of random digits are the most commonly used device today for drawing all kinds of probability samples.

Systematic Selection

The third procedure to be described is not actually a random selection procedure, although it will yield random results. It is systematic selection from a random list or process. This procedure might involve drawing every twentieth name from a list or taking a sample every half hour from a production process. If the arrangement of the items in the list or if the variations in the production process are random in character, a systematically drawn sample will have the characteristics of a random one. Many lists, particularly of people's names arranged alphabetically, seem to be random in character. As will be discussed further in Chap. 14, production processes which are "in control" have random variations only. In drawing systematically to obtain a random sample, one must always be careful to make sure that the systematic interval chosen does not correspond to a similar systematic arrangement in the data. For example, in studying absenteeism by days, one should not sample every seventh day since one would really be sampling only the same day of each week.

SOURCES OF ERROR IN PROBABILITY SAMPLING

Three factors basically determine the size or magnitude of the errors in probability sampling. We shall discuss these qualitatively here and show their specific quantitative effect in the later chapters. If one keeps these three factors in mind, it will help materially in understanding sampling theory and applications. Although we shall make no attempt to prove the validity of these factors, their logical character should be quite obvious.

Size of Sample

The first of these factors is the size of sample drawn. Sampling errors result from the fact that samples, as incomplete representations of the universe, are not identical with the universe. However, the larger the sample one draws, the better are the chances of representing all features of the universe. The better the representation, the less the size of the errors. Therefore, the magnitude of probability sampling error varies inversely with the size of the sample drawn.

Variability of the Universe

The second factor is the variability in the universe being sampled. If a universe were made up of completely identical items, sampling would be easy. Any size of sample would give the correct picture of the universe characteristics. However, as the variability in the universe increases, sampling becomes more difficult. The increased variability gives rise to more chances of error because there is an increasing number of values to be represented, placing a greater burden on the sampling procedure. The magnitude of probability sampling error, therefore, varies directly with the variability in the universe being sampled. This factor underlies the idea of stratified random sampling, where it is attempted to make the strata as homogeneous as possible and thereby reduce sampling error by reducing variability.

Portion of the Universe Sampled

The last factor in determining the magnitude of error in probability sampling is the portion of the universe sampled. As stated above, a sample of 1,000 items is less subject to error than a sample of 500 items. However, if the sample of 1,000 items is from a universe of 20,000 items, it will represent 5 percent of the universe, while, if it is from a universe of 10,000 items, it will be 10 percent of the universe. The larger percentage in the latter case increases the chances of getting good representation and thereby smaller errors. Therefore, we may state that the magnitude of probability sampling error varies inversely with the proportion of the universe sampled.

To summarize, let us repeat that three factors determine the magnitude of probability sampling error: (1) the size of sample drawn, (2) the variability of the universe being sampled, and (3) the proportion of the universe sampled. The magnitude of the error varies inversely with factors 1 and 3 and directly with factor 2. Note, in the following chapters, how these factors appear in the various formulas for quantitatively determining sampling error.

GENERAL CONSIDERATIONS OF SAMPLE SIZE

From the previous discussion we see that sample size and the magnitude of sampling error have an inverse relationship to each other. One can therefore reduce the error to any level of accuracy desired by increasing the sample size. One can also offset the errors resulting from high universe variability by increasing the sample size. However, increasing the sample size costs money, since it means that additional people will have to be interviewed or additional items tested. One should therefore always determine if the increased accuracy obtained from larger samples will yield savings commensurate with the increased cost. The proper size sample to use in a given problem is an interesting decision problem in itself.

STUDY GUIDE

Concepts Worth Remembering

Define:

1. Infinite universe
2. Statistical universe (population)
3. Frame
4. Convenience sample
5. Judgment (selective) sample
6. Probability sample
7. Random sample
8. Stratified random sample
9. Multistage sample
10. Cluster sample
11. Sequential sample
12. Random digits
13. Systematic selection
14. Random selection

Self-Test

Multiple-choice questions. Circle the letters of the statements which correctly complete the question. There may be one to four correct answers.

1 Sampling may be preferred to a complete enumeration because:
   (*a*) Sampling is less expensive than a complete enumeration.
   (*b*) There may be less total error even though the use of sampling introduces sampling error to the problem.
   (*c*) The universe being sampled may be infinite.
   (*d*) The results may be obtained more quickly.

2 A judgment sample is:

(*a*) A good type of sample to use when the composition of the universe is not known.

(*b*) A sample in which the items are deliberately selected by the investigator.

(*c*) A type of sample characterized by a small amount of sampling error.

(*d*) Often cheaper to use with a highly variable universe than a random sample.

3 A probability sample is:

(*a*) A sample in which the items are carefully chosen to give a cross-representation of the universe.

(*b*) A type of sample for which sampling errors can be measured.

(*c*) A sample chosen so that each universe item has a known chance of appearing in the sample.

(*d*) A type of sample of little use in statistical work.

4 A simple random sample is:

(*a*) A sample chosen so that every item in the universe has an equal chance of being in the sample.

(*b*) A type of sample for which sampling errors can be measured.

(*c*) A special type of probability sample.

(*d*) A type of sample the necessary size of which may be estimated in advance.

5 A table of random digits is:

(*a*) A haphazardly arranged set of digits.

(*b*) A device used to draw a random sample.

(*c*) Arranged so as to give each digit a 1-in-10 probability of appearing at any position in the table.

(*d*) Used to number items in a universe.

6 The items in a probability sample may be selected by:

(*a*) Using a table of random digits.

(*b*) Taking names at regular intervals (e.g., every fourth name) from an alphabetical list of people.

(*c*) Taking items in any regular pattern from a universe provided the universe itself is distributed at random.

(*d*) A goldfish-bowl selection procedure provided that the universe is not large.

7 The magnitude of random sampling error varies:

(*a*) Directly with the size of sample drawn.

(*b*) Inversely with the number of samples taken.

(*c*) Directly with the variability of the universe being sampled.

(*d*) Inversely with the portion of the universe sampled.

Questions to Think About

1. List the possible advantages of sampling over a complete enumeration and explain each advantage.
2. List the three basic types of samples discussed in the chapter. Distinguish clearly among the types, giving the advantages and disadvantages of each type.
3. Explain how a table of random digits is used to select a random sample.
4. What are the sources of error in probability sampling? Explain the effect of each source on the magnitude of possible error.

Student Project

Assume that you decided for the project described in the Study Guide for Chap. 2 to sample the student body to determine student opinion. Find out for your college what is available to use as a frame and describe how you could actually draw a random sample of your fellow students using this frame.

Answers to Self-Test

The following letters should have been circled:
1 $(a), (b), (c), (d)$;   **2** $(b), (d)$;   **3** $(b), (c)$;   **4** $(a), (b), (c), (d)$;   **5** $(a), (b), (c)$;
6 $(a), (b), (c), (d)$;   **7** $(c), (d)$.

TEN
SAMPLING DISTRIBUTIONS

LEARNING OBJECTIVES

The basic learning objective is to discover exactly what type of frequency distribution is meant by the term "sampling distribution." Specifically, you will learn:

1. The general nature of a sampling distribution, its importance in statistical inference, and the factors necessary to identify a specific distribution.
2. The exact nature of a random sampling distribution of arithmetic means:
   (*a*) Its pattern.
   (*b*) Its mean.
   (*c*) Its standard deviation.
3. The exact nature of a random sampling distribution of percentages:
   (*a*) Its pattern.
   (*b*) Its mean.
   (*c*) Its standard deviation.
4. The nature and use of the finite population correction.
5. The nature and importance of the central limit theorem.

INTRODUCTION

The basic tool necessary to the understanding and solution of problems of sampling is a device known as a sampling distribution. This entire chapter is devoted to clarifying this concept, for once it is mastered, other aspects of solving sampling problems, discussed in Chaps. 11 through 14, fall into place quite naturally.

DEFINITION OF THE CONCEPT

A sampling distribution is a frequency distribution showing the frequency, or probability, of *all* possible sample results for a specified sampling situation. It shows us, then, all the answers we should get in a given statistical problem if we were to draw samples over and over again until we had all that could be drawn. Such a procedure is obviously impractical, since it would entail more work than a complete enumeration; but if we could predict all possible results in advance of actual sampling, we should have a powerful tool for evaluating and predicting from the single sample actually drawn. Sampling distributions show just this, and in many cases can be predicted in advance.

THE SAMPLING SITUATION

A specific sampling distribution is identified by four basic factors: (1) the method of sample selection, (2) the statistical measure of interest in the problem, (3) the size of sample to be drawn, and (4) the universe from which the sample is to be taken. A change in any one of these four factors will result in a different sampling distribution.

As explained in Chap. 9, samples may be drawn in three general ways. Sampling distributions are generally associated with samples drawn by probability procedures, since it is for these that sampling distributions can be predicted in advance. Specifically, in this chapter, we shall consider only samples drawn by simple random sampling. Other methods, such as stratified random sampling or multistage sampling, yield different but predictable sampling distributions.

A separate sampling distribution results for each different statistical measure one wishes to use as the basis for making decisions. There is then a different distribution for arithmetic means, say, than for percentages or standard deviations. We shall illustrate several of these in our work.

The size of sample drawn (i.e., the number of items in a single sample) helps to determine a specific sampling distribution. This is related to the point made in Chap. 9 that the size of sample is an important factor in determining the probable amount of error in a sampling problem. We shall soon see how this factor operates through the sampling distribution in determining the expected error.

Similarly, the universe from which the sample is taken is a factor in identifying a specific sampling distribution in that, as indicated previously, the amount of variability in the universe being sampled is an important determinant of the probable amount of error. The specific universe defined for a particular statistical problem is obviously subject to a given amount of variability. This amount of variability again operates through the sampling distribution to determine the amount of expected error.

We shall now define a small hypothetical universe in order to illustrate these relationships. From this universe we shall actually draw all possible samples of a given size and construct sampling distributions for several measures. It should be emphasized that we are doing this for illustrative purposes and that in real sampling problems we draw only one sample and make inferences about unknown universe characteristics. The latter procedure is therefore essentially the reverse of our illustration, but deduction of sample behavior for a known universe should be helpful in making inferences from a sample about an unknown universe.

A CONTROLLED ILLUSTRATION

The Universe

The universe for our illustration will consist of four identical marbles having the values 7, 9, 11, and 13, respectively. Let us first compute some descriptive measures for this universe. The arithmetic mean (μ)[1] of this universe is

$$\mu = \frac{7 + 9 + 11 + 13}{4} = \frac{40}{4} = 10$$

The variance (σ^2) of this universe is

$$\sigma^2 = \frac{(7 - 10)^2 + (9 - 10)^2 + (11 - 10)^2 + (13 - 10)^2}{4}$$

$$= \frac{9 + 1 + 1 + 9}{4} = \frac{20}{4} = 5$$

The standard deviation, therefore, is

$$\sigma = \sqrt{5} = 2.25$$

The percentage of the values less than the mean is

$$\pi = 100 \times \tfrac{2}{4} = 50\%$$

A graph of the universe appears in Fig. 10-1.

It should be noted that the shape of the distribution, when plotted, is rectangular; that is, there are an equal number of frequencies of each value. The universe for our controlled illustration, then, is a rectangular one, composed of four marbles having an arithmetic mean value of 10, a standard deviation of 2.25, and 50 percent of its values less than the mean.

---

[1] We shall use Greek letters as symbols for universe measures, or parameters.

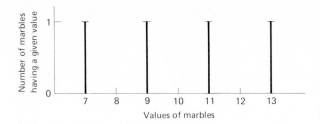

Figure 10-1 Universe of marbles.

Sampling Procedure

Our sampling procedure will be to draw simple random samples of size 2 with replacement. This sampling with replacement is comparable to sampling from an infinite universe. By replacing each item after it is drawn, and before drawing again, we have, in effect, an infinite universe. This will eliminate, for the time being, consideration of the effect of the portion of the universe being sampled on the errors in our results.

Statistical Measures

Our remaining choice is to pick a measure for which to sample. We shall try two of these and thereby construct two different sampling distributions. Our choices are the arithmetic mean and the percentage of the values less than the universe mean. Table 10-1 lists the 16 (all) possible samples of size 2 (from Chap. 7, the $_4M_2 = 4^2 = 16$), which can be drawn by simple random sampling with replacement from our specified

Table 10-1 All possible samples, sample means, and sample percentages for sample of size 2

Sample number	Sample values	Total (ΣX)	Sample mean ($\overline{X}$)	Percent less than μ
1	7, 7	14	7	100
2	7, 9	16	8	100
3	7, 11	18	9	50
4	7, 13	20	10	50
5	9, 7	16	8	100
6	9, 9	18	9	100
7	9, 11	20	10	50
8	9, 13	22	11	50
9	11, 7	18	9	50
10	11, 9	20	10	50
11	11, 11	22	11	0
12	11, 13	24	12	0
13	13, 7	20	10	50
14	13, 9	22	11	50
15	13, 11	24	12	0
16	13, 13	26	13	0

universe. For each sample the sample mean and the percentage of the sample values less than the universe mean have been computed.

Sampling Distributions

Distributions made out of the values in the last two columns of Table 10-1 would be distributions of all possible sample results for the given sampling situation and therefore would be designated as random sampling distributions. These are shown in Tables 10-2 and 10-3.

We have also calculated the means, variances, and standard deviations of the random sampling distributions in order that they may be compared with the values of the universe from which they were drawn. Earlier we noted that, to indicate an arithmetic mean symbolically, we merely place a bar over the symbol for the items being averaged.

Table 10-2   Random sampling distribution of arithmetic means

Sample mean ($\overline{X}$)	Number of samples having a given mean (f)	$f\overline{X}$	$\overline{X} - \overline{\overline{X}}$	$(\overline{X} - \overline{\overline{X}})^2$	$f(\overline{X} - \overline{\overline{X}})^2$
7	1	7	-3	9	9
8	2	16	-2	4	8
9	3	27	-1	1	3
10	4	40	0	0	0
11	3	33	1	1	3
12	2	24	2	4	8
13	1	13	3	9	9
Total	16	160	...	...	40

$$\overline{\overline{X}} = \tfrac{160}{16} \qquad \sigma^2_{\overline{X}} = \tfrac{40}{16} \qquad \sigma_{\overline{X}} = \sqrt{2.5}$$
$$= 10 \qquad\qquad = 2.5 \qquad\quad = 1.58$$

Table 10-3   Random sampling distribution of percentages

Sample percentage (p)	Number of samples having a given percent (f)	fp	$p - \overline{p}$	$(p - \overline{p})^2$	$f(p - \overline{p})^2$
0	4	0	-50	2,500	10,000
50	8	400	0	0	0
100	4	400	50	2,500	10,000
Total	16	800	....	.....	20,000

$$\overline{p} = \tfrac{800}{16} \qquad \sigma^2_p = \frac{20,000}{16} \qquad \sigma_p = \sqrt{1,250}$$
$$= 50 \qquad\quad = 1,250 \qquad\quad = 35.36\%$$

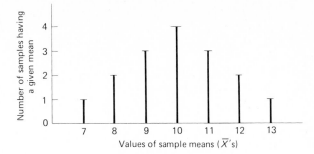

Figure 10-2 Random sampling distribution of arithmetic means.

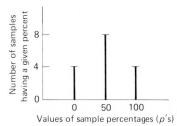

Figure 10-3 Random sampling distribution of percentages.

Here we have used $\overline{\overline{X}}$ for the arithmetic mean of the sample arithmetic means ($\overline{X}$) and $\overline{p}$ for the arithmetic mean of the sample percentages (p). We have used the lower case Greek sigma (σ) for our variances and standard deviations, indicating, by using $\overline{X}$ or p as a subscript, which distribution is in question. The distributions appear graphically in Figs. 10-2 and 10-3.

Some Interesting Comparisons

Let us now compare the results computed for the sampling distributions with those computed for the original universe by first considering the distribution means. We note that in both cases the arithmetic mean of the sampling distribution is equal to the true universe value; that is, $\overline{\overline{X}} = \mu = 10$ and $\overline{p} = \pi = 50$ percent. Many sampling distributions, but not all, exhibit this property, that the mean of the distribution is equal to the universe value. If such is the case, any single sample value is said to be an unbiased estimator of the universe value, since the complete set of sample values averages out to be equal to the true universe value.

Second, let us compare the variances of the sampling distributions with values from the universe. The variance of the sampling distribution of means is equal to one-half of the variance of the universe; i.e., $\sigma_{\overline{X}}^2 = \sigma^2/2 = \frac{5}{2} = 2.5$. Where does the factor of one-half come from? It derives from the fact that we drew samples of size 2 ($n = 2$). Therefore, we can write $\sigma_{\overline{X}}^2 = \sigma^2/n$ and $\sigma_{\overline{X}} = \sigma/\sqrt{n}$.

The variation in the universe percentages is reflected by the fact that there was a 50–50 chance in the universe for the value of an item to be less than the mean. We note similarly, therefore, that the variance of the sampling distribution of percentages is one-half of the variance of the universe; that is,

$$\sigma_p^2 = \frac{50 \times 50}{2} = \frac{2,500}{2} = 1,250$$

The factor of one-half again derives from the sample size 2, and therefore

$$\sigma_p^2 = \frac{\pi(100 - \pi)}{n} \qquad \text{and} \qquad \sigma_p = \sqrt{\frac{\pi(100 - \pi)}{n}}$$

STANDARD ERRORS

The standard deviation of any sampling distribution is a very important measure. Like any standard deviation, it measures the magnitude of the variability in the distribution in question. A sampling distribution, however, shows a unique kind of variation, namely, that of sample results. To the extent that the sample results are not equal to the corresponding universe value, they represent possible errors arising from the use of samples. The amount of variability in sample results, therefore, is the equivalent of the amount of error in sample results. Measuring the amount of variability in sample results, then, is equivalent to measuring the amount of error in sample results. The standard deviations of random sampling distributions can then be used not only as measures of the variability in such distributions, but also as measures of the amount of error to be found under conditions of random sampling. They are designated by the special term "standard error." The standard error of the arithmetic mean is the standard deviation of the random sampling distribution of means, and the standard error of the percentage is the standard deviation of the random sampling distribution of percentages. It is worth noting that values for both these standard errors (and most other standard errors) can be computed without having the entire sampling distribution. Specifically,

$$\sigma_{\bar{X}} = \frac{\sigma}{\sqrt{n}} \qquad \text{and} \qquad \sigma_p = \sqrt{\frac{\pi(100 - \pi)}{n}}$$

FINITE-UNIVERSE CORRECTION

Examination of the two preceding formulas supports our earlier conclusion that the magnitude of random sampling error will vary directly with the variation in the universe being sampled and inversely with the size of sample drawn (specifically, with the square root of the sample size). The third factor of the portion of the universe sampled does not enter here because we used an infinite universe. Both formulas would be adjusted by the same factor, the $\sqrt{(N - n)/(N - 1)}$, called either the "finite-universe correction" or the "finite-population correction," giving

$$\sigma_{\bar{X}} = \frac{\sigma}{\sqrt{n}} \sqrt{\frac{N - n}{N - 1}} \qquad \text{and} \qquad \sigma_p = \sqrt{\frac{\pi(100 - \pi)}{n}} \sqrt{\frac{N - n}{N - 1}}$$

where N equals the universe size, and n equals the sample size, if we were sampling from a finite universe. In practical sampling work, this factor is usually ignored unless the sample exceeds 10 percent of the universe. The same correction factor applies in most other kinds of probability sampling.

DISTRIBUTION PATTERNS

One more property of our sampling distributions is worth noting. Examination of Figs. 10-2 and 10-3 shows that the patterns of both our distributions are symmetrical and unimodal even though our universe (Fig. 10-1) was rectangular in shape. The patterns of many sampling distributions are of this general type. The specific patterns which they will have has been determined mathematically, and therefore is known in advance and separately from the actual drawing of all possible samples.

   In summary, we repeat the general properties of a random sampling distribution of means and of a random sampling distribution of percentages, some of which have been illustrated and derived in our controlled numerical experiment. Again it should be emphasized that they can be determined mathematically and are known without the necessity of drawing all possible samples. Three properties are important in each case: (1) the value of the mean of the distribution, (2) the value of the standard deviation of the distribution (the standard error), and (3) the pattern of the distribution.

THE SAMPLING DISTRIBUTION OF THE ARITHMETIC MEAN

The distribution of sample means has as its mean a value equal to the mean of the universe; that is, $\overline{\overline{X}} = \mu$. If the sampling is from an infinite universe, the formula for the standard error of the arithmetic mean is

$$\sigma_{\overline{X}} = \frac{\sigma}{\sqrt{n}}$$

The pattern of the distribution depends upon the pattern of the universe and upon the size of sample drawn. If the universe is a normal distribution, the sampling distribution is also a normal distribution for any size of sample. A remarkable theorem called the *central-limit theorem* states that even if the universe is not normal, the sampling distribution will approach normality as the size of the sample is increased. For most purposes a sample size of over 30 is considered sufficient to assume that the sampling distribution of means is normal.

THE SAMPLING DISTRIBUTION OF THE PERCENTAGE

The distribution of sample percentages has as its mean a value equal to the true percentage of the universe being sampled; that is, $\overline{p} = \pi$. If the sampling is from an infinite

Table 10-4   Values of n needed for use of normal approximation for various values of π

π, %	n (sample size)
50	30
40 or 60	50
30 or 70	80
20 or 80	200
10 or 90	600
5 or 95	1,400

Source: By permission from William G. Cochran, *Sampling Techniques*, John Wiley & Sons, Inc., New York, 1953, p. 41.

universe, the standard error of the percentage may be computed from the formula

$$\sigma_p = \sqrt{\frac{\pi(100 - \pi)}{n}}$$

The pattern of the distribution in this case is the binomial distribution. The latter may be approximated by the normal curve under certain conditions, depending on the value of π and the size of sample being used. These conditions are summarized in Table 10-4, modified from W. G. Cochran's table. If we use Table 10-4, we can be sure that the risks of error in making estimates when we use the normal curve differ from those made when we use the binomial by no more than a half of 1 percent.

The fact that the sampling distributions of both means and percentages may at least be approximated by the normal curve is fortunate, for, as noted in Chap. 8, this is an easy curve to work with. Actually, the normal curve can be used to approximate a very large number of sampling distributions other than these two. One must be careful, however, not to assume that it applies in all cases. Other patterns that occur, other than the normal and binomial, are the t distribution, the chi-square (χ^2) distribution, the F distribution, and the Poisson distribution. Although these are somewhat more difficult to work with than the normal, like the normal, they have been tabulated for at least the majority of situations encountered.

A FINAL COMMENT

The thoughtful student will have noted by now that, even though we know a great deal about the behavior of sample results through our knowledge of sampling distributions, and this knowledge is available without our having to draw all possible samples, we are still lacking important information for problem work. We do not actually know, in a real problem, the standard deviation of the universe or the true percentage of the universe. These values are needed to compute the standard errors of the mean and percentage, respectively. How do we solve this problem? It depends on the type of the real problem in question, which will be an important part of our discussion in the chapters to follow.

STUDY GUIDE

Concepts Worth Remembering

Define:

1. Sampling distribution
2. Sampling situation
3. Standard error of the arithmetic mean
4. Standard error of the percentage
5. Finite universe (population) correction
6. Central limit theorem

Self-Test

Multiple-choice questions. Circle the letters of the statements which correctly complete the question. There may be one to four correct answers.

1 A random sampling distribution:

(*a*) Is a frequency distribution made up of sample items.

(*b*) Is a frequency distribution made up of universe items.

(*c*) Depends in part on both the size of sample drawn and the universe being sampled.

(*d*) Gives the probability of occurrence of various sample results (outcomes) for the statistical measure of interest.

2 A random sampling distribution of arithmetic means:

(*a*) Is a binomial distribution.

(*b*) Has a mean equal to the mean of the universe being sampled.

(*c*) Is skewed to the right if the universe being sampled is skewed to the right.

(*d*) Has a standard deviation which is less than the universe standard deviation.

3 A random sampling distribution of percentages:

(*a*) Is a binomial distribution.

(*b*) Has a mean equal to the true percentage of the universe being sampled.

(*c*) Has greater variability the more variable the universe being sampled.

(*d*) Has less variability the larger the sample being used.

4 The standard error of the arithmetic mean:

(*a*) Varies inversely with the square root of the sample size.

(*b*) Varies inversely with the variability of the universe being sampled.

(*c*) Is the standard deviation of the random sampling distribution of arithmetic means.

(*d*) Measures the amount of sampling error for a given sampling situation.

5 The standard error of the percentage:

(*a*) Varies directly with the square root of the sample size.

(*b*) Varies directly with the variability of the universe being sampled.

(*c*) Is the standard deviation of the random sampling distribution of percentages.

(*d*) Is the same for both finite and infinite universes.

6 The finite universe (population) correction:

(*a*) Is used only when the sample exceeds 10 percent of the universe.

(b) Shows that the relative sample size is usually less important than the absolute sample size.

(c) Varies in form with the sample design being used.

(d) Applies only when sampling for arithmetic means.

7 The central-limit theorem:

(a) Applies only when sampling for percentages.

(b) Is effective for samples over 30 items.

(c) Allows the statistician to ignore the possible pattern of the universe.

(d) States that the random sampling distribution of arithmetic means approaches normality regardless of the pattern of the universe as the size of sample being used increases.

Questions to Think About

1. Explain the concept of a random sampling distribution and its importance to statistical inference. What basic factors identify a specific sampling distribution?
2. What are the basic properties of a random sampling distribution of arithmetic means?
3. What are the basic properties of a random sampling distribution of percentages?
4. Define the finite universe (population) correction. How and when should it be used?
5. State the central-limit theorem. What is its importance to statistical inference?
6. Explain under what conditions the normal curve may be used to approximate the binomial distribution in sampling.

Problem

1 Recalculate the values of Tables 10-1, 10-2, and 10-3 assuming simple random sampling *without* replacement. Compare the results of the Table 10-2 and Table 10-3 calculations with the results directly determinable by theory.

Answers to Self-Test

1 (c), (d); 2 (b), (d); 3 (a), (b), (c), (d); 4 (a), (c), (d); 5 (b), (c); 6 (a), (b); 7 (b), (c), (d).

ELEVEN
MAKING ESTIMATES FROM SAMPLE DATA

LEARNING OBJECTIVES

The basic learning objective is to study the process whereby estimates of population means and percentages are made using sample data. Specifically, you will become familiar with the following:

1. The difference between estimation and hypothesis testing problems.
2. How to estimate standard errors.
3. Point estimates.
4. Confidence intervals—their construction and interpretation.
5. The determination of sample size.

INTRODUCTION: KINDS OF SAMPLING PROBLEMS

We shall now employ our knowledge of sampling distributions, combining it with the information from a single sample, to do practical sampling problems and aid management in its decision making. Traditionally, these sampling problems are divided into two types: (1) making estimates and (2) testing hypotheses. If the problem requires a numerical answer, it is an estimation problem. For example, if the problem is to decide how long a new type of light bulb will last, a numerical answer of so many hours on the average is needed; hence, this would be an estimation problem. Another estimation problem is to determine the percentage of railroad shipments delayed through misrouting (a number). In contrast, problems requiring merely a yes or no answer are hypothesis testing problems. To decide whether or not the transverse strength of bricks exceeds a certain figure or whether or not the percentage of defectives in a lot of raw material is acceptable (less than specified on ordering) are examples of this type, for they call for a yes or no answer. Estimation problems will be discussed in this chapter, and hypothesis testing problems in Chap. 12. Both types represent the process of inference from sample information by combining that information with the knowledge of sample behavior deduced informally in Chap. 10. The use of samples in modern statistical (bayesian) decision making will be discussed in Chap. 13.

ESTIMATING STANDARD ERRORS

Chapter 10 concluded with the observation that one remaining obstacle was that the formulas for the standard error of the mean and the standard error of the percentage each depended on knowing a universe value. The expression for the standard error of the mean $(\sigma_{\bar{X}} = \sigma/\sqrt{n})$[1] required that the universe standard deviation (σ) be known, while the standard error of the percentage

$$\sigma_p = \sqrt{\frac{\pi(100 - \pi)}{n}}$$

depends on the universe percentage (π). Let us consider specifically each standard error in turn. The solution in both cases is to use the sample data to compute an estimate of the standard error desired.

Estimated Standard Error of the Mean

Our estimate of the standard error of the mean is basically determined by substituting the sample standard deviation s ($s = \sqrt{\Sigma x^2/n}$) as an estimate of our unknown universe standard deviation σ. One additional adjustment is needed in our formula since

---

[1] Here, and for the standard error of the percentage, we have assumed that the sampling is from an infinite universe or at least that the sample size is small relative to the universe. The finite-population correction $[\sqrt{(N - n)/(N - 1)}]$ is usually not applied unless the sample is greater than 10 percent of the universe; that is, $n/N > 10$ percent. We shall continue with this same assumption throughout the chapter.

s is not an unbiased estimator of σ. Actually, s tends to underestimate σ. In the sampling distribution of standard deviations, the mean of the distribution is less than the universe value; that is, $\bar{s} < \sigma$. The adjustment itself is a fairly simple one. As our numerator s is too small, we reduce the size of the denominator to compensate and give us an unbiased estimate of the standard error. The reduction needed is merely to subtract 1 from the sample size. Therefore, the expression for the estimated standard error of the mean $(\hat{\sigma}_{\bar{X}})$[1] is

$$\hat{\sigma}_{\bar{X}} = \frac{s}{\sqrt{n-1}}$$

Estimated Standard Error of the Percentage

In computing an estimate of the standard error of the percentage, the sample percentage (p) is substituted for the missing universe percentage (π). Generally, this is the only adjustment that needs to be made. Therefore, the expression for the estimated standard error of the percentage $(\hat{\sigma}_p)$ is

$$\hat{\sigma}_p = \sqrt{\frac{p(100-p)}{n}}$$

THE STUDENT t DISTRIBUTION

When one uses estimated rather than true standard errors, the patterns of the sampling distributions change. Specifically, the t distribution replaces the normal curve. The t distribution, like the normal, is a bell-shaped symmetrical curve, but it has greater variability to allow for the additional errors which might result from using only an estimate of the standard error. Just as the errors of estimation (sampling) decrease with increasing sample size, so the t distribution varies with sample size and approaches the normal curve as the sample size increases. A sample size of 30 is usually considered sufficient in the case of arithmetic means for using the normal curve as an approximation to the t distribution. The nature and use of the t distribution will be discussed further in Chap. 14. Here we shall keep our samples sufficiently large to enable us to use only the normal curve as the pattern of the sampling distributions.

POINT ESTIMATES AND MARGIN OF ERROR

If an estimate in a problem is given in the form of a single number, it is referred to as a "point estimate." Answers of 3,500 h for the new type of light bulb and of 7 percent for railroad shipments delayed through misrouting would be point estimates.

The difficulty with using this type of estimate may best be shown by a simple illustration. Suppose that we ask ourselves the question, "How many heads might

---

[1]We shall use a circumflex ($\wedge$) over the symbol for a value to indicate an estimate of that value.

appear in the tossing of a true coin 10,000 times?" There is almost an automatic tendency to say "about 5,000." However, if pushed to answer with a single number only (point estimate), we should be reluctant to say 5,000. Our reluctance stems from the fact that we have little expectation that there will be exactly 5,000 heads. In fact, we believe this to be very unlikely, and that is the reason we said "about 5,000" in the first place, i.e., to allow ourselves a margin of error. Statisticians, too, like to allow themselves a margin of error in making estimates. They do this either by giving the point estimate plus some indication of the error to which it is subject by indicating the value of the appropriate standard error, or, even more likely, by making the estimate in the form of an interval rather than a point. These latter estimates, called "confidence intervals," are discussed below. The numerical equivalent to the "about" in "about 5,000 heads" is 50. One could indicate that the estimate of the number of heads is 5,000 and that the standard deviation (equivalent here to the standard error) for this estimate is 50 heads. Assuming normality, the actual answer will fall within 50 heads of 5,000 exactly $68\frac{1}{4}$ percent of the time ($68\frac{1}{4}$ percent of the values in any normal curve fall within ± 1 standard deviation of the mean). Similarly, the standard errors for 3,500 h and 7 percent misrouted could be given and interpreted.

CONFIDENCE INTERVALS

Statisticians usually make their estimates in the form of a range, or interval. Such intervals are termed "confidence intervals," since they are constructed by statisticians so that the risks of making errors in the estimating procedure can be determined. Individual interval estimates may or may not be correct, but the probabilities of the estimating procedure being correct in repeated trials can be computed.

Confidence Intervals: The Mean

As an illustration of the construction of a confidence interval estimate of the universe mean, let us take a problem of the Frugal-Four Auto Company, makers of a four-cylinder automobile designed for economical gasoline consumption. The company is interested in determining gasoline consumption under actual operating conditions. To do this, a random sample of 37 Frugal-Four owners was chosen and data on the gasoline consumption of their cars were obtained. The mean and standard deviation of this sample were computed. The latter measure had a value of 3 miles per gallon ($s = 3$ mi/gal). From this we can compute an estimate of the standard error of the mean:

$$\hat{\sigma}_{\bar{X}} = \frac{s}{\sqrt{n-1}} = \frac{3}{\sqrt{37-1}} = 0.5 \text{ mi/gal}$$

Let us combine this information with our knowledge that *all* sample means for samples of size 37 for this problem would form a normal curve around our true unknown universe mean (μ) with a standard deviation (standard error) equal to this 0.5 mi/gal. Thus, if the true mean were 38 mi/gal, we should know from the table of areas of the normal curve that $95\frac{1}{2}$ percent of all sample means would fall between 37 and

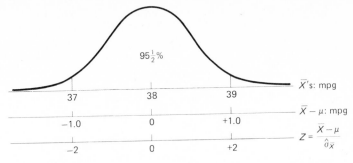

Figure 11-1 Random sampling distribution of $\overline{X}$'s for all samples of size $n = 37$ and $\mu = 38$ mi/gal.

39 mi/gal, that is, 38 mi/gal plus or minus 2(0.5). This is illustrated in Fig. 11-1. However, we do not know the true mean, and 38 mi/gal is just one possibility. If the true
mean were 39 mi/gal, the curve would look the same as before, except that it would be
centered around 39 mi/gal. In this case $95\frac{1}{2}$ percent of the sample means would fall
between 38 and 40 mi/gal. Statements of this type can be made indefinitely. Table
11-1 summarizes a collection of them. These statements are deduced from our knowledge of sample behavior. However, we have some information to help us to determine
which of these "ifs" is the most reasonable. This information is the mean of our sample of 37 Frugal-Four vehicles; this value was 40.5 mi/gal (i.e., $\overline{X} = 40.5$ mi/gal). On
the basis of this knowledge we find that our first "if" of 38 mi/gal is not particularly reasonable, since a universe mean of 38 mi/gal yields practically no sample means of 40.5
($95\frac{1}{2}$ percent of all sample means would have been between 37 and 39 mi/gal). The
"if" of 39 mi/gal would be better, but of those tabulated, only 40 and 41 mi/gal seem
likely to have yielded the observed sample value of 40.5 mi/gal. We therefore infer that
the universe mean is in the neighborhood of $40 \rightarrow 41$ mi/gal. More precisely, we
should set our limits as $\overline{X} - 2\hat{\sigma}_{\overline{X}}$ and $\overline{X} + 2\hat{\sigma}_{\overline{X}}$ (the use of $Z = 2$ here is purely arbitrary,
although fairly conventional). This will yield us values of 39.5 mi/gal [40.5 - 2(0.5)]
and 41.5 mi/gal [40.5 + 2(0.5)], respectively, for the limits of our confidence interval.
We should state that the true mean lies between 39.5 and 41.5 mi/gal and indicate that
this is a $95\frac{1}{2}$ percent confidence interval.

**Table 11-1 Sample mean values for selected hypothetical
value of the universe mean (miles per gallon)**

Hypothetical universe mean	Range of $95\frac{1}{2}\%$ of sample means
38	$37 \rightarrow 39$
39	$38 \rightarrow 40$
40	$39 \rightarrow 41$
41	$40 \rightarrow 42$
42	$41 \rightarrow 43$
43	$42 \rightarrow 44$

Let us briefly summarize the procedure before explaining the exact meaning of the confidence interval. A random sample of size n is chosen, and for this $\overline{X}$ and s are computed. From the sample data an estimate is made of the standard error of the mean $(\hat{\sigma}_{\overline{X}} = s/\sqrt{n-1})$. The actual estimate of the universe mean $(\hat{\mu})$ takes the form

$$\hat{\mu} = \overline{X} \pm Z\hat{\sigma}_{\overline{X}}$$

Different values may be used for Z, but each will give a different level of confidence.

The Meaning of Confidence Intervals

As indicated earlier, individual confidence intervals can be only correct or incorrect. As there is only one true universe mean, either it is in the interval 39.5 to 41.5 mi/gal, in which case the interval is correct, or it is not in the interval, in which case the interval is wrong. The degree of confidence, then, cannot apply to the individual answer in question. The degree of confidence lies in the estimating procedure. If samples of size 37 were drawn again and again and confidence intervals of two standard errors constructed around the respective sample means (these vary and would not all equal 40.5), $95\frac{1}{2}$ percent of the intervals so set up would include the true mean and $4\frac{1}{2}$ percent would not. Management of the Frugal-Four Auto Company is obviously going to act as if this particular interval we have constructed is correct. Their long-run risk of error in doing so is $4\frac{1}{2}$ percent.

Varying Confidence Intervals

Confidence intervals may be varied or changed either by changing the Z value or by changing the sample size. Changing the Z value also changes the confidence level, since different numbers of standard deviations under the normal curve would contain different percentages of sample results. If Z were changed from 2 to 3 in our illustration above, the interval would become 39 mi/gal [40.5 − 3(0.5)] to 42 mi/gal [40.5 + 3(0.5)]. This would be a 99.7 percent confidence interval. Note, however, that the increased confidence of 99.7 percent comes only at the loss of some precision in the estimate. Varying the sample size also changes the confidence interval, as it changes the size of the standard error. If the sample size in our example above were increased to 145 (roughly quadrupled), the standard error would be cut in two, becoming 0.25 mi/gal:

$$\hat{\sigma}_{\overline{X}} = \frac{s}{\sqrt{n-1}} = \frac{3}{\sqrt{145-1}} = 0.25$$

We could now have a $95\frac{1}{2}$ percent confidence interval, one-half the width of our old one (40 to 41 mi/gal, as opposed to 39.5 to 41.5 mi/gal), but only at a sampling cost roughly four times that of the original. The square-root sign over the n runs up the cost of sampling rapidly.

Confidence Intervals: The Percentage

Confidence intervals for the universe percentage (π) are constructed in the same manner as confidence intervals for the mean when sample sizes are sufficiently large to allow the use of the normal curve. The general procedure is to draw a random sample of size n and observe the number in the sample having the characteristic (r) in question. The sample percentage (p) is then computed as $p = 100(r/n)$. Next, an estimate of the standard error of the percentage ($\hat{\sigma}_p$) is determined from

$$\hat{\sigma}_p = \sqrt{\frac{p(100 - p)}{n}}$$

The actual limits of the confidence interval itself are derived from the expression $\hat{\pi} = p \pm Z\hat{\sigma}_p$.

To illustrate, let us assume that the management of the Frugal-Four Auto Company wanted to know what percentage of its sales was being made as the second car in a two-car family. At the request of the company statistician, management indicated that it desired a 95 percent confidence interval estimate. The statistician drew a random sample of 400 sales ($n = 400$) and discovered that 80 of these ($r = 80$) were second-car sales. Therefore,

$$p = 100 \, \frac{r}{n} = 100 \times \frac{80}{400} = 20\%$$

The estimate of the standard error is

$$\hat{\sigma}_p = \sqrt{\frac{p(100 - p)}{n}} = \sqrt{\frac{20(80)}{400}} = 2\%$$

The 95 percent confidence interval is

$$\hat{\pi} = p \pm Z\hat{\sigma}_p = 20 \pm 1.96(2)$$

($Z = 1.96$ will include exactly 95 percent of the values under a normal curve. See App. B_2.) The final answer is 16.1 to 23.9 percent. The interpretation is as before. This interval will be treated by management as correct, although it may not be correct. As it is a 95 percent confidence interval, there exists a long-run 5 percent chance that it is not correct.

FURTHER CONSIDERATIONS OF SAMPLE SIZE

In point of time, during an actual survey, the sample size must be determined in advance of its drawing and the constructing of the confidence interval estimate. We consider it second here, since methods for approximating appropriate sample size depend upon an understanding of confidence interval procedures of estimation. The method is essentially one of solving backward from an ideal confidence interval to the sample size (n).

A confidence interval has essentially two aspects: (1) the degree of confidence involved and (2) the precision or amount of error represented by the width of the interval. Data on both these aspects can be supplied to the statistician by management. Management must certainly decide the risks of error (and thereby the degree of confidence) it can tolerate in using a confidence interval to make decisions. It should also be able to indicate at least the approximate amount of precision needed in the estimate. Given these items of information, the statistician can usually work the standard error formulas backward to determine the approximate sample size needed to meet the requirements.

Sample Size: Arithmetic Mean

In setting confidence intervals for the arithmetic mean, the width of the interval (amount of error) is determined by the product of Z and the standard error. If we let E equal the amount of error, we may state that $E = Z\sigma_{\bar{X}}$. Substituting for $\sigma_{\bar{X}}$, we have $E = Z(\sigma/\sqrt{n})$. Solving this expression for n, we obtain

$$n_{\bar{X}} = \frac{Z^2 \sigma^2}{E^2}$$

(We have added an $\bar{X}$ subscript to the n to indicate that the sample is to be used to estimate a mean.) The values for Z and E are those given the statistician by management, as explained above. If the statistician can obtain a satisfactory approximation for σ, solving for the sample size to meet Z and E is simple. Fairly good approximations of σ are often available from past data on similar company studies or from outside sources. At times it is easier to estimate the range (R) than the standard deviation. If one believes the universe to be bell-shaped and not too skewed, one may approximate σ from the relationship that, for such curves, $\sigma \cong R/6$. If no other information is available, it is possible to make a small pilot-type study to estimate σ.

In order to bid on government defense work, the management of the Frugal-Four Auto Company needs to know the breaking strength of a type of weld. Management wants to be 99 percent certain $(Z = 2.58)$ of being within 5 lb $(E = 5$ lb$)$ of the correct answer. Investigation by the company statistician of past company studies shows that the standard deviation should be about 15 lb $(\sigma \cong 15$ lb$)$. Therefore, the size of sample needed for this study is

$$n_{\bar{X}} = \frac{Z^2 \sigma^2}{E^2} = \frac{(2.58)^2 (15)^2}{5^2} = 59.4 = 60 \text{ welds}$$

If 60 welds is feasible from a cost standpoint, the study can proceed. If not, management will have to settle for a lesser degree of confidence or less precision or abandon the study.

Sample Size: Percentage

The procedure for determining sample size when the sample is to be used to estimate a percentage is similar to that for the mean, differing in detail only. Again the amount of error is the product of Z and the standard error; that is, $E = Z\sigma_p$. Substituting for σ_p, we have

$$E = Z\sqrt{\frac{\pi(100 - \pi)}{n}}$$

When solved for n, the expression for the sample size to determine a percentage (n_p) becomes

$$n_p = \frac{Z^2\pi(100 - \pi)}{E^2}$$

If a satisfactory approximation for π can be found, the formula may easily be solved for n_p. Here again, past or outside information may give a good clue as to the value of π. However, if no idea of the value of π can be determined, there is an absolute upper limit on the amount of variation represented by $\pi(100 - \pi)$, and this limit can be used. The maximum amount of variability occurs when $\pi = 50$ percent and $\pi(100 - \pi) = 2,500$. Any other value for π represents less variability and gives a smaller cross product; e.g., if $\pi = 40$ percent, $\pi(100 - \pi) = 2,400$. Therefore, if no knowledge of π exists, one may use $\pi = 50$ percent and be certain of having a sufficiently large sample.

Management of the Frugal-Four Auto Company is considering bringing out a station-wagon model. It would like to know what percentage of Frugal-Four owners would have bought a station-wagon model if it had been available at the time they purchased their present model. It feels that it will be satisfactory to be $95\frac{1}{2}$ percent certain $(Z = 2)$ of being within 4 percent $(E = 4$ percent$)$ of the correct figure. Based on the sales of other automobiles, the company statistician estimates that the percentage preferring station wagons will not exceed 30 percent. Using this information, our sample size is computed as

$$n_p = \frac{Z^2(\pi)(100 - \pi)}{E^2} = \frac{2^2(30)(70)}{4^2} = 525 \text{ owners}$$

Since this is a fairly large sample, it must be determined if it is an economically feasible sample.

STUDY GUIDE

Concepts Worth Remembering

Define:

1. Types of sampling problems
   (a) Estimation problems
   (b) Testing problems
2. Estimated standard errors
3. t distribution
4. Point estimates
5. Confidence interval

Self-Test

Circle the proper letter to indicate whether the following statements are true or false.

T F   1 Estimation problems call for a yes or no answer.

T F   2 Testing problems use a different theory of sample behavior than do estimation problems.

T F   3 The sample standard deviation is a biased estimator of the universe standard deviation.

T F   4 The estimated standard error of the percentage is calculated by substituting the sample percentage value for the unknown universe percentage value.

T F   5 The t distribution may be approximated by the normal curve when using samples of 30 or more.

T F   6 Confidence intervals represent the form of making estimates usually used by statisticians.

T F   7 A 95 percent confidence interval established in estimating a universe mean indicates that the probability is 95 in 100 that the true mean falls in this interval.

T F   8 The precision of a confidence interval varies directly with the size of sample used.

T F   9 The precision of a confidence interval varies directly with the Z value used.

T F   10 In determining the sample size to use in a percentage estimation problem, a 50–50 percentage split must be assumed.

Questions to Think About

1. Distinguish clearly between the two traditional types of sampling problems.
2. Explain the difficulty of using a point estimation procedure.
3. Explain the meaning and interpretation of a 99 percent confidence interval.
4. What are the two types of information that must be supplied to the statistician by management in a sample-size problem?

Problems

1 For the purpose of checking the income tax paid by one-chair barber proprietors, the Bureau of Internal Revenue observed a random sample of 626 shops. The proprietors in the sample had a mean income of $9,500 per year, with a standard deviation of $200 per year. Determine for the Bureau the 95 percent confidence interval of the mean income of proprietors of this type.

2 The EC 70 Testing Company, a private testing company, was asked to estimate the arithmetic mean breaking strength of a particular type of carton. The company tested a random sample of 101 cartons, which were found to have a mean breaking strength of 50 lb, with a standard deviation of 3 lb. What would the testing company's estimate of the mean breaking strength be if the client wished to be 99 percent confident of the answer?

3 For auditing purposes, a sample of 226 accounts receivable is selected from the 11,317 accounts that a firm has, and the sample mean is found to be $142.35. The sample standard deviation is computed to be $2.50. Set up a 99.7 percent confidence interval estimate of the universe mean.

4 To study the transactions of its Ski Shop, the Deep Snow Ski Corporation drew a random sample of 101 transactions. The sample yielded a mean transaction's value of $27.50 with a standard deviation of $4.00. Within what limits would the Ski Corporation be $95\frac{1}{2}$ percent certain of finding the true mean value of the transactions?

5 A distributor of Christmas supplies sampled a shipment of Christmas-tree ornaments at random to determine the portion of broken ornaments received. The result was 60 broken ornaments in a random sample of 600 ornaments. Determine the 99.7 percent confidence limits for the true portion of broken ornaments.

6 The Beau Jardin Nursery is planning to market a new type of grass seed for shady areas. Tests on 400 plots with this seed showed that 80 percent of the seeds germinated. Assuming that the 400 plots represent a random sample, determine for the nursery the 95 percent confidence interval for the true percentage of the seeds that will germinate under shady conditions.

7 In a study conducted for a manufacturer of plastic tableware, a random sample of 200 families was drawn to estimate the portion of all families who regularly used 12-oz tumblers. Forty families reported that they regularly used such tumblers. Estimate for the manufacturer with $95\frac{1}{2}$ percent confidence the true portion of all families using 12-oz tumblers.

8 The Rainy Day Savings and Loan Association conducted a sample study to learn what portion of their savings accounts was held in joint names. A random sample of 600 accounts contained 240 joint accounts. Establish a 99 percent confidence interval for the Association of the percentage of joint accounts.

9 The EC 70 Testing Company has been asked to test the mean breaking strength of glass rods tempered by a new process. The client wishes to be $95\frac{1}{2}$ percent confident of knowing the true mean breaking strength of the rods with a range of error of 4 lb. The testing company's expert in this field estimates that the standard deviation of breaking strengths of rods of this type will be 15 lb. How large a sample should the testing company use to provide the answer the client desires?

10 The Botany Department of Agricultural University has requested that the Business Research Department make a survey for them of sweet potato prices. In response to questions by the Research Department, the Botany Department has indicated that it would like to be 99.7 percent certain of knowing the true mean price per pound with an error of no more than $0.03. A quick check of sweet potato prices by the Research Department showed that they ranged from $0.10 per pound to $0.70 per pound. What size of sample should the Research Department use for the Botany Department study?

11 An aircraft parts manufacturer wishes to determine the arithmetic mean strength of a certain type of weld in order to submit a bid for a contract to produce parts using this weld. What size of random sample is required so that the risk of exceeding an error of 18 lb or more is 3 in 1,000? Assume that the universe standard deviation is 100 lb.

12 The Deep Snow Ski Corporation wishes to study the mean incomes of holders of season passes. It would like to be $95\frac{1}{2}$ percent certain of learning their mean income within an error of $200. Other studies indicate that the standard deviation of the past holders' incomes will be about $2,000. What size of sample should be used to complete this particular study?

13 In a special study for the Biology Department of Agricultural University, the Business Research Department was asked to survey to find out what percentage of farmers raise white turkeys. The Biology Department informed the Research Department that it would like to be $95\frac{1}{2}$ percent certain of being within 4 percent of the right answer. It was thought that the percentage of farmers having white turkeys would not exceed 20 percent. Determine for the Research Department the proper size of sample needed for this survey.

14 The Absoraka State Board of Education needs an estimate of the appropriate size of sample to use in a study. This study is of the percentage of resident student graduates who go on to graduate school in the state. The Board feels the percentage will not exceed 20 percent but would like to be 99.7 percent certain of being within 6 percent of the correct figure when the study is actually conducted. Determine for the Board the size of sample needed for the study.

15 A small mail-order company wishes to make a study of what percentage of its customers place more than one order per year. The company has no idea what this percentage might be. They believe that to plan accurately, they must be 95 percent certain of being within 5 percent of the correct answer. Determine for the company the sample size needed for this study.

16 The Jones City Transit Company is considering the adoption of a special fare schedule for schoolchildren and would like you to determine what sample size they need to estimate the percentage of schoolchildren among their passengers. Management estimates that it needs to be $95\frac{1}{2}$ percent confident of being within 3 percent of the true figure. It is believed that the percentage of schoolchildren will not exceed 20 percent.

Answers to Self-Test

1 F; 2 F; 3 T; 4 T; 5 T; 6 T; 7 F; 8 T; 9 F; 10 F.

TWELVE
TESTING HYPOTHESES WITH SAMPLE DATA

LEARNING OBJECTIVES

The basic learning objective is to learn how sample data are used to test an hypothesis (to make a decision). Specifically, this will involve studying:

1. The classical approach to hypothesis testing, including:
    (a) The formulation of the null and alternative hypotheses.
    (b) A study of Type I and Type II errors.
    (c) The setting and determination of the risks involved in making each type of error.
    (d) Actual hypothesis testing for means and percentages.
2. The decision approach to testing, including:
    (a) Defining courses of action and states of the world.
    (b) The setting of the risks of incorrect decisions.
    (c) The development of a decision rule to meet problem requirements for both means and percentages.
3. A comparison and contrast of the two approaches.

INTRODUCTION

The subject of this chapter is the second type of sampling problem described in the introduction to Chap. 11. These are the statistical problems deriving from questions requiring a yes or no answer (decision) on management's part. Yes, the transverse strength of the bricks equals or exceeds 950 lb/in^2; no, the lot of raw material is not acceptable, i.e., does not meet specifications; yes, the filling machine is putting the correct amount of soap chips in each package. These are all examples of decision problems of the hypothesis testing type.

FORMULATING STATISTICAL HYPOTHESES

An hypothesis is a statement of one's belief with respect to some condition of the world. A statistical hypothesis is a statement about some condition with respect to a statistical universe. Testing procedures attempt to verify or refute the hypothesis. We speak of the hypothesis after testing as being accepted or rejected. In general, it is easier to amass evidence to refute an hypothesis than to verify it beyond doubt. If it is asserted (hypothesized) that there are no bad peaches in a given bushel, discovery of one bad peach is sufficient to cause rejection of the statement, but the entire bushel must be inspected to establish the statement's truth.

The formulation of the appropriate hypothesis for statistical testing depends in part upon the problem being studied and in part on statistical testing procedures. To test an hypothesis statistically, it is necessary to state it so that it can be tested by statistical procedures. In general, the hypothesis to be tested in statistics is called the "null hypothesis" (usually symbolized as H_0) and is so stated as to be testable in terms of random sampling procedures and errors. In addition to the null hypothesis, an alternative hypothesis (H_1) must be specified. This is the hypothesis that will be accepted if the null hypothesis is rejected. It may be stated specifically or as a general class of alternatives.

In the case of the transverse strength of the bricks, our null hypothesis is that the mean strength equals or exceeds 950 lb/in^2 $(H_0 : \mu \geqslant 950$ lb/in$^2)$ and, as we are going to test by sampling procedures, that any difference from 950 lb/in^2 can be attributed to random sampling errors. Our alternative might be specific, such as that the mean strength equals 925 lb/in^2 (a specific amount less than 950), or more likely, merely that the mean strength is less than 950 lb/in^2 (i.e., $H_1 : \mu < 950$ lb/in^2), without specifying a particular amount.

In the problem involving the lot of raw material, the null hypothesis is that the lot does meet specifications (e.g., $H_0 : \pi_0 \leqslant 10$ percent) and that any observed difference in sampling can be attributed to random sampling error. The alternative hypothesis in this type of problem is likely to be somewhat specific, as, for example, that the lot is at least 5 percent worse than specifications $(H_1 : \pi_1 = 15$ percent$)$.

In the case of our filling machine, the null hypothesis is that the machine is putting the correct amount in the container and that any observed difference in sampling can be attributed to random sampling error. The alternative is that the machine is not putting in the correct amount; i.e., it is either underfilling or over-filling. Note that this last alternative hypothesis is two-sided (over and under), in contrast to our previous examples, where the alternatives were one-sided, i.e., less than 950 lb/in^2, or 5 percent worse than specifications.

AN INFORMAL ILLUSTRATION

We shall first work out an illustration of hypothesis testing on an informal basis to develop certain concepts, and then we shall establish a more formal procedure for actual testing. For our problem, let us assume that the filling machine referred to previously is designed to fill boxes of soap chips with an average of 50 oz per box. Management would like to determine whether the machine is functioning properly. Overfilling is costly to the company, and underfilling may lead to legal difficulties, so management wishes to guard against both. The method of testing will be to open and weigh accurately the soap chips in a random sample of boxes from the machine's production. This is done for a sample of 37 boxes, and sample mean and standard deviation computed. The latter measure equaled 1.8 oz ($s = 1.8$ oz). Our null hypothesis states that the machine is operating properly. This is the equivalent of specifying $\mu = 50$ oz. Sample means form samples of size 37 will form a normal curve around this mean of 50 oz if the machine is functioning properly. We can calculate the estimated standard error of the mean to measure the variation in these sample results:

$$\hat{\sigma}_{\bar{X}} = \frac{s}{\sqrt{n-1}} = \frac{1.8}{\sqrt{37-1}} = 0.3 \text{ oz}$$

Let us suppose that our sample mean equaled 49 oz ($\bar{X} = 49$ oz). The sample distribution and this result are illustrated in Fig. 12-1. Notice that this 49 oz works out to be 3.3 standard errors below 50 oz; i.e., $Z = -3.3$ for 49 oz. We can determine from our table of areas of the normal curve (App. B$_1$) the probability of obtaining this value or one farther away. Here it is 0.05 percent. It is customary to double this value, since our alternative hypothesis is two-sided and a difference from 50 oz of $+ 1.0$ oz ($\bar{X} = 51.0$ oz) would be as important to us as our observed difference of $- 1.0$ oz. Therefore, the probability of observing a sample mean which differs from 50 oz by as much as or

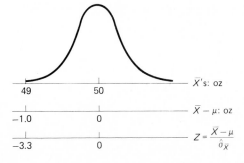

Figure 12-1 Random sampling distribution of $\bar{X}$'s for all samples of size $n = 37$.

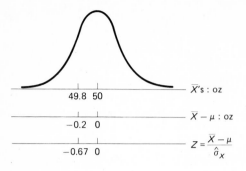

$\bar{X}$'s : oz

49.8 50

$\bar{X} - \mu$: oz

−0.2 0

$Z = \dfrac{\bar{X} - \mu}{\hat{\sigma}_{\bar{X}}}$

−0.67 0

Figure 12-2 Random sampling distribution of $\bar{X}$'s for all samples of size $n = 37$.

more than 1 oz is 0.1 percent, or 1/1,000. But we have observed such a sample mean. Therefore, either we have on a single trial achieved a very rare happening or our hypothesis that $\mu = 50$ oz is doubtful. We shall choose to conclude the latter. The risk in so doing (rejecting the hypothesis of 50 oz when it is true) is very small. In fact, it is our 1/1,000, for this is the probability of observing a difference of 1 oz if 50 oz is true. The error of rejecting a true hypothesis is called a Type I error.

An Informal Illustration: A Variation

Let us now suppose that our sample mean equals 49.8 oz ($\bar{X} = 49.8$ oz) instead of 49.0 oz. This situation is illustrated in Fig. 12-2. We still have under our null hypothesis a random sampling distribution of means around $\mu = 50$ oz, with $\hat{\sigma}_{\bar{X}} = 0.3$ oz. Our observed sample mean is now 0.67 of a standard error below 50 oz. From the normal curve table we can determine that the probability of drawing a sample mean as small as 49.8 or smaller from a universe with a mean of 50 oz is 25.14 percent. Doubling this, we find that the probability of obtaining a difference in sampling as large as or larger than 0.2 oz (the observed difference) is 50.28 percent. Our reaction now is different from what it was when our sample mean equaled 49 oz. Here we should undoubtedly accept the null hypothesis, since our sample evidence is quite consistent with it. We should run about a 50 percent chance of making a Type I error if we were to reject it, which is too great a risk for comfort. In accepting the null hypothesis, we do run the risk of making a Type II error, the error of accepting a false hypothesis. The actual probability of making this type of error depends on what the true (unknown) alternative hypothesis is, and can be estimated only by assuming specific values for the alternative hypothesis. We shall discuss this problem in greater detail below.

REJECTION REGION: ACCEPTANCE REGION: LEVEL OF SIGNIFICANCE

Somewhere between our relatively clear-cut cases of $\bar{X} = 49$ oz and $\bar{X} = 49.8$ oz lies the borderline point between rejection and acceptance. The decision as to where to draw this line should be made by management and in advance of actual testing (drawing of the sample). The line between acceptance and rejection is drawn on the basis of management's willingness to incur a Type I error, i.e., reject a true null hypothesis, since the placing of the line will set the risk of that type of error. Specifically, in the present example it would be the risk of concluding that the machine was functioning improperly (underfilling or overfilling) when it was actually putting in the desired amount of soap chips (50 oz.). Management should not choose this risk arbitrarily but in terms of its true nature and the potential costs of making an incorrect decision. If after study management decided in advance to reject the null hypothesis when the sample mean in a two-sided test occurred 5 percent or less of the time if that hypothesis were true, it would be drawing lines at ±1.96 standard errors. This is illustrated in Fig. 12-3.

The region between ±1.96 standard errors is called the "acceptance region," for if the sample mean drawn lies in this region, the null hypothesis will be accepted. The earlier sample mean of 49.8 oz resulted in a value of $Z = -0.67$, which would lead to automatic acceptance of the null hypothesis in that case, as such a Z value indicates that the sample mean fell in the acceptance region. The two rejection regions result from the two-sided nature of the alternative hypothesis; this type of problem is thus referred to as a "two-tailed test." Our first sample mean of 49 oz, with its $Z = -3.3$, falls in the lower rejection region and would, of course, result in automatic rejection of the null hypothesis. The 5 percent figure (often written 0.05) is called the "level of significance," and 1.96, the "critical ratio." A difference between $\bar{X}$ and μ sufficient to cause $\bar{X}$ to lie in the rejection region is termed a "significant difference." It is a difference so great that it is improbable that it is due to random sampling errors; hence the rejection of the hypothesis. A difference between $\bar{X}$ and μ lying in the acceptance region is termed an "insignificant difference." It is a difference which quite probably could have been due to random sampling errors. Levels of significance other than 5 percent are used. However, if one chooses a very low significance level, such as 0.1 percent, this increases the size of the acceptance region and thereby the risks of making a Type II error, i.e., accepting a false hypothesis.

An alternative approach defines the border lines on the $\bar{X}$ scale rather than the Z scale. In this approach, the critical ratio values are converted into values termed

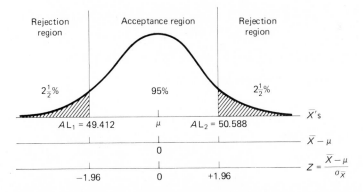

Figure 12-3 Acceptance and rejection regions for a two-sided test at the 5 percent level.

"action limits" (AL). The conversion is as follows:

$$AL = \mu_0 \pm Z\sigma_{\bar{X}}$$

where μ_0 is the value of the mean for the null hypothesis (H_0) and the Z is the critical ratio value that was set by management when choosing the risk of a Type I error. Here we would get

$$AL = 50 \text{ oz} \pm 1.96(0.3 \text{ oz})$$

$$= 50 \text{ oz} \pm 0.588 \text{ oz}$$

$$AL_1 = 49.412 \text{ oz} \quad \text{and} \quad AL_2 = 50.588 \text{ oz}$$

or

$$AL_1 = 49.4 \text{ oz} \quad \text{and} \quad AL_2 = 50.6 \text{ oz}$$

These action limits are shown in Fig. 12-3 and show that the null hypothesis will be accepted for values of $\bar{X}$ between 49.4 and 50.6 oz and that it will be rejected for $\bar{X}$'s outside this range. Our earlier $\bar{X} = 49.8$ oz lies in this range and, of course, will still lead to the null hypothesis being accepted. The $\bar{X} = 49$ oz lies below the action limit of 49.4 oz and again brings rejection of the null hypothesis.

A one-sided test (also called a "one-tailed test") is similar to the above except that there is only one rejection region. This region is either in the lower tail or in the upper tail of the curve, depending on the nature of the alternative hypothesis. Its size is determined by and represents the risk of making a Type I error. Obviously, there is also only one critical ratio or action limit.

TYPE I AND TYPE II ERRORS

Table 12-1 summarizes the nature of Type I and Type II errors. A Type I error is the rejection of the null hypothesis when it is true; a Type II error is the acceptance of the null hypothesis when it is false. As the action is either to accept or to reject the null hypothesis, only one kind of error can be made at a time; i.e., it is impossible to make both a Type I error and a Type II error in the same problem, because if you reject a true null hypothesis you cannot also accept a false null hypothesis, and vice versa. Testing procedures are designed to minimize the risks of making either type of error. The Greek letter alpha (α) is used to represent the risk of making a Type I

Table 12-1 Table of errors in hypothesis testing

State of the null hypothesis	Action on the null hypothesis	
	Accept	Reject
True	Correct action	Type I error
False	Type II error	Correct action

error. It corresponds to our level of significance. The Greek letter beta (β) is used to represent the risk of making a Type II error. The α risk in a given problem is automatically determined when one chooses the level of significance, because that choice represents the number of times (therefore the probability) that a result would fall in the rejection region when the null hypothesis is true. The β risk is harder to determine specifically, but depends on (1) the α risk, (2) the size of sample used, and (3) the specific alternative being considered. As suggested earlier, there is an inverse relationship between Type I and Type II errors, or between α and β. The smaller the α, the smaller the rejection region; the greater the acceptance region, and the greater the β risk. For example, if in our illustration above α were changed from 5 percent to 1 percent, new Z values of ± 2.58 would be needed for the critical ratios. This would result in new action limits of 49.2 oz and 50.8 oz. The new acceptance region lying between these limits is larger than the old acceptance region (49.4 to 50.6 oz) and would, therefore, increase the chances of accepting false values (the β risk). There is also an inverse relationship between the size of sample and the β risk. The larger the the sample, the smaller the standard error; the smaller the standard error, the smaller the acceptance region for any given α. This smaller acceptance region, of course, means less risk of a Type II error. To demonstrate this, let's use a sample of 145 boxes ($n = 145$). We now calculate our standard error to be

$$\hat{\sigma}_{\bar{X}} = \frac{s}{\sqrt{n-1}} = \frac{1.8}{\sqrt{145-1}} = 0.15 \text{ oz}$$

(Quadrupling the sample size will cut the standard error in half.) Using our original α of 5 percent ($Z = \pm 1.96$) our action limits are now 49.7 and 50.3 oz. This smaller acceptance region means fewer values lead to the acceptance of the null hypothesis, a false hypothesis will be accepted less often, and the risk of a Type II error is thereby reduced.

The Specific Alternative: Calculating Beta

To make a Type II error, the null hypothesis which is accepted must, in fact, be false. This means that some alternative hypothesis must be true. If the true alternative is close in value to the false null hypothesis value, the probability of discovering the difference is small and the chance of making a Type II error is great. Conversely, if the true alternative is substantially different from the false null hypothesis, the probability of discovering the difference is great and the β risk, therefore, small. Fortunately, the β risk is smallest for those situations where management most needs to avoid making a Type II error, i.e., where there is a material difference between the true alternative and the false null hypothesis. Usually, there is some critical difference between the false null hypothesis value and the true alternative for which management will want to have only a small risk of failing to detect the difference (of making the Type II error or accepting the false null value). If management can specify a critical difference of interest to them (a specific alternative value of μ, say μ_c) for which if true they would want only a small risk of accepting the false μ_0, we can compute the

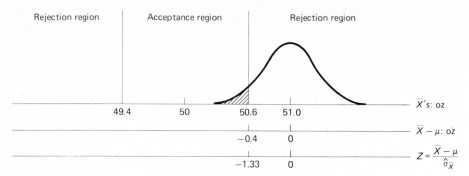

Figure 12-4 Calculation of β risk for $\mu_c = 51$ oz.

probability of such a false acceptance (β). As noted earlier, specific values for β can be computed only for specific alternative values of μ.

Let us illustrate such a calculation for our original testing procedure based on a sample of 37 boxes and a $\alpha = 5$ percent resulting in action limits of 49.4 and 50.6 oz. Assume that management indicates they would like to know the risk of failing to detect the fact that the machine is overfilling on the average by 1 oz. The question may be reworded as, "What is the probability of accepting the null hypothesis (H_0: $\mu = 50$ oz) when the true mean is 51 oz (H_1: $\mu_c = 51$ oz)?" Figure 12-4 illustrates our problem.

Changing μ changes only the location of our random sampling distribution of $\bar{X}$'s, moving it from 50 oz to 51 oz. The null hypothesis will still be accepted (incorrectly) for $\bar{X}$'s between 49.4 and 50.6 oz. The shaded lower tail of the distribution centered around 51 oz represents the probability desired. This value may be determined from App. B_1 after first determining the new Z for the action limit termed the critical Z (Z_c).

$$Z_c = \frac{AL - \mu_c}{\hat{\sigma}_{\bar{X}}} = \frac{50.6 - 51.0}{0.3} = \frac{-0.4}{0.3} = -1.33$$

The probability of falsely accepting the null hypothesis (H_0: $\mu = 50$ oz) turns out to be 9.18 percent. This is the β risk for the specific alternative $\mu = 51$ oz. Other alternative μ's would yield other β's. This will be illustrated below.

If 9 percent is a risk greater than management feels desirable, it may be reduced as explained earlier by either increasing α or increasing n. It should be noted that either of these represents in some sense a cost to management either in the form of a higher probability of a Type I error or in the form of increased sampling costs.

All the previous analysis of errors used an estimated standard error ($\hat{\sigma}_{\bar{X}}$) of 0.3 oz based on the sample standard deviation (s) of 1.8 oz. If a reasonable value for the population standard deviation (σ) is available, all of the analysis could (and probably should) be done in advance of any actual sampling to discover the testing procedure (customarily defined in terms of α and n) which best balances for management the costs of sampling and the risks and cost of errors. Such values of the population standard deviation are often available in advance of actual sampling, as discussed earlier in the sample-size section of Chap. 11.

Power Curves

The relationship between a whole set of specific alternatives and the probabilities of making Type II errors may be studied through a device known as a "power curve." The power curve applicable to our testing procedure for checking the operation of the filling machine using a sample of 37 boxes and $\alpha = 5$ percent is illustrated in Fig. 12-5. Values used to plot the curve are given in Table 12-2. The table gives values

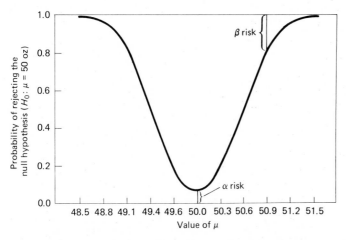

Figure 12-5 Power curve of the method used to test the operation of a filling machine.

for only the upper half of the power curve; as in a two-tailed test, the lower half is a mirror image of the upper half. As the entire sample space is divided into either regions of acceptance or rejection, the probabilities of accepting or rejecting the null hypothesis are complements of each other.

Table 12-2 Probabilities of rejecting and accepting the null hypothesis (H_0: μ = 50 oz) for n = 37 and α = 5%

Value of μ, oz	Z at AL_2	Probability of: Rejecting H_0, %	Accepting H_0, %
50.0	+1.96	5.00	95.00
50.3	+0.96	16.85	83.15
50.588 = AL_2	0.00	50.00	50.00
50.6	−0.04	51.60	48.40
50.9	−1.04	85.08	14.92
51.2	−2.04	97.93	2.07
51.5	−3.04	99.88	0.12

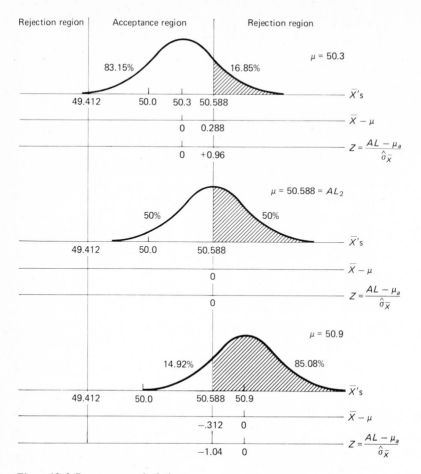

Figure 12-6 Power curve calculations.

Figure 12-6 illustrates the calculation of several of the Z values. However, if one selects values of μ at intervals equal to the standard error of the mean (0.3 oz in this case), the values of Z at the action limit will change by one each time and no calculations are really necessary to determine the Z's. The probabilities are obtained from App. B_1. The power curve of Fig. 12-5 is a plot of probabilities of rejecting the null hypothesis on the vertical axis against the alternative values of μ on the horizontal axis.[1]

The power curve therefore shows the probabilities of rejecting $\mu = 50$ oz for alternative values of the mean, the correct action except when $\mu = 50$ oz. The complements of these probabilities (1 – the probabilities of rejection) are the proba-

---

[1] A plot of the probabilities of accepting the null hypothesis against the alternative μ's would invert our graph. Such a curve is known as an "operating characteristic (OC) curve."

bilities of accepting the hypothesis of $\mu = 50$ oz for the given alternatives. If the alternative rather than the null hypothesis is true, the probabilities are those of making a Type II error for the specific alternative. In our illustration, the risk of accepting the hypothesis of 50 oz if, in fact, the mean equals 50.9 oz is about 15 percent (marked on the graph). We can determine the β risk for any other alternative from the graph. Note that these risks do decrease as we proceed farther and farther from the null hypothesis of 50 oz. This type of curve is a power curve, because it shows the power of the test to distinguish among alternatives to the null hypothesis.

Management must make the final decision as to whether the test is sufficiently sensitive in this respect. If not, the curve may be modified by changing α (raises the entire curve while maintaining its general shape) or by increasing the sample size (increases the steepness of the curve). The present testing procedure is reasonably certain ($\beta = 9$ percent) of detecting shifts of 1 oz in the mean.

STEPS IN TESTING HYPOTHESES

We shall now list and explain briefly the steps to follow in testing an hypothesis. In order, there are (1) management's question, (2) null and alternative hypotheses, (3) level of significance, (4) statistical test, (5) statistical conclusion, and (6) answer to management's question.

1. Management's Question

Lying behind any statistical problem is another problem or question to which management wishes an answer. The statistical problem must be formulated to give management a basis for reaching a decision on its related problem. If management's question is one requiring a yes or no answer, statistical testing procedures of the type discussed in this chapter may be helpful in aiding management in its decision making.

2. Null and Alternative Hypotheses

Management's problem is converted into a statistical problem by establishing the appropriate null hypothesis to be tested. In general, these hypotheses are stated by specifying certain numerical values of interest as population values (e.g., $\mu = 50$ oz or $\pi = 10$ percent defective) and explaining sample results in terms of random sampling error. The nature of the alternative hypothesis must also be established. It may be general or specific, one-sided or two-sided.

3. Level of Significance

A level of significance for the Type I errors must be decided upon. This should be chosen by management. The problem of the β risk must also be considered, and a tentative power or OC curve drawn if needed.

4. Statistical Test

The statistician must choose and apply the appropriate statistical methods for testing the hypothesis. Basic to this is the choosing of the appropriate sampling distribution. In this chapter we have been using sampling distributions having the normal curve as their pattern. In Chap. 14 we shall consider several other patterns of sampling distributions. Combining knowledge of the proper sampling distribution, the level of significance chosen, and the one-sided or two-sided nature of the alternative hypothesis, the statistician can establish cutoff points (critical ratios) as boundaries between the acceptance and rejection regions. The sample can now be drawn and the sample values computed. From these the standard error can be estimated and the test ratio established. Alternatively, the standard error can be used to establish action limits as boundaries between the acceptance and rejection regions.

5. Statistical Conclusion

The null hypothesis is accepted or rejected depending on whether the observed sample value being used for the test falls in the acceptance or rejection region as defined by either the critical ratios or the action limits.

6. Answer to Management's Question

Management must now make use of the statistical conclusion to answer its own question. This answer (decision) is subject to risks of error, but if based on statistical testing, these risks are known and were set in advance by management itself.

FORMAL ILLUSTRATION: THE MEAN

Management's Question

General Bridge Builders, Inc., builders of all types of bridges, has received a shipment of steel rods to be used in reinforced-concrete structures. In ordering the rods, the company specified that they must have an average tensile strength of more than 500 pounds per square inch (lb/in^2). Management's question is, "Does the shipment meet specifications with respect to average tensile strength?" As destructive testing is involved, a sampling test is to be made to answer the question.

Null and Alternative Hypotheses

As the problem involves a question of average tensile strength, we shall use a test involving the arithmetic mean. Our null hypothesis is that the universe of steel rods has a mean of only 500 lb/in^2, and any difference observed in sampling can be attributed to random sampling errors. In common symbolic shorthand, we would write $H_0: \mu \leqslant 500$ lb/in^2. The portion attributing differences to random sampling errors is understood, as it is part of all null hypotheses. We should state the hypothesis in this manner even if management reversed its question: "Does the shipment fail to meet specifications?"

The alternative hypothesis is $H_1 : \mu > 500$ lb/in^2. Here the alternative is one-sided, since management specified that the rods have a strength *greater than* 500 lb/in^2. Therefore, the test will involve a one-tailed rejection region. Notice that the alternative hypothesis must be accepted (i.e., the null hypothesis rejected) for the shipment to meet specifications. Notice also that the null hypothesis need not necessarily correspond to specifications.

Level of Significance

If management wishes to be quite certain that the shipment meets specifications (which they probably do), it should choose a very small α. Acceptance of a false hypothesis here means not using a satisfactory shipment of rods, which is probably less costly to the company than using a rod which is not strong enough (Type I error), although engineering standards usually have a large safety factor. Let us assume that management chooses $\alpha = 0.001$.

Statistical Test

If we use a sample greater than 30, the appropriate testing procedure involves use of the normal curve. The appropriate acceptance and rejection regions are illustrated in Fig. 12-7. We obtained the figure $Z = 3.09$ from App. B$_1$. If the Z of our test ratio $(\bar{X} - \mu)/\hat{\sigma}_{\bar{X}}$ is equal to or greater than 3.09, we shall reject the null hypothesis. If Z is less than 3.09, we shall accept it. A sample of 50 rods was tested, with the following results: $\bar{X} = 520$ lb/in^2 and $s = 28$ lb/in^2. The estimated standard error of the mean is

$$\hat{\sigma}_{\bar{X}} = \frac{s}{\sqrt{n-1}} = \frac{28}{\sqrt{50-1}} = 4 \text{ lb/in}^2$$

This value may be used to calculate either the test ratio or the action limit. The test ratio is

$$Z = \frac{\bar{X} - \mu}{\hat{\sigma}_{\bar{X}}} = \frac{520 - 500}{4} = \frac{20}{4} = 5$$

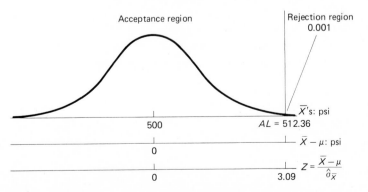

Figure 12-7 Random sampling distribution of $\bar{X}$ tensile strengths.

The action limit is

$$AL = \mu_0 + Z_\alpha \, \hat{\sigma}_{\bar{X}}$$
$$= 500 + 3.09(4) + 500 + 12.36 + 512.36 \text{ lb/in}^2$$

Statistical Conclusion

As 5 is greater than 3.09, or alternatively, as 520 lb/in^2 is greater than 512.36 lb/in^2, the sample mean of 520 lb/in^2 must fall in the rejection region. (In actual practice only one of the preceding comparisons need be made.) Therefore, our statistical conclusion is to reject the hypothesis that $\mu \leqslant 500$ lb/in^2 and accept the alternative hypothesis that $\mu > 500$ lb/in^2. A confidence interval estimate of the true mean strength could be made using the procedures of Chap. 11.

Answer to Management's Question

Management's question was, "Does the shipment meet specifications with respect to average tensile strength?" The answer is yes if the results of the statistical test are used. Before actually using the shipment, management may also wish to test whether the shipment is acceptable with respect to the variability in the strengths of the rods. This would involve a comparison of s with σ and will not be illustrated here.

FORMAL ILLUSTRATION: THE PERCENTAGE

Management's Question

The City Council of Pleasantdale must decide whether or not to submit a projected park bond issue to a vote of the citizens at this time. At least 60 percent of those voting must cast a favorable vote for the bond issue to carry. The Council's question is, "Will a park bond issue carry at this time?"

Null and Alternative Hypotheses

The null hypothesis is that the true percentage of the potential voters favoring the bond issue is at least 60 percent and that any difference observed in a sample can be attributed to random sampling errors; i.e., $H_0 : \pi \geqslant 60$ percent. The alternative hypothesis is that less than 60 percent of the potential voters favor the bond issue, i.e., $H_1 : \pi < 60$ percent. The test, therefore, will be a one-tailed test.

Level of Significance

The Council decides on an α risk of 5 percent. This is the risk of failing to hold an election when they should have. The Council is willing to let this risk be fairly high to help lower the β risk, since it feels an election will be held eventually, if not now. The β risk is the risk of holding an election when they should not have, and as this might be

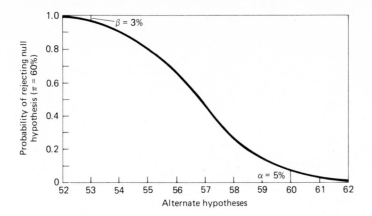

Figure 12-8 Power curve for bond-issue test.

very damaging to the cause of parks, the Council wishes to avoid this error. Shown in Fig. 12-8 is a tentative power curve drawn for the Council based on an α of 5 percent and a sample of 600. (The shape of this curve differs from our earlier curve because of the one-tailed nature of this test.) The β risks are again the complements of the probabilities of rejecting the null hypothesis ($\pi = 60$ percent) for the various alternative percentages. Illustrated is the fact that there would be a 3 percent chance of accepting the false hypothesis of 60 percent if the true percentage were 53. Let us assume that the Council feels that about 10 percent of the voters can be made to change their minds during the election campaign, so that this β risk is satisfactory.

Statistical Test

For a sample of 600 and percentages in the range being considered, the normal curve may be used to represent the sampling distribution of percentages. This distribution, our critical value for Z, and the acceptance and rejection regions are illustrated in Fig. 12-9. If $Z = (p - \pi)/\sigma_p$ is less than or equal to -1.64, we shall reject the null hypoth-

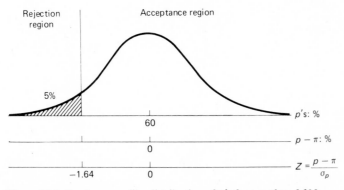

Figure 12-9 Random sampling distribution of p's for samples of 600.

esis. Otherwise, we shall accept it. The random sample of 600 voters was drawn, and 348 of them indicated they would vote in favor of the park bond issue. The sample percentage is

$$p = 100 \times \frac{348}{600} = 58\%$$

The standard error of the percentage is[1]

$$\sigma_p = \sqrt{\frac{\pi(100 - \pi)}{n}} = \sqrt{\frac{60(40)}{600}} = 2\%$$

$$\text{and } Z = \frac{p - \pi}{\sigma_p} = \frac{58 - 60}{2} = \frac{-2}{2} = -1$$

Statistical Conclusion

As -1 is greater than -1.64, our sample value of 58 percent must have fallen in the acceptance region. Therefore, the statistical conclusion is to accept the null hypothesis of $\pi = 60$ percent. Acceptance here is the equivalent of saying that there is not sufficient evidence to warrant rejecting the hypothesis.

Answer to Management's Question

The statistical results and conclusion in this problem do not provide the Council with a definite answer to the question, "Will a park bond issue carry at this time?" The sample evidence is not sufficiently strong to indicate that the bond issue will not carry, but since the sample result is less than 60 percent, it does not indicate that the bond issue is certain to carry. The election appears to be a close one. To reach its final decision on whether to hold the election, the Council must decide whether it truly feels it can influence at least a small percentage of people during the election campaign.

THE DECISION APPROACH TO TESTING PROBLEMS

A different approach to testing problems may be termed the decision approach. The differences are chiefly those of problem organization, since the same statistical theory underlies both approaches.

In the decision approach, a decision is thought of as a choice among alternative courses of action. These courses of action replace the null hypothesis and the alternative hypothesis. If the choice among the courses of action is to be made on the basis of an unknown universe statistical measure (called a decision parameter), the problem is a statistical decision problem.

---

[1] Note that we do not estimate the standard error of the percentage from the sample data, but compute the true standard error for our hypothetical value of 60 percent.

Table 12-3 A Simple decision problem

Alternative action	State of the world	
	Rain	No rain
Take umbrella	Correct decision	Incorrect decision
Leave umbrella	Incorrect decision	Correct decision

Whether the correct decision is made (correct alternative chosen) depends upon the true but unknown state of the real world. It is possible in choosing alternatives to make incorrect decisions similar to the errors described earlier under hypothesis testing. This is illustrated in Table 12-3 for the man who must decide in the morning upon leaving home whether or not to take his umbrella. The two types of incorrect decisions correspond to our two types of errors in hypothesis testing. As one course of action or the other must be chosen, the two types of incorrect decisions (errors) cannot occur at the same time. For convenience the terms Type I and Type II error and α and β risk are often used in describing the possible incorrect decisions, even though no longer strictly applicable, as no hypothesis exists. Which incorrect decision is designated by which term is immaterial as long as the correct numerical error risk is assigned to each.

Another difference in emphasis usually applied in the decision approach is to set the α risk and the β risk for a specific alternative and then determine the sample size needed to have those risks. In hypothesis testing the α risk and sample size are usually set and the β risk determined for various alternatives on the basis of these. As the sample size (n) is solved for in the decision approach, one is forced to do a complete analysis of the procedure in advance of actual sampling. In hypothesis testing, one may sample first and then worry about β later when it may be too late. Decision procedures do require a working value for the population standard deviation (σ) in advance. The procedures lead to what is termed a "decision rule."

One final difference in problem organization is that, in decision making, the critical value (one-tailed) or values (two-tailed) for decision making are usually computed in terms of the sample data. In hypothesis testing, in contrast, the critical value was in terms of the ratio of the difference to the standard error; for example,

$$Z = \frac{\overline{X} - \mu}{\sigma_{\overline{X}}} \quad \text{or as action limits.}$$

Statistical Decision Making: An Illustration—The Mean

Among its many products, the Ferrous Steel Company manufactures steel rods. The management of the company would like a statistical decision rule to check on the thickness of one type of such rods being produced by a particular rolling machine. The rods in question are specified to have an average thickness of 2.50 cm. If the rods differ from this by more than ±0.25 cm, they are considered unacceptable and corrective action to adjust the rolling machine will be taken. Of course, if the rods are satisfactory,

Table 12-4 Decision table for steel rod problem

Possible course of action	Possible state of the world	
	S_1: satisfactory rods $\mu_1 = 2.50$ cm	S_2: unacceptable rods $\mu_2 = 2.50 \pm 0.25$ cm
A_1: take no action	Correct decision	Incorrect decision ($\beta = 10\%$)
A_2: take corrective action	Incorrect decision ($\alpha = 1\%$)	Correct decision

no corrective action will be taken. These possible actions by management and the possible states of the world are summarized in Table 12-4. Such a table is an essential tool in solving decision problems. The table also shows that management decided that they wanted only a 1 percent risk of incorrectly taking corrective action (perhaps stopping production to adjust the rolling machine when no adjustment was needed). However, after discussion with the statistician working on the problem, management decided it could take a 10 percent risk of taking no action when the machine was producing unacceptable rods. This risk can be fairly large as it applies to one check of the machine and such checks are to be done frequently. The probability of not detecting unacceptable quality in two successive trials is much smaller. It is 10 percent squared (0.1^2) or 1 percent (0.01). Allowing β to be large will reduce the size of sample needed and thereby sampling costs.

The mechanics of the problem involve first solving for the needed sample size (n) and then for cutoffs $(\overline{X}'$ and $\overline{X}'')$ between $\mu_1 = 2.50$ cm and $\mu_2 = 2.50 \pm 0.25$ cm. Sample means close to 2.50 cm favor the state of the world satisfactory rods (S_1) and would lead to taking no action (A_1); sample means near 2.25 cm or 2.75 cm favor the state of the world unacceptable rods (S_2) and would lead to taking corrective action (A_2). The cutoffs $(\overline{X}'$ and $\overline{X}'')$ must be determined to decide which sample means between 2.50 cm and 2.50 ± 0.25 cm favor S_2 over S_1. Figure 12-10 illustrates this and the resulting division of the sample space into areas leading to action A_1 or action A_2. The A_2 region is in two parts, as corrective action will be taken if the rods are either too thin or too thick. This is analogous to a two-tailed test in hypothesis testing.

To solve for the sample size (n), two equations are determined for either $\overline{X}'$ or $\overline{X}''$, one based on how sample means would distribute themselves if S_1 were the true state of the world $(\mu_1 = 2.50$ cm$)$, and the second equation on how the means would be distributed if S_2 were the true state of the world $(\mu_2 = 2.25$ cm or $\mu_2 = 2.75$ cm$)$. We shall illustrate for $\overline{X}''$. This value, assuming S_1, would be

$$\overline{X}'' = \mu_1 + Z_\alpha \sigma_{\overline{X}}$$

A check of Table 12-4 tells us that 1 percent (α) of the sampling distribution around $\mu_1 = 2.50$ cm will be allowed to fall into the A_2 region. As there are actually two parts to the A_2 region, this means $\frac{1}{2}$ percent each (see Fig. 12-10). The necessary Z

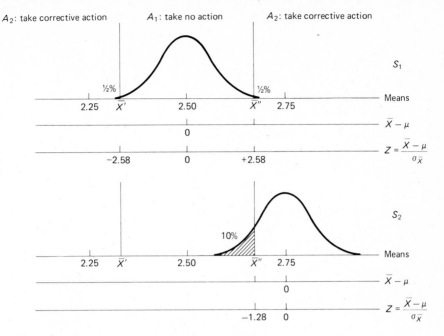

Figure 12-10 Random sampling distributions for S_1 and S_2.

values to cut off $\frac{1}{2}$ percent per tail are $Z = \pm 2.58$. Our first equation, therefore, can be rewritten as

$$\overline{X}'' = 2.50 \text{ cm} + 2.58\,\sigma_{\overline{X}}$$

We now proceed to a second equation based on S_2. We get

$$\overline{X}'' = \mu_2 + Z_\beta \sigma_{\overline{X}}$$

From Table 12-4 we find that 10 percent of a curve with $\mu_2 = 2.75$ may fall in the A_1 region. The 10 percent is not split, as there is only one A_1 region. The result is illustrated in Fig. 12-10 and the required Z is $Z = -1.28$. Therefore,

$$\overline{X}'' = 2.75 - 1.28\sigma_{\overline{X}}$$

We set our two equations equal to each other, getting

$$2.50 \text{ cm} + 2.58\,\sigma_{\overline{X}} = 2.75 - 1.28\sigma_{\overline{X}}$$

However, $\sigma_{\overline{X}} = \sigma/\sqrt{n}$ and if we can obtain a workable value for σ, the only unknown will be n. Let us assume that the Engineering Department uses the value $\sigma = 0.4$ cm for this type of rod. We get

$$2.50 + 2.58\,\frac{0.4}{\sqrt{n}} = 2.75 - 1.28\,\frac{0.4}{\sqrt{n}}$$

Solving for n,

$$2.50 + \frac{1.032}{\sqrt{n}} = 2.75 - \frac{0.512}{\sqrt{n}}$$

$$\frac{1.544}{\sqrt{n}} = 0.25$$

$$0.25 \sqrt{n} = 1.544$$

$$\sqrt{n} = \frac{1.544}{0.25} = 6.2$$

$$n = (6.2)^2 = 38.44 \text{ rods}$$

If n is a workable sample size, we may proceed to solve for the cutoffs $\overline{X}'$ and $\overline{X}''$. If the sample size turned out to be unsatisfactory (say too large and therefore too expensive), we could either abandon the project or try again with other values for α and β or with a greater difference between μ_1 and μ_2. This would be up to management. Remember, though, that one advantage of this procedure is that we have not yet drawn any rods.

As 39 rods appears to be a reasonable sample, we will solve for the cutoffs. Earlier,

$$\overline{X}'' = 2.50 + \frac{1.032}{\sqrt{n}}$$

But $\sqrt{n} = 6.2$, so we have

$$\overline{X}'' = 2.50 + \frac{1.032}{6.2} = 2.50 + 0.17 = 2.67 \text{ cm}$$

As $\overline{X}'$ is the same distance below μ_1 as $\overline{X}''$ is above, it would be

$$\overline{X}' = 2.50 - 0.17 = 2.33 \text{ cm}$$

Our final decision rule is:

Take a random sample of 39 rods from the rolling machine's production and compute the mean thickness of the sample ($\overline{X}$). If $\overline{X}$ lies between 2.33 cm and 2.67 cm, assume that the state of the world is S_1 and take no action. If $\overline{X}$ lies below 2.33 cm or above 2.67 cm, assume that the state of the world is S_2 and take corrective action.

A one-tailed (one-sided) decision rule differs from the rule above only in that a single cutoff is required and no error values are split in solving for n. This will be illustrated below for percentages.

Statistical Decision Making:
An Illustration—The Percentage

The Bubble Glass Company, Inc., a manufacturer of glass products, has been receiving complaints of excessive breakage during the shipment of its products due to poor

Table 12-5 Decision table for glass packaging problem

Possible course of action	Possible state of the world	
	S_1 : normal breakage $\pi_1 = 10\%$	S_2 : excessive breakage $\pi_2 = 15\%$
A_1 : leave packaging procedure alone	Correct decision	Incorrect decision ($\alpha = 0.01$)
A_2 : change packaging procedure	Incorrect decision ($\beta = 0.05$)	Correct decision

packaging. Management wishes to determine whether breakage is excessive, in which case it will take action to change the packaging procedure. However, if breakage is normal, it will leave the procedure alone. Past records indicate that normal breakage is 10 percent, and they decide to consider 15 percent as excessive. The problem and possible outcomes are summarized in Table 12-5. It is decided by the manufacturer and his statistician that the risk of taking no corrective action if breakage is excessive should be 0.01 and that of taking corrective action if breakage is normal, 0.05. These are also indicated in Table 12-5.

The mechanics of the problem involve solving first for a sample size and then for a critical value of the sample percentage (p') based on the two possible states of the world and the two risks of $\alpha = 0.01$ and $\beta = 0.05$. Assuming simple random sampling

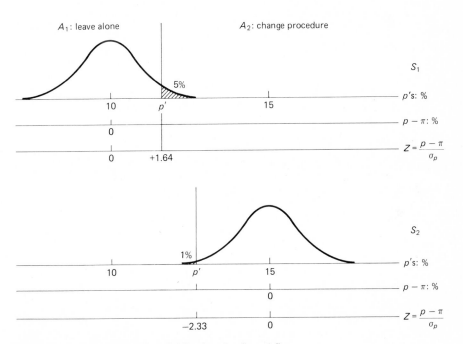

Figure 12-11 Random sampling distributions for S_1 and S_2.

and using a normal curve as the sampling distribution, the sampling distribution for $\pi_1 = 10$ percent is shown in Fig. 12-11. A normal deviate of 1.64 will have 5 percent of the curve beyond it. If the sample percentage p is equal to or greater than the critical value p', we shall change the method of packaging. As this can happen 5 percent of the time when $\pi_1 = 10$ percent, we have our 5 percent risk of error. The critical value p' is given by the expression

$$p' = \pi_1 + Z_\beta \sigma_p$$

$$= \pi_1 + Z_\beta \sqrt{\frac{\pi_1(100 - \pi_1)}{n}}$$

$$= 10 + 1.64 \sqrt{\frac{10(90)}{n}}$$

$$= 10 + \frac{49.2}{\sqrt{n}}$$

The second sampling distribution for $\pi_2 = 15$ percent is also shown in Fig. 12-11. The Z value to establish an error of 1 percent is $Z = 2.33$. Here the critical value p' is given by the expression

$$p' = \pi_2 + Z_\alpha \sigma_p$$

$$= \pi_2 + Z_\alpha \sqrt{\frac{\pi_2(100 - \pi_2)}{n}}$$

$$= 15 - 2.33 \sqrt{\frac{15(85)}{n}}$$

$$= 15 - \frac{83.18}{\sqrt{n}}$$

The two expressions for p' may be equated to solve for n:

$$10 + \frac{49.2}{\sqrt{n}} = 15 - \frac{83.18}{\sqrt{n}}$$

$$\sqrt{n} = \frac{132.38}{5} = 26.47$$

$$n = 26.5^2 = 702$$

This value of n may be substituted in either expression for p' to solve for the critical value. Here we have

$$p' = 10 + \frac{49.2}{\sqrt{702}} = 11.9\%$$

Our decision rule is to select a random sample of size 702 and compute the percentage breakage for the sample p. If p is greater than or equal to 11.9 percent, change the packaging procedure. If p is less than 11.9 percent, leave the procedure alone.

Statistical Decision Methods: A Summary

The following steps, demonstrated in the illustrations above, are used in establishing a statistical decision rule. First, the possible alternatives must be specified and the possible states of the world determined and quantified. Second, the risks of incorrect decisions must be decided upon. Third, the method of sampling must be chosen and the appropriate sampling distribution determined. Fourth, the sample size must be computed. Last, the critical value or cutoff or critical values or cutoffs for choosing between the alternatives must be computed. Two-tailed decision rules for either means or percentages are quite similar, but differ in that two critical values must be solved for. Sometimes decision rules are determined by specifying α and n. In these cases the procedure is almost identical with hypothesis testing.

SAMPLE SIZE (CONTINUED)

Previously, we discussed sample-size determination in general and in connection with estimating by the use of confidence intervals. Our illustrations under decision making show how the sample size may be determined for this type of problem or for an hypothesis testing problem. Of the three variables in a testing problem, α, β, and n, only two may be held fixed, and the third must be solved for in terms of the other two. Although it may seem more logical to set α and β and solve for n, the sample size which results may not be practicable in terms of sampling practice. The sample size may be so large as to be unduly expensive or as to require an unreasonable amount of time during sampling. If either of these were true, it would be necessary to settle for a smaller sample, even though accompanied by an increase in the risks involved. In all cases the determination of a test's power curve will show all the risks involved, serving as the basis for determining any adjustment in the risks management feels it is necessary to make, and thus will repay the expenditure of time and money.

A REVIEW AND A PREVIEW

In closing, it should be noted that the techniques studied in this chapter were strictly inferential in character; i.e., any decision on an hypothesis was made strictly on the basis of the sample evidence. Management was not necessarily bound by this sample evidence; however, its judgment was something separate from the sample evidence and often applied after the fact. Also, the techniques used included costs only implicitly in the setting of the risks. If costs of a wrong decision were particularly high, the risk of making that decision was set very low. In Chap. 13 we shall consider newer techniques which attempt to include management's judgments and explicit costs in the framework of the analysis itself.

STUDY GUIDE

Concepts Worth Remembering

Define:

1. Null hypothesis
2. Alternative hypothesis
3. One-tailed (sided) test: upper-tailed test; lower-tailed test
4. Two-tailed (sided) test
5. Acceptance region
6. Rejection region
7. Significant difference
8. Insignificant difference
9. Critical ratio
10. Action limit
11. Type I error
12. Type II error
13. α risk: level of significance
14. β risk
15. Power
16. Power curve
17. Operating characteristic (OC) curve
18. Decision
19. States of the world
20. Parameter
21. Statistic

Self-Test

Multiple-choice questions. Circle the letters of the statements which correctly complete the questions. There may be from one to four correct answers.

1 The null hypothesis in hypothesis testing problems:
(a) States that any difference from the hypothesized value observed while sampling can be attributed to the chance errors of random sampling.
(b) Is classified as one-sided or two-sided.
(c) Is symbolized by the symbol H_0.
(d) Is accepted if the alternative hypothesis is rejected.

2 An action limit (AL) in hypothesis testing problems:
(a) Is at the boundry between the acceptance and rejection regions.
(b) Is used in the calculation of α risks.
(c) May be on either side of μ_0 but not both.
(d) Serves the same purpose for testing as the critical ratio.

3 A significant difference found in hypothesis testing:
    (*a*) Leads to the acceptance of the null hypothesis.
    (*b*) Leads to the rejection of the alternative hypothesis.
    (*c*) Is a difference so great that it is improbable that it is the result of chance errors of random sampling.
    (*d*) Is a difference such that the sample value will lie in the rejection region.

4 A Type I error in hypothesis testing:
    (*a*) Is the error of accepting a false null hypothesis.
    (*b*) Is the error of rejecting a true null hypothesis.
    (*c*) Has a probability of occurrence designated by α.
    (*d*) Occurs less often for large samples than small samples.

5 A Type II error in hypothesis testing:
    (*a*) Is the error of accepting a false null hypothesis.
    (*b*) Is the error of rejecting a true null hypothesis.
    (*c*) Has a probability of occurrence designated by β.
    (*d*) Has a probability of occurrence which depends on the alternative hypothesis being considered.

6 In an hypothesis testing problem the α risk:
    (*a*) Is the risk of making a Type I error.
    (*b*) Is inversely related to the sample size.
    (*c*) Should be set before the sample is actually drawn.
    (*d*) Determines the size of the rejection region.

7 In an hypothesis testing problem the β risk:
    (*a*) Is the risk of making a Type I error.
    (*b*) Is inversely related to the size of the α risk.
    (*c*) Is the complement of the power value.
    (*d*) Determines the size of the acceptance region.

8 The power curve of a statistical testing procedure:
    (*a*) Is identical with the test's OC curve.
    (*b*) Shows the probability of correctly rejecting the null hypothesis when it is false.
    (*c*) Shows the probability of making Type II errors as complements of the values actually plotted.
    (*d*) Can be determined only after the sample is drawn.

9 The decision approach to testing problems:
    (*a*) Still requires the stating of a null and an alternative hypothesis.
    (*b*) Sets the risks of both types of errors and solves for the sample size.
    (*c*) Defines a decision as a choice among alternative courses of action.
    (*d*) Leads to a decision rule for testing.

Questions to Think About

1. What is the "null hypothesis"? What is the "alternative hypothesis"? Explain the use of each in hypothesis testing.
2. Define the types of errors which can occur in hypothesis testing. Explain how the risk of each type of error may be determined and controlled.

3. What is a "power curve"? What is an OC curve? Of what value and use are these curves in hypothesis testing?
4. List the steps to be followed in testing a statistical hypothesis. Explain what is happening at each step.
5. Compare and contrast the decision approach to testing problems with the conventional hypothesis testing approach.

Problems

1 A company ordered a shipment of "long-life" light bulbs for installation in inaccessible places. They specified that this shipment was to have a mean life of 10,000 h. A random sample of 65 bulbs used to test the shipment had a mean life of 9,986 h, with a standard deviation of 64 h.

(a) Testing at the 5 percent level, should the company accept or reject the shipment? Follow the six formal steps of hypothesis testing as outlined in the text in working this problem. Be sure to construct the power curve in step 3.

(b) What is the probability of accepting a shipment which has a mean 30 h less than that specified by the company?

2 In ordering ball bearings from a supplier, a manufacturer specified a mean diameter of 11 mm. A shipment of 10,000 arrived, and a random sample of 257 ball bearings had a mean diameter of 11.03 mm, with a standard deviation of 0.3 mm.

(a) At the 5 percent level, should he accept or reject the shipment? Demonstrate statistically.

(b) What is the probability of incorrectly accepting a shipment with a mean diameter of 11.07 mm?

3 The Frugal-Four Auto Company has decided to introduce a new six-cylinder car to be called the Saving-Six. Test runs on a sample of 50 cars showed a mean gas consumption of 30 mi/gal, with a standard deviation of 3.5 mi/gal.

(a) Test for the company at the 2 percent level of significance whether the new car has a gas consumption of more than 28 mi/gal.

(b) What is the probability of failing to conclude that the gas consumption is more than 28 mi/gal if, in fact, it is 30.5?

4 A machine automatically fills and closes cans of ground coffee, each of which is supposed to contain 1 lb of coffee. A random sample of 65 cans of coffee was selected from a day's output of the machine, and the amount of coffee in each can was weighed accurately. The arithmetic mean of this sample was 1.03 lb, and the standard deviation was 0.048 lb.

(a) Determine for the coffee company whether or not the machine is functioning properly. Let α equal 1 percent.

(b) What is the probability of concluding that the machine is functioning properly if it is putting in only an average of 0.97 lb per can?

5 The Mini-Max Dress Company has just received a shipment of thread from a supplier which was supposed to have a mean strength of at least 100 lb/in^2. A random sample of 50 lengths of thread showed a mean strength of 97 lb/in^2 with a standard deviation of 3.5 lb/in^2.

(a) Test for the company at the 1 percent level whether they should accept the shipment.

(*b*) Determine the company's probability of accepting a shipment with a mean of 98 lb/in^2

6 The Smooth-Smoke Pipe Tobacco Company has hired an independent testing agency to check on the percentage of white burley tobacco in its Junior Executive Mixture. This mixture is supposed to be 80 percent white burley. The testing agency analyzed a random sample of 200 units of the mixture and found the sample to be 85 percent white burley. Following the formal steps of hypothesis testing, determine whether the mixture sampled contains the proper portion of white burley. Let the α risk be 5 percent, and draw an approximate power curve for the test.

7 Over a long period of time the operators of bolt-threading machinery in a certain factory spoiled about 60 bolts per 1,000. Recently, inspectors have complained that spoilage has been excessive. A test run of 10,000 bolts resulted in 650 spoiled bolts.

(*a*) Assuming the test run to be a random sample of production, determine at the 1 percent level if spoilage was higher than normal during the test run.

(*b*) Calculate the probability of assuming that spoilage is normal if, in fact, it has increased to 6.8 percent.

8 Company records at Economics, Inc., show the percentage of control panels mis-wired when the wiring is by hand methods to be 12.5 percent. A random sample of 900 panels wired by machine methods contained 90 miswired panels.

(*a*) Determine for the company if machine wiring results in a significantly smaller percentage of miswired panels. Let α equal 5 percent.

(*b*) What is the probability of concluding that machine methods of wiring panels are no better than hand methods if, in fact, they produce 9.0 percent miswired panels?

9 The Modern Age Electronic Corp. has just received a shipment of transistors from its supplier. Specifications for these transistors require that at least 80 percent of them survive a particular pressure test. A random sample of 400 of the transistors was drawn and subjected to the pressure test. 306 of them passed the test.

(*a*) Test at the 2 percent level whether the Corporation should accept the shipment.

(*b*) Compute for the Corporation the probability of accepting a shipment of transistors of which only 71 percent will survive the pressure test.

10 A particular sewing operation at the Mini-Max Dress Company was expected to have no more than 10 percent mis-sewn items. When a random sample of 100 items from this operation was drawn, it was found to have 14 mis-sewn items.

(*a*) Determine for the company whether they may conclude the percentage of mis-sewn items to be excessive. Test at the 5 percent level.

(*b*) What is the probability that the company will conclude that the operation is operating satisfactorily when it is producing 18 percent mis-sewn items?

11 A manufacturer wishes to develop a statistical decision rule by which he will decide whether or not to accept large shipments of washers to be used in a pump assembly. These washers are specified to have a mean width of 0.2 in and a standard deviation of 0.03 in. After questioning by the company statistician, the manufacturer agrees that he is willing to run a 1 percent risk of rejecting a good shipment (meets specifications) and a 5 percent risk of accepting a bad shipment (differs from specifications by ±0.01 in or more). Formulate a statistical decision rule for the mean that meets the manufacturer's needs in this problem.

12 The quality control department of the Mini-Max Dress Company wants a decision rule for checking the weight of incoming bolts of cloth. The bolts are expected to have a mean weight of 50 lb per bolt. Unacceptable shipments are those which differ from this figure by ±4 lb or more. Management has agreed to take a 1 percent risk of rejecting bolts of satisfactory quality and a 10 percent risk of accepting bolts of unsatisfactory quality. Determine for the quality control department the needed rule. The standard deviation of the weights is thought to be 10 lb.

13 The Red and Green Tree-Lite company, manufacturers of a wide line of Christmas-tree lighting systems, wishes to develop a statistical decision rule for checking incoming shipments of fuses which are used in one of its lines of tree lights. Acceptable fuses according to specifications have a mean of 14 A. The Company wishes to run a risk of no more than 2 percent of accepting fuses which it considers inferior for its purposes (more than ±2 A from specifications). On the other hand, it is willing to take a 5 percent chance of not accepting some good fuses. The company statistician estimates that the population standard deviation must be about 5 A. Develop for the company a rule meeting the desired conditions.

14 The Beau Jardin Nursery is planning to stock a special type of hose for irrigating purposes and desires a statistical decision rule whereby they may check the quality of incoming shipments. The special hose was supposed to have a mean breaking strength of 150 lb/in^2. The nursery decided it was willing to run a 5 percent risk of not accepting good hose but only a 1 percent risk of accepting inferior hose (hose 5 lb/in^2 below specifications). It was estimated that the standard deviation of this type of hose would be about 10 lb/in^2. Develop the desired decision rule for the nursery.

15 The Ski-Lift Corporation, makers of chair lifts for ski areas, buys cable for its lifts from several suppliers. It would like you to develop a decision rule for checking the quality of incoming shipments of cable. Specifications for the cable call for it to have a mean tensile strength of 5,000 kg/cm^2. The corporation states that it can run only a 0.1 percent risk of accepting cable that has a mean 100 kg/cm^2 less than specified. However, it is willing to run a 5 percent risk of rejecting good cable. Corporation engineers determine that the cable has a standard deviation of approximately 150 kg/cm^2. Develop the desired rule for the corporation.

16 Economics, Inc., manufacturers of the EC 70 computer, is interested in a new process for producing magnetic cores which is thought to produce a smaller percentage of defective cores than the process currently being used. The present process is producing 20 percent defective cores. As the new process is somewhat more expensive than that currently being used, management does not want to introduce it unless it makes 5 percent fewer defectives. It has been decided to conduct a sample run of the new process to determine its capabilities and whether or not to introduce it. Develop for the management of the company a statistical decision rule which will have a 5 percent risk of failing to introduce the new process if it is superior, but only a 1 percent risk of changing the process if the new method is not superior.

17 The quality control department of Rain Gear, Inc., is interested in developing a statistical decision rule for checking the quality of outgoing rain hats for women. After discussion with management it was agreed that no more than 8 percent of these should have flaws and that management was willing to run a 5 percent risk of not shipping a lot of satisfactory quality. They further agreed that they would be willing

to accept a 10 percent risk of shipping a lot which had 12% flaws. Develop the desired rule for the quality-control department.

18 An auditing firm wishes to establish a statistical decision rule to help them in auditing a manufacturing firm's invoices for clerical errors. They feel that an error rate of 2 percent is to be expected. If the error rate should be as high as 4 percent, they call for follow-up action. The auditing firm is willing to run a 10 percent risk of taking follow-up action when not needed, but wishes to run only a 1 percent risk of failing to do so when the error rate is excessive. Construct for the auditing firm the needed rule.

19 The quality-control department of the Mini-Max Dress Company needs a decision rule for checking a cutting operation. The Company wishes to have 2 percent mis-cut pieces and is willing to run a $2\frac{1}{2}$ percent risk of incorrectly stopping the operation when it is performing at this level. On the other hand, they want to run no more than a 5 percent risk of not stopping the operation when it is producing 10 percent mis-cut pieces. Determine the needed decision rule.

20 The Uncle Gerry Company manufactures pancake mixes. A particular wholewheat mix is supposed to have 60 percent wholewheat flour. Too much wholewheat flour increases costs and too little affects the taste of the mix. Uncle Gerry wishes a statistical decision rule to check on the amount of wholewheat in the mix. He agrees that he is willing to run a 1 percent risk of both concluding the mix has the proper percentage of wholewheat when it does not (differs by more than ±10 percent) and of concluding that it has too little or too much wholewheat when it is actually all right. What should Uncle Gerry's decision rule be?

Answers to Self-Test

1 (a), (c); **2** (a), (d); **3** (c), (d); **4** (b), (c); **5** (a), (c), (d); **6** (a), (c), (d);
7 (b), (c); **8** (b), (c); **9** (b), (c), (d).

THIRTEEN
STATISTICAL DECISION MAKING

LEARNING OBJECTIVES

The basic learning objective is to acquire a knowledge of modern (bayesian) decision theory and methods. Specifically, you will become familiar with the following topics:

1. Decision making under certainty.
2. Decision making under uncertainty—discrete case
   (a) Prior analysis (without sampling):
       (1) Payoff analysis.
       (2) Opportunity loss analysis.
       (3) The expected value of perfect information.
   (b) Posterior analysis (with sampling)—the use of Bayes' theorem.
3. Decision making under uncertainty—continuous case
   (a) Prior analysis—the use of a normal prior.
   (b) Posterior analysis—the use of Bayes' theorem in the continuous case.
   (c) Determination of optimum sample size.

INTRODUCTION

In this chapter we shall give an introduction to "statistical decision theory" or "bayesian decision theory." The two terms have come to be used interchangeably. The term "bayesian" does emphasize the use of Bayes' theorem in the analysis to combine prior knowledge of some kind with information obtained from sampling. Either term characterizes the newer techniques discussed briefly at the end of Chap. 12. The techniques attempt to combine probabilities, expected monetary values (costs), statistical inference, and Bayes' theorem into an integrated whole to aid management in its decision-making function.

DECISION MAKING

In Chap. 12 a decision was defined as the choice between (or in general, among) alternative courses of action. The correct choice of action depended on knowing the true state of the world (of nature). The problem then and for most of this chapter is that we do not know which state of the world is (or will be) true. If such knowledge were available to us, the correct action (decision) would presumably be made.

Under Certainty

The term used to describe the decision problem when knowledge of the states of the world exists is "decision making under certainty." Such knowledge does not mean that the decision problem is trivial in terms of the necessary analysis; it does mean, however, that with proper analysis we should make the correct decision. Consider, for example, the problem of a manufacturer with three plants and five warehouses at varying locations who must decide from which plant and to and from which warehouse to ship goods to minimize transportation and storage costs in supplying the final market. Most factors in costs of storage and costs and routes for shipping are known well enough to be considered certain, yet finding the best combination to use among all possible combinations (alternatives) is not a simple one. The techniques of mathematical programming (particularly linear programming) are used to solve this kind of problem.

Under Uncertainty

Although the decisions represented by the term "decision making under uncertainty" are at times further subdivided, we shall use the term to describe all decisions where the states of the world are not known in advance and at best we have only the probabilities of their occurring. These probabilities may be objective in character, but are often of the subjective type. We shall develop the concepts and methods for this type of decision problem by means of a simple illustration.

Table 13-1 Payoff table for simple acceptance problem

Alternative course of action	Possible state of the world	
	S_1: good shipment $\pi_1 = 5\%$	S_2: bad shipment $\pi_2 = 15\%$
A_1: accept shipment	$5,000	-$2,000
A_2: reject shipment	-$500	0

Under Uncertainty without Sampling

We shall begin our illustration by considering how the best decision may be made before any additional information is collected by sampling. Later we shall see how sampling information may be added to improve the decision process. We shall limit our illustration to two courses of action and two states of the world, although the methods can be generalized to handle more actions and more states of the world.

The management of the Gamma Manufacturing Company has the familiar problem of trying to decide whether to accept or reject incoming shipments of raw material from one of its suppliers. This time we shall begin the analysis by constructing what is termed a "payoff table." This is illustrated in Table 13-1. This type of table attempts to evaluate the gains or losses (payoffs) associated with various decisions (acts) and various states of the world. We have limited ourselves to either accepting or rejecting an incoming shipment. The shipments may be classified as either good or bad, taken for convenience as 5 percent defective and 15 percent defective. The table shows that a $5,000 gain will be made in accepting and using a good shipment, while rejecting a good shipment will result in a $500 loss (lost production, perhaps). Accepting a bad shipment carries a loss of $2,000, resulting from increased production costs in using poor raw materials. Rejecting a bad shipment is assumed to have no monetary gain or loss. Note that in this type of analysis we have begun by explicitly introducing monetary values into the problem.

How should management use these data to make their decision? One generally accepted method that can be used if probabilities may be assigned to the states of the world is to choose the action having the greater expected monetary value (EMV). Let us assume that a review of the suppliers' past performance shows that he sends good shipments 80 percent of the time. Therefore, $P(S_1) = 0.8$ and $P(S_2) = 0.2$. Calculation of the EMVs is as follows[1]:

$$\text{EMV } (A_1) = 0.8(\$5,000) + 0.2(-\$2,000)$$
$$= \$4,000 - 400 = \$3,600$$

$$\text{EMV } (A_2) = 0.8(-\$500) + 0.2(0)$$
$$= -\$400 + 0 = -\$400$$

---

[1] The EMVs are the weighted averages of the payoffs for each action using the probabilities as weights.

If management always accepted incoming shipments from this supplier, it would have a long-term average gain of $3,600, which is much greater than the expected long-term average loss of $400 in rejecting shipments. Therefore, if action is to be taken without sampling, the shipments should always be accepted.

Decision criteria other than expected monetary values can be used. However, EMVs are particularly appropriate to repeated business problems. We have also assumed that a dollar gained is equal to a dollar lost (technically that management has a linear utility function for money). Advanced techniques are available to handle other utility functions if necessary.

Opportunity Losses: An Alternative

Once a payoff table has been constructed, an alternative form of analyzing the problem may be used. This form is in terms of what are called "opportunity losses" and is helpful in more general problems in studying the value of sampling.

An opportunity loss is defined as the difference between the payoff of the best (optimal) act that could have been selected given a state of the world and the payoff of any other act for the same state of the world. It is the profit foregone (opportunity lost) due to the failure to take the best action. Table 13-2 is the opportunity loss table derived from our payoff table, Table 13-1. There is no opportunity loss for accepting a good shipment or rejecting a bad shipment, as these are optimal acts for their respective states of the world. The opportunity loss for rejecting a good shipment is

$$\$5,000 - (-\$500) = \$5,500$$

The loss for accepting a bad shipment is

$$0 - (-\$2,000) = \$2,000$$

The decision to accept or reject the shipment without sampling can be made using the opportunity loss table, although this time we will choose the act which minimizes the expected opportunity loss (EOL). Using our earlier probabilities of $P(S_1) = 0.8$ and $P(S_2) = 0.2$, we get

$$\text{EOL } (A_1) = 0.8\,(0) + 0.2\,(\$2,000) = \$400$$

$$\text{EOL } (A_2) = 0.8\,(\$5,500) + 0.2\,(0) = \$4,400$$

Table 13-2 Opportunity loss table for simple acceptance problem

Alternative course of action	Possible state of the world	
	S_1: good shipment	S_2: bad shipment
A_1: accept shipment	0	$2,000
A_2: reject shipment	$5,500	0

In the absence of sampling, the best action is still to accept the shipment (A_1), as the expected loss of $400 is less than the expected loss of $4,400 for A_2. The $400 is referred to as the "cost of uncertainty," as it represents the expected long-run loss of even the best act.

Expected Value of Perfect Information

If somehow management could correctly determine the 80 percent of the shipments that were good and accept them and also determine the 20 percent that were bad and reject them, we would have no uncertainty. The expected value of certainty (EVC) thus obtained would be

$$EVC = 0.8\,(\$5{,}500) + 0.2\,(0) = \$4{,}000$$

However, we calculated earlier the expected monetary value of optimal act $[EMV\,(A_1)]$ here to be $3,600. The difference between these two values is defined as the expected value of perfect information (EVPI). Here we have

$$EVPI = \$4{,}000 - \$3{,}600 = \$400$$

This turns out to be equal to the cost of uncertainty (the expected opportunity loss of the best act). The latter method, using the expected opportunity loss, represents the easier way of obtaining this value. More important, this amount ($400) represents the most management should be willing to pay for additional information to aid in its decision making.

Under Uncertainty with Sampling

In the previous section we found the expected value of perfect information (EVPI) to be $400. Let us assume that this is sufficient to pay for sampling incoming shipments and that management decides to make its decision of acceptance or rejection after the sample is taken. Specifically we shall illustrate how the sample information may be used to modify our probabilities as to the states of the world and how these revised probabilities are used in the decision process. The revision process involves using Bayes' theorem (see Chap. 7), hence the term "bayesian decision theory." Our original probabilities of the states of the world will serve as the "prior probabilities" in Bayes' theorem and the revised ones after sampling will be the "posterior probabilities" derived by using the theorem. Our earlier analysis, therefore, is sometimes referred to as "prior analysis," while what follows may be termed "posterior analysis."

Revising Probabilities with Bayes' Theorem

To illustrate, let's assume that our sampling consisted of a random sample of 50 items $(n = 50)$ drawn from a large incoming shipment and that these items may be classified as either good or bad. These assumptions will allow us to use the binomial distribution to determine the probability of observing various sample outcomes, specifically the number classified as bad (x). Let us further assume that when an incoming shipment was sampled that eight bad items $(x = 8)$ were actually discovered.

Table 13-3 Computation of revised probabilities for simple acceptance problem

Possible state of the world	Prior probability $[P(S_i)]$	Likelihood $[P(x \mid S_i)]$	Joint probability $[P(S_i x)]$	Posterior probability $[P(S_i \mid x)]$
S_1: good shipment	0.8	0.0024	0.002	0.06
S_2: bad shipment	0.2	0.1493	0.030	0.94
Sum	1.0	–	0.032	1.00

From App. G for the binomial, we can determine for state of the world S_1 (good shipments: $\pi_1 = 5$ percent) the probability of drawing a sample having eight bad items. It is

$$P(x = 8 \mid n = 50 \text{ and } \pi_1 = 5\%) = 0.0024$$

For the state of the world S_2 (bad shipment: $\pi_2 = 15\%$) it is

$$P(x = 8 \mid n = 50 \text{ and } \pi_2 = 15\%) = 0.1493$$

The use of these probabilities derived from our sample result as the likelihoods in a bayesian revision of our prior probabilities is illustrated in Table 13-3 (see also Table 7-1). For this sample at least we see that its evidence has caused a major shift in the probabilities of the states of the world.

To complete our posterior analysis we need only recompute our expected opportunity losses to discover which action now has the minimum expected loss. Our opportunity losses are still those shown in Table 13-2, but these will now be weighted by our revised probabilities to get the new EOLs. The results are:

$$\text{EOL}(A_1) = 0.06(0) + 0.94(\$2,000) = \$1,880$$

$$\text{EOL}(A_2) = 0.06(\$5,500) + 0.94(0) = \$330$$

Not too surprisingly, we now find that the best action is to reject the shipment [EOL $(A_2) = \$330$ is less than EOL $(A_1) = \$1,880$].

Our illustration here used a sample of 50 items ($n = 50$). This may not be the best (optimum) size of sample to use. Unfortunately, determination of the best sample size to use in a discrete situation of this type is a somewhat tedious trial-and-error process. We shall not illustrate it here, but will consider the problem again in connection with the next illustration, which will use continuous data (specifically, the normal curve).

DECISION MAKING USING CONTINUOUS DATA

We shall now discuss and illustrate how bayesian decision methods may be applied using continuous data, particularly the normal curve. Our decision parameter will be an unknown value of the population mean (μ) which if known would allow us to make the correct decision. As we did earlier, we shall first illustrate how the decision may be made without sampling (prior analysis) and then illustrate the combined use of a sample and our prior information in a revised decision procedure (posterior analysis). This time, however, we shall extend our analysis to consider sample-size questions.

Continuous Prior Distributions

The correct decision in our problem depends on the unknown value of μ (the population mean). Although this value is actually unique, we shall assume for lack of knowledge a distribution of possible outcomes (values) for it. Classical theory assumed that when μ was unknown, all possible values of it were equally likely. We shall find it advantageous and more realistic to assume that our unknown values of μ are normally distributed with a mean μ_0 (our best prior estimate of the unknown population mean) and a standard deviation σ_0 (a measure of the degree of faith we have in our estimate).[1] Normality is not an unrealistic assumption in many business problems, as it basically implies that we feel that the possible errors in our estimate are symmetrical and that large errors are much less common than small errors.

Prior Analysis: An Illustration

To illustrate a normal prior, its use, and its later revision, let us assume that we have the problem of deciding whether or not to completely replace a set of existing air-conditioning units by new energy-saving ones.

The Better Burger and Fryes Company has been approached by a salesperson for the Super-kool Air Conditioning Company with a special deal to replace the combination heating/air conditioning units in its 1,000 stores with a new low-energy unit. The new units are priced at $1,440 each, and the salesperson predicts that they will save Better Burger an average of $50 per month per store over the next 3 years.

Simple straightforward analysis suggests that the units should be bought:

$$\text{Total cost} = \text{no. of units} \times \text{price}$$
$$= 1{,}000 \times \$1{,}440 = \$1{,}440{,}000$$

while

$$\text{Total savings} = \text{no. of units} \times \text{average savings per months} \times \text{no. of months}$$
$$= 1{,}000 \times \$50 \times 36 = \$1{,}800{,}000$$

giving a net saving over 3 years of

$$\$1{,}800{,}000 - \$1{,}440{,}000 = \$360{,}000$$

The Better Burger statistician concludes that the $50 estimate of average savings is about as good as any but that it is subject to quite a bit of variability as a result of varying store locations and the like. It is therefore necessary to get management's okay to set the problem up as a bayesian decision problem for further analysis.

---

[1] σ_0, the standard deviation of our prior distribution of μ, is not to be confused with σ, the standard deviation of our parent population. The former measures variability among our estimates of μ, while the latter measures variability among the actual items of the parent population.

The decision parameter will be the true but unknown average savings per month per store (μ). The statistician is willing to assume a normal prior distribution for this value with $\mu_0 = \$50$ (the salesperson's estimate). Further study convinces the statistician that a value of $10 is about right as a measure of the uncertainty in estimates of μ (i.e., $\sigma_0 = \$10$). This is based on the feeling that there is about a 1-in-3 chance that μ differs from $50 by more than $10 ($\mu_0 \pm \sigma_0 = \$50 \pm \$10$).

The next step is to determine a breakeven value for the mean (μ_b). For total savings to just equal total cost we have

$$\text{Total savings} = \text{no. of units} \times \text{average savings per month}$$
$$\times \text{no. of months} = \text{total cost}$$

$$1,000 \times \mu_b \times 36 = \$1,440,000$$

Therefore,

$$\mu_b = \frac{\$1,440,000}{1,000 \times 36} = \$40/\text{month}$$

We next consider possible opportunity losses. For the continuous case here, these may be presented as functions and are summarized in Table 13-4. Purchasing the new units when savings exceed costs or not purchasing them when costs exceed savings are correct decisions and hence result in zero opportunity losses. Failure to purchase the units when savings exceed costs will result in an opportunity loss (foregone savings) equal to the loss per store per month ($\mu - \mu_b$) times the number of stores (1,000) times the number of months (36). Purchase of the units when costs exceed savings will result in an opportunity loss (here an actual loss) of the loss per unit, again times the number of stores and the number of months. These opportunity loss functions are linear and symmetrical, a very common form in this type of problem.

It can be shown that for linear and symmetrical opportunity loss functions and a normal prior, the decision which minimizes the EOL (or maximizes the EMV) is that obtained by comparing μ_0 and μ_b. As this is essentially what we did earlier in our simple analysis, the decision at this stage is to purchase the units. However, the statistician is still worried about the variability of $\mu(\sigma_0)$ and decides to investigate if a sample would be helpful in making the final decision.

Table 13-4 Opportunity loss table for purchase problem

	Possible state of the world	
Alternative course of action	S_1: savings exceed costs $\mu > \mu_b$ ($40)	S_2: costs exceed savings $\mu < \mu_b$ ($40)
A_1: purchase new units	0	$(\mu_b - \mu) \times 1,000 \times 36$ $= 36,000 (\mu_b - \mu)$
A_2: do not purchase new units	$(\mu - \mu_b) \times 1,000 \times 36$ $= 36,000 (\mu - \mu_b)$	0

Expected Value of Perfect Information: The Continuous Case

When the prior distribution is normal and the opportunity loss functions are linear as in our case, the EOL of the best act, which is also the EVPI, may be obtained from the following expression:

$$EVPI = L\sigma_0 N(D_0)$$

with the help of the table of unit normal loss integrals $[N(D)]$ found in App. I. σ_0 is, of course, the standard deviation of our prior distribution. L is the absolute slope of our opportunity loss functions:

$$D_0 = \frac{|\mu_0 - \mu_b|}{\sigma_0}$$

It is a standardized version of the difference between our best estimate of the mean (μ_0) and the breakeven mean (μ_b).

To calculate the EVPI for our illustration, we begin by calculating D_0. Substituting our problem values, we get

$$D_0 = \frac{|\mu_0 - \mu_b|}{\sigma_0} = \frac{|\$50 - \$40|}{\$10} = \frac{\$10}{\$10} = 1$$

Referring to App. I for $D_0 = 1$, we find that $N(D_0) = 0.08332$. Substituting this value, $\sigma_0 = \$10$, and 36,000 (our slope value—see Table 13-4), we find that

$$EVPI = 36,000(10)(0.08332) = \$29,995.20$$

As this is a substantial amount, the statistician decides to proceed with a sample.

Posterior Analysis: An Introduction

To illustrate how sample information may be combined with prior data in our decision procedures for the continuous case, let us assume that our statistician was able to sample at random the performance of 50 units over a 3-month period. Upon completion of the trial period, he calculated the following results:

$$n = 50 \text{ units}$$
$$\overline{X} = \$36/\text{month/unit}$$
$$s = \$14/\text{month/unit}$$

While these data appear unfavorable for purchase of the new units, the analysis requires a combining of the sample information and the prior information for proper decision making. This combination is quite simple to do when both the prior data estimates and the distribution of sample results ($\overline{X}$'s) are normally distributed. We have assumed (realistically, we hope) a normal prior, and we know from the central limit theorem that our $\overline{X}$'s will tend to be normally distributed for our sample size (50) regardless of the distribution of our parent population. If we symbolize our revised estimate of the mean by μ_r, our formula for combining μ_0 and $\overline{X}$ is

$$\mu_r = \frac{I_0\mu_0 + I_{\overline{X}}\overline{X}}{I_0 + I_{\overline{X}}}$$

which is a weighted mean of our two values using the quantities represented by I as weights. The I's are termed "quantity of information" and are in general the reciprocal of the appropriate variance; i.e., the more variable our particular estimate, the less information it contains and the less weight we will give it in the final estimate. Here we have

$$I_0 = \frac{1}{\sigma_0^2} \quad \text{and} \quad I_{\overline{X}} = \frac{1}{\sigma_{\overline{X}}^2}$$

Also, $\sigma_{\overline{X}} = \sigma/\sqrt{n}$, but where (as here) we do not know the σ of the parent population, we may estimate it using the sample standard deviation (s), i.e.,

$$\hat{\sigma}_{\overline{X}} = \frac{s}{\sqrt{n-1}}$$

The value of the variance of our revised distribution may be obtained from the following relationship:

$$I_r = I_0 + I_{\overline{X}}$$

$$\frac{1}{\sigma_r^2} = \frac{1}{\sigma_0^2} + \frac{1}{\sigma_{\overline{X}}^2}$$

$$\sigma_r^2 = \frac{\sigma_0^2 \, \sigma_{\overline{X}}^2}{\sigma_0^2 + \sigma_{\overline{X}}^2}$$

If both the prior distribution and the sampling distribution are normal, the revised distribution will also be normal.

Posterior Analysis: Illustration Continued

For our illustration, we first estimate the standard error of the mean.

$$\hat{\sigma}_{\overline{X}} = \frac{s}{\sqrt{n-1}} = \frac{\$14}{\sqrt{50-1}} = \$2$$

Therefore,

$$I_{\overline{X}} = \frac{1}{2^2} = \frac{1}{4} = 0.25$$

The standard deviation of our prior distribution (σ_0) was \$10. Therefore,

$$I_0 = \frac{1}{10^2} = \frac{1}{100} = 0.01$$

We now find our revised mean (μ_r).

$$\mu_r = \frac{I_0 \mu_0 + I_{\overline{X}} \overline{X}}{I_0 + I_{\overline{X}}} = \frac{0.01(50) + (0.25)36}{0.01 + 0.25}$$

$$= \frac{0.5 + 9}{0.26} = \frac{9.5}{0.26} = \$36.54$$

Our revised variance is

$$\sigma_r^2 = \frac{\sigma_0^2 \, \sigma_{\bar{X}}^2}{\sigma_0^2 + \sigma_{\bar{X}}^2} = \frac{100(4)}{100 + 4} = \frac{400}{104} = 3.85$$

and
$$\sigma_r = \sqrt{3.85} = \$1.96$$

Our decision procedure still consists of comparing our best estimate of μ (now $\mu_r = \$36.54$) with the breakeven value of $\mu(\mu_b = \$40)$. This time, however, our decision would be to not purchase the new units if they are to have a 3-year payoff. This reversal of our earlier decision results of course from the particular illustrative mean used as our sample outcome combined with the high uncertainty of our prior estimate of μ (low I_0) and would not necessarily take place.

The methods above are based on a normal prior estimate and a normal sampling distribution. The latter can safely be assumed, based on the central-limit theorem, if the samples are kept large (generally over 30). The former assumption, while often realistic, many times is not critical, as σ_0^2 is typically large, leading to a small I_0 in the weighting procedure.

Determination of Optimum Sample Size

In our earlier discrete illustration, we begged off considering the determination of what size sample it would be best to use. We will now illustrate, though, for the continuous case, where the solution is considerably easier.

We begin by defining a new quantity, EVSI, the expected value of sample information. The EVSI measures the expected reduction in the cost of uncertainty that a particular sample will produce. This value, when computed for a range of sample sizes and compared with their costs of collection, will allow one to determine the optimum (in a return for cost sense) sample size.

The EVSI is obtained from an expression similar to that used earlier in calculating the EVPI. Here we have

$$\text{EVSI} = L\sigma_d N(D_d) \quad \text{where } D_d = \frac{|\mu_0 - \mu_b|}{\sigma_d}$$

The difference is the substitution for σ_0 of σ_d, which represents the decrease (improvement) in the prior variability anticipated from the use of the sample. Specifically, $\sigma_d^2 = \sigma_0^2 - \sigma_r^2$. As σ_d is less than σ_0, the EVSI is always less than EVPI.

Earlier we derived the following expression for the variance of the revised distribution (σ_r^2):

$$\sigma_r^2 = \frac{\sigma_0^2 \, \sigma_{\bar{X}}^2}{\sigma_0^2 + \sigma_{\bar{X}}^2}$$

This time, however, we would like to estimate the value of σ_r^2 before the sample is drawn rather than computing it afterward, as illustrated above. The problem here is one that we have encountered several times before. $\sigma_{\bar{X}}^2 = \sigma^2/n$. The key missing ingredient is a value for σ^2, the variance of the parent population of stores. This may be estimated from past data, a pilot study, or the best judgment of the statistician.

Substituting our expression for σ_r^2 in the one for σ_d^2, we get

$$\sigma_d^2 = \sigma_0^2 - \frac{\sigma_0^2\,\sigma_{\bar{X}}^2}{\sigma_0^2 + \sigma_{\bar{X}}^2} = \frac{\sigma_0^2\,\sigma_0^2}{\sigma_0^2 + \sigma_{\bar{X}}^2}$$

Taking the square root, we get the needed expression for σ_d:

$$\sigma_d = \sqrt{\frac{\sigma_0^2\,\sigma_0^2}{\sigma_0^2 + \sigma_{\bar{X}}^2}}$$

To illustrate numerically for a sample of 50, let us assume that our statistician estimated before sampling that $\sigma = \$15$. Substituting, we get

$$\sigma_{\bar{X}}^2 = \frac{\sigma^2}{n} = \frac{15^2}{50} = \frac{225}{50} = 4.5$$

Therefore,

$$\sigma_d = \sqrt{\frac{\sigma_0^2\,\sigma_0^2}{\sigma_0^2 + \sigma_{\bar{X}}^2}} = \sqrt{\frac{10^2(10^2)}{10^2 + 4.5}} = \sqrt{\frac{100(100)}{100 + 4.5}}$$

$$= \sqrt{\frac{10{,}000}{104.5}} = \sqrt{95.7} = 9.78$$

Then

$$D_d = \frac{|\mu_0 - \mu_b|}{\sigma_d} = \frac{10}{9.78} = 1.02$$

From App. I,

$$N(D_d) = 0.08019$$

so

$$\begin{aligned}
\text{EVSI}_{50} &= L\sigma_d N(D_d) \\
&= 36{,}000(9.78)(0.08019) \\
&= \$28{,}233.30
\end{aligned}$$

Suppose that our sampling costs consist of $10,000 in fixed setup costs and $75 per unit in variable costs. An expression for our cost of sampling would be

$$\text{Sample cost} = \$10{,}000 + \$75n$$

For our sample of 50 we get

$$\text{Sample cost} = 10{,}000 + 75(50) = 10{,}000 + 3{,}750 = \$13{,}750$$

The expected net gain from sampling (ENGS) for our sample of 50 is

$$\text{ENGS} = \text{EVSI} - \text{sample cost} = \$28{,}233 - 13{,}750 = \$14{,}483$$

Table 13-5 Calculation of expected net gains for selected sample sizes

Sample size	$\sigma_{\bar{X}}^2 = \dfrac{15^2}{n}$	$\sigma_d = \sqrt{\dfrac{10^2 \cdot 10^2}{10^2 + \sigma_{\bar{X}}^2}}$	$D_d = \dfrac{\lvert 50 - 40 \rvert}{\sigma_d}$	$N(D_d)$	EVSI $= 36,000\,\sigma_d N(D_d)$	Sampling cost $= 10,000 + 75n$	ENGS
20	11.250	9.43	1.06	0.07422	$25,196	$11,500	$13,696
30	7.500	9.64	1.04	0.07716	26,778	12,250	14,528
40	5.625	9.73	1.03	0.07866	27,553	13,000	14,553
50	4.500	9.78	1.02	0.08019	28,233	13,750	14,483
60	3.750	9.82	1.02	0.08019	28,349	14,500	13,849
70	3.214	9.84	1.02	0.08019	28,407	15,250	13,157

While our sample appears to be a good investment, EVSIs and sampling costs for other sample sizes must be determined to discover the optimum size (greatest ENGS). Table 13-5 presents an organized format for making the necessary comparisons. We find that the optimum sample size is about forty ($n = 40$). However, a curve of the expected net gains from sampling (ENGS) would be quite flat on top, as is often the case. Sampling is quite valuable here, but the exact size is not critical.

The methods for continuous data presented in the last several sections often make satisfactory approximations for the more complex discrete case.

Bayesian Decision Procedure: A Review

We have explained and illustrated the flavor of bayesian decision procedures with simple two-action problems both discrete and continuous. The procedures can be expanded, of course, to cover more complex situations (e.g., more than two possible acts). What we have attempted to show is how these newer techniques combine probabilities, monetary values, statistical inference, and Bayes' theorem into an integrated whole to aid management in decision making. Controversy does exist over the extensive use of subjective probabilities in the techniques, but not in how they are used if accepted. The use of management's judgment in the specific form of subjective probabilities would seem better than ignoring it. If management is quite uncertain of its prior estimates, these estimates will carry appropriately little weight in the final outcome after sampling. The determination of the appropriate cost data may often be more difficult than our examples imply. This is a comparatively new field, and more research into its possibilities is being (and needs to be) done.

STUDY GUIDE

Concepts Worth Remembering

Define:

1. Bayesian Decision Theory
2. Decision making under certainty
3. Decision making under uncertainty
4. Payoff
5. Expected monetary value (EMV)
6. Opportunity loss
7. Expected opportunity loss (EOL)
8. Cost of uncertainty
9. Expected value of certainty (EVC)
10. Expected value of perfect information (EVPI)
11. Prior analysis
12. Posterior analysis
13. Quantity of information
14. Expected value of sample information (EVSI)
15. Expected net gain from sampling (ENGS)

Self-Test

Circle the proper letter to indicate whether the following statements are true or false.

T F **1** "Bayesian decision theory" is so called because it makes use of Bayes' theorem to revise prior probabilities on the basis of sample evidence as part of the decision-making process.

T F **2** "Decision making under certainty" is a term used to describe a decision problem wherein knowledge of the states of the world exists.

T F **3** The values in a payoff table are the gains associated with the correct decision.

T F **4** The expected monetary value (EMV) of an action is the weighted average of the payoffs for that action using probabilities as weights.

T F **5** The value of an opportunity loss is determined from a company's accounting records.

T F **6** The expected value of perfect information (EVPI) turns out to be equal to the "cost of uncertainty."

T F **7** The correct decision in a problem is the one that maximizes the expected opportunity loss (EOL).

T F **8** The expected value of perfect information (EVPI) sets a ceiling on the amount management should be willing to pay for additional information to aid in its decision making.

T F **9** The expected value of sample information (EVSI) is the reduction in the cost of uncertainty shown by a sample after it is drawn.

T F **10** In the continuous case, bayesian decision theory uses only subjective probabilities as prior probabilities in the decision procedures.

T F **11** The weights, "quantity of information" (I), are reciprocals of appropriate variances.

T F **12** "Posterior analysis" is the term used to describe that portion of bayesian decision theory involving the revision of decision choices on the basis of sample evidence.

T F **13** Part of posterior analysis in the continuous case involves the recalculation of the break-even value of the mean (μ_b).

T F **14** The determination of the optimum sample size is a trial-and-error procedure for the continuous case, although it may be done easily for the discrete case.

T F **15** The expected net gain from sampling (ENGS) is equal to the expected value of sample information (EVSI) minus the cost of sampling.

Questions to Think About

1. Distinguish between decision making under certainty and decision making under uncertainty.
2. Compare and contrast payoff analysis with opportunity loss analysis.
3. Explain the relationship of the cost of uncertainty to the expected value of perfect information. What is the importance of the latter concept?

4. Distinguish between prior analysis and posterior analysis.
5. Explain the nature and importance of (1) a normal prior and (2) linear and symmetrical loss functions to continuous decision analysis.
6. Describe the procedure for determining the optimum sample size.

Problems

1 The Mini-Max Dress Company is faced with the problem of accepting or rejecting shipments of cloth. The quality criterion to be used for this particular cloth is the mean number of flaws per square yard of cloth. Shown here is the payoff table for two possible states of the world (good and bad cloth).

Payoff table for Mini-Max Dress Company problem

Alternative course of action	Possible state of the world	
	S_1: good cloth $\mu_1 = 1$ flaw	S_2: bad cloth $\mu_2 = 5$ flaws
A_1: accept shipment	$2,000	-$1,000
A_2: reject shipment	-$200	0

Historical records suggest that good cloth will be received 70 percent of the time and bad cloth received 30 percent of the time.

(a) Assuming that a decision is to be made at this stage, determine by two different methods the optimum decision.

(b) Calculate the expected value of certainty (EVC) and the expected value of perfect information (EVPI) for the data above.

(c) A sample of incoming cloth had four flaws in a square yard. Use this sample evidence to determine what is the optimum decision for this shipment. (*Hint:* Use the Poisson distribution to determine the likelihoods for Bayes' theorem.)

2 A company must decide whether to perform 100 percent inspection on incoming shipments of a particular part with removal of bad parts or to place the shipment into production without inspection and repair those assemblies containing defective parts later. Shipments are in lots of 1,000 parts and inspection costs are 20 cents per part. Repair at a later date costs $1.50 per unit. There is thought to be a 50–50 chance that incoming shipments are either 5 percent or 10 percent defective.

(a) Determine by two different methods the best decision under present conditions.

(b) Show two different ways of determining the expected value of perfect information (EVPI).

(c) Assume that the company decides to sample incoming shipments before making a decision. If a sample of 25 parts showed 1 defective part, what would be the company's best course of action?

3 A salesman from MPG, Inc., is trying to sell the Hither & Yon Taxi Company an attachment for the carburetors of their cabs which will save them money on fuel costs for their fleet of 500 cabs. The salesman predicts a mean savings of $4 per cab per month over the next 6 months. The attachments will cost $20 per cab installed.

(*a*) By conventional analysis, should Hither & Yon purchase the attachments?

(*b*) By bayesian (breakeven) analysis, should the attachments be purchased?

(*c*) Hither & Yon's statistician believes that the mean savings of $4 is probably a fair estimate, but it is close to the break-even mean and subject to variability. The variability in the estimate of the mean is judged to be about $1. Calculate the expected value of perfect information (EVPI) for this problem.

(*d*) The statistician asks for and receives permission to conduct a sample study before a final decision is made. The random sample of 37 cabs making up the study had a mean savings of $3 with a standard deviation of $3. Compute a revised value for the mean savings. What is now the optimum decision on purchasing the attachments?

(*e*) Calculate the expected net gains from sampling (ENGS) and the optimum sample size for this problem. The statistician's best estimate of the variability among cabs in savings is $3.50. Sampling costs are $4.00 per cab plus a fixed fee of $75.00.

4 Ventures, Inc., must decide whether or not to add a new product to its current line. The new product will require a fixed investment of $50,000 plus a manufacturing cost of $5 per unit to produce. It will be marketed through 200 dealers at a price of $10 per unit. Venture's president estimates mean sales of 54 units per dealer for the new product. Together he and the company statistician determine that the standard deviation for the estimate is 8 units per dealer.

(*a*) Show by two types of calculations whether the product should be produced if a decision is to be made at this stage.

(*b*) Compute the expected value of perfect information (EVPI) for the data above.

(*c*) A sample of 37 outlets had mean sales of 48 units with a standard deviation of 15 units. Calculate the revised estimate of mean sales. Did the decision of (*a*) change?

(*d*) Sampling costs are $4 per dealer plus a fixed cost of $500. The best estimate of the variability among dealer sales is that the standard deviation equals 15 units. What is the optimum sample size to use in this problem?

Answers to Self-Test

1 T; 2 T; 3 F; 4 T; 5 F; 6 T; 7 F; 8 T; 9 F; 10 F; 11 T; 12 T; 13 F; 14 F; 15 T.

FOURTEEN
SELECTED ADDITIONAL TOPICS
IN SAMPLING

LEARNING OBJECTIVES

The basic learning objective is to extend our knowledge of sampling by introducing continuous sampling distributions other than the normal curve and by introducing additional applications of sampling techniques. Specifically, you will learn about:

1. The t distribution and its uses.
2. Two sample tests for dependent and independent samples.
3. The chi-square distribution and its uses.
4. The F distribution and its uses.
5. The analysis of variance.
6. Statistical quality control.

INTRODUCTION

This chapter will survey a number of the more important sampling distributions and techniques which were not covered in previous chapters. It should serve both to introduce those distributions and techniques and to broaden the reader's appreciation of the nature of sampling and its applications. We shall begin with the Student t distribution, discussed briefly in Chap. 11.

THE NATURE OF THE t DISTRIBUTION

When pictured, the t distribution appears as a bell-shaped symmetrical curve looking very much like the normal. It differs from the normal in two basic respects: (1) it has greater dispersion than the normal, and (2) the amount of the dispersion varies inversely with a value termed "degrees of freedom" (df), which, for simple problems, is the sample size minus one ($n - 1$). Figure 14-1 illustrates these relationships by showing the normal curve and the t distribution for 2 and 20 df.

Since the t curve varies with the number of degrees of freedom, it is not possible to give a complete set of t values in the way that a complete set of normal curve values is given in App. B. Selected values of t for different degrees of freedom and for varying probability levels are given in App. D. For 10 df and a probability level of 0.05, $t = 2.228$. This indicates that, for 10 df, the probability is 0.05 (5 percent) of getting, through chance alone, a t value as large as or larger than 2.228.

Note that, as the number of degrees of freedom increases, the t values for all levels of probability approach the normal deviates for the corresponding levels. It is customary to use the normal curve as an approximation to the t curve for samples over 30, that is, at least 30 df.

Use of the t Distribution

In theory, the t distribution should be used to replace the normal curve as the pattern of the sampling distribution whenever the standard error is estimated from sample data. The extra dispersion of the t curve will protect against the added risks of error introduced in estimating the standard error. Also, proper use of the t distribution rests

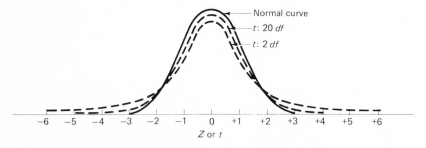

Figure 14-1 Comparison of the t distribution with the normal curve.

on the assumption that the sample was drawn from a normally distributed universe. In practice, the t distribution is used for those problems involving estimated standard errors when the samples are too small to permit approximating the t distribution by the normal curve and provided the universes from which the samples were drawn do not represent substantial departures from normality. The study of the t distribution is sometimes referred to as "the study of small samples," because its use is primarily with this size of sample.

In actual statistical problems using small samples, the values of t replace those of the normal deviates (Z) in establishing confidence limits or in testing hypotheses. Otherwise, the problems are handled as previously illustrated in Chaps. 11 and 12.

Using the t Distribution: Confidence Limits

The Pink Pill Drug Company, to determine the effectiveness of a new anesthetic, administered a measured dose to each of 10 monkeys and then timed the period during which they were unconscious. The company would now like to establish a 99 percent confidence interval for the arithmetic mean time for unconsciousness.

Such a confidence interval would be established exactly as in Chap. 11, except that the multiplier for the estimated standard error would be a t value rather than the Z value; i.e., the expression for our estimate is $\hat{\mu} = \overline{X} \pm t\hat{\sigma}_{\overline{X}}$ rather than, as formerly, $\hat{\mu} = \overline{X} \pm Z\hat{\sigma}_{\overline{X}}$. The appropriate t multiplier would be obtained from the t table in App. D. For 9 df $(n - 1 = 10 - 1 = 9)$ and $p = 0.01$ $(1.00 - 0.99)$, the t value for this problem is found to be 3.25.

The sample mean and standard deviation are computed from the data to be 57 and 6 min, respectively; that is, $\overline{X} = 57$ min and $s = 6$ min. The estimated standard error is next calculated:

$$\hat{\sigma}_{\overline{X}} = \frac{s}{\sqrt{n-1}} = \frac{6}{\sqrt{10-1}} = 2 \text{ min}$$

Therefore, our 99 percent confidence interval becomes

$$\hat{\mu} = \overline{X} \pm t\hat{\sigma}_{\overline{X}}$$
$$= 57 \pm 3.25(2)$$
$$= 57 \pm 6.5 \quad \text{or} \quad 50.5 \text{ to } 63.5 \text{ min}$$

As before, the degree of confidence refers to the procedure rather than to this specific interval.

Using the t Distribution: Testing Hypotheses

The Pink Pill Drug Company would like to test a batch of completed drug compound to see whether it has an average of at least 100 cm^3 of miracle drug Y per unit. Because drug Y is expensive, a sample of only 20 units can be analyzed. We shall follow the six steps in testing hypotheses listed in Chap. 12 to solve this problem.

Management's question The drug-company management would like to determine whether or not there is at least an average of 100 cm³ of drug Y per unit of the compound.

Null and alternative hypotheses The null hypothesis is that there is an arithmetic mean amount of 100 cm³ of drug Y per unit of the compound (i.e., $H_0: \mu \geq 100$ cm³) and that any difference observed in sampling is the result of chance sampling errors. The alternative hypothesis (H_1) is that $\mu < 100$ cm³. The test is a one-tailed one.

Level of significance Management decides, after discussing the problem with the statistician, that the hypothesis should be tested at the 1 percent significance level.

Statistical test Since it was decided that a sample of 20 was to be used and an estimated standard error must be computed, the appropriate testing procedure involves the use of the t distribution. The distribution based on 19 df appropriate to this problem is shown in Fig. 14-2. As before, the curve is symmetrical around $\mu = 100$ cm³. The acceptance region, rejection region, and critical ratio (in terms of t) are shown on the graph. As our test in this problem is a one-tailed one and as the table of t values is for two tails, the t value given was found from the table by looking under $p = 0.02$ (twice 1 percent) and 19 df. When the random sample of 20 was drawn, it was found to have a mean of 94.6 cm³ ($\overline{X} = 94.6$ cm³) and a standard deviation of 3.5 cm³ ($s = 3.5$ cm³). The estimated standard error becomes

$$\hat{\sigma}_{\overline{X}} = \frac{s}{\sqrt{n-1}} = \frac{3.5}{\sqrt{20-1}} = 0.80 \text{ cm}^3$$

The test ratio is

$$t = \frac{\overline{X} - \mu}{\hat{\sigma}_{\overline{X}}} = \frac{94.6 - 100}{0.80} = \frac{-5.4}{0.80} = -6.75$$

Statistical conclusion Since our computed t value of -6.75 falls in the rejection region, our statistical conclusion is to reject the null hypothesis and accept the alternative hypothesis that $\mu < 100$ cm³.

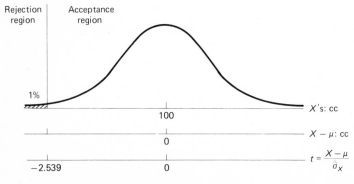

Figure 14-2 Random sampling distribution of means.

Answer to management's question Acceptance of the alternative hypothesis should lead the management of the drug company to conclude that, for some reason, the compound fails to contain the anticipated average of at least 100 cm^3 of miracle drug Y.

This illustration, using the t distribution in hypothesis testing, and the one preceding it, illustrating the use of the t distribution in establishing confidence intervals, both show that resulting changes in the problem are chiefly mechanical in the substitution of the t values for the normal deviates (Z's) and that the logic of the problem in combining knowledge of sample behavior with the results of a single sample remains the same.

TESTS COMPARING TWO SAMPLE MEANS

In this and the following sections we shall broaden our knowledge of sampling by considering problems involving the use of information obtained, not just from a single sample, but from two samples. Such problems will be illustrated by considering the statistical testing procedures for comparing two sample means. These procedures divide into two types, depending on whether the two samples are independent (nonpaired) or dependent (paired). Both will be discussed below.

DEPENDENT SAMPLES

The procedure for comparing the means of dependent, or paired, samples is quite similar to that used when testing an hypothesis involving a single sample mean. This is because, in comparing paired-sample results, the differences between the various sample pairs are treated as a single series, and tests are made in terms of this new series. Samples are dependent, or paired, when the choice of an item for one sample automatically includes a corresponding or related item for the other sample. This might be the case if one wished to determine the effectiveness of a special training program and chose to do so by administering the same test before and after training to the same sample of trainees. Inclusion in the first (before) sample means automatic inclusion in the second (after) sample; hence, the sample test results are paired, or dependent. Such pairing is likely to be desirable in a problem of this type, since giving the tests to an identical group removes several sources of variability, such as intelligence and background, from the problem.

Dependent Samples: An Illustration

As suggested above, the approach to this type of problem is to make a new series composed of the differences between the paired results and to use this latter series in testing hypotheses about the difference between the two samples. To illustrate, consider the problem of deciding whether a new method developed by the methods engineers for assembling a product is faster than the old method. As some workers are naturally faster than others, data were collected for a random sample of workers each of whom

Table 14-1   Sample test data on production times by a new and by an old method

Worker	New method (X_1), min	Old method (X_2), min	Difference ($D = X_1 - X_2$), min	D^2
A	3	6	−3	9
B	5	6	−1	1
C	4	8	−4	16
D	9	10	−1	1
E	6	4	2	4
F	2	1	1	1
G	1	2	−1	1
H	3	2	1	1
I	1	4	−3	9
J	2	2	0	0
Total	36	45	−9	43
Mean	3.6	4.5	−0.9	

$$s_D = \sqrt{\frac{\Sigma D^2}{n} - \overline{D}^2} = \sqrt{\frac{43}{10} - (-0.9)^2} = 1.87 \text{ min}$$

used both the old and the new method in order that variability attributable to workers might be removed from the problem. The results are shown in Table 14-1. Note that the mean of the differences $(\overline{D})$ between the new and old methods equals the difference between the means of the new and old methods; that is, $\overline{D} = \overline{X}_1 - \overline{X}_2$. The series of differences may be treated as a separate series, and we may test an hypothesis concerning the mean difference $(\overline{D})$ of −0.9 min. We shall do this, again following the six-step procedure of Chap. 12.

Management's question   The question here is whether the new method of assembly is faster than the old.

Null and alternative hypotheses   We shall hypothesize that the true difference $(\Delta = \mu_1 - \mu_2)$ between the mean time for the new and that for the old method is zero and that our observed difference $(\overline{D} = \overline{X}_1 - \overline{X}_2)$ of −0.9 min can be attributed to chance errors of random sampling. Our alternative hypothesis is that the new method is faster than the old method (i.e., $\mu_1 < \mu_2$). Our test, therefore, is a one-sided one.

Level of significance   Management believes that either a Type I or a Type II error would affect it about equally. A Type I error (adopting the new method when it is not faster) would involve unnecessary training costs. A Type II error (failure to adopt the new method when it is actually superior) would increase manufacturing costs because of the failure to use the most efficient production method. It was eventually decided to set $\alpha = 0.05$ and test a sample of 10 workers; the data are given in Table 14-1.

Statistical test The appropriate sampling distribution for this problem is the t distribution, since a sample of size 10 is being used and it will be necessary to estimate the standard error. The standard error to be used will be the same as that used in testing a mean of a single sample, since the distribution of $\overline{D}$'s for paired samples is like that of $\overline{X}$'s for single samples. The formulas for the true and estimated standard errors of the mean were

$$\sigma_{\overline{X}} = \frac{\sigma}{\sqrt{n}} \quad \text{and} \quad \hat{\sigma}_{\overline{X}} = \frac{s}{\sqrt{n-1}}$$

These may be rewritten for this problem as

$$\sigma_{\overline{D}} = \frac{\sigma_D}{\sqrt{n}} \quad \text{and} \quad \hat{\sigma}_{\overline{D}} = \frac{s_D}{\sqrt{n-1}}$$

where σ_D and s_D are the population and sample standard deviations of the differences, respectively. The sampling distribution for this problem, along with the acceptance region, rejection region, and critical value of t, are shown in Fig. 14-3.

Referring to Table 14-1, we find that the sample standard deviation (s_D) is equal to 1.87 min. We may now estimate the standard error to be

$$\hat{\sigma}_{\overline{D}} = \frac{s_D}{\sqrt{n-1}} = \frac{1.87}{\sqrt{10-1}} = 0.62 \text{ min}$$

The t ratio for the problem is

$$t = \frac{\overline{D} - \Delta}{\hat{\sigma}_{\overline{D}}} = \frac{-0.9 - 0}{0.62} = \frac{-0.9}{0.62} = -1.45$$

Statistical conclusion As our computed t value of -1.45 is greater than the critical value of -1.833, our result must lie in the acceptance region, and therefore we shall accept the null hypothesis that there is no difference between the new and old methods.

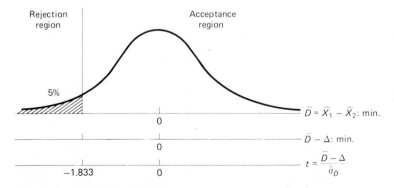

Figure 14-3 Sampling distribution of differences between paired means.

Answer to management's question The test evidence is not sufficient to indicate that the new method is superior in speed to the old method, and on this basis there is no ground for instituting it. If the new method represents a substantial cost saving, management may desire to introduce it anyway, since there is no evidence that the new method is any slower than the old method.

INDEPENDENT SAMPLES

Now we shall consider the second case of comparing two sample means of independent (nonpaired) samples. Sample values are independent when the selection of an item for one sample in no way determines the selection of an item for the second sample.

Problems involving independent samples differ from those discussed above for dependent samples chiefly in the nature of the appropriate sampling distribution and standard error to be used. Where the samples were paired, the problem could be handled as if only a single series were involved and the sampling distribution and standard error formulas for single arithmetic means were used. For independent samples we need a new sampling distribution and its corresponding standard error which will represent a pooling of the information obtained from the two samples. The distribution itself is made up of all possible differences between sets of two sample means and is called the "sampling distribution of the differences between means." If the sample values are sufficiently large, the distribution will tend to be normal in pattern. The distribution's mean will be zero if we are testing the hypothesis that both samples were drawn from the same population. Otherwise, it will be the value of the hypothesized difference between the means of the two populations from which the samples are drawn. The standard deviation of the sampling distribution of differences (the standard error of the difference) is computed by pooling the error of two samples; i.e., $\sigma_{\bar{X}_1 - \bar{X}_2} = \sqrt{\sigma_{\bar{X}_1}^2 + \sigma_{\bar{X}_2}^2}$. As we shall illustrate below, this new distribution and its sampling error are used in practice like the other distributions we have encountered.

Independent Samples: An Illustration

For our illustration we shall take the problem of a market-research firm which is conducting a study for one of its clients to determine whether there is a greater average expenditure for home maintenance in urban or rural areas. Once again we shall follow the six steps of Chap. 12 in presenting our illustration.

Management's question The client wishes to know if there is a greater average expenditure in one type of area or the other and, if so, in which area.

Null and alternative hypotheses For our null hypothesis we shall state that both samples were drawn from the same universe of home-maintenance expenditures (i.e., H_0: $\mu_u = \mu_r = \mu$) and that any observed difference between sample means is the result of chance errors of random sampling. Our alternative hypothesis is that the mean home-maintenance expenditure is greater in one type of area than in the other (i.e., H_1: $\mu_u \neq \mu_r$). The test will be a two-sided one, since the alternative hypothesis does

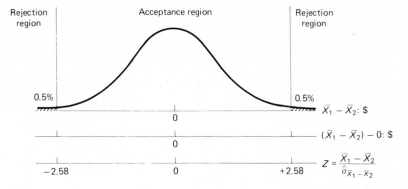

Figure 14-4 Random sampling distribution of differences between means.

not specify which area has the greater expenditures, but merely that one area has greater expenditures than (not the same as) the other.

Level of significance The client is desirous of not assuming that a difference exists when it does not, so the market-research firm chose an $\alpha = 0.01$. In addition, it also decided to sample 100 homes of each type.

Statistical test The test will be based on the use of the random sampling distribution of differences between means and the standard error of the difference discussed above. For samples as large as those taken, the normal curve may be used to set the critical ratio, even though the standard error will have to be estimated. Shown in Fig. 14-4 is the graph of the sampling distribution. The critical Z value for $\alpha = 0.01$ for a two-tailed test is 2.58. The first two scales of the curve are the same because of our particular null hypothesis, but need not be, since a specific difference other than zero may be hypothesized.

The two samples were drawn, and the results are summarized as follows:

	Urban	Rural
n	100	100
$\overline{X}$	$600	$540
s	$120	$100

The difference between the sample means is $600 - 540$, or $60.
Our formula for the standard error of the difference is

$$\sigma_{\overline{X}_1 - \overline{X}_2} = \sqrt{\sigma_{\overline{X}_1}^2 + \sigma_{\overline{X}_2}^2}$$

This may be squared and rewritten as

$$\sigma_{\overline{X}_1 - \overline{X}_2}^2 = \frac{\sigma_1^2}{n_1} + \frac{\sigma_2^2}{n_2}$$

If the samples are from the same universe or from universes with the same variance though different means,[1] $\sigma_1^2 = \sigma_2^2 = \sigma^2$, and we may write

$$\sigma_{\bar{X}_1 - \bar{X}_2}^2 = \frac{\sigma^2}{n_1} + \frac{\sigma^2}{n_2} = \sigma^2 \left(\frac{1}{n_1} + \frac{1}{n_2} \right)$$

Where σ^2 is unknown, it must be estimated from the sample variances, and an estimate made of the standard error. A pooled estimate of the universe variance may be obtained from the expression

$$\hat{\sigma}^2 = \frac{n_1 s_1^2 + n_2 s_2^2}{n_1 + n_2 - 2}$$

Substituting in the previous expression, we have

$$\hat{\sigma}_{\bar{X}_1 - \bar{X}_2}^2 = \frac{n_1 s_1^2 + n_2 s_2^2}{n_1 + n_2 - 2} \left(\frac{1}{n_1} + \frac{1}{n_2} \right)$$

The square root of this result will be our estimated standard error of the difference, $\hat{\sigma}_{\bar{X}_1 - \bar{X}_2}$. Substituting the results of the survey, we obtain

$$\sigma_{\bar{X}_1 - \bar{X}_2}^2 = \frac{n_1 s_1^2 + n_2 s_2^2}{n_1 + n_2 - 2} \left(\frac{1}{n_1} + \frac{1}{n_2} \right)$$

$$= \frac{100(14{,}400) + 100(10{,}000)}{100 + 100 - 2} \left(\frac{1}{100} + \frac{1}{100} \right) = 246.5$$

$$\hat{\sigma}_{\bar{X}_1 - \bar{X}_2} = \sqrt{246.5} = \$15.7$$

Our test ratio becomes

$$Z = \frac{\bar{X}_1 - \bar{X}_2}{\hat{\sigma}_{\bar{X}_1 - \bar{X}_2}} = \frac{600 - 540}{15.7} = \frac{60}{15.7} = 3.81$$

Statistical conclusion The computed test value 3.81 is greater than the critical value 2.58, so the difference of $60 must fall in the rejection region. The null hypothesis is rejected, and the alternative hypothesis is accepted.

Answer to management's question Because the alternative hypothesis is accepted, the market-research firm can tell the client that there is a significant difference in average home-maintenance expenditures and that expenditures are greater in urban areas.

Further Comments on Independent Samples

The illustration above made use of the normal curve in testing because the sample sizes were large. When sample sizes are small, the t distribution should be used in-

---

[1]Such a condition of equal variances is termed homoscedasticity.

stead if the problem employs an estimated standard error (which it probably will). It is not necessary to have both samples the same size as in our illustration. In using the t distribution, we have $n_1 + n_2 - 2$ df. The assumption of equal variances can (and should) be tested by methods discussed later in this chapter, specifically by use of the F test. If the variances are not equal, there is no entirely satisfactory procedure for the test.

TESTS INVOLVING VARIANCES

Introduction

To this point our discussion of sampling has focused on either arithmetic means or percentages. However, as observed at the beginning of Chap. 6, many business decisions depend as much on a knowledge of variability as on information on averages. Also, a number of the techniques we have studied for arithmetic means (e.g., those of the previous section) required making assumptions about variances. Therefore, to overcome these deficiencies and further broaden the reader's appreciation of sampling and its applications, we shall now turn our attention to the techniques used to test hypotheses about variances.

Single-sample Tests: Chi-square Distribution

Brief mention was made of the chi-square (χ^2) distribution as a continuous probability distribution at the end of Chap. 8. This distribution, like the t distribution, varies with the number of degrees of freedom (df) so is conventionally tabled for only certain selected probability levels. Such a table is to be found in App. F. However, looking at Fig. 14-5, we see that the χ^2 distribution is not symmetrical like the t distribution, but is right-skewed (even a reverse J for 1 and 2 df). The skewness decreases as the degrees of freedom increase and the curve may eventually be approximated by a normal curve. The table in App. F is a one-tailed table which shows the chance prob-

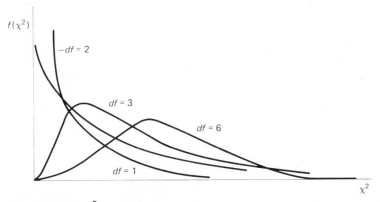

Figure 14-5 The χ^2 distribution.

ability of obtaining a χ^2 equal to or greater than one appearing in the table. For example, consulting the table with $P = 0.1$ and df $= 14$, we find that $\chi^2 = 21.06$, indicating that the chance probability of obtaining a $\chi^2 \geqslant 21.06$ for 14 degrees of freedom is 10 percent.

For testing purposes, if we may assume that we are sampling from a normal universe, we define

$$\chi^2 = \frac{ns^2}{\sigma^2} \quad \text{where } s^2 = \frac{\Sigma x^2}{n}$$

This ratio may then be used to compare a sample variance (s^2) with an hypothesized population variance (σ^2) in a single-sample test. The appropriate number of degrees of freedom is again sample size minus one (i.e., df $= n - 1$).

Single-sample Test: An Illustration

To illustrate, let us assume that the management of Wide World Manufacturing Company feels that it has a problem with raw-material shipments of fiber from one of its suppliers, The Small Company. Recent shipments, although of the same general quality level as past shipments, appear to be more variable, which could cause delays in the manufacturing process. These delays would be due to excessive downtime for machine adjustment resulting from the suspected increase in variability. Management asks the company statistician to check on their feelings. Checking past records, he found that incoming shipments in the past had a variance of 40. A random sample of 20 units of fiber from the most recent shipment showed a variance of 70 ($s^2 = 70$). We shall use our formal steps of Chap. 12 to complete the illustration.

Management's question Management of the Wide World Manufacturing Company would like to know if there has been an increase in the variability of the raw material fiber from the Small Company.

Null and alternative hypotheses The null hypothesis is that there has been no increase in the variability as measured by the variance, and that any difference observed in sampling is the result of chance sampling errors (H_0: $\sigma^2 \leqslant 40$). The alternative hypothesis is that there has been an increase (H_1: $\sigma^2 > 40$). The test is a one-tailed test, as management specifically suspects an increase in variability.

Level of significance After discussion, the decision was made to test at the 5 percent level ($\alpha = 0.05$).

Statistical test Since our problem involves a single-sample test for a variance, it will be based on the χ^2 distribution. The particular χ^2 distribution for a test based on 19 df is illustrated in Fig. 14-6. It has been divided into an acceptance region and a rejection region using our $\alpha = 0.05$. The critical $\chi^2 = 30.14$ was obtained from App. F using $P = 0.05$ and df $= 19$. We must now calculate our test χ^2 to discover if it is in the

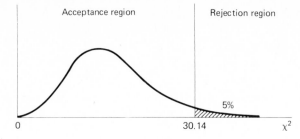

Figure 14-6 χ^2 distribution for fiber variability test.

acceptance or rejection region. It is

$$\chi^2 = \frac{ns^2}{\sigma^2} = \frac{20(70)}{40} = 35$$

Statistical conclusion Since our test χ^2 is in the rejection region, we will reject the null hypothesis ($\sigma^2 \leqslant 40$) in favor of the alternative hypothesis ($\sigma^2 > 40$).

Answer to management's question It would appear that management's suspicions are well founded. Perhaps a "nasty" letter to the Small Company is in order.

Other Uses of χ^2

The chi-square distribution is quite a remarkable distribution. In addition to the use described above, it may be used in a number of goodness-of-fit tests involving fitting to theoretical curves and contingency tables. These uses, however, will not be illustrated here.

Two-sample Tests: The F Distribution

Another continuous probability distribution used in testing variances is the F distribution. As F is defined as the ratio of two sample variances from normal populations (i.e., $F = s_1^2/s_2^2$ with $s_1^2 > s_2^2$ and $n - 1$ df for each variance), it may be used in two sample tests of variances particularly to test to see if it may be assumed both samples come from the same normal population with respect to variability. If the two variances in question are from the same universe, the expected value for the F ratio would be 1. Tables of F values (App. E) show the probabilities of getting various departures from 1 as the result of chance factors of sampling, in terms of the degrees of freedom applicable to each sample variance. The table gives values of F which would result from chance alone at selected probability (significance) levels for varying values of the 2-df figures. By comparing the test F of a problem with the appropriate table F, one may determine if the test F is significant or not at the probability level chosen for testing. When graphed, the F distribution resembles χ^2 in that it is generally right-skewed, but will be a reverse J for small df's.

Two-sample Test: An Illustration

For illustration, let us look at a problem of the Good Health Chemical Company. The management of the Company wishes to determine whether or not there is any difference between the variability of the output of two new alternate processes for producing vitamin Q. A random sample of 25 units from process 1 had a variance of 144 ($s_1^2 = 144$) while a similar-sized sample from process 2 had a variance of 100 ($s_2^2 = 100$). We shall once again follow our formal steps in hypothesis testing to solve management's problem:

Management's question Management would like to know if the two processes have the same variability.

Null and alternative hypotheses Our null hypothesis will be that there is no difference in the variability of the two processes and that any observed difference is the result of chance sampling error (H_0: $\sigma_1^2 = \sigma_2^2$). Our alternative hypothesis is that one process has greater variability than the other (H_1: $\sigma_1^2 \neq \sigma_2^2$). As it is not known which process might have greater variability, we shall have a two-sided test.

Level of significance Management decided that they would like the test performed at the 10 percent level ($\alpha = 0.10$).

Statistical test As the problem involves comparing two sample variances, it will be done as an F test. Figure 14-7 shows the F curve for this problem and its division into an acceptance region and a rejection region at a critical F of 1.98. This critical value was actually found in the 5 percent table at the intersection of 24 df for the numerator and 24 df for the denominator. Owing to the convention of placing the larger s^2 in the numerator when calculating (and tabling) F, the α of a two-tailed test must be cut in half when determining the critical F, as the convention has resulted in transferring the lower tail F's to the upper tail of the curve. Cutting off 5 percent in the upper tail then also includes 5 percent for the lower tail and gives us our desired $\alpha = 10$ percent. We can now calculate our test F to discover whether it is in the acceptance region or

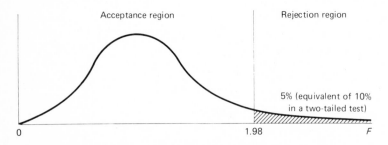

Figure 14-7 F distribution for vitamin problem.

the rejection region. For our data we get

$$F = \frac{s_1^2}{s_2^2} = \frac{144}{100} = 1.44$$

Statistical conclusion Our test F is in the acceptance region, so we accept the null hypothesis ($\sigma_1^2 = \sigma_2^2$).

Answer to management's question On the basis of the statistical evidence, there appears to be no difference in the two processes for producing vitamin Q, so a choice between them should be made on some other basis (e.g., cost).

An Additional Use of F

The primary use of the F test is in the analysis of variance, a technique to be discussed in the next several sections.

TESTS INVOLVING MORE THAN TWO SAMPLE MEANS

Somewhat different procedures than those we discussed earlier in the chapter are used if our decision problem involves comparison of more than two arithmetic means. The techniques used for this type of problem are termed "analysis of variance." These techniques have much wider application than we shall discuss and illustrate here, although our discussion should serve as a general introduction to the technique, as well as a demonstration of the handling of the problem involving more than two means.

ANALYSIS OF VARIANCE: AN INTRODUCTION

In general, the analysis of variance procedures are used to divide the total variance of a series of observations into component parts, each of which is associated with a possible source of variation, and to assess the importance of the various sources in order to locate significant sources of variation. Mechanically, the procedure compares variances by the use of the F test. Even so, it is possible to use it as a test for means if the problem has been properly set up. This may best be shown by illustration.

Analysis of Variance: An Illustration

As our illustration we shall consider the problem of testing the wearing properties of four types of floor wax. The test data are given in Table 14-2. The mean wearing times of the four types of wax differ, and we should like to develop a technique to see if these differences are significant, i.e., if variations in wearing times are significantly related to type of floor wax. To do this we take the total variance and divide it into two component parts, one associated with the type of floor wax and one associated with sampling error. These are compared, and if the former significantly exceeds the latter, we may conclude that a difference exists among the floor waxes.

Mechanics of Calculations

The first step in the mechanics is to compute the "sums of squares" (the sum of the squared deviations from the mean, the numerator used in calculating a variance) for the total and for each possible source of variation. Our possible sources of variation are the type of floor wax, which in our problem appears as variation among the columns of Table 14-2, since each column gives data for a different floor wax; and sampling error, which can be measured free of wax effects by combining the information within columns where no wax effect exists. Therefore, we need a total sum of squares, an among column sum of squares (that associated with type of floor wax), and a within column sum of squares (that associated with sampling error).

Altogether there are 24 samples of floor wax lasting a total of 96 months. The grand mean $(\overline{\overline{X}})$ for computing the total sum of squares, therefore, is $\frac{96}{24}$, or 4 months. The calculation of the total sum of squares is most easily done by a variation of the adjustment method of computing the standard deviation (see Chap. 6). Table calculations are shown in Table 14-3. The total sum of squares (total SS) is given by

$$\text{Total SS} = \Sigma X^2 - \frac{(\Sigma X)^2}{n}$$

Substituting from the table, we have

$$\text{Total SS} = 522 - \frac{(96)^2}{24} = 138$$

This is the sum of the squared deviations for all items from the grand mean of 4 months.

Table 14-2 Wearing times, in months, of samples of four types of floor wax

	Type A	Type B	Type C	Type D
	2	3	6	5
	3	4	8	6
	1	3	7	6
	4	5	4	4
	1	0	10	3
	2	. . .	. . .	6
	1	. . .	. . .	. . .
	2	. . .	. . .	. . .
Total	16	15	35	30
Mean	2	3	7	5

Table 14-3 Calculations for analysis of variance

	Type A		Type B		Type C		Type D		Grand total	
	X_A	X_A^2	X_B	X_B^2	X_C	X_C^2	X_D	X_D^2		
	2	4	3	9	6	36	5	25		
	3	9	4	16	8	64	6	36		
	1	1	3	9	7	49	6	36		
	4	16	5	25	4	16	4	16		
	1	1	0	0	10	100	3	9		
	2	4	...	...	...	...	6	36		
	1	1	...	...	...	...	...	...		
	2	4	...	...	...	...	...	...		
ΣX	16	...	15	...	35	...	30	...	96	...
$\Sigma (X)^2$	...	40	...	59	...	265	...	158	...	522

The among column sum of squares is the sum of the weighted squared deviations of the column means about the grand mean; i.e.,

$$\text{Among SS} = \Sigma [n_i (\overline{X}_i - \overline{\overline{X}})^2]$$

where the subscript i refers to a particular column. For our problem we have

$$\text{Among SS} = 8(2 - 4)^2 + 5(3 - 4)^2 + 5(7 - 4)^2 + 6(5 - 4)^2$$
$$= 8(4) + 5(1) + 5(9) + 6(1)$$
$$= 32 + 5 + 45 + 6 = 88$$

The within column sum of squares may be calculated as the difference between the total sum of squares and the among sum of squares; i.e.,

$$\text{Within SS} = \text{total SS} - \text{among SS}$$

Substituting, we get

$$\text{Within SS} = 138 - 88 = 50$$

This last value equals the sum of the sums of the squared deviations of the items in each column from its own column mean.

Once the sum of squares for each source of variation has been computed, the number of degrees of freedom for each source must be determined. For the total variation, this is the total number of items minus one (24 - 1 = 23). For the among column variation, it is the number of columns minus one (4 - 1 = 3). For the within column variation, we may again use the difference between the total and among figures (23 - 3 = 20).

Finally, the sums of squares and degrees of freedom are used to compute an among column variance estimate and a within column variance estimate, and these are used in

Table 14-4 Variance table for wearing times of floor wax

Source of variation	Sums of squares	Degrees of freedom	Variance estimate	F
Total	138	23		
Among	88	3	29.3	11.7
Within	50	20	2.5	

turn to compute an F value:

$$F = \frac{\text{Among variance estimate}}{\text{Within variance estimate}}$$

for test purposes. These calculations and our previous ones are summarized in Table 14-4, which is a typical variance table for the analysis of variance procedure.

Hypothesis Tested

The hypothesis to be tested here is of a threefold nature. We hypothesize (1) that the mean wearing times of all four types of floor wax are the same, $\mu_A = \mu_B = \mu_C = \mu_D$; (2) that the variances for all four types are the same, $\sigma_A^2 = \sigma_B^2 = \sigma_C^2 = \sigma_D^2$; and (3) that the population distributions are normally distributed. For the procedure to be used as a test for means, parts 2 and 3 of the hypothesis must be true, particularly part 2, since the test procedure involves comparing variance estimates. If there is doubt as to the validity of this part of the hypothesis, it should be tested prior to testing for the means. Departures from normality affect the exactness with which levels of significance may be determined when testing, but moderate departures will cause little difficulty.

   We divided the total variation into two sources in this problem. The within column variation is free of any variation attributable to wax type because it is based entirely on deviations from the respective column means. If part 2 of our hypothesis is true, our pooling of the individual column figures will allow us to use the within column variance estimate as an estimate of sampling error free of wax effects. The among column variation is designed to reflect variations attributable to both wax type and sampling error. Under part 1 of our hypothesis, however, this is reduced to sampling error alone, since that part states that there is no difference in mean wearing times of the four types of wax. Therefore, we may use our among variance estimate as an independent estimate of sampling error and compare it with the within variance estimate. If only sampling error is present, these should be similar. If they are not similar, it is evidence that there is a difference in the mean wearing times of the wax types.

Statistical Test

As our problem here is that of comparing two sample variances, we shall make use of the F test studied in the previous section. Referring to Table 14-4, we recall that we had an F value of 11.7 with 3 and 20 df. Let us assume that management desires a test at the 1 percent level ($\alpha = 0.01$). Reference to App. E shows that, for 3 and 20 df, the 0.01 value for F is 4.94. This is interpreted to mean that a value of F as large as or larger than 4.94 will occur only 1 in 100 times as a result of chance sampling errors if the hypothesis is true. As the F of our example ($F = 11.7$) is greater than that of the table, we reject statement 1 of the hypothesis and conclude that there is a difference in the mean wearing times of the wax types. This merely indicates that at least one wax mean differs significantly from one other mean. Individual differences between means may be tested for significance by using the t test as described earlier in the chapter.

A Final Comment

The foregoing discussion of the analysis of variance illustrated only one of many potential types of problems for which it is useful. It is in general a most powerful technique for locating significant sources of variation. The F test also has wider application than is indicated by the illustration above. We shall illustrate an additional use of the analysis of variance when we study regression and correlation in Chaps. 15 and 16.

STATISTICAL QUALITY CONTROL

The final sections of this chapter will present a brief introduction to statistical quality control. The use of statistical techniques to control the quality level of manufactured product first developed in the 1930s but gained wide use and acceptance as the result of World War II. Today these techniques are highly developed and widely used in industry.

Techniques of statistical quality control are divided into two broad categories: (1) acceptance sampling or product or lot control and (2) process control. The former deals with the problem of whether a completed lot meets certain specifications; i.e., is the lot acceptable? The second type attempts to control the manufacturing process while it is operating, thereby preventing the production of poor-quality product.

Acceptance Sampling

Quality-control problems of this type resemble the hypothesis testing (or more specifically the decision problems) discussed in Chap. 12. Therefore, we shall not discuss them in detail here. However, we shall point out several interesting features of this type of problem.

Problems of this type involve two points of view, that of the producer of the product and that of the potential consumer, and the relation between them. The producer may be a raw-materials supplier, and the consumer a manufacturer using the raw material, or the producer may be one department in a plant, and the consumer another department in the same plant or the producer may be a manufacturer and the consumer the final user. In any case the producer runs the risk of having a good lot rejected and the consumer runs the risk of accepting a poor lot. These risks correspond to the probabilities of making Type I and Type II errors, or α and β risks discussed in Chap. 12.

Actual testing procedures resemble those of the decision-making illustration in that alternative values of the quality level are specified and α and β set for these. The size of the test sample is then determined. Large portions of the necessary calculations have been tabulated, and extensive use is made of these tables.

Much of acceptance sampling makes use of double sampling or sequential sampling techniques. The idea here is that a very good or bad lot can be identified quickly with a small sample (reducing sampling costs), while larger samples are needed only for doubtful lots. These sampling plans are more costly to operate, however.

Acceptance sampling techniques are widely used in industry. Where testing procedures are destructive, they are a must. They are also used extensively elsewhere, however, to keep down inspection costs and because in practice they are often more effective than 100 percent inspection.

Process Control

As indicated above, the objective of this type of quality control is to ensure a satisfactory product while the manufacturing process is in actual operation. The problem stems from the fact that all manufactured products vary. The problem is to determine whether the existing variation in the process and its product at any given time may be attributed to chance variations in the process and hence are beyond the immediate control of the manufacturer or whether the variation appears to have been greater than that attributable to chance, in which case the process may be operating improperly and a search is made for an assignable cause, e.g., tool wear, a new operator, or a new source of raw material. The device used in process control to study the variations in the process is a control chart or charts. As a by-product of process control, one may also study the process's ability to meet specifications.

State of Control

Before beginning the operation of a control chart for a particular manufacturing process, one must first determine that a "state of control" exists; i.e., the process must be studied to ensure that it is subject to chance variations only. This is accomplished by setting up a preliminary control chart based on about 25 samples[1] and establishing tentative control limits. The sample measures (e.g., means) are then plotted and studied to determine if a state of control appears to exist. If not, the process is reviewed until all assignable causes are removed and a state of control does exist. Such a state is necessary to proper operation of the control system and to ensuring its effectiveness in detecting nonchance sources of variation.

---

[1] Process control generally utilizes small samples (as small as four or five items per sample) taken at fairly frequent intervals.

Control Charts: An Illustration

Control charts are constructed for the control of quality by measuring some quality characteristic of the product or by counting the number of the product having or not having some property. The former are called control charts for variables; the latter are called control charts for attributes. We shall use control charts for variables for our illustration.

Two charts are generally employed, one for the average level of measurement (arithmetic mean) and one for the variability in measurement (range or standard deviation). Table 14-5 gives data from 25 samples of five items each on inside washer diameters. For each sample the mean and the range have been computed. With samples as small as these, the range is a good measure of variability, since it will give reliable estimates of the population standard deviation (σ) and is easier to compute. If the sample is greater than about 15, the sample standard deviations should be used.

Table 14-5 Data for construction of control charts for variables (inside washer diameters) (values as deviations from 0.50 in in hundredths of an inch)

Sample number	Sample values	Sample mean	Sample range
1	1, 5, 8, 1, 9	4.8	8
2	2, 2, 3, 9, 6	4.4	7
3	2, 10, 6, 8, 5	6.2	8
4	7, 7, 9, 8, 4	7.0	5
5	8, 2, 6, 2, 1	3.8	7
6	3, 10, 8, 9, 2	6.4	8
7	8, 3, 7, 4, 8	6.0	5
8	5, 6, 10, 4, 9	6.8	6
9	4, 6, 3, 7, 5	5.0	4
10	6, 7, 4, 8, 8	6.6	4
11	10, 9, 2, 8, 1	6.0	9
12	10, 5, 5, 8, 2	6.0	8
13	7, 2, 9, 5, 10	6.6	8
14	8, 8, 5, 7, 9	7.4	4
15	9, 5, 8, 6, 1	5.8	8
16	1, 1, 6, 5, 2	3.0	5
17	7, 10, 5, 5, 5	6.4	5
18	10, 8, 7, 6, 7	7.6	4
19	6, 4, 7, 2, 3	4.4	5
20	8, 2, 9, 3, 4	5.2	7
21	4, 1, 1, 2, 10	3.6	9
22	7, 7, 5, 5, 6	6.0	2
23	3, 4, 4, 10, 6	5.4	7
24	7, 2, 4, 8, 6	5.4	6
25	1, 8, 8, 2, 4	4.6	7
Total	702	. . .	156

Table 14-6 Factors useful in construction of control charts [†]

Number of items in sample, n	Chart for averages: factors for control limits, A_2	Chart for ranges		
		Factors for central line, d_2	Factors for control limits	
			D_3	D_4
2	1.880	1.128	0	3.267
3	1.023	1.693	0	2.575
4	0.729	2.059	0	2.282
5	0.577	2.326	0	2.115
6	0.483	2.534	0	2.004
7	0.419	2.704	0.076	1.924
8	0.373	2.847	0.136	1.864
9	0.337	2.970	0.184	1.816
10	0.308	3.078	0.223	1.777
11	0.285	3.173	0.256	1.744
12	0.266	3.258	0.284	1.716
13	0.249	3.336	0.308	1.692
14	0.235	3.407	0.329	1.671
15	0.223	3.472	0.348	1.652

[†]These factors assume a normal distribution.

Source: By permission from the American Society for Testing and Materials. (Adapted from *ASTM Manual on Presentation of Data and Control Chart Analysis*, 1976, STP 15d, p. 83, table 2.)

Each control chart consists of a central line and upper and lower control limits. The values of these are easily computed from the data in the table with the aid of special factors shown in Table 14-6.

The $\bar{X}$ Chart

The $\bar{X}$ chart is a special application of the random sampling distribution of arithmetic means. The mean chart for our washer data is shown in Fig. 14-8. The central line is theoretically at μ, the population mean. As this is unknown, we use $\bar{\bar{X}}$, the mean of the sample means, to estimate it. Standard practice is to place the upper control limit (UCL) and the lower control limit (LCL) at a distance of $3\sigma_{\bar{X}}$ above or below the mean. As the distribution of means is at least approximately normal, these limits will contain 99.7 percent of the sample means as distributed by chance. Table 14-6 provides factors for estimating the value of $3\sigma_{\bar{X}}$ from $\bar{R}$ (the average range) for varying size samples. For our data, $\bar{\bar{X}} = \frac{702}{125} = 5.62$, so our central line is at 5.62. We estimate $3\sigma_{\bar{X}}$ as $3\sigma_{\bar{X}} = A_2\bar{R}$. For samples of five, $A_2 = 0.577$, and for our data, $\bar{R} = \frac{156}{25} = 6.24$, so we obtain $A_2\bar{R} = 0.577(6.24) = 3.60$. Therefore,

$$UCL = \bar{\bar{X}} + A_2\bar{R} = 5.62 + 3.60 = 9.22$$

and

$$LCL = \bar{\bar{X}} - A_2\bar{R} = 5.62 - 3.60 = 2.02$$

The results of these calculations are shown in the $\bar{X}$ chart of Fig. 14-8.

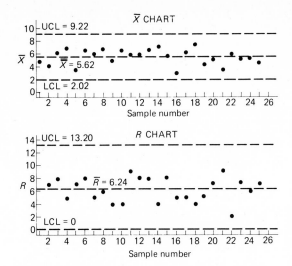

Figure 14-8 Control charts for inside washer diameters (data are given in hundredths of an inch as deviations from 0.50 in).

The Range Chart

The R chart of Fig. 14-8 is a range chart. The central line of the chart is at the value of the average range $(\overline{R})$ of our data. The control limits are placed at $\pm 3\sigma_R$ (σ_R is the standard deviation of the distribution of sample ranges), even though the distribution of sample ranges is not normal, but positively skewed. These limits seem to work well in practice, however, and only a small percentage of the sample ranges will fall outside them if only chance factors are in operation.

Actual computation of the values of the control limits is again done with the aid of factors from Table 14-6. Thus,

$$UCL = \overline{R} + 3\sigma_R = D_4\overline{R} = 2.115(6.24) = 13.20$$

and
$$LCL = \overline{R} - 3\sigma_R = D_3\overline{R} = 0(6.24) = 0$$

These limits are shown on the chart.

A study of our two charts shows this process to be "in control," since all points are within the control limits and no patterns or runs appear. If one or more points had been out of control (outside the limits), they would have been investigated for assignable causes and eliminated and revised control limits computed.

Control Charts in Operation

Once a state of control has been established, the control chart may be used to control the quality of current production. Samples are drawn at specified intervals, the length of which depends on the production process. The sample mean and sample range are computed and plotted on their respective charts. If only chance variations are present, very few means or ranges will fall outside the control limits, and if one does, it is immediately investigated for assignable cause, and correction of the process is made where necessary. The probability of making an investigation where not needed (the

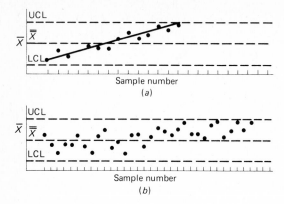

Figure 14-9 Control charts evidencing lack of control.

equivalent of a Type I error) is very small because of the use of the 3σ control limits. The risk of not detecting a change in the process (the equivalent of a Type II error) is large for any one sample, but is quickly reduced by the repetitive nature of the sampling.[1]

The charts are also studied for evidence of potential trouble even when no points fall outside the control limits. Figure 14-9a and b gives examples of what might happen. The points plotted on the control chart in Fig 14-9a show a gradual trend toward a higher average. This is typically the result of tool wear. The second half of Fig. 14-9 shows the excessive number of points above the centerline, indicating a shift in the process average. Constant watch is maintained on the control charts to spot difficulties before they become serious and before substantial quantities of poor product can be produced.

Control Charts and Specifications

Once a state of control has been established, it is possible to determine from the control chart information the ability of a given process to meet specifications. This is done by comparing process behavior and specifications. Process behavior can be derived from the control-chart data. The central line of the mean chart shows average process behavior. This can be compared with the value specified for the product. The variability of the process may be determined from the data on the average range. Factors are available for the conversion of $\overline{R}$ into an estimate of the population standard deviation ($\hat{\sigma}$). These are shown in Table 14-6. $\hat{\sigma} = \overline{R}/d_2$. A range of $6\hat{\sigma}$ ($\pm 3\hat{\sigma}$) may then be compared with the tolerances provided by the specifications to determine if the process can produce within the tolerances. Practically all production will fall within the limits of $\overline{\overline{X}} \pm 3\hat{\sigma}$.

If process behavior does not meet specifications, either the specifications will have to be revised (relaxed) to conform with the actual performance possibilities of the process or the process must be changed. The change may be simple, such as resetting a

---

[1] If the probability of a Type II error is 0.50 on a single drawing, the probability of repeating the error four consecutive times is $0.5^4 = 0.0625$.

machine, but often can be quite expensive, involving a complete revision of process and new machinery. The only remaining alternative is to accept a product of unsatisfactory quality.

STUDY GUIDE

Concepts Worth Remembering

Define:

1. t distribution
2. Degrees of freedom (df)
3. Independent (non paired) samples
4. Dependent (paired) samples
5. Standard error of the difference
6. Analysis of variance
7. Sum of squares
8. Homoscedasticity
9. Chi-square distribution
10. F distribution
11. Statistical quality control
12. Acceptance sampling
13. Process control
14. State of control
15. Control chart

Self-Test

Multiple-choice questions. Circle the letters of the statements which correctly complete the questions. There may be from one to four correct answers.

1 The t distribution:
    (a) Should, in theory, be used for all problems involving estimated standard errors.
    (b) Is tabled as a one-tailed distribution.
    (c) May be approximated by the normal curve for degrees of freedom greater than 30.
    (d) Is symmetrical and bell-shaped when plotted.

2 Two sample tests involving the use of dependent samples:
    (a) Revert to a one-sample test of the mean difference.
    (b) Require a pooling of sample variances in the calculation of the standard error.
    (c) Require a pairing of the observations of the first and second samples.
    (d) Control unwanted variability by the pairing of observations.

3 The random sampling distribution of differences between means:
    (a) Generally has a mean of zero.
    (b) Is used for problems involving dependent samples.
    (c) Takes the pattern of either a t distribution or a normal curve.
    (d) Has $n_1 + n_2 - 2$ degrees of freedom.

4 The chi-square distribution:
  (a) Is tabled for selected probability levels only.
  (b) Is the ratio of two sample variances drawn from the same population.
  (c) Is generally right-skewed when plotted.
  (d) Is used to perform single-sample variance tests.

5 The F distribution:
  (a) Varies with the number of degrees of freedom.
  (b) Is symmetrical and bell-shaped when plotted.
  (c) Has an expected value of 1.
  (d) Is the ratio of two sample arithmetic means drawn from the same population.

6 Analysis of variance procedures:
  (a) Allocate the total variance to its possible sources and evaluate their importance.
  (b) May be used as a test for differences among means even though the test is based on variances.
  (c) May be thought of as the study of the correlation between qualitative variables.
  (d) Use the chi-square test to compare variances.

7 In computing the "sums of squares" in the analysis of variance:
  (a) The total sum of squares represents the sum of the squared deviations of all items from the grand mean.
  (b) The among column sum of squares is based on deviations between the column means and the grand mean.
  (c) The within column sum of squares is based on deviations from the column means only.
  (d) The last sum of squares may be obtained by subtraction as sums of squares (variances) are additive.

8 In determining the "degrees of freedom" in the analysis of variance:
  (a) The among column df equals the number of items minus the number of columns.
  (b) The same number is used for both the among column and within column degrees of freedom.
  (c) The total degrees of freedom is always $n - 1$.
  (d) The final degrees of freedom may be obtained by subtraction.

9 Process control:
  (a) Is like ordinary hypothesis testing.
  (b) Must be based on a "state of control."
  (c) Searches for assignable causes for variations in process behavior.
  (d) Makes use of control charts.

10 Control charts in statistical quality control:
  (a) May be constructed for variables only.
  (b) May be used to determine if a process can meet specifications.
  (c) Consist of a centerline and upper and lower control limits.
  (d) Indicate the process is out of control only when points fall outside the control limits.

Questions to Think About

  1. Explain the nature and use of the t distribution.
  2. Explain the nature and use of the chi-square distribution.

3. Explain the nature and use of the F distribution.
4. Compare and contrast the two kinds of two-sample tests discussed in this chapter.
5. Explain how the analysis of variance may be used to test an hypothesis about means even though the test itself is made using variances.
6. Compare and contrast the two categories of quality control discussed in this chapter.
7. What is a "state of control"? What is its importance in process control techniques?

Problems

1 Economics, Inc., made a study of the diodes being received from several of its suppliers. A random sample of 26 diodes from supplier A had a mean life of 550 h, with a standard deviation of 15 h. Estimate for the company the range within which management might expect the true mean life of the diodes to fall all but 1 percent of the time.

2 Probability, Inc., a statistical consulting firm, has been asked by Faultless Steel, Inc., to estimate the hardness of a new alloy they have developed. A random sample of 17 pieces of the new alloy had a mean hardness of 25 Brennell units with a standard deviation of 2 Brennell units. Estimate for Faultless Steel with 95 percent confidence the true mean hardness.

3 Faultless Steel hoped that the new alloy (of Prob. 2) would have a tensile strength greater than 500 kg/cm^2. The sample of the hardness study was tested for tensile strength and found to have a mean strength of 510 kg/cm^2 with a standard deviation of 20 kg/cm^2.

    (*a*) Test at the 5 percent level whether the steel meets the desired strength.

    (*b*) What is the approximate probability of concluding the steel is unsatisfactory if in fact it has a mean strength of 515 kg/cm^2?

4 The engineering department at the Roll-Ever Tire Company has designed a new tire which they expect to have a life in use of more than 50,000 miles. The research department has had a sample of 26 of these new tires made up. When tested, the sample had a mean of 50,800 miles with a standard deviation of 2,000 miles.

    (*a*) May the company safely assume the tire will last more than 50,000 miles? Test at the 5 percent level.

    (*b*) What is the approximate probability of concluding the tire will have a life in use of only 50,000 miles if in fact, the tire will last an average of 52,000 miles?

5 High Temper Metals, Inc., has developed a new experimental alloy wire for one of its customers. The customer has asked for a wire having an average breaking strength of more than 1,200 lb. When a sample of 17 pieces of the new wire was tested, it had an arithmetic mean of 1,210 lb and a standard deviation of 20 lb.

    (*a*) Test statistically with α equal to 5 percent whether the new wire will meet the customer's specifications.

    (*b*) Determine the approximate probability of concluding that the wire will not meet specifications when, in fact, it has a mean of 1,215 lb.

6 Twelve different pieces of metal were split in half and assigned at random to one or the other of two different treatments for the prevention of rust. All pieces were then subjected to a variety of weather conditions until the first signs of rust appeared. The results of the tests are shown in the accompanying table. Test to see if there is a

**Results of weathering tests on pieces of metal treated
by two different methods**

Piece number	Weeks to rust	
	Treatment 1	Treatment 2
1	8	12
2	6	15
3	11	14
4	7	10
5	10	10
6	11	13
7	10	15
8	14	16
9	8	14
10	11	9
11	7	7
12	8	15

significant difference in the average rusting time of the two different treatments. Let α equal 2 percent.

7 Faultless Steel has developed a new treatment which they hope will reduce scratches on the stainless plate steel they produce. Ten pieces of plate were split in half and the new treatment applied to one half of each piece. The pieces were then subjected to wear and then counted for scratches. The results are given in the accompanying table.

Piece number	Nontreated	Treated
1	4	2
2	4	1
3	3	3
4	3	5
5	5	2
6	3	2
7	7	3
8	1	3
9	3	1
10	1	2

The numbers are scratches per square meter. Test at the 1 percent level whether the treatment reduces the number of scratches.

8 A manufacturer wishes to test a new sleeping pill before marketing it. He chooses 20 individuals at random, 10 of whom are given the new sleeping pill and 10 of whom are given a sugar pill. The first group shows an average increase in sleeping time of 50 min, with a standard deviation of 5 min. The second group shows a mean increase in sleeping time of 44 min, with a standard deviation of 6 min. Test at the 1 percent level whether the new sleeping pill induces a significant increase in the number of minutes slept. State your conclusion.

9 To help the marketing department, the research department of the Roll-Ever Tire Company compared a sample of Roll-Ever Super Deluxes to a sample of competing tires manufactured by the Wear-Never Tire Company. A summary of test results is given in the accompanying table. Mileages are in 1,000s of miles. Test at the 5 percent level to see if there is a significant difference in the tires.

Result	Roll-Ever	Wear-Never
n	10	10
$\overline{X}$	37	35
s	2	1.5

10 Probability, Inc., has been asked by a client to test to see if there is a significant difference in the mean length of life of an electronic component which can be supplied by either of two suppliers. A sample of 12 parts from supplier A showed a mean life of 1,200 h with a standard deviation of 10 hr. A sample of 12 parts from supplier B had a mean life of 1,212 h with a standard deviation of 12 hr. Test at the 2 percent level whether or not there is a significant difference in mean length of life.

11 A company engaged in manufacturing various types of hose needed cord for the manufacture of garden hose. Having requested samples from various suppliers, the company received cord from supplier A which tested as follows:

Breaking strength, lb	Number of pieces broken
36.0–39.9	4
40.0–43.9	10
44.0–47.9	21
48.0–51.9	30
52.0–55.9	18
56.0–59.9	12
60.0–63.9	5

Another sample of 100 pieces from supplier B had a mean breaking strength of 52 lb and a standard deviation of 7 lb. On the basis of the information given, does either supplier have a cord of a superior average breaking strength? Test at the 5 percent level.

12 Specifications for a particular yarn being manufactured by Spinning, Inc., called for a standard deviation of 6 lb. The Company's quality control department, when checking a particular production run before shipment to a customer, found a standard deviation of 8 lb for a sample of 18 pieces. Test at the 0.025 level if the shipment should be sent to the customer.

13 Upon receipt of a shipment of "long-life" light bulbs by a company, they were tested to see if they met specifications as to average length of life and variability in length of life. The shipment proved satisfactory as to average life. Specifications on variability required a standard deviation of no more than 50 hr. A sample of 25 bulbs showed a standard deviation of 60 hr. Do the bulbs meet specifications as to variability? Test at the 5 percent level.

14 Problems 8, 9, and 10 assumed that both samples involved were drawn from the same universe or from universes with the same variance, although different means (i.e., $\sigma_1^2 = \sigma_2^2 = \sigma^2$). Use F tests to test this assumption. Test at the 10 percent level.

15 The engineers at High Temper Metals, Inc., have developed a new wire-drawing process which they feel will reduce the variability in the strength of the wire the company manufactures. A sample of 25 pieces of wire from each process (old and new) was drawn and studied. The standard deviation of the old process was 20 lb while that of the new process was 12 lb. Test at the 1 percent level if there has been a significant reduction in process variability.

16 The accompanying table gives the weight losses in pounds after a 4-week period of a random sample of persons on three different diets. Test at the 5 percent level to

Diet A	Diet B	Diet C
7	7	9
6	3	7
5	5	11
6	. . .	7
. . .	. . .	11

see if there is a significant difference in the mean weight losses associated with the various diets.

17 The Seek and Find Research Agency has been hired to settle a disagreement concerning the population densities of four cities, Greenville, Pleasantdale, Clearview, and Popular City. The agency selected a random sample of the blocks in each city and determined the number of family units in each block. The results of the survey are shown in the accompanying table. Test at the 1 percent level to determine if there is a significant difference among the cities in the population densities.

Greenville	Pleasantdale	Clearview	Popular City
5	5	3	6
3	8	4	8
4	7	2	10
4	6	3	7
2	4	. . .	9
6	. . .	. . .	. . .

18 In a study Probability, Inc., was asked to determine if there was a significant difference in the mean failure rates of an electronic part. Given in the table are the failure rates for this part for four different suppliers. Test at the 1 percent level whether there is a significant difference or not.

A	B	C	D
2	10	8	6
1	6	2	8
4	9	2	6
1	7	4	4

19 The accompanying table gives the results of strength tests performed by the research department of the Roll-Ever Tire Company on samples of four new types of cord to be used in tire construction. The data are in kg/cm^2. Test at the 5 percent level to see if there is a significant difference in the mean strength of the four types of cord.

Cord type			
A	B	C	D
5	3	1	7
7	4	3	9
8	6	2	5
4	7	5	...
...	...	4	...

20 Given in the following table are the resistances in ohms of an electrical part being produced by a manufacturing process.

Sample number	Sample values	Sample number	Sample values
1	82, 82, 80, 83, 86	14	80, 82, 87, 86, 83
2	89, 81, 89, 81, 86	15	87, 82, 82, 88, 84
3	80, 82, 84, 86, 89	16	81, 89, 87, 86, 88
4	83, 85, 87, 81, 82	17	82, 84, 88, 86, 86
5	82, 82, 85, 83, 83	18	83, 88, 86, 85, 82
6	80, 82, 81, 89, 85	19	83, 80, 86, 85, 86
7	81, 83, 80, 84, 82	20	86, 89, 82, 81, 84
8	87, 83, 84, 89, 84	21	82, 82, 89, 86, 87
9	80, 81, 81, 79, 82	22	84, 88, 86, 81, 89
10	82, 80, 88, 80, 81	23	83, 80, 81, 83, 89
11	81, 85, 89, 80, 80	24	86, 86, 80, 88, 84
12	85, 81, 85, 82, 86	25	87, 86, 80, 86, 80
13	83, 83, 84, 85, 80		

(*a*) Use the data above to determine the central lines and control limits for an $\overline{X}$ chart and an R chart for this production process.

(*b*) Plot the means and ranges of the 25 samples to see if a state of control exists. If such a state does not exist, remove the out-of-control data and establish revised values for the central lines and control limits.

(c) Specifications for the process are 85 ± 8 Ω. Determine from the data given the ability of this process to meet specifications.

Answers to Self-Test

1 (a), (c), (d); **2** (a), (c), (d); **3** (a), (c), (d); **4** (a), (c), (d); **5** (a), (c); **6** (a), (b); **7** (a), (b), (c), (d); **8** (c), (d); **9** (b), (c), (d); **10** (b), (c).

FOUR

REGRESSION AND CORRELATION ANALYSIS

FIFTEEN
SIMPLE REGRESSION AND CORRELATION ANALYSIS

LEARNING OBJECTIVES

The basic learning objective is to learn about simple regression and correlation analysis—the techniques for studying the relationships between two quantitatively classified variables. Specifically, you will become familiar with:

1. The basic objectives of the analysis:
   (*a*) To determine the pattern of the relationship.
   (*b*) To determine the closeness of the relationship.
2. The descriptive measures used in the analysis, their calculation, their interpretation, and their use:
   (*a*) Regression line.
   (*b*) Standard error of estimate.
   (*c*) Coefficient of determination.
3. Statistical inference for regression and correlation:
   (*a*) Hypothesis testing.
   (*b*) Estimation.
4. Certain general cautions applicable to all regression and correlation analysis.

INTRODUCTION

Many decision problems require a knowledge of relationships for the making of a decision. Whether a man is overweight at 205 lb depends in part upon his height. It is well known that a relationship exists between weight and height, so a tall man may well weigh 205 lb. Knowledge of this relationship, then, is helpful in deciding whether the man is overweight.

A less well-known relationship is that between the hardness and tensile strength of a piece of metal. Knowledge of the nature of this relationship is of value in studying tensile strengths, however, since tensile-strength tests are destructive while hardness tests are not. The close relationship between tensile strength and hardness allows one to substitute nondestructive hardness tests when attempting to determine tensile strength.

Many statistical techniques exist for the study of relationships. We have already encountered one such technique in Chap. 14, when we studied the analysis of variance. There we were concerned with an example of the relationship between type of floor wax and wearing time. The analysis of variance was used to determine the relationship between a variable classified qualitatively (type of wax) and one classified quantitatively (wearing time). In this chapter we shall study the statistical techniques for determining and evaluating the relationships between two or more series which have both been classified quantitatively. These techniques are termed "regression and correlation." In this chapter we shall limit our discussion to the two-variable case ("simple" regression and correlation) while in Chap. 16 we shall expand it to include more than two variables ("multiple" and "partial" regression and correlation).

BASIC OBJECTIVES OF THE ANALYSIS

There are two basic objectives in a regression and correlation analysis. One is to determine the pattern, or functional nature, of the relationship between the variables. The second is to determine the closeness, or degree of relationship, between the variables. The first answers the question, "What kind of relationship exists between the variables?" The second answers the question, "How good is the relationship?"

In the first case we are interested in discovering such things as whether the variables move (change) in the same direction (i.e., as one increases, the other increases, as would be the case for height and weight) or in opposite directions (i.e., as one increases, the other decreases, as, for example, with temperatures and fuel-oil consumption). The former pattern is termed direct, or positive; the latter pattern is called inverse, or negative. We should also like to learn whether the changes have the general pattern of a straight line (linear) or a curved line (curvilinear).

There are two aspects to the second question, "How good is the relationship?" We are interested in answering it both in absolute terms (i.e., in terms of the units of the original data) and in relative (percentage) terms.

The study of the pattern of the relationship and closeness of the relationship in absolute terms is regression analysis. The term "correlation analysis" technically applies only to the study of the relative closeness of the relationship, although it is often used to include regression analysis as well.

MEASURES USED IN THE ANALYSIS

Three basic descriptive measures are computed in a regression and correlation analysis: (1) the regression line, (2) the standard error of estimate, and (3) the coefficient of determination (or the coefficient of correlation, which is the square root of the former).

The Regression Line

Regression lines are computed to show the pattern of the relationship. Several regression lines are shown in Fig. 15-1a and b. The graphs illustrated are called "scatter diagrams," because they show the scatter pattern of the relationship. Each point on the scatter diagram represents one item for which two characteristics have been observed. The vertical axis (Y) is used for the characteristic whose variations we wish to explain (termed the "dependent variable"), while the horizontal axis (X) is used for the characteristic being introduced (independent variable) to explain the variations in the dependent variable. The characteristics must be related in some logical way for the results to have meaning. For example, on the height and weight graph (Fig. 15-1a), each point logically represents one individual, not a pairing of one person's height with another person's weight. Similarly, in Fig. 15-1b, the points should represent the price and quantity supplied for a given market or time.

The regression line is also termed "the line of average relationship." The reason for this is well illustrated in Fig. 15-1a and b, where individual points vary, but the line shows their behavior in general or on the average. The line is also referred to as "the estimating equation," for, once established, it can be used to make estimates of the dependent variable from known values of the independent variable.

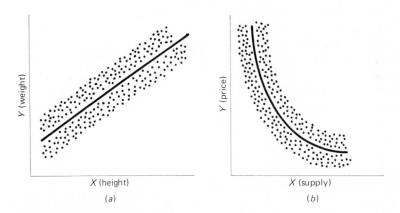

Figure 15-1 Illustrative scatter diagrams.

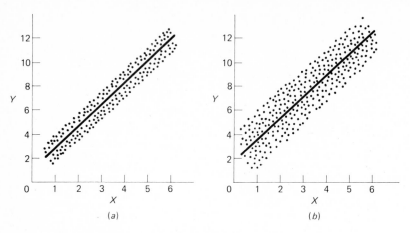

Figure 15-2 Illustration of varying amounts of scatter.

Both relationships illustrated in Fig. 15-1a and b are simple (two-variable). Figure 15-1a also illustrates a positive, or direct, linear relationship. Figure 15-1b illustrates a negative, or inverse, curvilinear relationship.

The Standard Error of Estimate

The second measure, the standard error of estimate,[1] is a measure of the scatter, or variation, of the points around the regression line. In measuring this variation, it measures the closeness of the relationship. This is illustrated in Fig. 15-2a and b.

Both scatter diagrams have the same scales and the same regression line. The pattern of the scatter in Fig. 15-2a is much more concentrated than that of Fig. 15-2b. Figure 15-2b exhibits much greater scatter, or variation. Because of the concentration of the points about the regression line in Fig. 15-2a, the relationship is comparatively close. That of Fig. 15-2b is poorer, since the greater variation means a comparatively poorer relationship. The standard error of estimate measures this scatter, or variation, around the regression line and would have a greater numerical value in Fig. 15-2b than in a. As the standard error of estimate is in the units of the dependent variable (Y), it is our measure of the absolute closeness of the relationship.

The standard error of estimate derives its name from the use to which it is customarily put. It is used in qualifying estimates made by means of the regression line. Estimates made from the regression line of Fig. 15-2a, while identical with those made from the regression line of Fig. 15-2b, would be of more general value, since they would be subject to less variation (error).

---

[1] Despite the use of the term "standard error," this is not a measure of sampling error. It corresponds to the sample standard deviation rather than to the standard error of the arithmetic mean.

Coefficient of Determination

Our final measure, the coefficient of determination, is used to measure the relative closeness of the relationship. Correlation seeks to explain the variations in the dependent variable. For example, to what factors may variations in weights or prices (the dependent variables in Fig. 15-1a and b) be attributed? The variations in the dependent variable are taken as a base, or total amount of variation, and the coefficient of determination measures what portion of that total may be attributed to or explained by variations in the independent variable, i.e., by height, in the case where weight is the dependent variable, or by quantity supplied, where price is the dependent variable.

Although computations may become involved and auxiliary sampling measures called for, the three measures just discussed are the basic descriptive measures and all that are needed to complete a regression and correlation analysis.

AN ILLUSTRATION: SIMPLE LINEAR CASE

Let us now illustrate the calculation for a sample of the three basic measures for the simple linear case. The method which we shall illustrate is that known as "the method of least squares," for mathematically, it has the property of making the sum of the squared deviations of points from the regression line a minimum. (It may be recalled from Chap. 5 that the arithmetic mean had this property.) This method is strictly applicable only when the line is fit to a set of random points, in which case the method guarantees the line of best fit, but it is widely used for all types of data in all types of correlation problems. The method has many variations in the actual mechanics, only one of which will be illustrated here. The variation to be illustrated is not the easiest one for all cases, but has proved to be a good all-around method for a large variety of problems, and extends itself nicely to multiple and partial regression and correlation. We shall concentrate in this section on mechanics only and reserve further explanation and interpretation of the measures until the next section.

To illustrate the mechanics of computing the basic correlation measures, let us consider the problem of the Happy Home Fuel Oil Company in scheduling oil deliveries to one of its customers. Table 15-1 gives data for a 10-day sample on the average daily temperatures and resulting fuel-oil consumption at this home. The company wishes to study the relationship between this customer's fuel-oil consumption and temperature in order to be able to schedule fuel-oil deliveries based on estimates of consumption from observed temperatures. Fuel-oil consumption, then, is the dependent variable (Y), and temperature is the independent variable (X).

The first step is to draw a scatter diagram of our data, to determine if our regression appears to be a linear one. This scatter diagram appears as Fig. 15-3. At this stage of the problem our graph would not have the lines appearing in Fig. 15-3, but would consist of only the 10 points. As these seem to scatter themselves in a straight line, we may proceed with linear techniques. If they had scattered themselves in a curved line, different techniques from those to be illustrated would have to be used.

Table 15-1 Temperature data and fuel-oil consumption customer H. Jones

Day	Average daily temperature (X), °F	Gallons consumed per day (Y)	XY	X^2	Y^2
1	32	10	320	1,024	100
2	28	11	308	784	121
3	23	17	391	529	289
4	26	12	312	676	144
5	18	18	324	324	324
6	20	19	380	400	361
7	14	22	308	196	484
8	12	26	312	144	676
9	10	27	270	100	729
10	3	30	90	9	900
Total	186	192	3,015	4,186	4,128

The second step is to compute the figures for the additional columns shown in Table 15-1, i.e., columns XY, X^2, and Y^2, and to total all five columns.

The third step is to reduce column, or item, totals to corresponding deviation totals. The deviations referred to are deviations from the respective arithmetic means of the X and Y series ($\overline{X}$ and $\overline{Y}$). We shall use a capital X and a capital Y to represent the original items or observations. We shall use a lowercase x and a lowercase y to represent deviations from the means; that is, $x = X - \overline{X}$ and $y = Y - \overline{Y}$. It is not necessary to determine the individual deviations in order to obtain deviation totals. These

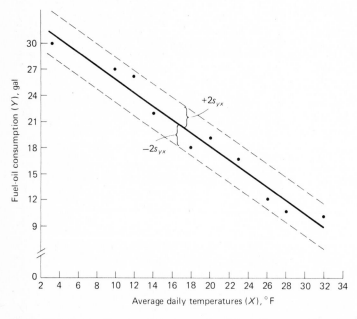

Figure 15-3 Scatter diagram of temperatures and fuel-oil consumption.

may be more efficiently derived from the following relationships:

$$\Sigma x^2 = \Sigma X^2 - \frac{(\Sigma X)^2}{n}$$

$$\Sigma y^2 = \Sigma Y^2 - \frac{(\Sigma Y)^2}{n}$$

$$\Sigma xy = \Sigma XY - \frac{\Sigma X \, \Sigma Y}{n}$$

For our data we obtain

$$\Sigma x^2 = 4{,}186 - \frac{186^2}{10} = 4{,}186 - 3{,}459.6 = 726.4$$

$$\Sigma y^2 = 4{,}128 - \frac{192^2}{10} = 4{,}128 - 3{,}686.4 = 441.6$$

$$\Sigma xy = 3{,}015 - \frac{186(192)}{10} = 3{,}015 - 3{,}571.2 = -556.2$$

The first two results must be positive since they represent the sums of squared deviations, which themselves are all positive because of the squaring. The latter result may be positive or negative, depending on the problem. As our scatter diagram shows an inverse, or negative, pattern, we should expect the negative value in this case.

The fourth step is the actual computation of the regression and correlation measures. We shall begin with the regression line. We shall use a linear equation of the form $Y_e = a + bX$. The subscript on the Y indicates that the values in question are estimated, or line, values of Y as distinguished from actual, or item, values. Our specific mechanical problem here is to solve numerically for values for a and b. Solution equations for a and b are

$$b = \frac{\Sigma xy}{\Sigma x^2} \quad \text{and} \quad a = \overline{Y} - b\overline{X}$$

Substituting the values of our problem, we have

$$b = \frac{-556.2}{726.4} = -0.766 = -0.77$$

$$a = 19.20 - (-0.766)(18.6) = 19.20 + 14.25 = 33.45$$

The equation of our problem's regression line is

$$Y_e = 33.45 - 0.77X$$

It is possible to determine the goodness of the fit of our regression line to the data and to check our arithmetic by plotting the regression line on our scatter diagram. As the method of least squares is foolproof for straight lines, we are primarily checking our arithmetic in this case. To plot a linear regression line, we may substitute any two convenient values of X and solve for the corresponding Y_e's. These will be the coordinates of two points on the regression line, which may be plotted on the scatter diagram, and then the line itself drawn through these two points. Substituting $X = 4$, we get

$$Y_e = 33.45 - 0.77(4) = 30.37$$

Substituting $X = 30$, we get

$$Y_e = 33.45 - 0.77(30) = 10.35$$

These two points and the regression line are plotted on the scatter diagram of Fig. 15-3. The fit appears to be a good one.

To compute our two remaining regression and correlation measures (the coefficient of determination and the standard error of estimate) it is convenient to first partition (divide) the sum of squares (the sum of the squared deviations from the mean) for the dependent variable (Y) into two parts: one associated with the independent variable (X) and one representing all other variables not specifically included in the problem.[1] The sum of squares for the dependent variable (Y) is referred to as the "total sum of squares." That part of the total sum of squares associated with the independent variable (X) is termed the "explained" or "regression" sum of squares while that part associated with all other variables is called the "unexplained" or "residual" sum of squares.

We already have the value of the total sum of squares as we computed it as part of our third step when computing deviation totals. Therefore, the

$$\text{Total SS} = \Sigma(Y - \bar{Y})^2 = \Sigma y^2 = 441.6$$

The explained sum of squares may be computed from the following:

$$\text{Explained SS} = \Sigma(Y_e - \bar{Y})^2 = \Sigma y_e^2 = b\Sigma xy$$

Substituting the values of our problem, we have

$$\text{Explained SS} = \Sigma y_e^2 = -0.766(-556.2) = 426.0$$

The unexplained sum of squares is most easily determined as a residual as our total is being divided into only two parts. Hence, we have

$$\text{Unexplained SS} = \text{total SS} - \text{explained SS} = \Sigma(Y - Y_e)^2$$

$$= \Sigma y^2 - \Sigma y_e^2 = \Sigma y_s^2$$

Substituting for our problem, we get

$$\Sigma y_s^2 = 441.6 - 426.0 = 15.6$$

The coefficient of determination, symbolized by r^2, is the ratio of the explained sum of squares to the total sum of squares, i.e.,

$$r^2 = \frac{\Sigma y_e^2}{\Sigma y^2}$$

---

[1] Compare analysis of variance procedures on page 205 and following.

Substituting, we find

$$r^2 = \frac{426.0}{441.6} = 0.965$$

The standard error of estimate is a special form of standard deviation and is represented by the symbol s_{yx}, indicating that it measures variability in the dependent variable (Y) after provision for the independent variable (X). It is given by the following formula:

$$s_{yx} = \sqrt{\frac{\Sigma y_s^2}{n}}$$

For our data, we get

$$s_{yx} = \sqrt{\frac{15.6}{10}} = \sqrt{1.57} = 1.25 \text{ gal}$$

Bands of $\pm 2 s_{yx}$ have been plotted on the scatter diagram (Fig. 15-3). Because s_{yx} is in the units of Y(gal), it is plotted parallel to the Y axis. As the distribution of the points about the regression line may be assumed to be approximately normal in linear regression, about $95\frac{1}{2}$ percent of the points on the scatter diagram should fall within these bands. In our case all points do, as might be expected with only 10 points.

Interpretation and Use of the Regression Line and Standard Error of Estimate

The b value of the regression line is termed the "coefficient of regression." It is a useful summary measure of the pattern of the relationship, particularly in the linear case. Geometrically, the b value is the slope coefficient of the line representing the change in the estimated values of the dependent variable (Y_e) for a unit change in the independent variable (X). For our problem the estimated (average) decrease in daily fuel-oil consumption for each additional degree Fahrenheit rise in the average daily temperature is 0.77 gal. This relationship applies only in the observed average daily temperature range of 3 to 32°F. Outside this range the relationship will undoubtedly change. Above some higher temperature, for example, fuel oil will cease to be consumed at all.

The a value is geometrically the Y intercept (i.e., the point where the line crosses the Y axis). It is usually of no particular interpretive value in regression analysis. It serves geometrically to determine the general height of the line, since two parallel lines have the same slope value, b, but differing a values.

As previously mentioned, the line itself, in addition to showing the pattern of the relationship, is used to make estimates of the dependent variable. The Happy Home Fuel Oil Company can use the regression line to estimate customer Jone's daily fuel-oil comsumption and thereby plan their fuel-oil deliveries to him. If the average temperature (X) on a given day is 16°F, Jones's estimated daily consumption would be 21.13 gal:

$$Y_e = 33.45 - 0.77X = 33.45 - 0.77(16) = 21.13$$

The standard error of estimate is used to qualify the estimate. As the measure of the dispersion of the points about the regression line, it will show how much variation in our estimate can be reasonably expected. These variations would result from factors affecting fuel-oil consumption other than the temperature, as, for example, wind direction and velocity. If our standard error of estimate is large, our estimate is subject to a great deal of variation and may not be too useful. Conversely, when the standard error of estimate is small, our estimate is subject to only a small amount of variation, is more precise, and hence is generally more useful.

The standard error of estimate is used to qualify estimates made from the line in much the same way as a sampling standard error is used to establish a confidence interval. The line estimate is a point estimate, and the probability of its being exactly correct is small, and hence the need to qualify it. The estimates in regression are not confidence intervals, however, despite the name given to our measure of dispersion ("standard error of estimate"), since they do not involve estimates of sample measures (for example, $\overline{X}$'s, p's). The similarity further occurs in that many confidence intervals and linear regression use the normal curve in determining probabilities in making the estimates.

We estimated that customer Jones would use 21.13 gal of fuel oil on a 16°F day. Our standard error of estimate is 1.26 gal. Using this, we may qualify our estimate to state that $95\frac{1}{2}$ percent of the time (assuming normality) customer Jones will use between 18.61 and 23.65 gal on a 16°F day[1]:

$$Y_e \pm Zs_{yx} = 21.13 \pm 2(1.26)$$

Interpretation and Use of the Coefficient of Determination

The coefficient of determination (r^2), as stated previously, is used to measure the relative closeness of the relationship, and thereby the extent to which we have been able to explain variations in the dependent variable, by correlating it with the independent variable. r^2 was computed as the ratio of the explained sum of squares to the total sum of squares. The total sum of squares is a measure of the amount of variation that exists in the dependent variable before relating it to (correlating it with) the independent variable. (Dividing the total sum of squares by the number of items in the problem would actually give one the "variance" of the dependent variable, $s_y^2 = \Sigma y^2/n$.) The explained sum of squares is that part of the total sum of squares which can be associated with the independent variable. (Division by n would again convert this value to a "variance.") The explained sum of squares, therefore, shows the amount of variation in the dependent variable attributable to the independent variable. By dividing it by the total sum of squares in the computation of r^2, we obtain a ratio which shows the portion (percentage) of the total variation which is explained by, associated with, or attributable to the independent variable.

For our problem $r^2 = 0.965$ or 96.5 percent. That is, we find that 96.5 percent of the total variation (variance) in our dependent variable, gallons of fuel oil consumed

---

[1]Strictly speaking, the procedure illustrated here should not be applied to a sample as small as that of our problem (10), but reserved for large samples ($n > 30$) only. Proper small-sample methods are illustrated later in the chapter.

per day, is explained by the introduction of the independent variable, average daily temperature. Since the most we could explain would be 100 percent, we obviously have a good correlation here. r^2 is used to indicate the importance of the independent variable (or variables in multiple correlation) as a factor in explaining the variation in the dependent variable.

The Coefficient of Correlation

An alternative measure of the degree of correlation in relative terms is the coefficient of correlation (r). This measure, as its symbol indicates, is the square root of the coefficient of determination (r^2). It will therefore measure essentially the same thing. Its interpretation, however, is somewhat more arbitrary, for as the square root of a percentage, it cannot itself be interpreted as a percentage. One can merely conclude that the larger the r value (closer to 1, which is its limit), the better the positive correlation, the closer to -1, the better the negative correlation, and the smaller the r (closer to 0), the poorer the correlation. If computed directly from the data, r will come out automatically having the same sign as the regression. If computed from r^2, we give it the sign of the regression as indicated by our scatter diagram and b value. For our problem,

$$r = \pm\sqrt{0.965} = -0.982$$

THE LIMITING CASES

Figure 15-4a and b shows the scatter diagrams for the two possible extremes of perfect correlation (Fig. 15-4a, 1 and 2) and no correlation (Fig. 15-4b). Figure 15-4a-1 represents perfect positive correlation; Fig. 15-4a-2 is perfect inverse correlation. Appropriate values of the various regression and correlation measures are also indicated below the diagrams. For perfect correlation all points of the scatter diagram lie on the

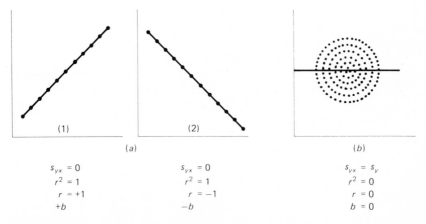

$s_{yx} = 0$	$s_{yx} = 0$	$s_{yx} = s_y$
$r^2 = 1$	$r^2 = 1$	$r^2 = 0$
$r = +1$	$r = -1$	$r = 0$
$+b$	$-b$	$b = 0$

Figure 15-4 Scatter diagrams showing perfect and no correlation.

regression line; there are no unexplained variations, and therefore $s_{yx} = 0$ and $r^2 = 1$. r also equals 1, but has the sign of the correlation, as does the b value. The scatter of points in no correlation has no pattern, and a regression line fit to such a pattern has no slope (b value equal to zero), but is a horizontal line at the mean of the Y's. The variation around the line therefore equals the variation around the mean, and the total variance is unexplained. As the total variance equals the unexplained variance, both r^2 and r equal zero.

PROBLEMS OF STATISTICAL INFERENCE IN REGRESSION AND CORRELATION ANALYSIS

Our discussion to this point has been within the framework of a single sample only. If the sample in question is a properly chosen (random) one, we can use it and sampling theory to answer some additional questions about our data. We shall consider two such questions: (1) Might the degree of correlation shown by our sample have resulted from chance alone? and (2) what additional modifications need to be made in our estimating procedures (p. 233) to allow for sampling error in addition to the variation already allowed for by our standard error of estimate (unexplained variation, i.e., variations from factors other than average daily temperature, e.g., wind direction and velocity)?

The first of these two questions is usually answered by a formal hypothesis test, and the second is answered by modifying our estimating procedures to include both sampling error and provision for unexplained (nontemperature) variations. Each will be illustrated in turn.

Hypothesis Testing

Figure 15-5 illustrates the problem posed by our first question. It shows a hypothetical universe characterized by *no* correlation ($\rho^2 \neq 0$).[1] If by chance we were to draw as a sample the circled points, we would discover that we had a sample which showed perfect correlation ($r^2 = 1$). While this is an extreme illustration, it shows the nature of our problem: any universe having no correlation will yield some samples which show a degree of correlation ($r^2 > 0$) due only to the chance factors of sampling.

While several methods exist for testing whether or not a given sample r^2 is greater than chance alone would produce, one simple and straightforward procedure for this problem uses analysis of variance techniques. This is true because most of the mechanical work of an analysis of variance was done when we partitioned the sum of squares in computing r^2 and s_{yx}.

All that remains to be done is to set up the variance table, determine the proper degrees of freedom, and compute F as a test of our hypothesis. We will now proceed to illustrate the test for the fuel-oil-consumption problem.

---

[1] As in all sampling work, we use Greek letters for universe measures, or parameters. Here the lowercase Greek rho (ρ), when squared, symbolizes the universe coefficient of determination.

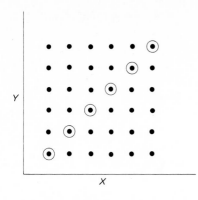

Figure 15-5 Hypothetical universe with no correlation.

F Test: An Illustration

Our null and alternative hypotheses for our test will be

$$H_0: \quad \rho^2 = 0$$

$$H_1: \quad \rho^2 \neq 0$$

In effect our null hypothesis says there is no "real" correlation and our sample value is the result of chance errors of random sampling. Our alternative hypothesis merely states the obvious—that as a general class the only alternative to no correlation is some correlation. We will test this null hypothesis at the 1 percent level (i.e., $\alpha = 0.01$).

Table 15-2 is our variance table for the test. The numerical values of the sums of squares are those derived earlier when we partitioned the total sum of squares to compute r^2 and s_{yx}. The total degrees of freedom (df) is always $(n-1)$. For our sample of $n = 10$, we therefore get $n - 1 = 10 - 1 = 9$ df for the total variation. The degrees of freedom for the explained variation is always equal to the number of independent variables being used to explain variations in the dependent variable. In simple correlation there is only one independent variable; hence, the variance table shows only 1 df for the explained variation. The degrees of freedom for the unexplained variation may be obtained by subtraction. For our illustration we have $9 - 1 = 8$ df for the unexplained variation.

If the null hypothesis is true (i.e., there is no correlation in the universe being sampled), we can compute two independent estimates of the universe variance, one using the values for the explained variation and one using the values for the unex-

Table 15-2 Variance table for significance of correlation test

Source of variation	Sums of squares	Degrees of freedom	Variance estimate	F
Total	441.6	9	. . .	. . .
Explained	426.0	1	426.0	218.5
Unexplained	15.6	8	1.95	. . .

plained variation by dividing the sum of squares by the degrees of freedom in each case.

As actually computed the explained sum of squares contains two elements of variation: (1) the independent variable, average daily temperature, and (2) the sampling variation. The unexplained sum of squares reflects sampling variation only. However, if the null hypothesis of no correlation is true, element (1) of the explained variation does not exist, and hence we would have two estimates of the universe variance based on sampling variation only.

The test value of F for this type of problem is defined as

$$F = \frac{\text{Explained variance estimate}}{\text{Unexplained variance estimate}}$$

and: if the null hypothesis is true, the expected value of F would be 1. Our test value of F works out to be

$$F = \frac{426.0}{1.95} = 218.5$$

Appendix E gives values of F for various significance levels and various degrees of freedom. Referring to the 1 percent table in App. E, we find that for 1 df and 8 df, $F = 11.26$; i.e., the chance probability is 1 percent of getting an $F \geqslant 11.26$ if the null hypothesis is true. Our test $F = 218.5$, being much greater than this, we reject our null hypothesis of no correlation and conclude that the relationship between fuel oil consumed and average daily temperature is significant, that is, that it is improbable that the relationship found could have resulted from chance errors of sampling only.

F Test: An Alternative Form

As the test just illustrated is based on a ratio (F), an alternative form based on the use of relative sums of squares rather than absolute sums of squares may at times be advantageous. The total sum of squares on a relative basis is taken as 100 percent; i.e., the total sum of squares is 100 percent of itself. The explained sum of squares on a relative basis is our sample r^2, here equal to 96.5 percent. The figure for the unexplained sum of squares is the difference between the other two, or 3.5 percent (100.0 - 96.5 = 3.5). The use of these figures to obtain F is illustrated in Table 15-3. Our new $F = 219.3$ differs only slightly from the previous $F = 218.5$ because of rounding. Here again, of course, we would reject the null hypothesis.

Table 15-3 Alternative variance table

Source of variation	Sums of squares	Degrees of freedom	Variance estimate	F
Total	100.0	9	. . .	. . .
Explained	96.5	1	96.5	(219.3)
Unexplained	3.5	8	(0.44)	. . .

Small-sample Estimation

Two changes from the estimation procedure illustrated earlier are needed for small samples. First the standard error of estimate must be adjusted for bias (compare with the discussion of estimating the standard error of the mean in Chap. 11), and second specific allowance must be made for sampling errors in using our sample regression line ($Y_e = a + bX$).

To adjust our sample standard error of estimate (s_{yx}) for bias, we must multiply it by a factor $\sqrt{n/(n-2)}$. We have, therefore,[1]

$$s'_{yx} \text{ (unbiased standard error of estimate)} = s_{yx} \sqrt{\frac{n}{n-2}}$$

For our illustration we get

$$s'_{yx} = s_{yx} \sqrt{\frac{n}{n-2}} = 1.25 \sqrt{\frac{10}{8}} = 1.25 \sqrt{1.25} = 1.25(1.12) = 1.40 \text{ gal/day}$$

Sampling error is allowed for by the use of the following formula for the standard error of the estimate of an individual Y ($\hat{\sigma}_{\hat{Y}}$):

$$\hat{\sigma}_{\hat{Y}} = s'_{yx} \sqrt{1 + \frac{1}{n} + \frac{(X - \overline{X})^2}{\Sigma x^2}}$$

The 1 under the radical serves to combine the unexplained variation with the sampling error in our overall estimate. The $1/n$ provides for any sampling error in the a term of our regression line which affects the height of our sample regression line. The $(X - \overline{X})^2/\Sigma x^2$ term allows for any sampling error in the b term which controls the slope of our sample regression line. The whole formula, therefore, combines in a single expression for estimating purposes both unexplained variation and sampling errors resulting from the use of our sample regression line. The X in the third term under the radical is the value of the independent variable used in making the particular estimate under question. $\Sigma x^2 = \Sigma(X - \overline{X})^2$ was computed earlier as part of our reductions.

We shall now recalculate our estimate of customer Jones' fuel-oil consumption when the temperature is $16°F$ ($X = 16$) using small-sample techniques. Again, we first have

$$Y_e = 33.45 - 0.77x$$

$$= 33.45 - 0.77(16)$$

$$= 21.13 \text{ gal}$$

---

[1]s'_{yx} could be obtained directly by dividing our unexplained sum of squares (Σy_s^2) by ($n - 2$), i.e., $s'_{yx} = \sqrt{\Sigma y_s^2/(n-2)}$. The $n - 2$ divisor represents $n - 2$ degrees of freedom and corresponds to the number of degrees of freedom used in calculating the unexplained variance estimates of Tables 15-2 and 15-3.

We shall now modify this point estimate using the standard error of the estimate of an individual Y.

$$\hat{\sigma}_{\hat{Y}} = s'_{yx} \sqrt{1 + \frac{1}{n} + \frac{(X - \bar{X})^2}{\Sigma x^2}}$$

For our data we get

$$\hat{\sigma}_{\hat{Y}} = 1.4 \sqrt{1 + \frac{1}{10} + \frac{(16 - 18.6)^2}{726.4}}$$

$$= 1.4 \sqrt{1 + 0.1 + \frac{(-2.6)^2}{726.4}}$$

$$= 1.4 \sqrt{1 + 0.1 + 0.01}$$

$$= 1.4 \sqrt{1.11} = 1.4(1.05) = 1.47 \text{ gal}$$

To estimate an individual value of the dependent variable $(\hat{Y})$, we use $\hat{Y} = Y_e \pm t\hat{\sigma}_{\hat{Y}}$. We need a t multiplier here rather than a normal curve multiplier (Z) because of our small sample. The appropriate degrees of freedom are $(n - 2)$, our divisor for the unbiased standard error of estimate. Substituting the values of our illustration and choosing a 95 percent probability level to determine a t value from App. D, we have

$$\hat{Y} = Y_e \pm t\hat{\sigma}_{\hat{Y}}$$

$$= 21.13 \pm 2.306(1.47)$$

$$= 21.13 \pm 3.39$$

$$= 17.74 \longrightarrow 24.52 \text{ gal/day}$$

Therefore, the probability is 95 percent that customer Jones will consume between 17.74 and 24.52 gal of fuel oil on a $16°$ day. The somewhat wider interval than previously found results from the proper allowance for bias and sampling error, both of which are critical in small samples. The earlier technique illustrated on page 234 might be characterized a "large-sample approximation" as both types of sampling error tend to zero as the sample size increases and the effect of the bias also becomes negligible in large samples. The t curve is also approximated by the normal curve for larger samples.

Other Sampling Problems

The techniques shown here for testing for the significance of correlation also serve to test for the significance of regression. This may be done separately by testing to see if the slope of the regression line differs significantly from zero (no regression). We need not do this, however, for if the correlation tests are significant, the regression will be significant also.

Additional techniques exist for constructing confidence intervals for r or r^2, but they will not be illustrated here.

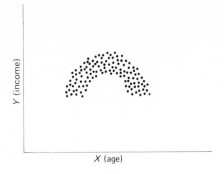

Figure 15-6 Scatter diagram of income and age.

A LIMITATION OF THE CHAPTER DISCUSSION

It would be well to remind the reader at this point that the techniques illustrated in this chapter are for linear patterns only. If they are applied blindly, they may lead to serious errors. Figure 15-6 illustrates an extreme example of this. The scatter diagram shows a definite relationship between the variables income and age, but it is curvilinear in character. A linear regression line fit to these data would be a horizontal one ($b = 0$), indicating incorrectly no regression or correlation. To avoid this error one must always begin by drawing a scatter diagram to see the pattern of the relationship before attempting to fit a line of a particular type.

Fortunately, many regressions turn out to be linear or at least linear in the ranges of interest. If they are not linear, they may often prove to be linear for some transformation of the variables (e.g., log Y vs. X or log Y vs. log X) and the techniques illustrated above may be applied to the transformed variables. Alternatively, techniques beyond the scope of our discussion do exist for fitting curvilinear regression lines.

CAUTIONS REGARDING CORRELATION IN GENERAL

Certain general cautions should be observed in applying or interpreting all correlation results, whether for linear or curvilinear or for simple or multiple correlations. The first concerns the use of the regression line in making estimates. Valid estimates can be made only when employing values of the independent variable (or variables in multiple regression; see Chap. 16) within the extremes observed for that variable when fitting the regression line. To do otherwise is to assume that the regression line maintains the same pattern outside the observed data as within the observed data. Although this is not impossible, it is obviously an incorrect assumption in many cases. For example, in our first illustrative problem, where the observed temperatures ranged from 3 to 32°F, extension of the line beyond 32°F leads to an estimate of -5.05 gal for a temperature of 50°F; but negative consumption is obviously impossible. Valid use of regression lines for making estimates is limited to those values of the independent variable lying within the range of the observed data.

A second caution is with regard to extreme values in the data, which may distort the results of the analysis. The regression line as an average possesses properties analogous to the arithmetic mean and, like the arithmetic mean, may be distorted by extreme values. These extremes are often most readily spotted on the scatter diagram. This is illustrated in Fig. 15-7a and b, where the extreme point is circled in both cases. In Fig. 15-7a the point will cause the regression line's slope to be shifted to that of the solid line rather than that of the dashed line, where it would be without the extreme point. In Fig. 15-7b the regression line is not distorted by the extreme value, but the r^2 would have a much higher value with the point than without it.

There is no clear-cut solution to the problem of the extreme value in correlation. The point may be eliminated, and the correlation done without it, if sufficient grounds can be presented to establish it as a heterogeneous item. However, it should be eliminated only for some specific reason, not simply because it is an extreme item. For example, one would feel free to eliminate one frame house from a study of the correlation of house size and value if all other houses in the study were brick. If no grounds can be presented for eliminating the point, it must be left in. Rank correlation (illustrated in Chap. 16) might then be used in place of ordinary correlation in determining the *amount* of correlation, since it would not be distorted by the extreme. However, rank correlation cannot be used as a device to eliminate distortion in the *pattern* of the regression.

For our final caution we shall consider the often misunderstood relationship between correlation and causation. Many are aware that the existence of a correlation between variables does not prove a causal relationship between these variables. From this they conclude that there is then no connection at all between correlation and causation. Assuming that the correlation is not the result of sampling error, this conclusion is obviously not correct, for the correlation must have been the result of some relation between the variables. The possible relationships may be divided into three categories: (1) cause and effect, (2) common cause, and (3) mutual cause. Variables that are related in an immediate cause-and-effect relationship most certainly will show correlation. An example would be the relationship between dividends paid and the price of railroad stocks. One factor very definitely affecting the price of a railroad stock is the dividends the railroad company pays. If data for these two variables were analyzed, they most certainly would show correlation. Less direct cause-and-effect relationships will also give rise to correlation. A positive correlation might well exist

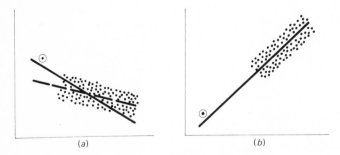

(a)   (b)

Figure 15-7 Extreme values which distort the correlation.

among workers between their number of weeks of employment on a job and their hourly production rate in that job. Additional weeks of employment, however, are not an immediate cause of increased production but operate through an intermediate factor of increasing skill. Both direct and indirect causal chains then give rise to correlations when the variables involved are so analyzed.

Many correlations observed between two variables may, upon further analysis, be found to be the result of a common variable affecting both. A drugstore might find a positive correlation between its fountain sales and its sales of bottled soft drinks. This should not be taken to mean that expanding the soda fountain will likewise expand the sales of bottled soft drinks; a more likely explanation lies in the effect of the common factor of weather on both. Hot weather would increase sales in both categories, while cold weather would cause sales to fall off. Partial correlation techniques would allow one to study the correlation between the two types of sales after both had been adjusted for weather effects.

Many correlations in economics and business result from a mutual-cause situation. This is the situation where the two variables interact with changes in one causing changes in the other, which, in turn, cause changes in the first variable, and so on. Price and production relationships may be of this type. Price influences volume of production, which in turn influences price.

The relationships alternative to pure cause and effect just discussed explain why one may not point to the existence of a correlation between variables as proof of a causal relationship between those variables. This does not mean that correlations should not be performed to test causal hypotheses. If one hypothesizes that X causes Y, one may test this by correlating values of X and Y. If one discovers a correlation, it merely supports, but does not prove, the hypothesis. Failure to discover a correlation, however, will most certainly discredit the hypothesis.

STUDY GUIDE

Concepts Worth Remembering

Define:

1. Regression analysis
2. Correlation analysis
3. Simple regression and/or correlation
4. Regression line
5. Scatter diagram
6. Standard error of estimate
7. Coefficient of determination
8. Method of least squares
9. Regression coefficient
10. Coefficient of correlation
11. Standard error of the estimate of an individual Y

Self-Test

Multiple-choice questions. Circle the letters of the statements which correctly complete the question. There may be one to four correct answers.

1 The coefficient of regression (b value):

(*a*) Equals one if there is perfect correlation.

(*b*) Measures the estimated change in the dependent variable for a unit change in the independent variable within the limits observed for the latter variable.

(*c*) Measures the dispersion of the points around the regression line.

(*d*) Cannot be negative.

2 A scatter diagram in a regression and correlation problem may be used to:

(*a*) Check the computation of the values for the regression line.

(*b*) Decide whether to eliminate an extreme value.

(*c*) Determine the pattern of the regression.

(*d*) Determine the degree of the correlation.

3 The regression line of a regression analysis:

(*a*) May be used to estimate values of the independent variable from values of the dependent variable.

(*b*) Is usually fit by the method of least squares.

(*c*) Shows the degree of correlation.

(*d*) Shows the pattern of the relationship between the dependent and independent variables.

4 An extreme item appearing on a scatter diagram:

(*a*) Will affect the b value only.

(*b*) Should be eliminated if it can be shown to be heterogenous.

(*c*) Is of importance to correlation analysis only.

(*d*) Will not distort the answer if rank correlation is used.

5 A correlation between X and Y found to be significant indicates:

(*a*) Y causes X.

(*b*) X causes Y.

(*c*) That both X and Y are caused by a common factor.

(*d*) That the relationship between X and Y is too strong to have been the result of chance.

6 The standard error of estimate is:

(*a*) Equal to one if there is perfect correlation.

(*b*) Used to measure the unexplained variation in a correlation problem.

(*c*) Used to qualify estimates made using the regression line.

(*d*) Equal to the standard deviation of the dependent variable if there is no correlation.

7 The coefficient of determination (r^2):

(*a*) Is the ratio of the unexplained variance to the total variance.

(*b*) Measures the variability of the points around the regression line.

(*c*) Equals one for perfect correlation and equals zero for no correlation.

(*d*) Takes the sign of the b value if not computed directly from the data.

8 Valid estimates may be made with the regression line:

(*a*) Only for X values within the limits of the original data.

(*b*) Only for Y values within the limits of the original data.

(*c*) Only if $r^2 > 0.8$.

(*d*) Only for values of the independent variable within the limits of the original data.

9 In testing for the significance of a simple correlation:

(*a*) The null hypothesis is that there is no correlation.

(*b*) The test ratio is the explained variance estimate divided by the unexplained variance estimate.

(*c*) There are $n - 2$ degrees of freedom for the unexplained variance.

(*d*) The explained degrees of freedom equal the number of independent variables.

10 In estimating the value of an individual $Y(\hat{Y})$:

(*a*) The first step is to estimate an average Y using the regression line.

(*b*) Allowance is made for both unexplained variation and sampling errors.

(*c*) The F distribution is used.

(*d*) The appropriate number of degrees of freedom to use is $n - 1$.

Questions to Think About

1. State the basic objectives of a regression and correlation analysis.
2. What are the three descriptive measures of a regression and correlation analysis? To what use may each measure be put?
3. What is a "scatter diagram"? Explain its importance to and uses in a regression analysis.
4. What are the inferential problems of a regression and correlation analysis, and how are they handled?
5. What general cautions must be observed regarding regression and correlation analysis? Discuss each in detail.

Problems

1 Use data from the accompanying table to do (a) to (f) below.

Estimated and actual shrinkage of 12 lots of fine Texas wool

Lot	Appraiser's estimate of percent shrinkage	Mill results: actual percent shrinkage
A	62.0	64.0
B	59.0	57.5
C	60.4	62.0
D	59.0	56.8
E	60.0	60.5
F	59.8	61.4
G	64.0	66.6
H	63.0	65.6
I	62.0	60.9
J	63.5	63.5
K	65.0	67.1
L	66.0	68.9

Source: U.S. Senate, Special Committee to Investigate the Production, Transportation, and Marketing of Wool, *Hearings*, part 6 (1945).

(a) Plot the following:
    (1) Scatter diagram.
    (2) Regression line.
    (3) Bands of ±2 standard errors of estimate.
(b) Compute:
    (1) Regression line.
    (2) Standard error of estimate.
    (3) Coefficient of determination.
(c) Interpret the following in terms of these data:
    (1) Regression coefficient.
    (2) Coefficient of determination.
(d) Estimate with 95 percent confidence the actual percentage of shrinkage for a lot with an appraiser's estimate of 61.0 percent shrinkage.
(e) Test at the 1 percent level whether there is significant correlation.
(f) Would you be willing to make an estimate of the actual percentage of shrinkage if the appraiser's estimate had been 57.0 percent? Why or why not?

2 The data in the accompanying table represent a random sample from the records of the sales department of a large manufacturing company.

Salesperson	Sales aptitude test score	First year's sales (thousands)
A	71	$167
B	52	108
C	38	82
D	49	92
E	32	84
F	74	190
G	44	109
H	66	151
I	32	84
J	76	154
K	59	149
L	66	136

(a) Plot the following:
    (1) Scatter diagram.
    (2) Regression line.
    (3) Bands of ±2 standard errors of estimate.
(b) Compute:
    (1) Regression line.
    (2) Standard error of estimate.
    (3) Coefficient of determination.
(c) Interpret the following in terms of these data:
    (1) Regression coefficient.
    (2) Coefficient of determination.
(d) Estimate with 99 percent confidence the dollar amount of first year's sales of a prospective salesperson who scored 57 on the aptitude test.
(e) Test at the 1 percent level whether there is significant correlation.

(f) Suppose that the original data contained another salesperson, M, who scored 36 on the aptitude test and had first year's sales of $140,000. Plot this salesperson's data on your scatter diagram. Discuss how you would handle the problem created by such a point.

3 The following table gives the annual dividend paid and the closing price on May 3, 1978, for a sample of railroad stocks:

Railroad	Dividend	Closing price
Burlington Northern	$1.60	$39
Canadian Pacific	0.95	16
Chessie	2.32	33
Illinois Central	1.52	24
Katy	0.00	9
Milwaukee	0.00	7
Missouri Pacific	2.10	50
Norfolk & Western	1.84	27
Rio Grande	0.80	24
St. Louis & San Francisco	2.50	41
Santa Fe	2.20	39
Southern	2.60	49
Southern Pacific	2.40	32
Union Pacific	2.00	49
Western Pacific	1.00	26

Source: The Wall Street Journal.

(a) Plot the following:
   (1) Scatter diagram.
   (2) Regression line.
   (3) Bands of ±2 standard errors of estimate.
(b) Compute:
   (1) Regression line.
   (2) Standard error of estimate.
   (3) Coefficient of determination.
(c) Interpret in terms of these data:
   (1) Regression coefficient.
   (2) Coefficient of determination.
(d) Estimate with 98 percent confidence the price of a railroad stock paying an annual dividend of $1.50.
(e) Test at the 1 percent level whether there is significant correlation.
(f) Since dividends do not completely explain the variations in price, what other independent variables might be added to the problem to help explain the price variations if the problem were changed to a multiple correlation problem?

Answers to Self-Test

1 (b); **2** (a), (c); **3** (b), (d); **4** (b), (d); **5** (d); **6** (b), (c), (d); **7** (c); **8** (a), (d); **9** (a), (b), (c), (d); **10** (a), (b).

SIXTEEN
MULTIPLE REGRESSION AND CORRELATION ANALYSIS

LEARNING OBJECTIVES

The basic learning objective is to expand our knowledge of regression and correlation analysis by studying the techniques of multiple and partial regression and correlation and of rank correlation. Specifically, you will study:

1. The following descriptive measures, their calculation, interpretation, and use.
   (a) Multiple regression line.
   (b) Multiple standard error of estimate.
   (c) Multiple coefficient of determination.
   (d) Partial coefficients of determination.
2. The testing of hypotheses for multiple and partial correlation.
3. The coefficient of rank correlation, its determination, and uses.

INTRODUCTION

We shall continue the discussion by turning our attention to regressions and correlations, including more than two variables, i.e., to what are termed "multiple" and "partial" regressions and correlations. In this type of analysis we still have only one dependent variable, but we add additional independent variables to improve both our ability to estimate that dependent variable and to explain more fully its variations. If we reconsider an earlier example from simple regression and correlation in which weight was the dependent variable and height the independent variable, we might well conclude that height alone gave us neither satisfactory estimates of weight nor sufficient explanation of its variability. To remedy these shortcomings we could add a second independent variable, e.g., age. The addition of this second independent variable changes our analysis into a multiple regression and correlation and should provide us with a basis for better estimates of weight (i.e., a better estimate of weight can be made when we know both a person's height and age than when we know only his height) and with a better explanation of the variability in weight as shown by a larger coefficient of determination. If additional independent variables can be obtained, even better estimates and explanations should be forthcoming.

Terms, Objectives, and Measures

In regression and correlation analysis the adjective "simple" was used to designate the two-variable (one dependent and one independent) case. The adjectives "multiple" and "partial" are used in the more-than-two-variable (one dependent and two or more independent) case. The term "multiple" is used when designating measures showing the relationship between the dependent variable and the independent variables taken as a group, e.g., when relating weight to *both* height and age. The term "partial" is used when designating measures showing the relationship between the dependent variable and any one independent variable when both have been adjusted for their relationship with all other independent variables in the problem, e.g., when relating weight to just height when both have been adjusted for age effects or when relating weight to age when both have been adjusted for height.

Our objectives in a multiple and partial analysis remain as before, i.e., (1) to determine the pattern, or functional nature, of the relationship and (2) to determine the closeness, or degree of relationship.

The descriptive measures of a multiple analysis are essentially those discussed and illustrated in Chap. 15 for a simple analysis. A multiple regression line (technically a plane) is computed to show the pattern of the relationship and to be used as an "estimating equation." A multiple standard error of estimate is determined to measure the closeness of the relationship in absolute terms and to serve in qualifying the estimates made from our multiple regression line. A multiple coefficient of determination is calculated to measure the relative closeness of the relationship, i.e., what portion of the total variation in the dependent variable may be explained by the independent variables as a group.

Only somewhat different descriptive measures are computed for the partial analysis. Partial coefficients of regression are automatically determined when computing the multiple regression line. These show the estimated change in the dependent variable for a unit change in a particular independent variable adjusted for and assuming no change in the other independent variables. For example, such a coefficient might show the estimated change in weight for a 1-in change in height if there were no change in age. In addition, partial coefficients of determination are computed to discover the value (gain in explanation) of adding additional independent variables to the problem. For example, one partial coefficient of determination might show the gain in explanation from adding our variable age to the previous correlation based on only weight and height. The number of partial coefficients in any given problem depends on the number of independent variables used in that problem.

As was the case previously, various sampling measures may be needed in addition to the descriptive measures outlined above.

A Digression on Symbols

In simple regression and correlation the dependent variable was designated by the letter Y and the independent variable by X.

The letter X is used for all variables in a multiple and partial analysis along with a system of numerical subscripts to identify a particular variable. The dependent variable is designated by the symbol X_1; the symbols $X_2, X_3, X_4, \ldots, X_P$ are used to represent the various independent variables.

Let us illustrate how this new system operates for a three-variable and a four-variable linear problem.

$$
\begin{array}{lll}
X_1 & \text{Dependent variable} & \text{Three-} \\
\left.\begin{array}{l} X_2 \\ X_3 \end{array}\right\} & \text{Independent variables} & \begin{array}{l}\text{variable} \\ \text{problem}\end{array}
\end{array}
$$

$$
\begin{array}{lll}
X_1 & \text{Dependent variable} & \text{Four-} \\
\left.\begin{array}{l} X_2 \\ X_3 \\ X_4 \end{array}\right\} & \text{Independent variables} & \begin{array}{l}\text{variable} \\ \text{problem}\end{array}
\end{array}
$$

Multiple regression line:

$$X_{e1.23} = a_{1.23} + b_{12.3}X_2 + b_{13.2}X_3$$

or

$$X_{e1.234} = a_{1.234} + b_{12.34}X_2 + b_{13.24}X_3 + b_{14.23}X_4$$

The subscript e in the X_1 symbol again indicates estimated values of the dependent variable, in contrast to the data values of X_1 used in determining the regression line. The numerals 2 and 3, or 2, 3, and 4, listed after the point identify the number and designation of the independent variables used in the analysis.

The b coefficients are partial (or net) coefficients of regression. The numerals before the point (termed "primary subscripts") identify the dependent variable and the particular independent variable with which the coefficient is associated. The numerals after the point (termed "secondary subscripts") list what additional independent variables have been used in the analysis. For example, the symbol $b_{13.24}$ shows that this is the partial coefficient relating the independent variable X_3 to the dependent variable X_1 in a problem involving two additional independent variables, X_2 and X_4.

The a constant carries a subscript similar to that of X_1, as it is a general constant associated with all variables.

$s_{1.23}$ or $s_{1.234}$ symbolizes the multiple standard error of estimate, depending on whether we have two independent variables (X_2 and X_3) or three (X_2, X_3, and X_4).

A capital R^2 is used for the multiple coefficient of determination. For the three-variable analysis we would have $R^2_{1.23}$, while the four-variable coefficient would be $R^2_{1.234}$.

The partial coefficients of determination use a small r^2 and a subscript system similar to that of the partial regression coefficients. For example, $r^2_{14.23}$ would indicate a partial coefficient measuring the relative gain in explanation in adding the variable X_4 to a problem which had previously used X_2 and X_3 to explain the variations in X_1.

Although the symbol system may seem a bit complex, it is quite straightforward and extends easily to additional variables. It may also be simplified somewhat within the context of a particular problem, as will be shown in our illustration below.

A THREE-VARIABLE LINEAR ILLUSTRATION

Multiple Methods

The mechanics of a multiple regression and correlation analysis are a straightforward extension of those previously illustrated for simple regression and correlation. Briefly, the steps followed earlier and to be repeated here are:

1. Draw scatter diagrams.
2. Compute table totals.
3. Reduce item totals to corresponding deviations totals.
4. Compute regression and correlation measures starting with the regression line and followed by the coefficient of determination and the standard error of estimate after partitioning the sum of squares.

For our illustration, consider the data of Table 16-1 where the variables are:

X_1	Final hospital bill in \$10s	Dependent variable
X_2	No. of days in the hospital	Independent variables
X_3	No. of special-procedure charges on the bill	

Table 16-1 Multiple correlation illustration

Item	X_1	X_2	X_3	X_1^2	$X_1 X_2$	$X_1 X_3$	X_2^2	$X_2 X_3$	X_3^2
A	32	3	2	1,024	96	64	9	6	4
B	18	2	4	324	36	72	4	8	16
C	50	5	2	2,500	250	100	25	10	4
D	6	1	5	36	6	30	1	5	25
E	42	4	3	1,764	168	126	16	12	9
F	48	6	9	2,304	288	432	36	54	81
G	80	9	8	6,400	720	640	81	72	64
H	35	3	7	1,225	105	245	9	21	49
I	52	5	2	2,704	260	104	25	10	4
J	68	7	4	4,624	476	272	49	28	16
	431	45	46	22,905	2,405	2,085	255	226	272

First, we draw scatter diagrams of the dependent variable with each of our independent variables. We then have the two graphs of Fig. 16-1 a and b showing the pattern of X_1 vs. X_2 and of X_1 vs. X_3. Our purpose here, as earlier, is to determine if our relationships are linear ones. (We will again limit our illustration to linear techniques only.)

As neither figure shows a curvilinear pattern, we shall proceed to our second step, which is to compute the values for the additional columns of Table 16-1 (i.e., the columns headed X_1^2, $X_1 X_2$, $X_1 X_3$, X_2^2, $X_2 X_3$, and X_3^2) and to total all nine columns.

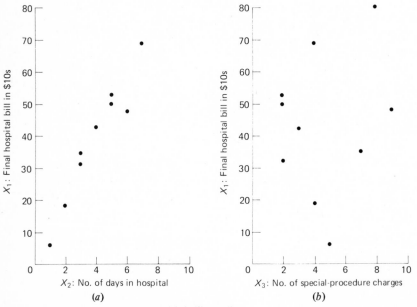

Figure 16-1 Scatter diagrams for multiple illustration.

The third step is to reduce column, or item, totals to the corresponding deviation totals. As earlier, the deviations are those from the respective arithmetic means of the X_1, X_2, and X_3 variables, i.e., $\overline{X}_1$, $\overline{X}_2$, and $\overline{X}_3$. These deviation totals are most efficiently derived from the following relationships, which are those used previously except for the obvious need to change the symbols (letters) used. These may be written in general as:

$$\Sigma x_i^2 = \Sigma X_i^2 - \frac{(\Sigma X_i)^2}{n} \qquad i = 1, 2, \text{ or } 3$$

and

$$\Sigma x_i x_j = \Sigma X_i X_j - \frac{\Sigma X_i \, \Sigma X_j}{n} \qquad \begin{array}{l} i \neq j \\ i = 1, 2, \text{ or } 3 \\ j = 1, 2, \text{ or } 3 \end{array}$$

For our data, we obtain

$$\Sigma x_1^2 = \Sigma X_1^2 - \frac{(\Sigma X_1)^2}{n} = 22{,}905 - \frac{(431)(431)}{10} = 22{,}905 - 18{,}576.1 = 4{,}328.9$$

$$\Sigma x_2^2 = \Sigma X_2^2 - \frac{(\Sigma X_2)^2}{n} = 255 - \frac{45(45)}{10} = 255 - 202.5 = 52.5$$

$$\Sigma x_3^2 = \Sigma X_3^2 - \frac{(\Sigma X_3)^2}{n} = 272 - \frac{46(46)}{10} = 272 - 211.6 = 60.4$$

$$\Sigma x_1 x_2 = \Sigma X_1 X_2 - \frac{\Sigma X_1 \, \Sigma X_2}{n} = 2{,}405 - \frac{431(45)}{10} = 2{,}405 - 1{,}939.5 = 465.5$$

$$\Sigma x_1 x_3 = \Sigma X_1 X_3 - \frac{\Sigma X_1 \, \Sigma X_3}{n} = 2{,}085 - \frac{431(46)}{10} = 2{,}085 - 1{,}982.6 = 102.4$$

$$\Sigma x_2 x_3 = \Sigma X_2 X_3 - \frac{\Sigma X_2 \, \Sigma X_3}{n} = 226 - \frac{45(46)}{10} = 226 - 207 = 19$$

The first three results must again be positive, as they represent sums of squares. The latter three may be positive or negative, depending on the relationship between the variables in question.

The fourth step is the actual computation of the regression and correlation measures, starting as before with the regression line. The form of our line will be[1]

$$X_{e1} = a + b_2 X_2 + b_3 X_3$$

Our specific mechanical problem here is to solve numerically for values for a, b_2, and b_3. Solution equations are

$$\Sigma x_1 x_2 = b_2 \, \Sigma x_2^2 + b_3 \, \Sigma x_2 x_3$$

[1] As suggested above, we may simplify our symbol subscripts within the context of an actual problem, e.g., b_2 for $b_{12.3}$ and b_3 for $b_{13.2}$.

and

$$\Sigma x_1 x_3 = b_2 \Sigma x_2 x_3 + b_3 \Sigma x_3^2$$

which are solved simultaneously for b_2 and b_3.[1] Then,

$$a = \overline{X}_1 - b_2 \overline{X}_2 - b_3 \overline{X}_3$$

which may be solved for a after the b_2 and b_3 values have been obtained.

Substituting our deviations totals, we have

$$465.5 = 52.5b_2 + 19.0b_3 \tag{1}$$

$$102.4 = 19.0b_2 + 60.4b_3 \tag{2}$$

Multiplying (2) by 2.7632, which equals 52.5/19.0, we get

$$465.5 = 52.5b_2 + 19.0b_3 \tag{1}$$

$$283.0 = 52.5b_2 + 166.9b_3 \tag{2}$$

Subtracting (2) from (1)

$$182.5 = -147.9b_3 \quad \text{and} \quad b_3 = \frac{182.5}{-147.9} = -1.23$$

Substituting this value back in (2),

$$102.4 = 19.0b_2 + 60.4(-1.23)$$

$$102.4 = 19.0b_2 - 74.3$$

$$19.0b_2 = 176.7$$

$$b_2 = \frac{176.7}{19.0} = 9.30$$

Using both b values and the values of our means in our a equation,

$$a = 43.1 - 9.30(4.5) - (-1.23)\,4.6$$

$$= 43.3 - 41.8 + 5.7 = 7.0$$

Our multiple regression line is

$$X_{e1} = 7.0 + 9.3X_2 - 1.2X_3$$

We next proceed to partition the sum of squares (SS) for the dependent variable (X_1) in order to be able to compute our multiple coefficient of determination and multiple standard error of estimate.

---

[1] Technically, least squares procedures involve solving simultaneously as many equations as there are constants in the regression equation. The use of deviation totals rather than items totals reduces the order of the solution by one. Here we need solve only two equations instead of three and earlier one instead of two.

Our total sum of squares is already available as part of our reductions.

$$\text{Total SS} = \Sigma x_1^2 = 4{,}328.9$$

The explained sum of squares may be computed from the following:

$$\text{Explained SS} = \Sigma x_{e1}^2 = b_2 \, \Sigma x_1 x_2 + b_3 \, \Sigma x_1 x_3$$

Substituting our values, we have

$$\text{Explained SS} = \Sigma x_{e1}^2 = 9.3(465.5) + (-1.23)\,102.4$$

$$4{,}329.2 - 126.0 = 4{,}203.2$$

The unexplained sum of squares is again obtained as a residual.

$$\text{Unexplained SS} = \text{total SS} - \text{explained SS}$$

$$= \Sigma x_1^2 - \Sigma x_{e1}^2 = \Sigma x_{s1}^2$$

Substituting we get,

$$\text{Unexplained SS} = \Sigma x_{s1}^2 = 4{,}328.9 - 4{,}203.2 = 125.7$$

As in simple correlation, the coefficient of determination, here symbolized by $R_{1.23}^2$ or just R^2, is the ratio of the explained sum of squares to the total sum of squares. For our data we have

$$R_{1.23}^2 = \frac{\Sigma x_{e1}^2}{\Sigma x_1^2} = \frac{4{,}203.2}{4{,}328.9} = 0.971 = 97.1\%$$

The multiple standard error of estimate $(s_{1.23})$, like the simple standard error of estimate $(s_{y.x})$, is derived from the unexplained sum of squares.

$$s_{1.23} = \sqrt{\frac{\Sigma x_{s1}^2}{n}} = \sqrt{\frac{125.7}{10}} = \sqrt{12.57} = 3.55 \; (\$10\text{s})$$

An unbiased estimate of the universe standard error of estimate would be

$$s'_{1.23} = \sqrt{\frac{\Sigma x_{s1}^2}{n-3}} = \sqrt{\frac{125.7}{7}} = \sqrt{17.96} = 4.24 \; (\$10\text{s})$$

Note that the addition of the second independent variable has cost us another degree of freedom and that we now have $n-3$ degrees of freedom for the unexplained variance.

It is worth reemphasizing that the mechanics illustrated above for the multiple measures represent a straightforward extension of those illustrated earlier for simple regression and correlation.

Illustration Continued: Partial Correlation

Partial coefficients of regression were computed automatically in determining the multiple regression line. Additional computations are needed to find the partial coefficients of determination. (In our three-variable illustration there will be two partial coefficients symbolized as $r^2_{12.3}$ and $r^2_{13.2}$).

Several ways exist for calculating the partial coefficients, but one straightforward and relatively simple approach begins with determining simple coefficients of determination from the following expression:

$$r^2_{ij} = \frac{(\Sigma x_i x_j)^2}{\Sigma x_i^2 \; \Sigma x_j^2} \qquad i \neq j$$

For our data and making use of deviation totals derived earlier for the computation of the multiple regression line, we have

$$r^2_{12} = \frac{(\Sigma x_1 x_2)^2}{\Sigma x_1^2 \; \Sigma x_2^2} = \frac{(465.5)^2}{4,328.9(52.5)} = \frac{216,690.25}{227,267.25} = 0.953$$

$$r^2_{13} = \frac{(\Sigma x_1 x_3)^2}{\Sigma x_1^2 \; \Sigma x_3^2} = \frac{(102.4)^2}{4,328.9(60.4)} = \frac{10,485.76}{261,465.56} = 0.040$$

$$r^2_{23} = \frac{(\Sigma x_2 x_3)^2}{\Sigma x_2^2 \; \Sigma x_3^2} = \frac{(19.0)^2}{52.5(60.4)} = \frac{361.00}{3,171.00} = 0.114^1$$

Our two partial coefficients of determination can now be computed from the following relationships:

$$r^2_{12.3} = \frac{R^2_{1.23} - r^2_{13}}{1 - r^2_{13}} \qquad \text{and} \qquad r^2_{13.2} = \frac{R^2_{1.23} - r^2_{12}}{1 - r^2_{12}}$$

In our illustration we get

$$r^2_{12.3} = \frac{R^2_{1.23} - r^2_{13}}{1 - r^2_{13}} = \frac{0.971 - 0.040}{1 - 0.040} = \frac{0.931}{0.960} = 0.970 = 97.0\%$$

$$r^2_{13.2} = \frac{R^2_{1.23} - r^2_{12}}{1 - r^2_{12}} = \frac{0.971 - 0.953}{1 - 0.953} = \frac{0.018}{0.047} = 0.383 = 38.3\%$$

This completes the computation of descriptive measures for our illustration.

INTERPRETATION AND USE

Multiple Regression Line and Standard Error of Estimate

The b values of our multiple regression line are partial coefficients of regression, and as such, each tells only part of the story. However, they are slope values and can be interpreted in a fashion similar to the regression coefficient of a simple problem. Our

---

[1] r^2_{23} is not actually needed to calculate the partial coefficients of determination, but is useful in interpreting the results, as it shows the degree of overlap (duplication) between the independent variables.

b values were:

$$b_2 = b_{12.3} = 9.30 \ (\$10s) = \$93.00$$

$$b_3 = b_{13.2} = -1.23 \ (\$10s) = -\$12.30$$

The first value $(b_{12.3})$ tells us that the final hospital bill (X_1) increases an estimated $93 for each additional day spent in the hospital (X_2) if the number of special procedure charges on the bill remains constant. This relationship applies only in the observed range of one to nine days.

The second value $(b_{13.2})$ tells us that the final hospital bill (X_1) actually decreases an estimated $12.30 for each additional special procedure charge (X_3) if the number of days spent in the hospital (X_2) remains constant. The applicable range of the relationship here is two to nine such charges. The somewhat surprising negative relationship shown here is of a type often encountered in partial regression. The simple regression between X_1 and X_3 is positive, as shown by the fact that $\Sigma x_1 x_3$ was positive. However, we are now dealing with a relationship between X_1 and X_3 after both have been adjusted for their relationship with X_2, i.e., a partial relationship. When the effect of the number of days in the hospital (X_2) has been allowed for in both the final bill (X_1) and the number of special charges (X_3), the latter two variables now show a negative relationship.

The multiple regression equation in its entirety may once more be used to make estimates. This time these would be of the dependent variable from given values of both independent variables. For example, if one wished to estimate the final bill of a patient staying in the hospital 8 days (X_2) and requiring four special procedure charges (X_3), we would have

$$X_{e1} = 7.0 + 9.3X_2 - 1.2X_3$$

$$= 7.0 + 9.3(8) - 1.2(4)$$

$$= 7.0 + 74.4 - 4.8 = 76.7 \ (\$10s) = \$767$$

The multiple standard error of estimate may be used to qualify the estimate for the effect of variables, not specifically included in our analysis. Using our unbiased estimate of the standard error $[s'_{1.23} = 4.24 \ (\$10s)]$, assuming normality, and not properly allowing for the sampling error of our small sample, we could qualify our estimate as follows:

$$\hat{X}_1 = X_{e1} \pm Zs'_{1.23}$$

$$= 76.7 \pm 2(4.24)$$

$$= 76.7 \pm 8.5$$

$$= 68.1 \rightarrow 85.1 \ (\$10s) = \$681 \rightarrow \$851$$

The probability is $95\frac{1}{2}$ percent that the patient's bill would be between $681 and $851. Such an estimate would be useful to an insurance company in setting its premiums.

Multiple Coefficient of Determination

The multiple coefficient of determination $(R_{1.23}^2)$ measures the overall closeness of the relationship in relative terms, and thereby our success in explaining the variations in the dependent variable by correlating it with *both* independent variables. As in simple correlation, it was computed as the ratio of the explained sum of squares to the total sum of squares.

In our illustration, $R_{1.23}^2 = 0.971$. This tells us that 97.1 percent of the variance in the final hospital bill (X_1) is explained by the two variables, number of days in the hospital (X_2) and the number of special procedure charges on the bill (X_3). This is a good correlation as the largest R^2 we could obtain is still 100 percent.

Partial Coefficients of Determination

The interpretation of the partial coefficients of determination follows directly from the formulas used for their calculation. These were:

$$r_{12.3}^2 = \frac{R_{1.23}^2 - r_{13}^2}{1 - r_{13}^2} = \frac{0.971 - 0.040}{1 - 0.040} = \frac{0.931}{0.960} = 0.970$$

and

$$r_{13.2}^2 = \frac{R_{1.23}^2 - r_{12}^2}{1 - r_{12}^2} = \frac{0.971 - 0.953}{1 - 0.953} = \frac{0.018}{0.047} = 0.383$$

The denominators in both cases tell us the portion of the total variance in X_1 that remains unexplained after the computation of a simple correlation between the dependent variable (X_1) and either of the independent variables $(X_2$ or $X_3)$. $r_{13}^2 = 0.040$ indicates that only 4 percent of the variance in X_1 is explained by X_3. $1 - r_{13}^2 = 1 - 0.040 = 0.960$ tells us then that 96 percent of the variance in X_1 was not explained by X_3 and, therefore, could possibly be explained by the addition of further independent variables. Similarly, $r_{12}^2 = 0.953$ tells us that 95.3 percent of the X_1 variance is explained by X_2. Hence, only 4.7 percent $(1 - 0.953 = 0.047)$ remains unexplained in the second case to be possibly explained by the addition of another independent variable. These denominators, although different in value, give the only fair basis for determining the value of adding an additional independent variable (going from a simple correlation to a multiple correlation), as a second independent variable can explain no more of the variance in the dependent variable than remains unexplained after correlation with the first independent variable.

Both numerators show the increase in total explanation that takes place in changing from the simple correlation to the multiple correlation. In the first case $R_{1.23}^2 - r_{13}^2 = 0.971 - 0.040 = 0.931$ shows that the use of X_2 as well as the previously used X_3 increases our explanation of the total variance from 4 percent to 97.1 percent, or by 93.1 percent. In the second case, $R_{1.23}^2 - r_{12}^2 = 0.971 - 0.953 = 0.018$ shows us that using X_3 in addition to X_2 increases our explanation from 95.3 percent to 97.1 percent, or by 1.8 percent.

A direct comparision of our first increase of 93.1 percent to our second increase of only 1.8 percent would be unfair, however, as the portion remaining unexplained after the simple correlations was quite different in both cases (96 percent in the first case, as against 4.7 percent in the second case.)

The partial coefficients are designed to show the true value of an additional independent variable as they give the ratio of the *actual* increase in the total explanation to the *possible* increase in that explanation (i.e., to the portion of the total variance left unexplained after the correlation with the first independent variable). $r^2_{12.3} = 0.931/0.960 = 0.970$ indicates that the use of X_2 as well as X_3 explains 97 percent of what X_3 when used alone failed to explain. In contrast, $r^2_{13.2} = 0.018/0.047 = 0.383$ tells us that the use of X_3 in addition to X_2 explains 38.3 percent of what was unexplained when using only X_2. The partials show us our gain in explanation from adding an additional independent variable as a percentage of the total possible gain.

Interpreting our partials in terms of the actual variables of our illustration, we find first that the use of the independent variable number of days in the hospital (X_2) explains 97 percent of what remained unexplained when we correlated the dependent variable hospital bill (X_1) with the independent variable number of special charges on the bill (X_3). In contrast, the use of the independent variable number of special charges (X_3), in addition to the independent variable number of days in the hospital (X_2), explains 38.3 percent of what was unexplained by the simple correlation of the dependent variable final hospital bill (X_1) with the number of days in the hospital (X_2). Like other coefficients of determination, the partial coefficients of determination can range from 0 to 1 (or 0 percent to 100 percent). The first partial of 97 percent obviously indicates there is a major gain in explanation in adding the X_2 variable to a problem previously correlating X_1 with X_3 while the second partial of 38.3 percent indicates that there is a lesser gain in adding X_3 to a problem originally correlating X_1 with X_2.

In summary, the value and use of the partial coefficients of determination is in measuring the gains made in adding additional independent variables in a correlation analysis.

STATISTICAL INFERENCE IN MULTIPLE AND PARTIAL CORRELATION

Introduction

For multiple and partial correlation, we shall illustrate only the extension of analysis of variance techniques to test hypotheses concerning the multiple and partial coefficients of determination and shall omit illustrating small-sample estimation procedures. Large-scale approximate estimating methods were illustrated above in the section "Interpretation and Use."

Illustration: Multiple Coefficient of Determination

A simple extension of the analysis of variance techniques and F test used in testing the hypothesis of no correlation for simple correlation (see Chap. 15) may be used to perform the same test for multiple correlation. As before, our null and alternative

Table 16-2 Analysis of variance table for multiple correlation

Sources of variation	Sums of squares	Degrees of freedom	Variance estimate	F
Total	100.0	9		
Explained (X_2 and X_3)	97.1	2	48.55	118.4
Unexplained	2.9	7	0.41	

hypotheses are:

$$H_0: \quad \rho^2_{1.23} = 0$$

$$H_1: \quad \rho^2_{1.23} \neq 0$$

The null hypothesis says, in effect, that no correlation existed in the universe from which our sample was drawn, attributing our sample result ($R^2_{1.23} = 97.1$ percent) to chance errors of sampling. The alternative hypothesis merely specifies that if we reject the null hypothesis of no correlation, we must assume that some correlation exists. We shall test at the 1 percent level ($\alpha = 0.01$).

Mechanics of the test are contained in Table 16-2, where we find the use of the relative sums of squares more convenient than using their absolute values.

The total degrees of freedom (df) still equals ($n - 1$), so we have ($10 - 1$) = 9 df total. The explained degrees of freedom is once again the number of independent variables. As indicated in the table, we have two independent variables (X_2 and X_3); hence, we have 2 df for the calculation of the explained variance estimate. Unexplained degrees of freedom are once again the difference between the other values, so we have $9 - 2 = 7$ df for unexplained variance estimate. Our variance estimates are the respective sums of squares divided by the appropriate df's. As previously:

$$F = \frac{\text{Explained variance estimate}}{\text{Unexplained variance estimate}}$$

or

$$F = \frac{48.55}{0.41} = 118.4$$

Consulting the 1 percent table of App. E for 2 and 7 df's, we find the critical value of $F(F')$ to be $F' = 9.55$. As our $F = 118.4$ is much greater than $F' = 9.55$, we reject our null hypothesis and conclude that significant correlation exists between the dependent variable (X_1), the final hospital bill, and both independent variables (X_2 and X_3), the number of days in the hospital and the number of special procedure charges on the bill.

Illustration: Partial Coefficients of Determination

The procedures for testing the no-correlation hypothesis for our two partial coefficients are an expansion of the test just shown. These are illustrated in Tables 16-3 and 16-4.

Table 16-3 Analysis of variance table for partial correlation ($r_{12.3}^2$)

Source of variation	Sums of squares	Degrees of freedom	Variance estimates	F
Total	100.0	9		
Explained (X_2 and X_3)	97.1	2		
Explained (X_3)	4.0	1		
Increase (X_2)	93.1	1	93.10	227.1
Unexplained	2.9	7	0.41	

H_0: $\rho_{12.3}^2 = 0$ $F' = 12.25$ for 1 and 7 df's

H_1: $\rho_{12.3}^2 \neq 0$ $F > F'$ Reject H_0

$\alpha = 0.01$

Table 16-4 Analysis of variance table for partial correlation ($r_{13.2}^2$)

Source of variation	Sums of squares	Degrees of freedom	Variance estimates	F
Total	100.0	9		
Explained (X_2 and X_3)	97.1	2		
Explained (X_2)	95.3	1		
Increase (X_3)	1.8	1	1.80	4.39
Unexplained	2.9	7	0.41	

H_0: $\rho_{13.2}^2 = 0$ $F' = 12.25$ for 1 and 7 df's

H_1: $\rho_{13.2}^2 \neq 0$ $F < F'$ Accept H_0

$\alpha = 0.01$

Rows 1, 2, and 5 of both tables are those of Table 16-2 for testing the multiple coefficient. The sum of squares in row 3 is the simple coefficient of determination (r_{13}^2 or r_{12}^2) for the independent variable used as the prior variable in the computation of the particular partial. The sum of squares in row 4 (labeled "increase") is the numerator previously calculated for the partial coefficient in question (i.e., the difference between the multiple coefficient and the specified simple coefficient). The degrees of freedom in both rows 3 and 4 are one, as they represent the allocation of the two degrees of freedom for row 2 to their respective independent variables. F is defined as:

$$F = \frac{\text{Increase variance estimate}}{\text{Unexplained variance estimate}}$$

and has been computed in both tables.

For Table 16-3 we find our computed $F = 227.1$ greater than the critical $F' = 12.25$, so we reject the null hypothesis. We thereby conclude there is a significant increase in correlation (explanation) by adding the independent variable X_2, number of days in the hospital, to an analysis previously correlating the dependent variable X_1, final hospital bill, with the independent variable X_3, number of special procedure charges.

In contrast in Table 16-4, we find that our $F = 4.39$ is less than the critical $F' = 12.25$ and accept our null hypothesis. We, therefore, must conclude that there is no significant increase (i.e., no increase greater than may be attributed to sampling error) in correlation obtained by adding the independent variable X_3, number of special procedure charges, to the simple correlation between final hospital bill (X_1) and number of days in the hospital (X_2).

A REMINDER

The reader is reminded to refer back to the sections of Chap. 15 entitled *A Limitation* and *Cautions*, as both apply to multiple regression and correlation as much as to simple regression and correlation.

RANK CORRELATION: INTRODUCTION

We shall conclude this chapter with a discussion of rank correlation. As indicated previously, this technique can be used only to measure the (relative) closeness of the relationship. This is because, as the name implies, we correlate the data in the form of rankings only. These rankings may be the natural form of the data, or they may be the ranked form of some measured data. In the former case, only rank correlation can be employed, since we have the data only in the form of the rankings. In the latter case, least squares techniques could possibly be employed, using the original observations.

Rank Correlation: Illustrations

We shall use r' as a symbol for the coefficient of rank correlation. The formula for the coefficient of rank correlation is

$$r' = 1 - \frac{6\Sigma D^2}{n(n^2 - 1)}$$

where n, as usual, refers to the number of items, and D symbolizes the differences between the rankings of the items. The application of the formula is illustrated in Table 16-5 for data whose natural form was rankings. The data represent the rankings of the abilities of 10 employees by their immediate supervisors. The problem is to correlate the rankings to determine the consistency of the supervisor's ratings. Our $r' = 0.85$ indicates a reasonably high degree of consistency, since the maximum value is 1. The coefficient of rank correlation has possible values like the least squares coefficient of correlation; i.e., it ranges from -1 for perfect negative correlation, through 0 for no correlation, to $+1$ for perfect positive correlation.

Table 16-5 Rankings of ten employees by two supervisors

Employee	Supervisor 1's ranking	Supervisor 2's ranking	D	D^2
A	2	3	−1	1
B	1	2	−1	1
C	3	1	2	4
D	4	4	0	0
E	6	6	0	0
F	5	7	−2	4
G	8	5	3	9
H	7	9	−2	4
I	10	10	0	0
J	9	8	1	1
Total	...	...	0	24

$$r' = 1 - \frac{6\,\Sigma D^2}{n(n^2 - 1)} = 1 - \frac{6(24)}{10(100 - 1)} = 1 - 0.15 = 0.85$$

The computation of the coefficient of rank correlation for measured data is illustrated in Table 16-6. Two variations from our previous illustration are worth noting. The first is that, since the data do not come naturally as rankings, the first step in our procedure is to rank them. This is usually done on a small-to-large basis. The second is the handling of the tie in the traffic-flow index rankings. It is conventional to assign the average of the tied ranks to both, e.g., $(4 + 5)/2 = 4.5$. Our result, $r' = 0.97$, indicates a very high degree of rank correlation between traffic flow and site cost.

Table 16-6 Rank correlation of service-station site cost and traffic–flow index

Site	Traffic-flow index (X)	Site cost (Y)	Ranking		D	D^2
			X	Y		
1	100	$10,000	1	1	0	0
2	110	11,500	2	2	0	0
3	119	12,000	3	3	0	0
4	123	14,000	4.5	5	−0.5	0.25
5	123	13,500	4.5	4	0.5	0.25
6	127	17,500	6	6	0	0
7	130	21,000	7	8	−1	1.00
8	132	20,000	8	7	1	1.00
Total	...	...	...	...	0	2.50

$$r' = 1 - \frac{6\,\Sigma D^2}{n(n^2 - 1)} = 1 - \frac{6(2.5)}{8(64 - 1)} = 1 - 0.03 = 0.97$$

Uses of Rank Correlation

The basic use of rank correlation is with ordered data, i.e., with data for which the items have been assigned an order of merit without being given a numerical measure of worth. For such data least squares correlation cannot be applied. The ordering (ranking) of the data may result from a lack of time, money, instruments, or adequate units for measurement.

Rank correlation is sometimes used as a preliminary device before undertaking a least squares correlation. A good estimate is gained of the value to be expected for r if the data are linear and free of extreme values.

Rank correlation may be used where large departures from normality exist in one of the variables (fairly common in economics and business) since the formal correlation model assumes normality of the variables. The use of rank correlation involves no such assumption.

Finally, rank correlation may be used to give a better picture of the correct amount of correlation in a problem involving an extreme item which cannot be eliminated as being heterogeneous.

STUDY GUIDE

Concepts Worth Remembering

Define:
1. Multiple regression and/or correlation
2. Partial regression and/or correlation
3. Multiple regression line
4. Multiple standard error of estimate
5. Multiple coefficient of determination
6. Partial regression coefficient
7. Partial coefficient of determination
8. Rank correlation
9. Coefficient of rank correlation

Self-Test

Circle the proper letter to indicate whether the following statements are true or false.

T F 1 Multiple regression analysis uses a free-hand fitting procedure because of the large number of variables involved.

T F 2 Multiple regression analysis cannot be performed for other than linear relationships.

T F 3 There is one dependent and several independent variables in a multiple regression and correlation analysis.

T F 4 In a multiple regression and correlation analysis, the same descriptive measures are used as for a simple analysis.

T F **5** The multiple coefficient of determination ($R^2_{1.23}$) is equal to the sum of the two partial coefficients of determination ($r^2_{12.3}$ and $r^2_{13.2}$).

T F **6** The partial coefficient of determination ($r^2_{13.2}$) gives the portion of the variance in X_1 not explained by X_2 which can be explained by the introduction of X_3.

T F **7** The partial coefficient of determination ($r^2_{12.3}$) is a measure of the correlation between X_1 and X_2 when both have been adjusted for their regression with X_3.

T F **8** The partial regression coefficient ($b_{12.3}$) is the coefficient of the X_3 value in a multiple regression equation.

T F **9** In testing the null hypothesis for $R^2_{1.23}$ the explained variance estimate has 2 degrees of freedom.

T F **10** In testing the null hypothesis for $r^2_{12.3}$ the F-test ratio is the ratio of the explained variance estimate to the unexplained variance estimate.

T F **11** Values of the coefficient of rank correlation range from −1 to +1.

T F **12** The basic use of rank correlation is with ordered data, i.e., with data for which the items have been assigned an order of merit without being given a numerical measure of worth.

T F **13** Rank correlation may be used to determine the pattern of the relationship in a problem containing an extreme value.

Questions to Think About

1. Explain the similarities and the differences between a simple and a multiple regression and correlation analysis.
2. Explain the nature and use of the partial coefficients of determination.
3. Discuss the nature of rank correlation and its uses.

Problems

1 The following data are a random sample from a McGraw-Hill catalog:

Textbook	Price (X_1)	Number of pages (X_2)	Years since copyright (X_3)
A	$15.00	480	2
B	14.50	679	11
C	12.50	322	4
D	14.95	758	7
E	13.95	608	1
F	12.50	304	2
G	13.50	288	7
H	13.50	450	5
I	16.50	710	1
J	13.50	435	3

(a) Plot:
   (1) X_1 vs. X_2.
   (2) X_1 vs. X_3.
(b) Compute:
   (1) Multiple regression line.
   (2) Multiple standard error of estimate.
   (3) Multiple coefficient of determination.
   (4) Partial coefficients of determination.
(c) Interpret in terms of these data:
   (1) Partial regression coefficients.
   (2) Multiple coefficient of determination.
   (3) Partial coefficients of determination.
(d) Estimate (large-sample approximation) with $95\frac{1}{2}$ percent certainty the price of a 2-year-old book of 400 pages.
(e) Test for significance at the 1 percent level:
   (1) Multiple coefficient of determination.
   (2) Partial coefficients of determination.
(f) What other independent variables might be added to this problem to improve the correlation?

2 The following table gives data for a random sample of the sales territories of a large national baking company.

Territory	Weekly sales (thousands)	Total number of stops	Number of salespersons
1	11.0	105	5
2	16.4	205	8
3	14.5	187	7
4	10.4	132	4
5	7.6	95	4
6	12.8	111	6
7	14.7	166	9
8	18.0	214	12
9	14.2	78	3
10	16.1	150	7
11	17.7	142	8
12	22.4	211	11

Source: Company records.

(a) Plot:
   (1) X_1 vs. X_2.
   (2) X_1 vs. X_3.
(b) Compute:
   (1) Multiple regression line.
   (2) Multiple standard error of estimate.
   (3) Multiple coefficient of determination.
   (4) Partial coefficients of determination.

(c) Interpret in terms of these data:
  (1) Partial regression coefficients.
  (2) Multiple coefficient of determination.
  (3) Partial coefficients of determination.
(d) Estimate (large sample approximation) with 99% certainty the weekly sales of a territory with 200 stops and 10 salespersons.
(e) Of what use might this analysis be to the company?

3 Compute the coefficient of rank correlation for the data of Prob. 1, Study Guide of Chap. 15. Of what use is this measure in a problem of this type?

4 The table below gives the rankings of the students in a statistics class on their first two hourly exams. Use rank correlation techniques to determine the consistency of the students' performances on the two exams. How does your use of rank correlation for this problem differ from that of Prob. 3?

Student rankings on first two hourly exams, Economics 70

Student	First exam rank	Second exam rank
A	6	1
B	17	9
C	9	15
D	4	3
E	11	5
F	14	10
G	18	16
H	10	14
I	16	17
J	15	6
K	8	13
L	7	4
M	5	11
N	13	18
O	2	2
P	12	7
Q	1	8
R	3	12

Answers to Self-Test

1 F; **2** F; **3** T; **4** T; **5** F; **6** T; **7** T; **8** F; **9** T; **10** F; **11** T; **12** T; **13** F.

FIVE

THE ANALYSIS OF DATA CLASSIFIED THROUGH TIME

SEVENTEEN
TREND ANALYSIS

LEARNING OBJECTIVES

The basic learning objective is to study the methods of measuring the patterns of long-term growth (trend) in time series data. Specifically, you will learn about:

1. The classical time series model of trend, cycle, seasonal, and irregular.
2. Semilogarithmic graph paper.
3. The purposes for fitting trend lines.
4. The methods of fitting trend lines.
5. The following types of trend lines:
    (*a*) Straight lines: arithmetic and logarithmic.
    (*b*) Parabolas: arithmetic and logarithmic.
    (*c*) Growth curves: Gompertz and logistic.
6. Measuring rates of growth and rates of acceleration.

INTRODUCTION TO TIMES SERIES ANALYSIS

If the observations being studied are each for a different consecutive time period, we have data classified over time, or a "time series." Here we are particularly interested in those time series whose observations have economic and business significance and whose dates are actually historical. We shall study methods for analyzing and making decisions on the basis of economic, historic time series. The separate methods which exist for the analysis of other types of time series, such as those found in physics dealing with falling bodies from time of release, will not be discussed here.

Two distinct sets of methods have been developed for analyzing economic data classified over time. Both sets are essentially descriptive in character. The first of these is a set of decomposition techniques wherein a time series is taken apart to better understand the causal factors underlying its movements; the second is a set of composition techniques wherein artificial time series are constructed from individual time series in order to better follow the general movement of a related set of series such as prices. The first of these is considered the formal technique of time series analysis and is the subject of this chapter (Chap. 17) and the next (Chap. 18). The second is index number construction and will be covered in Chap. 19.

THE CLASSICAL MODEL

Before we consider the mechanics of decomposing a time series, we must first consider the nature of a time series and establish a model of its behavior and composition as a guide to our analysis. The problem here is analogous to studying the behavior of sample results (i.e., sampling distributions) prior to the study of the use of samples in decision making. However, the analogy breaks down at about this point, for while in sampling we could definitely establish the character of the sampling distribution, we cannot definitely establish the nature of a time series. We shall consider a widely used model which has proved helpful in many problems. Unfortunately, there is no way to check the validity of this or any other time series model.

Our model derives in part from a logical study and grouping of the factors and forces which would produce a given value of the data at a point in time and cause it to change with changes in time. These include such things as changes in the weather and changes in the population. In addition, our model derives from empirical observation of a large number of time series. These show certain consistent types of movements

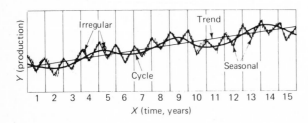

Figure 17-1 Hypothetical time series and its components.

which correspond to what one would expect from the logical analysis. Figure 17-1 shows an hypothetical time series and identifies graphically the four basic components of the classical time series model: (1) trend, (2) cycle, (3) seasonal, and (4) irregular. We shall discuss briefly the nature of each.

Trend

We shall define "trend" as the long-term underlying growth movement of a time series. It is generally conceived of as being smooth, continuous, and irreversible in form. It is thought of as the basic movement of the time series, the other movements being departures from it. The period of time needed for trend analysis varies with the series, but easily runs 20 to 25 years or longer. Trend movement may easily be represented by lines if we conceive of it as smooth and continuous. Requiring it to be irreversible aids in separating it from the cycles.

Trend movements are attributed to two broad classes of causal factors, population and technology. In studying an individual trend movement these must be broken down and looked at in greater detail. Population factors include such things as total population growth, growth in particular areas, and numbers in various age groups. Technological factors must be considered both internal to and external to the company or industry being studied.

Cycle

"Cycle" may be defined as a roughly repetitive wavelike movement with a duration greater than a year. Individual cycles generally average 3 to 5 years in length, although they vary greatly in duration both within and among series. They also vary widely in amplitude of swing. Because of their varied nature, cycles are often analyzed indirectly as a residual in the decomposition process.

To study the causal factors of cycles in a specific time series it is generally necessary first to establish the relationship of the cycles in the series being studied to the general business cycle. If conformity with the general business cycle is good, the causes of the cycles in the individual series are those of business in general. If conformity is low, the individual series must be studied for unique factors.

Seasonal

"Seasonal" is a repetitive fluctuating movement with a duration of a year. Although the patterns of seasonal movements may not be perfectly regular, they exhibit a generally high degree of regularity and stability over time. The movement completes itself within the year and repeats itself year after year.

Seasonal is the least controversial of the time series components. This in part is because the causal factors and their immediate effect as shown by the movement of individual series are so obvious. Seasonal movements are the result of climate or weather factors and of customary forces, such as Christmas.

Irregular

The three components discussed above are all characterized by smooth regular patterns. The original time series itself possessed many discontinuities and quick changes. Several of these are circled in Fig. 17-1. These movements, because of their lack of a definite pattern, are called "irregulars."

Irregulars are caused by such things as strikes, other work stoppages, heat waves, and wars. Where the effect on the series is pronounced, as in the case of a major strike or a war, the specific cause of the particular movement is easily identified. Causes of smaller irregulars are harder to identify, but are obviously of less importance.

The Model Itself

To complete our model it is necessary to specify how the components of trend (T), cycle (C), seasonal (S), and irregular (I) are combined. The model most generally accepted and used specifies that values of the time series (Y) are the product of all the components; i.e.,

$$Y = T \times C \times S \times I$$

Since the separation of cycle and irregular movements is difficult and the effect of an irregular factor on the series is similar to that of cycle, the model may be rewritten

$$Y = T \times S \times CI$$

where the cycle and irregular are combined as a single component.

Decomposition According to the Model

Our general approach to the analysis of a specific time series will be to decompose it into representations of the trend, seasonal, and cycle-irregular components in order to better study and understand the related causal factors for use in decision making. Specifically, we shall attempt to represent trend as a line, computing it directly from the data by methods similar to those used in fitting a regression line. A representation of seasonal in the form of an index will also be obtained directly from the data by the elimination of the other components. The cycle-irregular component will be studied as a remainder, or residual. It will be calculated by dividing the original data through by our measures of trend and seasonal, thereby eliminating them and leaving only the cycle-irregular. In symbols,

$$\frac{Y}{T \times S} = \frac{T \times S \times CI}{T \times S} = CI$$

TREND ANALYSIS

The choice of mechanical methods for determining trend lines depends in part on the purposes for fitting the trend line and in part on the nature of the data.

Purposes for Fitting Trend Lines

Purposes for fitting trend lines are basically (1) as an aid to forecasting, (2) for historical description, and (3) to aid in studying cycles. The first two purposes have in common primary interest in the trend itself, while the third purpose has as its primary interest a study of cycles. The purposes are obviously not mutually exclusive, as a complete time series analysis involves a study of both trend and cycle.

Trend lines are extended into the future as the basis for long-term (five or more years) forecasting. Their predictions should be modified by judgment and the results of other methods where necessary. Forecasting is subject to many risks of error at best, but it is impossible for a business manager to operate without forecasts. The extension of trend lines into the future is a basic form of long-term forecasting. (For the short-run or intermediate forecast, knowledge of seasonal and cycle is more important than knowledge of the trend.) When extending trend lines to forecast, the mathematical nature of the line must be made to correspond with the expected growth behavior of the series.

The fitting of a trend line for purposes of historical description is an attempt to describe the time series growth for some fixed period of time only, with no extension of the line contemplated. Here one need not be as concerned with whether the mathematical nature of the line is economically logical as long as it gives a good description, for no attempt will be made to extend it as in forecasting. Of course, the general purpose of any historical study is to serve as a guide to the future, and in this sense historical time series analysis is for future business decisions. A knowledge of the past growth patterns exhibited by known products after their introduction might be of much value when planning to introduce a new product.

When studying trend as an aid to forecasting or for historical description, the emphasis is on the trend which is usually represented by the mathematical equation of a line. If we are interested in trend as an aid in studying cycles, we use any form of trend representation which allows for an easy separation of trend and cycle. This may be a mathematical line, or it may be a moving average. The general objective is to find a trend representation which bisects the cycles through time, and while a mathematical line may do this if the cycles are fairly regular, the flexibility of the moving average may be needed for other problems.

To summarize, mathematical lines are desirable for our first two purposes, while either a mathematical line or a moving average may be used for the third purpose. In addition, forecasting calls for a mathematical line which is "logical," i.e., has growth behavior similar to that expected of our time series.

Graphing Time Series Data

The nature of time series data, the second consideration in the mechanics of fitting a trend line, is best shown by plotting the series. A graph will show the general shape of the growth pattern of the time series we are studying.

In trend analysis we are interested both in amounts of growth (i.e., growth in the units of the original data such as dollars, tons, and number of sets) and in the per-

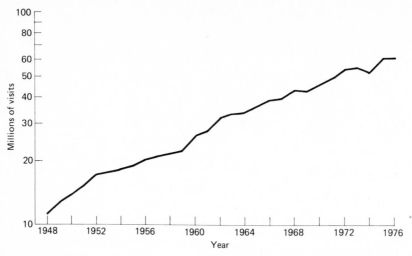

Figure 17-2 Visits to U.S. National Parks, 1948–1976 (logarithmic vertical scale). SOURCE: Survey of Current Business.

centage rates of growth (i.e., percentages of increase or decrease from one time period to another). This calls for two types of graphs, one for studying amounts and one for studying rates. Ordinary arithmetic graph paper ruled in equal spacings on both axes is appropriate for studying amounts of growth. The time element is plotted on the horizontal, and equal spaces on the vertical are assigned equal amounts. A series increasing by constant amounts appears as a straight line on such paper and serves as a reference for comparison with other series.

A different type of graph paper is needed for studying rates. Semilogarithmic paper may be used for this purpose.[1] This paper has an ordinary arithmetic horizontal scale to be used for plotting time but a logarithmically ruled vertical scale constructed so that equal vertical distances will represent equal percentages of increase or decrease.

Figure 17-2 shows a series plotted on semilogarithmic paper. Note that the spacings on the vertical are no longer equal. However, a quick check of the scale shows that a given vertical distance always represents a given percentage. For example, the distance from 30 to 60 is the same as that from 50 to 100, since both represent 100 percent increases; or the distance from 20 to 30 is the same as that from 40 to 60, since both are 50 percent increases.

Semilogarithmic vertical scales are easy to use and work with as long as one uses the guide numbers provided along the edge of the vertical scale. These guide numbers repeat themselves in what are known as cycles from 1 to 10 (or 1 again), and paper may be purchased with varying numbers of cycles on the vertical as needed. Any one cycle will allow for a 900 percent increase (1 to 10). Figure 17-3 shows the guidelines of a cycle and some examples of possible values assigned to them. Any number may be assigned to the bottom of the cycle, and then twice that number is opposite guide number 2, three times that number is opposite guide number 3, and so on. If 100 is

[1] If semilogarithmic paper is unavailable, the same result may be obtained by plotting the logs of the series on arithmetic paper.

10	100	1,000	50	200	250
9	90	900	45	180	225
8	80	800	40	160	200
7	70	700	35	140	175
6	60	600	30	120	150
5	50	500	25	100	125
4	40	400	20	80	100
3	30	300	15	60	75
2	20	200	10	40	50
1	10	100	5	20	25

Figure 17-3 Possible values for a logarithmic scale.

opposite guide number 1, the scale runs 100, 200, 300, 400, and so on. If 5 is opposite guide number 1, the scale runs 5, 10, 15, 20, and so on. The top of any cycle is always 10 times the number on the bottom.

A straight line on semilogarithmic paper implies a series increasing (or decreasing) at a constant rate (percentage). This can be used as a reference guide to see if an actual series is increasing (or decreasing) at an increasing, constant, or decreasing rate of increase (or decrease). The steeper the line, the greater the rate of increase or decrease.

Fitting Procedures

Mathematical lines for forecasting or historical description may be fit either by the method of selected points or by the method of least squares.[1] The actual shape or type of mathematical line will depend on the specific purpose and the shape of the data when plotted.

Selected-point procedures consist of forcing the trend line to pass through certain predetermined (selected) points. These points may be chosen by the statistician on the basis of his best judgment as to the nature of the trend, or they may represent the results of averaging the data for a period of years.

Least squares procedures are those used and illustrated in Chap. 15 for fitting a regression line. Their application to trend analysis is not based on theoretical grounds as it was in regression analysis, but merely on the fact that they are easy and convenient to use and give satisfactory trend representations in many problems. Even though they may appear less arbitrary in character than selected-point procedures, they are not necessarily so, as the entire choice of the method is arbitrary where time series analysis is concerned.

Both methods will be illustrated in the sections that follow for a variety of trend shapes.

[1] Moving averages are discussed later, with seasonal analysis.

Trend Types

Before illustrating the fitting methods, however, we need to take a brief look at the forms of mathematical lines that are commonly used to represent the trend component of a time series. These may be divided into two types: (1) simple polynomials and (2) growth curves.

Four polynomials are in common use. They are:

1. $Y_T = a + bx$: a straight-line fit to the natural numbers.
2. $\log Y_T = \log a + x \log b$: a straight-line fit to the logarithms of the data.
3. $Y_T = a + bx + cx^2$: a parabola (second-degree curve) fit to the natural numbers.
4. $\log Y_T = \log a + x \log b + x^2 \log c$: a parabola (second-degree curve) fit to the logarithms of the data.

The T subscript on Y is necessary to distinguish trend values from data values; x is used to indicate time values from any arbitrary convenient origin. The actual fitting problem is to derive numerical values for the constants a, b, and c or $\log a$, $\log b$, and $\log c$ from the data to which one is attempting to fit a trend line. All four may be fit by the method of selected points or the method of least squares, although in practice the latter three are generally fit by least squares only.

All four polynomials are generally used for historical description and/or cycle study. They may be used for short-term forecasting; but, as their mathematical patterns are not those of expected economic growth, their use in long-term forecasting would be dangerous.

Two growth curves are in common use. They are:

1. $\log Y_T = \log L + \log a(b)^x$: the Gompertz.
2. $Y_T = L/(1 + 10^{a+bx})$: the logistic.

These are curves that possess mathematical properties which logically correspond to the processes of economic growth in a firm or industry. These curves, given certain signs for the constants, have no negative values with a lower limit of zero, as would the production or sales of a firm or industry. They have fixed upper limits representing the natural market saturation faced in business. Their growth patterns are a function of their present level and the distance from the upper limit. Similarly, industry growth reflects the current level of operations, being limited by current capacity, and slows as the saturation level is reached. When drawn, these curves have the patterns shown in Fig. 17-4.

Both curves are generally fit by selected points. Three such points are needed, since both equations have three constants. The L constant is the fixed upper limit. These curves are particularly useful in long-term forecasting because their growth behavior is similar to that logically expected of a company or industry. They may also be used for historical description and/or cycle study. They should be used with care and judgment, however, as their use implies that one expects the future to grow according to a pattern established in the past.

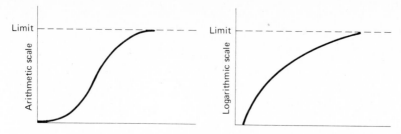

Figure 17-4 Growth curve patterns on arithmetic and semilog paper.

We shall now illustrate the actual fitting of a number of the trend types we have just described.

Illustration: Straight Line, Selected Points

A straight line is the simplest form of a mathematical line. As noted above, it is chiefly used for historical description or cycle study, since it lacks the necessary mathematical properties for forecasting. A straight line in terms of natural numbers implies a series which is increasing by constant amounts of growth. The trend of an economic time series would generally have this property for only a fairly limited time period. Again, our equation will be of the form

$$Y_T = a + bx$$

Data and table calculations for fitting a straight line by selected points are given in Table 17-1. Ten years of data are generally not adequate for studying trend, but

Table 17-1 Fitting a straight line by selected points to sales of the Antique Chair Company, 1970–1979

Year (X)	Sales (Y), $10,000s	Semitotal	Semiaverage	Arbitrary time scale (x)
1970	10			−2
1971	12			−1
1972	14	62	12.4	0
1973	11			1
1974	15			2
1975	14			3
1976	12			4
1977	14	70	14.0	5
1978	16			6
1979	14			7

Source: Hypothetical.

will suffice for illustrative purposes. Trend lines are very often fit to annual data or, for longer series, to 5-year averages. The use of annual data eliminates seasonal variations from the data since they are entirely within the year.

Prior to the actual fitting of a trend line, a graph (or graphs) of the data should be drawn to determine whether a straight line can be used to describe the trend of the data or whether a curve is called for. The data of Table 17-1 are graphed in Fig. 17-5. Although the data show ups and downs, these are cyclical in character, and the series does have a pronounced upward trend, for which a straight line seems to be an adequate description.

Two points only are needed to determine a straight line. We have chosen the averages of the first and second halves of the series. When this is done, the method of selected points is termed the "method of semiaverages." The points could have been chosen by judgment, however. The calculation of the two averages is shown in Table 17-1, the results being 12.4, which is centered at 1972, and 14.0, located at 1977. These points are plotted on the graph, and a line passed through them and extended to the ends of the data. As this line appears to be a good description of trend, we may proceed to obtain numerical values for a and b in order to have its equation.

To facilitate obtaining values for a and b, an arbitrary time scale has been set up in the last column of Table 17-1. The origin for this scale is the date of the first semiaverage. The scale has been kept in annual values, as was the original scale, although this is not necessary for all problems. As the a value in any straight line equation is the value of Y_T when x equals zero, we now know that our $a = 12.4$. The b value is the slope of the line, or the change in Y_T for a unit change in x. $Y_T = 12.4$ in 1972, and $Y_T = 14.0$ in 1977. Y_T therefore increases 1.6 (14.0 - 12.4) in the 5-year period 1972 to 1977. The annual increase is $1.6/5 = 0.32$ per year. As a unit of x is 1 year, this is our b value. The semiaverage trend equation for our data is

$$Y_T = 12.4 + 0.32x$$

$$x = 0 \text{ in } 1972$$

$$1x = 1 \text{ year}$$

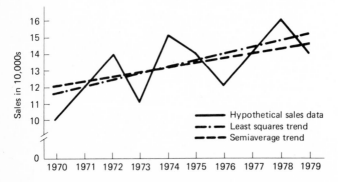

Figure 17-5 Hypothetical sales data and straight line trends.

The last two items of information on the origin and units of the equation are necessary to identify the equation completely and are an integral part of the answer.

The b value of 0.32 indicates that the trend of sales increased $3,200 per year from 1970 to 1979.

Trend values for any year other than the semiaverage points may be obtained by substituting the appropriate x value in the equation. For example, the x value for 1978 is +6, so Y_T for 1978 is

$$Y_T = 12.4 + 0.32x = 12.4 + 0.32(6) = 14.32$$

This procedure may also be used to extend the line for forecasting purposes if it is anticipated that the series will continue to grow as in the past.

Illustration: Straight Line, Least Squares

We shall now use the same data to illustrate the fitting of a straight line trend by the method of least squares. The data are reproduced in Table 17-2, along with the necessary calculations. Again the data should be plotted to determine the appropriate trend shape before fitting. The data have been graphed in Fig. 17-5.

The equations for the constants a and b when fitting by least squares are

$$a = \frac{\Sigma Y}{n} \qquad b = \frac{\Sigma x Y}{\Sigma x^2}$$

These equations are valid only for an arbitrary time scale which sums out to zero (i.e., where $\Sigma x = 0$). When fitting to an odd number of points, the arbitrary time scale can easily be made to sum to zero by choosing the middle item as the origin (zero value) and counting backward and forward in consecutive integers. This is illustrated below

Table 17-2 Fitting a straight line by least squares to sales of the Antique Chair Company, 1970–1979

Year (X)	Sales (Y), \$10,000s	x	xY	x^2
1970	10	−9	−90	81
1971	12	−7	−84	49
1972	14	−5	−70	25
1973	11	−3	−33	9
1974	15	−1	−15	1
1975	14	+1	14	1
1976	12	+3	36	9
1977	14	+5	70	25
1978	16	+7	112	49
1979	14	+9	126	81
Total	132	0	+66	330

Source: Hypothetical.

for two different situations:

(1)		(2)	
X	x	X	x
1975	-2	1957	-2
1976	-1	1962	-1
1977	0	1967	0
1978	+1	1972	+1
1979	+2	1977	+2
Total	0		0

These differ in that in situation (1), $1x$ equals 1 year, and in (2), $1x$ equals 5 years, but for both, $\Sigma x = 0$.

To make the $\Sigma x = 0$ when fitting to an even number of points, the origin is taken as halfway between the two central points, and the counting is in consecutive odd integers. This is illustrated below for annual data and for data at 5-year intervals.

(1)		(2)	
X	x	X	x
1974	-5	1952	-5
1975	-3	1957	-3
1976	-1	1962	-1
1977	+1	1967	+1
1978	+3	1972	+3
1979	+5	1977	+5
Total	0		0

Here $x = 0$ in $1976\frac{1}{2}$ and $1x = \frac{1}{2}$ year in situation (1), while $x = 0$ in $1964\frac{1}{2}$ and $1x = 2\frac{1}{2}$ years in (2).

Since we are fitting to an even number of points (10) in our illustration, our arbitrary time scale x has been set up on an odd-integer basis in Table 17-2. Column xY is the cross product of the x and the Y values in the preceding columns. The final column of the table contains squares of the x values. The values are now totaled and substituted in the formulas to solve for a and b.

$$a = \frac{\Sigma Y}{n} = \frac{132}{10} = 13.2$$

$$b = \frac{\Sigma xY}{\Sigma x^2} = \frac{66}{330} = 0.2$$

The least squares trend equation therefore is

$$Y_T = 13.2 + 0.2x$$

$$x = 0 \text{ in } 1974\tfrac{1}{2}$$

$$1x = \tfrac{1}{2} \text{ year}$$

To check the goodness of fit and our arithmetic, we may substitute any two values of x, solve for values of Y_T, and plot these and the trend line on the graph. Substituting $x = -9$ (x value for 1970), we obtain

$$Y_T = 13.2 + 0.2x = 13.2 + 0.2(-9) = 11.4$$

Substituting $x = +9$ (x value for 1979), we get

$$Y_T = 13.2 + 0.2x = 13.2 + 0.2(9) = 15.0$$

These two points and the resulting trend line have been plotted in Fig. 17-5. The trend line appears to fit the data satisfactorily.

A study of Fig. 17-5 shows that our two straight line trends are similar in character and that either appears to give a satisfactory fit. Unfortunately, there is no commonly agreed on criterion in trend analysis to determine which line gives the better fit. Goodness of fit is generally determined subjectively by inspection, and in this case either line appears satisfactory. The least squares line is the steeper of the two, since it has an annual trend increase of $4,000 per year [$b = 0.2$ ($10,000s) per half-year, or 0.4 ($10,000s) per year] as compared with $3,200 per year for the semi-average line.

Illustration: Logarithmic Straight Line, Least Squares

We shall next illustrate the fitting of trend lines with a logarithmic straight line, or exponential curve. This type of line appears as a curve on arithmetic paper, but as a straight line on semilogarithmic paper. As such it may be used to describe the trend of a time series, which appears to be increasing at a constant rate. The early phases of the growth of many companies and industries and certain aspects of the economy at large tend to exhibit such growth.

Although the natural number form of the equation is $Y_T = ab^x$, giving rise to the term "exponential," the more common form of the equation used for fitting is its logarithmic transformation,

$$\log Y_T = \log a + x \log b$$

If the trend is to be fit by least squares procedures, the following equations may be used to determine the constants $\log a$ and $\log b$:

$$\log a = \frac{\Sigma \log Y}{n}$$

$$\log b = \frac{\Sigma x \log Y}{\Sigma x^2}$$

Table 17-3 Logarithmic straight line trend illustration, federal expenditures for airways in the United States, 1959–1976

Year	Expenditures (Y), millions of $	log Y	x	x log Y	x^2
1959	385	2.5855	−17	−43.9535	289
1960	462	2.6646	−15	−39.9690	225
1961	558	2.7466	−13	−35.7058	169
1962	574	2.7589	−11	−30.3479	121
1963	634	2.8021	−9	−25.2189	81
1964	670	2.8261	−7	−19.7827	49
1965	635	2.8028	−5	−14.0140	25
1966	722	2.8585	−3	−8.5755	9
1967	870	2.9395	−1	−2.9395	1
1968	788	2.8965	1	+2.8965	1
1969	936	2.9713	3	8.9139	9
1970	1192	3.0763	5	15.3815	25
1971	1468	3.1668	7	22.1676	49
1972	1513	3.1798	9	28.6182	81
1973	1446	3.1602	11	34.7622	121
1974	1589	3.2012	13	41.6156	169
1975	1695	3.2292	15	48.4380	225
1976	1868	3.2714	17	55.6138	289
Total	· · ·	53.1373	0	37.9005	1938

Source: Annual budgets of the U.S. government.

as long as $\Sigma x = 0$. These equations are the same as those used to obtain a and b previously, except that log Y replaces Y. The procedure, therefore, is sometimes described as fitting to the logs of the series. Data and table calculations are shown in Table 17-3. The series is plotted in Fig. 17-6.

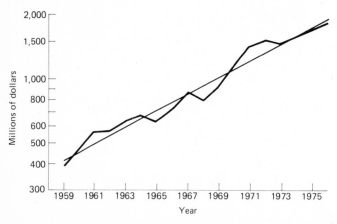

Figure 17-6 Logarithmic straight line illustration.   SOURCE: Federal Expenditures for Airways, 1959–1976.

Inspection of Fig. 17-6 shows that the trend movement of the series might well be represented by a straight line. As Fig. 17-6 is on semilogarithmic paper, this means that our straight line must be in terms of the logs of the data. Necessary table calculations for fitting appear in Table 17-3. The Y values are first transformed into log Y values. We next set up our arbitrary time scale x. The next column, x log Y, is the product of the two preceding columns. The final column, x^2, contains the squares of our time values. Totaling the columns and substituting in our formulas for log a and log b, we obtain

$$\log a = \frac{\Sigma \log Y}{n} = \frac{53.1373}{18} = 2.9521$$

$$\log b = \frac{\Sigma(x \log Y)}{\Sigma x^2} = \frac{37.9005}{1938} = 0.0196$$

Our trend equation, therefore, is

$$\log Y_T = 2.9521 + 0.0196x$$

$$x = 0 \text{ in } 1967\tfrac{1}{2}$$

$$1x = \tfrac{1}{2} \text{ year}$$

To solve for values of Y_T for purposes of checking goodness of fit and our arithmetic, we must first solve for values of log Y_T by substituting appropriate values of x in our equation and then determine Y_T as the antilog of log Y_T. Substituting $x = -17$ (x value for 1959) and $x = +17$ (x value for 1976), the results are

$$\log Y_T = 2.9521 + 0.0196(-17) = 2.9521 - 0.332 = 2.6189$$

and

$$Y_T = \text{antilog (log } Y_T) = \text{antilog } 2.6189 = 415.9 \text{ for } 1959$$

$$\log Y_T = 2.9521 + 0.0196(+17) = 2.9521 + 0.332 = 3.2853$$

and

$$Y_T = \text{antilog (log } Y_T) = \text{antilog } 3.2853 = 1929 \text{ for } 1976$$

These two Y_T's were plotted on the graph of Fig. 17-6 and connected by a straight line. The fit appears good.

As a logarithmic straight line represents a series which is increasing at a constant rate, we should like to know the numerical value of that rate. This may be determined easily from the log b value. The antilog of the log b value gives the relative change (R) per unit of x. If we subtract 1 from the R value, we have the rate of change (r). Here we have

$$R = \text{antilog log } b = \text{antilog } 0.0196 = 1.046$$

$$r = R - 1 = 1.046 - 1 = 0.046 \quad \text{or} \quad 4.6\%/\tfrac{1}{2} \text{ yr}$$

This is the constant rate at which the trend increases per half-year to go from \$415.9 million in 1959 to \$1,929 million in 1976. If one desires a rate of change for a period of time differing from the basic unit of x, the log b value is adjusted appropriately *before* taking the antilog. Here, for example, a rate of change per year would probably be more useful than our rate per half-year. Such a rate would be computed by doubling the log b value before taking the antilog. Specifically, we get

$$R = \text{antilog } [2(\log b)] = \text{antilog } 0.0392 = 1.094$$

$$r = R - 1 = 1.094 - 1 = 0.094 \quad \text{or} \quad 9.4\%/\text{yr}$$

Parabolas, or Second-degree Curves

By no means all data, when plotted, form a straight line either on arithmetic paper or on semilog paper. Many data exhibit a curved pattern on both arithmetic and semilog paper. To describe the trend of data where the trend is a curve, wide use is made of the parabola, or second-degree curve, especially when the purpose is historical description. This curve, which is generally fit by least squares, may be fit either to the natural numbers or to the logarithms of the series.

In its natural-number form the trend equation would be

$$Y_T = a + bx + cx^2$$

Least squares equations for solving for the constants a, b, and c are

$$\Sigma Y = na + c\Sigma x^2 \tag{1}$$

$$\Sigma x^2 Y = a\Sigma x^2 + c\Sigma x^4 \tag{2}$$

$$b = \frac{\Sigma x Y}{\Sigma x^2} \tag{3}$$

Equations (1) and (2) are solved simultaneously for a and c. These equations assume that the arbitrary time scale has been made to sum to zero.

The log form of the equation is

$$\log Y_T = \log a + x \log b + x^2 \log c$$

Solution equations for $\log a, \log b$, and $\log c$, if $\Sigma x = 0$, are

$$\Sigma \log Y = n \log a + (\log c) \Sigma x^2$$

$$\Sigma (x^2 \log Y) = (\log a)\Sigma x^2 + (\log c)\Sigma x^4$$

$$\log b = \frac{\Sigma (x \log Y)}{\Sigma x^2}$$

In its entirety the parabola is a comet-shaped curve, but segments of it may be used to describe possible trend lines. Figure 17-7 shows some possible segment shapes and the corresponding signs of the b and c constants (a is always positive). The same relationships hold for log curves and log b and log c. The two increasing curves (+b value) are the most common.

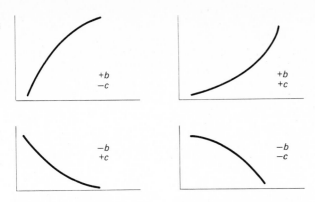

Figure 17-7 Possible parabola trend shapes and corresponding signs of b and c constants.

Illustration: Natural Number Parabola, Least Squares

The original data for our natural number parabola illustration are given in Table 17-4. A plot of the data is given in Fig. 17-8. A study of Fig. 17-8 shows us that we will need a curved line to represent the trend of our data.

When fitting a trend line to so many years of data, the actual mechanics are often done in terms of centered five-year averages (averages of consecutive sets of five data values each located date-wise at the middle year of the set), to cut down on the calculations. However, upon completion, goodness of fit is checked against the original annual values, as it is their trend we are trying to describe.

Table 17-4 Crude petroleum production in the United States, 1947–1976

Year	Production 10s of millions of barrels	Year	Production 10s of millions of barrels
1947	186	1962	268
1948	202	1963	275
1949	184	1964	279
1950	197	1965	285
1951	225	1966	304
1952	229	1967	322
1953	236	1968	333
1954	232	1969	336
1955	248	1970	382
1956	262	1971	348
1957	262	1972	346
1958	245	1973	335
1959	257	1974	320
1960	257	1975	305
1961	262	1976	298

Source: Survey of Current Business.

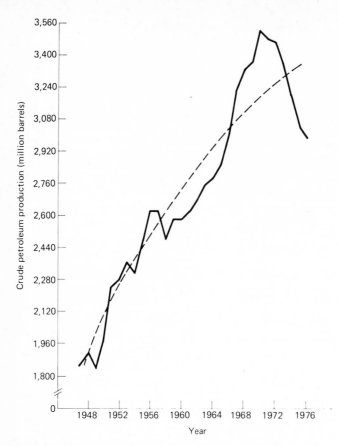

Figure 17-8 Natural number parabola illustration: Crude petroleum production in the United States, 1947–1976. SOURCE: Survey of Current Business.

Table 17-5 is the work table for our illustration. The first column gives the dates at which our centered 5-year averages are located. The second column gives the values of the centered 5-year averages (Y) themselves. These were derived from the data of Table 17-4. We use an odd-integer time scale in the third column as we are fitting to an even number of points (6) and our solution equations require that $\Sigma x = 0$. The xY column values are the cross-products of the Y and x columns and the $x^2 Y$ values are the cross-products of the x and xY columns. The last two columns give the values of x^2 and x^4. All columns are totaled to get the sums needed in the solution equations.

Using these totals and $n = 6$ (we are fitting to the six five-year averages) in our simultaneous equations for a and c:

$$\Sigma Y = na + c\Sigma x^2 \tag{1}$$

$$\Sigma x^2 Y = a\Sigma x^2 = c\Sigma x^4 \tag{2}$$

we get

$$1{,}644 = 6a + 70c \tag{1}$$

$$18{,}804 = 70a + 1414c \tag{2}$$

Table 17-5 Work table for fitting a parabola to United States crude petroleum production

Year	Centered 5-yr averages (Y)	x	xY	x^2Y	x^2	x^4
1949	199	-5	-995	4,975	25	625
1954	241	-3	-723	2,169	9	81
1959	257	-1	-257	257	1	1
1964	282	1	282	282	1	1
1969	344	3	1,032	3,096	9	81
1974	321	5	1,605	8,025	25	625
Total	1,644	0	944	18,804	70	1,414

Multiplying Eq. (1) through by 20.2 and subtracting Eq. (2) from the result, we have

$$33,208.8 = 121.2a + 1414c \tag{1}$$
$$18,804.0 = 70.0a + 1414c \tag{2}$$

$$14,404.8 = 51.2a$$

and $a = 281.3$. We now substitute this value in Eq. (1) to solve for c.

$$1,644 = 6(281.3) + 70c \tag{1}$$
$$1,644 = 1,687.8 + 70c$$
$$-70c = 43.8$$
$$c = -0.6$$

Using Eq. (3) to solve for b, we get

$$b = \frac{\Sigma xY}{\Sigma x^2} = \frac{944}{70} = 13.5 \tag{3}$$

Our trend equation is

$$Y_T = 281.3 + 13.5x - 0.6x^2$$

$$x = 0 \text{ in } 1961\tfrac{1}{2}$$

$$1x = 2\tfrac{1}{2} \text{ years}$$

Note that we have $a + b$ value and $a - c$ value, as would be anticipated from the sketch of our expected trend shape as shown in Fig. 17-7. Note also that our $a = 281.3$ does appear to be about right for the trend level in $1961\tfrac{1}{2}$ (i.e., when $x = 0$). After these preliminary checks on our constants, we may solve for a set of Y_T values to check the goodness of fit of our trend line to our original 30 years of data. For curved trend lines such solutions can be most efficiently handled in a table. Table 17-6 is such a table for our illustration.

The choice of years in the first column is somewhat arbitrary, but sufficient years must be used to establish the curvature of our trend line. The particular choice of the

Table 17-6 Computation of trend values for a parabola fit to United States crude petroleum production

Year	x	x^2	$a =$ 281.3	$bx =$ 13.5x	cx^2 $= -0.6x^2$	Y_T
1947	−5.8	33.64	281.3	−78.3	−20.2	182.8
1948	−5.4	29.16	281.3	−72.9	−17.5	190.9
1949	−5.0	25.00	281.3	−67.5	−15.0	198.8
1954	−3.0	9.00	281.3	−40.5	− 5.4	235.4
1959	−1.0	1.00	281.3	−13.5	− 0.6	267.2
1964	1.0	1.00	281.3	13.5	− 0.6	294.2
1969	3.0	9.00	281.3	40.5	− 5.4	316.4
1974	5.0	25.00	281.3	67.5	−15.0	333.8
1975	5.4	29.16	281.3	72.9	−17.5	336.7
1976	5.8	33.64	281.3	78.3	−20.2	339.4

first two and the last two years will be explained in a later section. The x values for dates not in our work table can be obtained by taking the difference between the year desired and the origin and dividing the difference by the value of $1x$. For example, for 1947, we get

$$x_{47} = \frac{1947 - 1961\frac{1}{2}}{2\frac{1}{2}} = \frac{-14.5}{2.5} = -5.8$$

Values are first determined vertically by columns, and then the a, bx, and cx^2 columns are added horizontally to obtain Y_T values.

The Y_T values of Table 17-6 have been plotted on Fig. 17-8 and seem to give a fair description of the trend for the 30 years in question. Common knowledge and the sharp drop in the data during the last 3 years would definitely suggest against extending this trend for forecasting purposes.

Illustration: Logarithmic Parabola, Least Squares

The data we shall use to illustrate a logarithmic parabola (a second-degree curve to the logs) are given in Table 17-7. The data have been plotted on semilog graph paper in Fig. 17-9. We see again the need for a curved trend line. As our plot is on semilog paper, we shall try a second-degree curve to the logs.

We shall again use centered 5-year averages to simplify our calculations. These are shown in Table 17-8, which is our work table for this illustration. Table 17-8 differs from our earlier natural-number parabola work table (Table 17-5) chiefly in that logarithms of the 5-year averages must be determined before the cross products can be computed. These appear in the third column. This time we are fitting to an odd number of points (5), so consecutive integers were used for the x values in the fourth column to make $\Sigma x = 0$.

Substituting our table totals in our simultaneous solution equations for log a and log c:

$$\Sigma \log Y = n \log a + \log c\Sigma x^2 \tag{1}$$

$$\Sigma x^2 \log Y = \log a\Sigma x^2 + \log c\Sigma x^4 \tag{2}$$

we get

$$12.0386 = 5 \log a + 10 \log c \tag{1}$$

$$24.3029 = 10 \log a + 34 \log c \tag{2}$$

Table 17-7 U.S. fish stocks in cold storage at year's end, 1952–1976

Year	Fish stocks millions of lb	Year	Fish stocks, millions of lb
1952	193	1965	230
1953	176	1966	271
1954	194	1967	253
1955	175	1968	285
1956	196	1969	275
1957	191	1970	306
1958	215	1971	302
1959	232	1972	415
1960	230	1973	459
1961	197	1974	433
1962	231	1975	356
1963	244	1976	366
1964	215		

Source: *Survey of Current Business.*

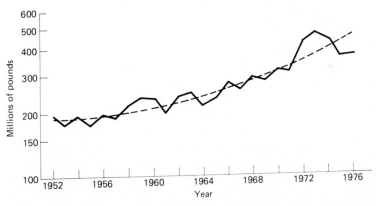

Figure 17-9 Logarithmic parabola illustration: fish stocks (cold storage) in the United States, 1952–1976. SOURCE: Survey of Current Business.

Table 17-8 Work table for fitting a logarithmic parabola to United States fish stocks

Year	Centered 5-yr averages (Y)	log Y	x	x log Y	x^2 log Y	x^2	x^4
1954	187	2.2718	-2	-4.5436	9.0872	4	16
1959	213	2.3284	-1	-2.3284	2.3284	1	1
1964	238	2.3766	0	0.0000	0.0000	0	0
1969	284	2.4533	1	2.4533	2.4533	1	1
1974	406	2.6085	2	5.2170	10.4340	4	16
total	...	12.0386	0	0.7983	24.3029	10	34

Multiplying Eq. (1) through by 2 and subtracting it from Eq. (2), we have

$$24.3029 = 10 \log a + 34 \log c \qquad (2)$$
$$\underline{24.0772 = 10 \log a + 20 \log c} \qquad (1)$$
$$0.2257 = \qquad\qquad 14 \log c$$

Therefore, $\log c = 0.0161$. Substituting this value in Eq. (1) and solving for $\log a$, we get

$$12.0386 = 5 \log a + 10(0.0161) \qquad (1)$$

$$12.0386 = 5 \log a + 0.1610$$

$$5 \log a = 11.8776$$

$$\log a = 2.3755$$

Using Eq. (3) to solve for $\log b$, we get

$$\log b = \frac{\Sigma x \log Y}{\Sigma x^2} = \frac{0.7983}{10} = 0.0798$$

Our trend equation is

$$\log Y_T = 2.3755 + 0.0798x + 0.0161x^2$$

$$x = 0 \text{ in } 1964$$

$$1x = 5 \text{ years}$$

A check of Fig. 17-7 shows that we have the right signs for our $\log b$ and $\log c$ values. The value of $\log a$ (2.3755) appears very good. Table 17-9 shows the computation of a selected set of trend values using our logarithmic parabola trend equation. The steps are the same as those of Table 17-6 except that adding across gives values for $\log Y_T$. Antilogs of these values must be taken to get the actual Y_T's. The Y_T's have been plotted on the graph in Fig. 17-9. We seem to have an acceptable trend line.

Table 17-9 Computation of trend values for a logarithmic parabola fit to United States fish stocks

Year	x	x^2	$\log a =$ 2.3755	$x \log b =$ 0.0798x	$x^2 \log c =$ 0.0161 x^2	$\log Y_T$	Y_T
1952	-2.4	5.76	2.3755	-0.1915	0.0927	2.2767	189.1
1953	-2.2	4.84	2.3755	-0.1756	0.0779	2.2778	189.6
1954	-2.0	4.00	2.3755	-0.1596	0.0644	2.2803	190.7
1959	-1.0	1.00	2.3755	-0.0798	0.0161	2.3118	205.0
1964	0.0	0.00	2.3755	0.0000	0.0000	2.3755	237.4
1969	1.0	1.00	2.3755	0.0798	0.0161	2.4714	296.1
1974	2.0	4.00	2.3755	0.1596	0.0644	2.5995	397.6
1975	2.2	4.84	2.3755	0.1756	0.0779	2.6290	425.6
1976	2.4	5.76	2.3755	0.1915	0.0927	2.6597	456.7

Illustration: Growth Curve, Gompertz

As our final trend illustration, we shall fit a Gompertz to a set of data to show the general procedure for fitting a growth curve. As mentioned earlier, the fitting is usually done by the method of selected points. The equation for a Gompertz trend line is

$$\log Y_T = \log L + \log a(b)^x$$

Note that the time value (x) appears in the equation as an exponent of the b value. Figure 17-4 shows the general shape of a Gompertz on both arithmetic and semilogarithmic paper.

Table 17-10 gives data on the production of cigarettes in the United States which we shall use for our Gompertz illustration. These data have been plotted in Fig. 17-10.

The selected points (y) to which we shall force fit the trend are given in Table 17-11, which is the work table for this illustration. Three points are needed in fitting a three-constant equation. Here we have used centered 10-year averages for our points. However, often the points are chosen on the basis of the statistician's best judgment as to what the trend should be. The methods we intend to illustrate here do require that the selected points be equidistant timewise. This is because our solution equations are based on an arbitrary time scale (x scale) of the 0, 1, 2 type illustrated in Table 17-11. Also, the percentage increase in the y's (selected points) must be greater in the first time period than in the second for the curve to have the proper shape. For example, here, the increase from 405 to 519 is 26 percent, while the increase from 519 to 613 is only 18 percent.

The origin for the x scale is always placed at the date of the first selected point (in this case, of our first 10-year average, $1951\frac{1}{2}$). The count of the scale is then in consecutive integers. The first selected point is designated y_0, with the second and third points becoming y_1 and y_2.

The first step in our calculations is to determine the logarithms of the selected points (given in the work table, Table 17-11). We next compute differences between consecutive $\log y$'s, i.e.:

$$d_1 = \log y_1 - \log y_0 = 2.7152 - 2.6075 = 0.1077$$

$$d_2 = \log y_2 - \log y_1 = 2.7875 - 2.7152 = 0.0723$$

This is followed by the calculation of the b value. We have

$$b = \frac{d_2}{d_1} = \frac{0.0723}{0.1077} = 0.6713$$

Table 17-10 United States cigarette production, 1947-1976

Year	Billions of cigarettes	Year	Billions of cigarettes
1947	370	1962	536
1948	387	1963	551
1949	385	1964	540
1950	392	1965	556
1951	419	1966	569
1952	434	1967	577
1953	424	1968	577
1954	402	1969	558
1955	412	1970	584
1956	424	1971	578
1957	442	1972	598
1958	470	1973	646
1959	490	1974	635
1960	507	1975	651
1961	528	1976	729

Source: Survey of Current Business.

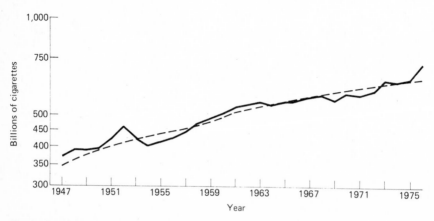

Figure 17-10 Gompertz trend illustration: United States cigarette production, 1947-1976. SOURCE: Survey of Current Business.

Table 17-11 Work table for fitting a Gompertz to United States cigarette production

Year	x	Centered 10-year averages, y	$\log y$
$1951\frac{1}{2}$	0	405	2.6075
$1961\frac{1}{2}$	1	519	2.7152
$1971\frac{1}{2}$	2	613	2.7875

Once we have b, we may calculate $\log a$ from

$$\log a = \frac{d_1}{b-1} = \frac{0.1077}{0.6713 - 1} = \frac{0.1077}{-0.3287} = -0.3277$$

Finally, we determine $\log L$ from

$$\log L = \log y_0 - \log a = 2.6075 - (-0.3277) = 2.9352$$

As checks on our arithmetic, we might note that b must be less than 1, that $\log a$ must be negative, and that $\log L$ must be greater than $\log y_2$. Our answer is

$$\log Y_T = 2.9352 + (-0.3277)(0.0713)^x$$

$$x = 0 \text{ in } 1951\tfrac{1}{2}$$

$$1x = 10 \text{ years}$$

Table 17-12 contains the values for calculating Y_T's to check the goodness of fit of the trend line and to check our arithmetic. The latter check comes from the fact that we must obtain as Y_T values the values of our original selected points (centered 10-year averages) when we substitute the corresponding x values (0, 1, and 2) in the

Table 17-12 Computation of trend values for a Gompertz fit to United States cigarette production

Year	x	$x \log b =$ $x(9.8269 - 10)$	$b^x =$ $(0.0713)^x$	$\log a(b)^x =$ $-0.3277(0.0713)^x$	$\log Y_T$	Y_T
1947	-0.45	0.0771	1.194	-0.3919	2.5439	350
1948	-0.35	0.0600	1.148	-0.3762	2.5590	362
$1951\frac{1}{2}$	0.00	0.0000	1.000	-0.3277	2.6075	405
$1956\frac{1}{2}$	0.50	4.9134 - 5	0.8192	-0.2685	2.6667	464
$1961\frac{1}{2}$	1.00	9.8269 - 10	0.6713	-0.2200	2.7152	519
$1966\frac{1}{2}$	1.50	14.7404 - 15	0.5500	-0.1802	2.7550	569
$1971\frac{1}{2}$	2.00	19.6538 - 20	0.4506	-0.1477	2.7875	613
1975	2.35	234.5932 - 235	0.3919	-0.1284	2.8068	641
1976	2.45	244.5759 - 245	0.3766	-0.1234	2.8118	648

equation as we are using a forced-fit procedure. Of course, our trend line checks out satisfactorily.

The selection of dates and resulting x values is again somewhat arbitrary, although some other than our original dates must be chosen to learn the true pattern of our trend line.

Solving a Gompertz equation requires raising the b value to various powers represented by the x's. As some of these are fractional, the only way to accomplish this is by logarithms—using the relationship b^x = antilog (x log b). Log b was taken as 9.8269-10 for the x's 0 through 2 and as 99.8269–100 for x = 2.35 and x = 2.45. For the negative x's of 0.35 and 0.45, we used log b = -0.1731 obtained by combining +9.8269 and -10 into a single number.

After the x log b products are obtained, their antilogs are taken to determine the b^x values of the fourth column. These values are next multiplied by log $a(-0.3277)$ to get the values of the fifth column. To obtain the log Y_T values of the next column, the log $a(b)^x$ values are added to the value of log L (2.9532). The Y_T's of the last column are, of course, the antilogs of the log Y_T numbers. The plot of these values appears in Fig. 17-10.

A Note on the Logistic

The procedure for fitting a logistic trend line,

$$Y_T = \frac{L}{1 + 10^{a+bx}}$$

is quite similar to that illustrated for the Gompertz. The fitting is to a set of three selected points. If these points are again equidistant from each other timewise and subject to decreasing rates of growth, we may use the following solution equations:

$$d_1 = \frac{1}{y_0} - \frac{1}{y_1}$$

$$d_2 = \frac{1}{y_1} - \frac{1}{y_2}$$

$$b = \log \frac{d_1}{d_2}$$

$$\frac{1}{L} = \frac{1}{y_0} - \frac{d_1^2}{d_1 - d_2}$$

$$a = \log \left[\left(\frac{d_1^2}{d_1 - d_2} \right) L \right]$$

The fit this time is in terms of reciprocals rather than logs. For most series, the final results (Y_T's) are about the same.

Rates of Change and Rates of Acceleration

Average rates of change $(\bar{r})$ and average rates of acceleration $(\bar{a})$ are useful measures for summarizing the growth patterns of trend lines. The former measures give the rate at which the trend would have grown if it had grown at a constant rate (i.e., if it had appeared as a straight line on semilogarithmic paper). The latter measures, which are actually measures of the rate of change in the trend line's actual rates of change, can be used as measures of the direction and degree of curvature in a trend line. The former measures give an *average* rate of growth which would be comparable to the constant rate of growth of a logarithmic straight-line trend. The latter measures are something of a measure of variability, being equal to zero for the logarithmic straight line where the average rate is constant and increasing in value the greater the curvature of a trend line, i.e., when the actual rates differ more and more from the average rate.

Formulas for determining the average relative change $(\bar{R})$, a necessary first step, and the average rate of change $(\bar{r})$ on an annual basis for any type of trend line are

$$\bar{R} = \sqrt[n-1]{\frac{T_n}{T_1}} \quad \text{and} \quad \bar{r} = \bar{R} - 1$$

where n is the number of possible annual trend values, T_n is the trend value of the last year, and T_1 is the trend value of the first year.

Formulas for the average relative acceleration $(\bar{A})$ and the average rate of acceleration $(\bar{a})$ are

$$\bar{A} = \sqrt[n-2]{\frac{T_n/T_{n-1}}{T_2/T_1}} \quad \text{and} \quad \bar{a} = \bar{A} - 1$$

T_2 is the trend value in the second year and T_{n-1} is the trend value of the next-to-last year.

We shall illustrate the application of these formulas for our two parabola trend lines and for the Gompertz. Referring to Table 17-6 containing the trend computations for our natural-number parabola for pertroleum production, we find that $T_1 = 182.8$ (1947), $T_2 = 190.9$ (1948), $T_{n-1} = 336.7$ (1975), and $T_n = 339.4$ (1976). The series covered 30 years, so $n = 30$. Therefore,

$$\bar{R} = \sqrt[n-1]{\frac{T_n}{T_1}} = \sqrt[29]{\frac{339.4}{182.8}} = \sqrt[29]{1.857} = 1.022 \quad \text{or} \quad 102.2\%/\text{yr}[1]$$

and $\bar{r} = \bar{R} - 1 = 1.022 - 1 = 0.022$, or 2.2%/year.

On the average, each trend value is 102.2% *of* the trend value for the previous year, or 2.2% *greater* than the trend of the previous year.

For our rate of acceleration, we get

$$\bar{A} = \sqrt[n-2]{\frac{T_n/T_{n-1}}{T_2/T_1}} = \sqrt[28]{\frac{339.4/336.7}{190.9/182.8}} = \sqrt[28]{\frac{1.008}{1.044}}$$

$$= \sqrt[28]{0.9655} = 0.9989 \quad \text{or} \quad 99.89\%/\text{yr}$$

[1] The higher-valued roots are obtained by using logarithms.

and

$$\bar{a} = \bar{A} - 1 = 0.9989 - 1 = -0.0011, \text{ or } -0.11\%/\text{year}$$

Our calculations show that our actual rates of growth have fallen from 4.4% (T_2/T_1) to 0.8% (T_n/T_{n-1}). The rate of change in these growth rates needed to bring about this reduction is given by our $\bar{a}$ value. Each growth rate is 99.89 percent of the previous rate, or 0.11 percent less than the previous rate. The negative acceleration value was expected, as Fig. 17-8 shows our trend to be increasing at decreasing rates.

As both our logarithmic parabola and Gompertz are fit to logs, a variation of our rate formulas will be useful in determining their rates. Writing the expression for $\bar{R}$ and $\bar{A}$ in logarithms, we get

$$\log \bar{R} = \frac{\log T_n - \log T_1}{n - 1}$$

and

$$\log \bar{A} = \frac{(\log T_n - \log T_{n-1}) - (\log T_2 - \log T_1)}{n - 2}$$

The log T values are available from our trend computation tables. Checking our fish-stock trend computations found in Table 17-9, we find that log T_1 = 2.2767 (1952), log T_2 = 2.2778 (1953), log T_{n-1} = 2.6290 (1975), and log T_n = 2.6597 (1976). Substituting for log $\bar{R}$,

$$\log \bar{R} = \frac{\log T_n - \log T_1}{n - 1} = \frac{2.6597 - 2.2767}{24} = \frac{0.3830}{24}$$

$$= + 0.0160$$

$$\bar{R} = \text{antilog } (\log \bar{R}) = \text{antilog } 0.0160 = 1.038 \quad \text{or} \quad 103.8\%/\text{yr}$$

$$\bar{r} = \bar{R} - 1 = 1.038 - 1 = 0.038 \quad \text{or} \quad 3.8\%/\text{yr}$$

Our calculations for $\bar{a}$ are

$$\log \bar{A} = \frac{(\log T_n - \log T_{n-1}) - (\log T_2 - \log T_1)}{n - 2}$$

$$= \frac{(2.6597 - 2.6290) - (2.2778 - 2.2767)}{23}$$

$$= \frac{0.0307 - 0.0011}{23} = \frac{0.0296}{23} = 0.0013$$

$$\bar{A} = \text{antilog } (\log \bar{A}) = \text{antilog } 0.0013 = 1.003 \text{ or } 100.3\%/\text{yr}$$

$$\bar{a} = \bar{A} - 1 = 1.003 - 1 = 0.003 \quad \text{or} \quad 0.3\%/\text{yr}$$

Note that our $\bar{a}$ is positive this time. A check of Fig. 17-9 shows that this time our trend is increasing at increasing rates. The sign of the $\bar{a}$ indicates the direction of the curvature, while its numerical value measures the degree.

Finally, checking Table 17-12 (the trend computation table for the Gompertz), we find that log T_1 = 2.5439 (1947), log T_2 = 2.5590 (1948), log T_{n-1} = 2.8068 (1975), and log T_n = 2.8118 (1976). Substituting for log $\overline{R}$,

$$\log \overline{R} = \frac{\log T_n - \log T_1}{n-1} = \frac{2.8118 - 2.5439}{29}$$

$$= \frac{0.2679}{29} = 0.0092$$

$$\overline{R} = \text{antilog } (\log \overline{R}) = \text{antilog } 0.0092 = 1.022 \quad \text{or} \quad 102.2\%/\text{yr}$$

$$\overline{r} = \overline{R} - 1 = 1.022 - 1 = 0.022 \quad \text{or} \quad 2.2\%/\text{yr}$$

Substituting for log $\overline{A}$,

$$\log \overline{A} = \frac{(\log T_n - \log T_{n-1}) - (\log T_2 - \log T_1)}{n-2}$$

$$= \frac{(2.8118 - 2.8068) - (2.5590 - 2.5439)}{28}$$

$$= \frac{0.0050 - 0.0151}{28} = \frac{-0.0101}{28}$$

$$= -0.0004 = 9.9996 - 10$$

$$\overline{A} = \text{antilog } (\log \overline{A}) = \text{antilog } (9.9996 - 10) = 0.9990 \text{ or } 99.9\%/\text{yr}$$

$$\overline{a} = \overline{A} - 1 = 0.9990 - 1 = -0.0010 \quad \text{or} \quad -0.1\%/\text{yr}$$

The trend of U.S. cigarette production grew at an average rate of 2.2 percent per year over the 30 years studied. The actual rates of growth were subject to a slight negative acceleration of 0.1 percent per year.

Uses of Trend Lines

The uses of trend lines correspond to the purposes for which they are fit. To use a trend line as an aid to forecasting, one merely substitutes the appropriate time value in the trend equation and solves for the trend estimate. When fit for historical description, the resulting trend equation is of course the basic device for describing the trend. This is often compared with related trend equations. Constants of the equations, such as the *b* value and log *b* value and rates of growth and rates of acceleration, may be used as illustrated above to show the more interesting features of the trend growth. If the trend line has been computed to aid in studying cycles, the original values of the data are divided by the appropriate trend values to remove the trend from the original data. This will be illustrated in Chap. 18 when cycle analysis is discussed in greater detail.

STUDY GUIDE

Concepts Worth Remembering

Define:

1. Trend
2. Cycle
3. Seasonal
4. Irregular
5. Classical model
6. Semilogarithmic graph paper
7. Method of selected points
8. Method of least squares
9. Parabola (second-degree curve)
10. Growth curves
11. Gompertz curve
12. Logistic curve
13. Rate of change
14. Rate of acceleration

Self-Test

Matching questions. Listed in Group 1 below are the components of the "classical" time series model. In Group 2 are listed some definitions or properties of the measures in Group 1. In the blanks provided, indicate the number of the component in Group 1 referred to by the Group 2 descriptions.

Group 1

1. Trend
2. Cycle
3. Seasonal
4. Irregular

Group 2

—— 1 A movement lasting many years.
—— 2 A movement caused in part by climate or weather.
—— 3 A movement attributed in part to population factors.
—— 4 A movement generally 3 to 5 years in length.
—— 5 A movement associated with wars and strikes.
—— 6 A movement with a roughly repetitive pattern.
—— 7 A movement often left combined with cycle during analysis.
—— 8 A movement complete within the period of a year.
—— 9 A movement characterized as being smooth and continuous.
—— 10 A movement generally analyzed as a residual.
—— 11 A movement important to long-term forecasting.
—— 12 A movement characterized by no predictable pattern.
—— 13 A movement measured in the form of an index.

—— **14** The least controversial component of the time series model.
—— **15** A movement generally measured by a line.
—— **16** A movement caused in part by customary calendar factors.
—— **17** A movement attributed in part to changes in technological forces.
—— **18** A movement whose conformity to general business conditions is carefully studied.

Questions to Think About

1. Discuss the "classical" time series model particularly as to its derivation, the nature of its parts, and how they are combined to produce the final time series.
2. What are the factors affecting the choice of mechanical methods of determining trend lines?
3. List the possible purposes for fitting a trend line. Explain how the purpose affects the type of line used in fitting.
4. Explain the nature of semilogarithmic graph paper and how it differs from ordinary arithmetic paper. How is it used in trend analysis?
5. Compare and contrast the two different fitting procedures used in the chapter for fitting trend lines.
6. Give examples of and explain the nature of "growth" curves. For what purpose are these curves particularly useful?
7. Of what use in trend analysis are rates of growth and rates of acceleration?

Problems

1

Ton miles of freight per freight car day carried by class I railroads in the United States, 1963–1976

Year	Ton-miles	Year	Ton-miles
1963	1,113	1970	1,418
1964	1,160	1971	1,373
1965	1,250	1972	1,482
1966	1,310	1973	1,621
1967	1,271	1974	1,646
1968	1,360	1975	1,510
1969	1,426	1976	1,645

Source: Yearbook of Railroad Facts, 1977 Edition, p. 44.

(a) Plot the data above on a sheet of arithmetic graph paper.
(b) Fit a straight line trend to the data above by the method of semiaverages. Plot the trend line on the graph drawn in (a).
(c) Fit a straight line trend to the data above by the method of least squares. Plot the trend line on the graph drawn in (a).
(d) What generalizations can you make about the trend of ton miles per freight car day during this period?

2

Average daily freight car mileage in the United States, 1964-1976

Year	Average daily car mileage	Year	Average daily car mileage
1964	50.0	1971	53.3
1965	51.7	1972	56.1
1966	53.0	1973	57.7
1967	51.5	1974	54.4
1968	53.5	1975	53.5
1969	54.9	1976	56.9
1970	54.6		

Source: Yearbook of Railroad Facts, 1977 Edition, p. 43.

(*a*) Plot the data above on a sheet of arithmetic graph paper.

(*b*) Fit a straight line trend to the data above by the method of semiaverages. Use the 1970 value of 54.6 in both averages. Plot the trend line on the graph drawn in (*a*).

(*c*) Fit a straight line trend to the data above by the method of least squares. Plot the trend line on the graph drawn in (*a*).

(*d*) What generalizations can you make about the trend of average daily car mileage during this period?

3

New plant and equipment expenditures for all industries in the United States, 1958-1976

Year	Billion dollars	Year	Billion dollars
1958	30.5	1968	64.1
1959	32.5	1969	71.2
1960	35.7	1970	79.7
1961	34.4	1971	81.2
1962	37.3	1972	88.5
1963	39.2	1973	99.7
1964	44.9	1974	112.4
1965	52.0	1975	112.8
1966	60.6	1976	120.5
1967	61.7		

Source: Survey of Current Business.

(*a*) Plot the data above on a sheet of semilogarithmic graph paper.

(*b*) Fit a logarithmic straight line trend to the series above by the method of least squares. Plot the trend line on the graph drawn in (*a*).

(*c*) Compute the average rate of change per year in the trend of new plant and equipment expenditures.

4

United States production of automobile tires, 1952–1976

Year	Millions	Year	Millions
1952	90.4	1967	163.2
1953	96.1	1968	203.1
1954	84.1	1969	207.8
1955	112.1	1970	190.4
1956	100.4	1971	213.1
1957	106.9	1972	229.6
1958	96.6	1973	223.4
1959	118.0	1974	211.4
1960	119.8	1975	186.7
1961	116.8	1976	188.0
1962	133.9		
1963	139.0		
1964	158.1		
1965	167.9		
1966	117.2		

Source: Survey of Current Business.

(*a*) Plot the data above on a sheet of semilogarithmic graph paper.

(*b*) Compute 5-year averages of the data above.

(*c*) Fit a logarithmic straight line trend to the 5-year averages by the method of least squares. Plot the trend line on the graph drawn in (*a*).

(*d*) Compute the annual rate of growth in the trend of automobile tire production.

5

United States paper products production, 1947–1976

Year	Millions of short tons	Year	Millions of short tons
1947	21.1	1962	37.6
1948	21.9	1963	39.0
1949	20.3	1964	41.7
1950	24.4	1965	44.1
1951	26.0	1966	47.1
1952	24.4	1967	46.9
1953	26.5	1968	49.5
1954	26.9	1969	53.5
1955	30.2	1970	52.2
1956	31.4	1971	54.6
1957	30.7	1972	59.3
1958	30.8	1973	61.8
1959	34.0	1974	60.2
1960	34.4	1975	52.4
1961	35.7	1976	59.5

Source: Survey of Current Business.

(a) Plot the data above on a sheet of semilogarithmic graph paper.

(b) Compute 5-year averages of the data above.

(c) Fit a logarithmic straight line trend to the 5-year averages by the method of least squares. Plot the trend line on the graph drawn in (a).

(d) Compute the annual rate of growth in the trend of paper products production.

6

Piggyback loadings, Western District, 1957–1976

Year	Revenue cars loaded, thousands	Year	Revenue cars loaded, thousands
1957	113	1967	459
1958	130	1968	511
1959	202	1969	524
1960	269	1970	491
1961	254	1971	457
1962	272	1972	485
1963	309	1973	565
1964	334	1974	560
1965	379	1975	467
1966	430	1976	589

Source: Car Service Division, Association of American Railroads.

(a) Plot the data above on a sheet of arithmetic graph paper.

(b) Fit a parabola to the data above by the method of least squares.

(c) Compute trend values for each year and plot the trend line on the graph drawn in (a).

(d) How would you characterize the growth trend of this series?

7

Total sales of the Gillette Company, 1957–1976

Year	Dollars, 100,000s	Year	Dollars, 100,000s
1957	194.9	1967	428.4
1958	193.9	1968	553.2
1959	209.3	1969	609.6
1960	224.7	1970	672.7
1961	253.5	1971	729.7
1962	276.2	1972	870.5
1963	295.7	1973	1064.4
1964	299.0	1974	1246.4
1965	339.1	1975	1406.9
1966	396.2	1976	1462.6

Source: Moody's *Handbook of Common Stocks.*

(*a*) Plot the data above on a sheet of semilogarithmic graph paper.

(*b*) Compute 5-year averages of the data above.

(*c*) Fit a logarithmic parabola trend to the 5-year averages by the method of least squares.

(*d*) Compute trend values for 1957, 1958, 1959, 1964, 1969, 1974, 1975, and 1976. Plot the trend line on the graph drawn in (*a*).

(*e*) Compute the average annual rate of growth in the trend of Gillette Company sales.

(*f*) Compute the average annual rate of acceleration in the trend of Gillette Company sales.

8

United States production of margarine, 1952–1976

Year	Billions of pounds	Year	Billions of pounds
1952	1.29	1967	2.11
1953	1.29	1968	2.14
1954	1.36	1969	2.18
1955	1.33	1970	2.23
1956	1.37	1971	2.29
1957	1.46	1972	2.36
1958	1.57	1973	2.36
1959	1.61	1974	2.40
1960	1.70	1975	2.40
1961	1.72	1976	2.63
1962	1.73		
1963	1.79		
1964	1.86		
1965	1.90		
1966	2.11		

Source: Survey of Current Business.

(*a*) Plot the data above on a sheet of semilogarithmic graph paper.

(*b*) Compute 5-year averages of the data above.

(*c*) Fit a logarithmic parabola trend to the 5-year averages by the method of least squares.

(*d*) Compute trend values for 1952, 1953, 1954, 1959, 1964, 1969, 1974, 1975, and 1976. Plot the trend line on the graph drawn in (*a*).

(*e*) Compute the average annual rate of growth in the trend of margarine production.

(*f*) Compute the average annual rate of acceleration in the trend of margarine production.

9

Asphalt production in the United States, 1947–1976

Year	Millions of barrels	Year	Millions of barrels
1947	49.3	1962	109.6
1948	51.9	1963	111.9
1949	49.0	1964	114.9
1950	58.2	1965	123.6
1951	66.3	1966	129.6
1952	70.3	1967	127.8
1953	72.4	1968	135.5
1954	74.9	1969	135.7
1955	83.1	1970	146.7
1956	90.6	1971	157.0
1957	85.7	1972	155.3
1958	89.4	1973	167.9
1959	97.6	1974	164.2
1960	98.7	1975	144.0
1961	101.8	1976	139.7

Source: Survey of Current Business.

(a) Plot the data above on a sheet of semilogarithmic graph paper.

(b) Compute centered 10-year averages for the data above.

(c) Fit a Gompertz trend line to the centered 10-year averages by the method of selected points.

(d) Compute trend values for 1947, 1948, $1951\frac{1}{2}$, $1956\frac{1}{2}$, $1961\frac{1}{2}$, $1966\frac{1}{2}$, $1971\frac{1}{2}$, 1975, and 1976. Plot the trend line on the graph drawn in (a).

(e) Compute the average annual rate of growth in the trend of asphalt production.

(f) Compute the average annual rate of acceleration in the trend of asphalt production.

Student Project—Times Series, Part I

Contact your nearest National Park for annual data on the number of park visits to that park for the past 30 years. Use these data as the basis for determining the trend in the number of visits.

Also collect data on the monthly number of park visits for the past 10 years. Save this data for Part II of this project at the end of the Study Guide of Chap. 18.

Answers to Self-Test

1	1	4	7	3	13
3	2	3	8	3	14
1	3	1	9	1	15
2	4	2	10	3	16
4	5	1	11	1	17
2	6	4	12	2	18

EIGHTEEN
SEASONAL AND CYCLICAL ANALYSIS

LEARNING OBJECTIVES

The basic learning objective is to extend our knowledge of time series analysis by studying the methods of seasonal analysis and of cycle analysis. Specifically, you will become familiar with:

1. The computation of seasonal indexes by the ratio to moving average method.
2. The interpretation and use of seasonal indexes.
3. Cycle analysis by the residual method.
4. Cycle analysis by the National Bureau of Economic Research's methods.
5. The use of the results of cycle analysis.

INTRODUCTION

In this chapter we continue our discussion of the decomposition techniques of formal time series analysis. We shall first turn our attention to seasonal analysis and then conclude with a discussion of cycle analysis.

SEASONAL ANALYSIS

Seasonal analysis, like trend analysis, determines a measure of this type of variation, starting with the data. It differs in that, where trend lines are computed directly from the data, our measure of seasonal variation is computed by eliminating the other components from the data, so that only seasonal remains. Although several methods of measuring seasonal variation have been developed, most seasonal index computations today are variations of the ratio to moving average method. The basic form of this method will be discussed and illustrated in the sections which follow.

Ratio to Moving Average Method: An Explanation

The basic ratio to moving average method, like most methods, measures the seasonal component in the form of an index. The method employs three steps in the computation of the index: (1) computing an annual moving average of the series being studied, (2) dividing the values of the original data through by the corresponding moving average values, and (3) averaging and adjusting the ratios computed in step 2 to obtain the seasonal index.

Normally, a seasonal index is computed on a monthly basis using 12 to 15 years of original data. The same general procedure may be used, however, to compute a seasonal index by quarters or weeks. The first step is to compute a moving average of annual duration (i.e., 12 months, 4 quarters, or 52 weeks). If the data begin in year 1 with a January value, the first average would be based on the monthly data from January through December of that year. The second average moves over 1 month. It is computed from the monthly values starting with February of year 1 through January of year 2. The third average is based on values from March of year 1 through February of year 2. This process is continued until all the data are exhausted.

The annual moving average thus computed will contain none of the original seasonal variation. "Seasonal" was defined as a movement of only 1 year's duration and therefore will average out when an annual moving average is computed. However, as a trend is a movement of many years' duration, and even determined from annual values in many cases, practically all of it will be contained in the moving average. The amount of the cyclical variation which will remain in the moving average depends on the duration and amplitude of the cycles. The moving average will always overcut the troughs and undercut the peaks of the cycles, but the extent of this overcutting and undercutting varies with the type of cycle, being more pronounced when the cycles are of short duration and/or pronounced amplitude. In most cases, however, most of the cycle is contained in the moving average. Short irregulars will tend to be averaged out by the moving average, but longer ones will be reflected in the average. In general, the moving average will contain or show the movements of the trend and most of the cycle, but only a small portion of the irregular and no seasonal.

The second step of dividing the original data values by the corresponding moving average values serves to cancel out or eliminate from the original data all components contained in the moving average. The resulting ratios therefore should contain all the seasonal and most of the irregular, but only a little cycle and no trend.

In step 3 the ratios are averaged for like time periods, i.e., all Januaries, all Februaries, all first quarters, and so on. These averaging procedures are designed to eliminate any nonseasonal elements remaining, leaving only a measure of seasonal variation.

The procedure is quite flexible and may be changed to meet the needs of a specific series at several points. The averaging techniques in step 3 in particular may be adapted to conditions of a constant seasonal pattern (i.e., one that remains the same over a period of years) or a moving seasonal pattern (i.e., one that exhibits a systematic change in timing, amplitude, or both).

Ratio to Moving Average Method: An Illustration

Table 18-1 contains quarterly data on agricultural employment in the United States and the calculations of the first two steps in computing a quarterly seasonal index. The data are plotted in Fig. 18-1.

The first step is the computation of a centered four-quarter moving average. This begins with the computation of moving four-quarter totals shown in column 2 of Table 18-1. These have been arbitrarily placed opposite the third item in each total, although they should be centered between the second and third items. Next, a two-

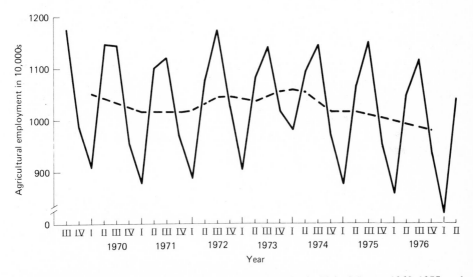

Figure 18-1 Seasonal illustration: agricultural employment in the United States, 1969–1977, and four-quarter moving average. SOURCE: Survey of Current Business.

Table 18-1 **Seasonal illustration, agricultural employment in the United States, 1969–1977**

Year and quarter	(1) Agricultural employment, 10,000s	(2) Moving four-quarter total	(3) Moving two-item total	(4) Moving average	(5) Ratio of original data to moving average, %
1969 III	1176				
IV	987				
1970 I	908	4217	8401	1050	86.5
II	1146	4184	8338	1042	110.0
III	1143	4154	8276	1034	110.5
IV	957	4122	8200	1025	93.4
1971 I	876	4078	8131	1016	86.2
II	1102	4053	8117	1015	108.6
III	1118	4064	8139	1017	109.9
IV	968	4075	8127	1016	95.3
1972 I	887	4052	8161	1020	87.0
II	1079	4109	8275	1034	104.4
III	1175	4166	8350	1044	112.6
IV	1025	4184	8370	1046	98.0
1973 I	904	4186	8340	1042	86.8
II	1082	4154	8298	1037	104.3
III	1143	4144	8365	1046	108.4
IV	1015	4221	8454	1057	96.0
1974 I	981	4233	8467	1058	92.7
II	1094	4234	8425	1053	103.9
III	1144	4191	8275	1034	110.6
IV	972	4084	8143	1018	95.5
1975 I	877	4059	8125	1016	86.3
II	1066	4066	8114	1014	105.1
III	1151	4048	8074	1009	114.1
IV	954	4026	8033	1004	95.0
1976 I	855	4007	7980	998	85.7
II	1047	3973	7930	991	105.7
III	1117	3957	7877	985	113.4
IV	938	3920	7837	980	95.7
1977 I	818	3917			
II	1044				

Source: Survey of Current Business.

item moving total is computed of the four-item totals. These results are shown in column 3. They are placed opposite the first item in the total. The two-item totals are needed to line up the dates of the moving average values with those of the original data. For example, the first two-item total of 8,401 is written opposite the first quarter of 1970 and is the total of 4,217 and 4,184. Although written opposite the first quarter, the 4,217 should appear between the fourth quarter of 1969 and the first quarter of 1970. The value of 4,184 is written opposite the second quarter of 1970 (the third quarter of its set of four), but should be centered between the first and second quarters of 1970. The total of 4,217 and 4,184, therefore, should appear opposite the first quarter of 1970, which is where it has been written. These relationships are as follows:

$$
\begin{array}{lll}
\text{1969 III} & 1{,}176 \\
 \text{IV} & 987 \\
\text{1970 I} & 908 & \rightarrow 4{,}217 \quad 8{,}401 \\
 \text{II} & 1{,}146 & \rightarrow 4{,}184 \\
 \text{III} & 1{,}143
\end{array}
$$

To complete the computation of the moving average, each two-item total of column 3 is divided by 8 to obtain the moving average values shown in column 4. Division is by 8, as this is the number of original quarter-sized values in each two-item total. The moving average is plotted with the original data in Fig. 18-1. Notice how the pronounced seasonal apparent in the original data has been averaged out and how the moving average itself follows the downward trend of employment. If the computations were for monthly data, the second column would have 12-month moving totals, the third would contain two-item totals of the 12-month totals to center on the proper month, and the moving average of the fourth column would be obtained by dividing by 24.

The second step of the method is to divide the original data by the moving average values to eliminate those components contained in the moving average. The resulting ratios expressed as percentages are given in the fifth column of Table 18-1.

The final step in the ratio to moving average procedure is to average the ratios by quarters in an attempt to average out any remaining nonseasonal elements (mostly irregulars, but also some cycle). The actual averaging techniques employed depend upon the data of the problem itself. A great deal of flexibility is introduced into the general method by the variety of approaches which may be employed here in step 3. A preliminary analysis of the ratios is needed to decide what averaging technique to employ. Such an analysis is generally graphical. The ratios have been rearranged in Table 18-2 in order that they may be grouped by quarters and have also been plotted in Figs. 18-2 and 18-3.

Table 18-2 Ratios of original data to moving average by quarters

	Quarter			
Year	I	II	III	IV
1970	86.5	110.0	110.5	93.4
1971	86.2	108.6	109.9	95.3
1972	87.0	104.4	112.6	98.0
1973	86.8	104.3	108.4	96.0
1974	92.7	103.9	110.6	95.5
1975	86.3	105.1	114.1	95.0
1976	85.7	105.7	113.4	95.7

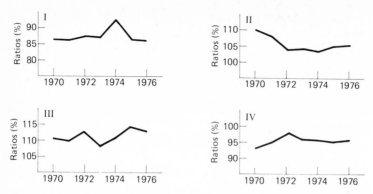

Figure 18-2 Ratios to moving averages by quarters by years, 1970–1976.

Figure 18-2 shows the ratios for each quarter plotted consecutively by years. This type of graph is used to study whether there has been any change in the general level of any quarter's seasonal value over time. If the values for the quarters show no consistent pattern, but merely fluctuate around a horizontal line (as ours do), it is evidence of a stable seasonal pattern. Changing seasonals will be discussed briefly later in the chapter. They would appear here as some form of pattern in the ratios when plotted.

Figure 18-3 is drawn to aid us in determining how to average the ratios to obtain a stable seasonal index. As we generally deal with a small number of items, a straight arithmetic mean is seldom used, because it might be excessively distorted by an extreme irregular. Most often a modified mean is used; i.e., the mean of the remaining items after the extremes have been eliminated. This usually takes the form of a positional mean, since, for every high item eliminated, the corresponding low item is also eliminated. A study of Fig. 18-3 shows that quarter I in particular and quarter II also have values (high ones) which might distort an arithmetic mean. Therefore, we shall

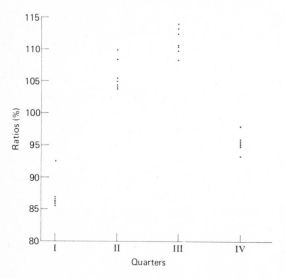

Figure 18-3 Ratios to moving average arrayed for each quarter.

Table 18-3 Mean of middle three ratios and seasonal index for agricultural employment

Quarter	Mean middle three ratios	Seasonal index
I	86.5	86.9
II	105.1	105.5
III	111.2	111.7
IV	95.5	95.9
Total	398.3	400.0

average the middle three ratios for each quarter to obtain our seasonal index. (There is a bit too small a number for averaging, but it results here from the shorter-than-usual period used for illustration.) Table 18-3 shows the results of such averaging. To complete our seasonal index, we must adjust the values of the averages to total 400.0 so they average to 100.0. This is necessary so that, when the index is used to adjust data for seasonal variation, it will not change the total of the series for any given year. To adjust, we multiply each three-ratio average by the factor 400/398.3 = 1.0042681. The results of this adjustment, our completed seasonal index, are also shown in Table 18-3. The index of 86.9 for the first quarter indicates that that quarter is only 86.9 percent of (or 13.1 percent below) the average quarter because of seasonal influences (poor weather). Other quarters would yield similar interpretations.

The modifications needed in steps 2 and 3 to determine a monthly seasonal index are obvious. Figures 18-2 and 18-3 would be for 12 months each rather than for four quarters. After averaging ratios by months, the results must be adjusted to total 1,200.0 rather than 400.0.

Comments on Moving Seasonals

Although a large number of seasonal patterns are constant or stable over long periods of time, others show changes with time. These changes may be gradual and consistent, in either the amplitude or timing of the pattern, or in some cases abrupt, because of some shift in the company or industry's operating methods. All these changes should show up in graphs similar to Fig. 18-2. As the possibilities are numerous and varied, each problem must be handled individually. In general, the modified mean procedure employed in our illustration is replaced by an attempt to establish the trend of the change in the ratios of the moving seasonal.

The computation of all forms of seasonal indexes is greatly facilitated by the existence and use of electronic computers, which can do a computer variation of the ratio to moving average method for 15 years of monthly data in less than 2 minutes. The use of an electronic computer also bypasses the problem of moving versus stable seasonal patterns, as the ratios are averaged by a five-ratio moving average (with highest and lowest ratios omitted from the average) which will remain the same if the pattern is stable or will change as needed with a moving pattern.

Uses of Seasonal Indexes

Seasonal indexes (SI) are used to adjust a time series for seasonal variation (i.e., remove the seasonal effects on the series) and to aid in short-term forecasting.

According to our model, we may remove the effects of seasonal variation from a time series by dividing the original data for the series through by the seasonal index. In symbols we have

$$\frac{Y}{SI} = \frac{T \times \cancel{S} \times CI}{\cancel{S}} = T \times CI$$

Therefore, if we wish to study the movement of a time series free from seasonal effects, we divide each month or quarter of the series through by the seasonal index for the corresponding month or quarter. Study of the movements of a time series free from seasonal variation is desirable because, in the short run, seasonal effects may outweigh and run counter to some longer-term effects, such as cycle and trend, whose movement we are trying to study. Such would be the case, for example, near the bottom of a cycle when one was evaluating whether an increase in sales or employment in a given month was a sign of recovery or merely the expected seasonal increase for that period.

Knowledge of seasonal patterns and the indexes themselves is useful in short-term forecasting and planning. If a company is expecting a sales peak in July (high seasonal index for July sales), it can plan its production in advance to meet this peak by manufacturing excess product earlier in the year during a slack sales season and keeping it in inventory for July. Similarly, a department store which is placing orders in the spring for goods to be sold in the fall will make use of the fall seasonal index to forecast possible fall sales.

CYCLE ANALYSIS

More attention has probably been devoted to the study of the cyclical movements in a time series than to any of the other components. Even so, nothing like complete agreement exists on the way to best measure cycles or on the causes of cycles. We shall discuss the conventional "residual" approach and the approach developed by the National Bureau of Economic Research.

Residual Method: An Explanation

This method was described briefly in our discussion of the classical time series model at the beginning of Chap. 17. For annual data, that model is $Y = T \times CI$. To obtain a measure of the cycle in the annual data, we first compute a measure of trend. The original data are then divided through by this measure of trend, canceling out trend and leaving only the cycle-irregular component. In symbols, we have

$$\frac{Y}{Y_T} = \frac{\cancel{T} \times CI}{\cancel{T}} = CI$$

The model for monthly or quarterly data is $Y = T \times S \times CI$. To obtain the cyclical residual in this case, we must first compute both a measure of trend and a seasonal index. Dividing the original data by both again leaves only the cycle-irregular component.

$$\frac{Y}{Y_T(SI)} = \frac{\not{T} \times \not{S} \times CI}{\not{T} \times \not{S}} = CI$$

Generally, no attempt is made to separate the cycle and irregular components in annual data, but the irregular in monthly data is sometimes smoothed out by using a 3-month moving average, giving double weight to the central item.

The residual approach, while quite straightforward in its logic, is subject to several difficulties. To be successful, it requires that one obtain a trend line which fits well, bisecting all the cycles. This is not always easy to do. Also, if monthly data are being used, an adequate seasonal index must be determined. To the extent that our seasonal index and trend line are incomplete, we shall not obtain a true measure of cycle. In addition, there is the more basic problem of whether we have the correct model at all. Despite these difficulties, the method does often yield a useful measure of the apparent cyclical element in many series.

Residual Method: An Illustration

To illustrate the computation of a measure of cyclical variation, we shall again use the sales data of the Antique Chair Company from our first trend illustration (Table 17-1 or 17-2). These data are reproduced in Table 18-4. In addition, the trend values of the least squares trend line have been computed for each year. The final column of the table contains our measure of cyclical variation. These values are termed "cyclical relatives" and are obtained by dividing the sales figure for each year by the corresponding trend figure for the year. The results are conventionally expressed as percentages. These values have been plotted in Fig. 18-4 in order that the cyclical pattern

Table 18-4 Computation of cyclical relatives for sales of the Antique Chair Company, 1970–1979

Year (X)	Sales (Y), $10,000s	Least squares trend values (Y_T)	Cyclical relative ($100Y/Y_T$)
1970	10	11.4	87.7
1971	12	11.8	101.7
1972	14	12.2	114.8
1973	11	12.6	87.3
1974	15	13.0	115.4
1975	14	13.4	104.5
1976	12	13.8	87.0
1977	14	14.2	98.6
1978	16	14.6	109.6
1979	14	15.0	93.3

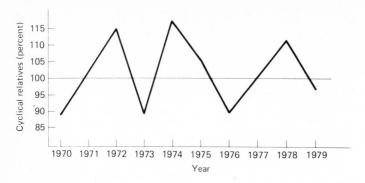

Figure 18-4 Cycle chart of the sales of Antique Chair Company, 1970–1979.

may be more readily observed. This pattern may be compared with that of business in general to determine if the specific series conforms with the general business cycle. If it does, attempts to forecast the cyclical behavior of this series will be related to forecasts of general business conditions.

To illustrate the interpretation of a specific year's value, let us consider 1972's cyclical relative of 114.8 percent. This indicates that sales in 1972 were 14.8 percent above trend because of cyclical and irregular factors in the data. 1973's relative of 87.3 percent indicates that sales were 87.3 percent of trend, or 12.7 percent below trend in 1973 because of cyclical and irregular factors.

Methodology of the National Bureau of Economic Research

The most extensive empirical research into the behavior of business cycles has been done by the National Bureau of Economic Research (NBER). The Bureau has analyzed over 1,000 different time series to study their cyclical patterns. While the average individual will have little occasion to do an analysis following Bureau procedures, a knowledge of the nature of the procedure is of value to anyone studying cycles and forecasting business conditions.

As data for its cycle analysis, the NBER starts with data adjusted for seasonal variation only. No attempt is made in the beginning to separate the trend element from the cyclical element, although the method does contain provision for later evaluation of the former element.

The basic unit of experience in the Bureau's analysis of an individual time series is the cycle itself, irrespective of its actual duration through time. Two types of cycles are developed and studied. One of these is the specific cycle, and the other, the reference cycle.

For specific cycle analysis the series adjusted for seasonal variation is plotted and the turning points (peaks and troughs) of the cycles identified. The values making up each cycle are then averaged to obtain a base for that cycle. These values are next divided by the cycle base for that cycle to convert them to relatives. Each cycle, irrespective of its actual duration in time, is now divided into nine stages. Stage I is the initial trough, and Stage IX the terminal trough. Stage V marks the cycle peak. Stages II, III, and IV represent equal periods in the expansion phase, while Stages VI, VII, and VIII are equal periods in the contraction phase. Values for each stage are determined by averaging appropriate specific cycle relatives. Once the stages for all the specific cycles have been determined, they may be combined and averaged to obtain the average specific cycle and its pattern. Both the average level of each stage and the average duration between stages may be determined. Measures of dispersion are developed to help evaluate how typical these various averages are.

Reference cycle analysis follows the same mechanical format of nine-stage analysis, with the important exception that the dating of the turning points (peaks and troughs) of the reference cycles is on the basis of a reference chronology established by the Bureau.[1] The turning points of this chronology and the cycles determined by them are the basis for establishing the cycle units to be used in the reference analysis of a particular series, irrespective of whether the series in question has cycles conforming to the reference chronology or not. The analysis again proceeds through the determining of a cycle base, reference cycle relatives, and stage averages for each cycle, and finally an average reference cycle pattern. An important addition to the reference cycle analysis is a variety of measures to show the degree of conformity of the series analyzed to the reference cycle chronology. These include measures of lead or lag. Knowledge of the former behavior is obviously of value in forecasting business conditions.

Uses of the Results of Cycle Analysis

Cycle analysis is performed chiefly to gain knowledge which will aid in forecasting. The form this aid takes may be quite varied, however. To the business manager, the problem of cycle forecasting differs from that of trend and seasonal in that, while the latter factors tend to be specific to the company or industry, a specific cycle forecast based on company data alone would be of doubtful value. Most companies and industries are affected by the cycles in general business conditions, and their own forecasts should be related to forecasts of general business conditions. A company's analysis of its own past cycles will help to establish the nature of its relationship to general business cycles. Cycle analysis of the type done by the NBER has established a number of series which have a good record as leaders of general business conditions and which may be watched to forecast turns in general business. The Department of Commerce's Index of Leading Indicators is based on the research of the National Bureau. Cycle forecasting is, of course, for periods of an intermediate duration between those for which seasonal is the dominant factor and those for which trend is dominant. Correct anticipation of the turning points is very important to successful business decisions, and forecasts of cyclical conditions are made and revised almost constantly.

[1] The reference chronology represents the Bureau's best estimate of the turning points in general business activity. These turning points have been established by extensive research of both a qualitative and quantitative nature into business records, newspapers, and trade journals.

STATE OF THE ART

In closing, we should like to note what was apparent in our discussion—that the art of analyzing a time series is not as highly developed as our other statistical techniques previously discussed. Sampling and correlation techniques, for example, have sound theoretical bases. Time series techniques, on the other hand, are highly pragmatic in character. One widely used model exists, but its validity cannot be proved, and it is not accepted by all analysts.

Underlying most of time series analysis is a desire to forecast the future. It is absolutely essential for a business manager to make forecasts in order to make intelligent decisions about the future. Failure to forecast consciously is a forecast itself; i.e., it assumes that the status quo will hold.

The state of our analysis varies with the component (granted the model), being best for seasonal and poorest for cycle. New approaches to the problem are being studied, and better techniques will undoubtedly be developed in the future.

STUDY GUIDE

Concepts Worth Remembering

Define:
1. Ratio to moving average method
2. Moving averages
3. Constant (stable) seasonal
4. Moving (changing) seasonal
5. Residual method of cycle analysis
6. Cyclical relative

Self-Test

Multiple-choice questions. Circle the letters of the statements which correctly complete the questions. There may be one to four correct answers.

1 The seasonal component of the time series model is:
   (a) The least controversial element in the model.
   (b) Important to short-term forecasting.
   (c) The result of climate and custom.
   (d) An intrayear movement which does not appear in annual data.

2 The cyclical component of the time series model:
   (a) Cannot be separated from the trend component.
   (b) Is usually studied as a residual or remainder.
   (c) Results from population movement and growth.
   (d) Is a wavelike movement with a duration of more than a year.

3 The ratio to moving average method of determining a seasonal index:
   (a) Is widely used partly because of its great flexibility, being easily adapted to either a constant or a moving seasonal pattern.

(b) Computes a moving average of a year's duration as its initial step.

(c) Is so called because the second step in the method consists of dividing the original data through by the moving average.

(d) Is easily adaptable to computer calculations.

4 The first step in the ratio to moving average method of computing a quarterly seasonal index involves:

(a) Computing a two- of a four-quarter moving average to line up the dates properly.

(b) Dividing each year's values by four after eliminating the high and low items.

(c) Computing a centered four-quarter moving average as a measure of trend and most cycle.

(d) Combining all values for like time periods for averaging.

5 The second step in the ratio to moving average method of computing a quarterly seasonal index:

(a) Has as its purpose the elimination of the trend and most of the cycle from the data.

(b) Is the multiplication of the original data through by the centered four-quarter moving average.

(c) Produces a set of ratios which contain primarily seasonal and irregular movements.

(d) Is done differently for a stable seasonal.

6 The final step in the ratio to moving average method of computing a stable quarterly seasonal index:

(a) Requires the fitting of freehand trend lines to the ratios plotted on the panel graphs.

(b) Uses a moving average when done on a computer.

(c) Involves the use of positional means to average out all foreign elements in the ratios.

(d) Requires that the final averages be adjusted to total 400.

7 A moving seasonal pattern:

(a) Can be recognized by plotting the ratios computed in step 2 of the ratio to moving average method.

(b) Is one which shows a systematic change of pattern over time.

(c) Has the same index value for each month or quarter in consecutive years.

(d) Cannot be computed on an electronic computer.

8 The residual method of studying cycles:

(a) Can only be applied to annual data.

(b) Involves the calculation of values termed "cyclical relatives."

(c) Was developed by the National Bureau of Economic Research.

(d) Usually leaves the irregular component combined with the cyclical component.

Questions to Think About

1. Outline the steps in the ratio to moving average method of determining a quarterly seasonal index. Explain the purpose of each step.
2. Explain how the last step in the computation of a seasonal index differs for a moving seasonal from that used for a stable seasonal.
3. List and discuss the uses of seasonal indexes.

4. Explain the logic and assumptions underlying the residual approach to studying cycles. What are the method's strengths and weaknesses?
5. Contrast the National Bureau of Economic Research's method of studying cycles with the residual method.
6. Explain how cycle forecasting differs from forecasting based on trend or seasonal.

Problems

1

United States paper products production by quarters, 1969–1976

Year and quarter		Millions of short tons	Year and quarter		Millions of short tons
1969	I	13.3	1973	I	15.4
	II	13.6		II	15.9
	III	13.1		III	15.1
	IV	13.4		IV	15.4
1970	I	13.4	1974	I	15.6
	II	13.5		II	16.0
	III	12.5		III	15.1
	IV	12.5		IV	13.4
1971	I	13.4	1975	I	12.1
	II	13.7		II	12.5
	III	13.4		III	13.3
	IV	14.0		IV	14.4
1972	I	14.7	1976	I	15.1
	II	15.0		II	14.9
	III	14.6		III	14.4
	IV	15.0		IV	14.5

Source: Survey of Current Business.

(*a*) Use the ratio to moving average method to compute quarterly seasonal indexes for the data above.
(*b*) Interpret the index values for each of the four quarters.
(*c*) Use the indexes computed in (*a*) to adjust these data for seasonal variation.

2

Quarterly sales of the Gillette Company, 1969–1976

Year and quarter		Dollars, 100,000s	Year and quarter		Dollars, 100,000s
1969	I	149.9	1973	I	231.9
	II	138.5		II	248.5
	III	156.3		III	260.8
	IV	165.4		IV	323.2

Quarterly sales of the Gillette Company, 1969–1976 (*Continued*)

Year and quarter		Dollars, 100,000s	Year and quarter		Dollars, 100,000s
1970	I	162.5	1974	I	285.5
	II	162.0		II	298.5
	III	164.0		III	316.9
	IV	184.2		IV	345.5
1971	I	168.0	1975	I	318.4
	II	170.8		II	352.3
	III	186.1		III	374.3
	IV	204.8		IV	361.9
1972	I	196.3	1976	I	361.0
	II	206.0		II	357.5
	III	228.3		III	378.8
	IV	239.9		IV	365.3

Source: Moody's *Handbook of Common Stocks.*

(*a*) Use the ratio to moving average method to compute quarterly seasonal indexes for the data above.

(*b*) Interpret the index values for each of the four quarters.

(*c*) Explain how the Gillette Company might use the indexes computed in (*a*).

3

Asphalt production in the United States by quarters, 1969–1976

Year and quarter		Millions of barrels	Year and quarter		Millions of barrels
1969	I	20.2	1973	I	26.3
	II	37.4		II	43.6
	III	45.2		III	54.7
	IV	32.9		IV	43.2
1970	I	22.8	1974	I	29.1
	II	38.3		II	43.9
	III	48.2		III	50.5
	IV	37.4		IV	40.9
1971	I	26.0	1975	I	24.9
	II	42.5		II	36.9
	III	51.0		III	47.6
	IV	37.6		IV	34.4
1972	I	26.2	1976	I	22.3
	II	42.3		II	37.7
	III	51.2		III	46.9
	IV	35.6		IV	32.7

Source: Survey of Current Business.

(*a*) Use the ratio to moving average method to compute quarterly seasonal indexes for the data above.

(b) Interpret the index values for each of the four quarters.

(c) Use the index computed in (a) to adjust these data for seasonal variation.

4

New housing units started in the United States by quarters, 1969–1976

Year and quarter	Thousands of units	Year and quarter	Thousands of units
1969 I	336	1973 I	488
II	468	II	643
III	387	III	552
IV	308	IV	371
1970 I	264	1974 I	323
II	399	II	460
III	408	III	341
IV	391	IV	229
1971 I	389	1975 I	194
II	604	II	326
III	579	III	351
IV	511	IV	300
1972 I	510	1976 I	283
II	667	II	441
III	643	III	437
IV	557	IV	409

Source: Survey of Current Business.

(a) Use the ratio to moving average method to compute quarterly seasonal indexes for the data above.

(b) Interpret the index values for each of the four quarters. To what causes would you attribute the pattern discovered in (a)?

(c) Use the indexes computed in (a) to adjust these data for seasonal variation.

5   (a) Use your least squares trend line from Prob. 1 of the Study Guide for Chap. 17 (ton-miles of freight per freight car day) to compute a complete set of annual trend values from 1963 through 1976.

(b) Use your trend values from (a) to compute annual cyclical relatives from 1963 through 1976.

(c) Construct a cycle chart of the values computed in (b).

(d) Interpret the cyclical relatives for 1967 and 1974.

(e) Does the cycle pattern of ton miles per freight-car day seem to conform to that of the general business cycle?

6   (a) Use your least squares trend line from Prob. 2 of the Study Guide for Chap. 17 (average daily freight-car mileage) to compute a complete set of annual trend values from 1964 through 1976.

(b) Use your trend values from (a) to compute annual cyclical relatives from 1964 through 1976.

(c) Construct a cycle chart of the values computed in (b).

(d) Interpret the cyclical relatives for 1969 and 1975.

(e) Does the cycle pattern of average daily freight-car mileage seem to conform to that of the general business cycle?

7   (a) Use your logarithmic straight line trend from Prob. 3 of the Study Guide for Chap. 17 (new plant and equipment expenditures) to compute a complete set of annual trend values from 1958 through 1976.

(b) Use your trend values from (a) to compute annual cyclical relatives from 1958 through 1976.

(c) Construct a cycle chart of the values computed in (b).

(d) Interpret the cyclical relatives for 1961 and 1969.

(e) Does the cycle pattern of new plant and equipment expenditures seem to conform to that of the general business cycle?

8   (a) Use your logarithmic straight line trend from Prob. 4 of the Study Guide for Chap. 17 (production of automobile tires) to compute a complete set of annual trend values from 1952 through 1976.

(b) Use your trend values from (a) to compute annual cyclical relatives from 1952 through 1976.

(c) Construct a cycle chart of the values computed in (b).

(d) Interpret the cyclical relatives for 1958 and 1972.

(e) Does the cycle pattern of automobile tire production seem to conform to that of the general business cycle?

9   (a) Use the annual trend values computed in (c) of Prob. 6 of the Study Guide for Chap. 17 (piggyback loadings) to compute annual cyclical relatives from 1957 through 1976.

(b) Construct a cycle chart of the values computed in (a).

(c) Interpret the cyclical relatives for 1969 and 1975.

(d) Does the cycle pattern of piggyback loadings in the western district seem to conform to that of the general business cycle?

10 (a) Use your logarithmic straight line trend from Prob. 5 of the Study Guide for Chap. 17 (paper products production) to compute a complete set of annual trend values from 1947 through 1976.

(b) Use your trend values from (a) to compute annual cyclical relatives from 1947 through 1976.

(c) Construct a cycle chart of the values computed in (b).

(d) Interpret the cyclical relatives for 1949 and 1973.

(e) Use your same trend line to compute a complete set of quarterly trend values from 1969 through 1976.

(f) Use your trend values from (e) and the seasonally adjusted values from (c) of Prob. 1 of this study guide to compute quarterly cyclical relatives from 1969 through 1976. Why must the seasonally adjusted values be used in this computation?

(g) Construct a cycle chart of the values computed in (f) and compare it with the chart drawn in (c).

Student Project—Time Series Part II

Use the monthly data on park visits collected during Part I of this project to determine monthly seasonal indexes for park visits.

Determine if there is a cyclical pattern to park visits by calculating annual and monthly cyclical relatives for your data.

Explain and illustrate how the results of your various time series analyses may be of use to park authorities in planning for the future.

Answers to Self-Test

1 $(a), (b), (c), (d)$; 2 $(b), (d)$; 3 $(a), (b), (c), (d)$; 4 $(a), (c)$; 5 $(a), (c)$; 6 $(b), (c), (d)$; 7 $(a), (b)$; 8 $(b), (d)$.

NINETEEN
INDEX NUMBERS

LEARNING OBJECTIVES

The basic learning objective is to learn about index numbers, the second technique for analyzing data classified over time. Specifically, you will become familiar with:

1. Simple and composite indexes.
2. Price, quantity, and value indexes.
3. The sampling problem in index number construction.
4. The following methods of index number construction:
   (a) Weighted relative of aggregates.
   (b) Weighted arithmetic mean of relatives.
   (c) Unweighted geometric mean of relatives.
5. Link and chain indexes.
6. The following important government indexes:
   (a) The Wholesale Price Index.
   (b) The Consumer Price Index.
   (c) The Industrial Production Index.
7. The uses of index numbers.

INTRODUCTION

Index numbers are the second of our two bodies of techniques for analyzing data classified over time. Two types of index numbers may be distinguished, simple and composite. A simple index number is merely the result of converting the consecutive values of a single series, e.g., the price of bread or the production of steel, into percentages of the value for some one time period chosen as the base. Simple index numbers present no problems of interpretation since they are interpreted like the single series itself. The conversion into the percentages making up the index is done to allow easier comparisons.

A composite index number is the result of combining the information of a number of related time series into a new single series. The new series, usually in percentage form, attempts to show the general movement of the entire group over time, even though individual series in the group may have divergent movements. This is the type of index number we shall deal with in this chapter. Most well-known indexes, such as the Consumer Price Index and the Federal Reserve Board Production Index, are composite indexes.

Index numbers may be further classified by the subject or field covered. On this basis three types are of interest to the business manager: (1) price indexes, (2) quantity indexes, and (3) value indexes.

Price indexes, as the name implies, deal with sets of related price series. They show changes in prices only. The two best-known price indexes are the Consumer Price Index and the Wholesale Price Index, both constructed by the U.S. Bureau of Labor Statistics. Other examples would include the various indexes of stock market prices and those of agricultural commodities. We shall use price indexes to illustrate the methods by which index numbers are constructed, although the methods may be used for the other types as well.

Quantity indexes attempt to measure changes only in the physical volume of various activities. The Federal Reserve Board's Index of Industrial Production is the best-known example. Another example is the F. W. Dodge Division of McGraw-Hill Informations Systems Co. Construction Contracts Awarded (Number).

Value indexes measure changes in the total value of related series whether the change results from a price change, a quantity change, or some combination of the two. The Gross National Product series may be thought of as a value index, even though it is not expressed in percentage form. The Federal Reserve Board Index of Department Store Sales is an additional example.

THE SAMPLING PROBLEM IN INDEX NUMBER CONSTRUCTION

The major problem in constructing a composite index number is not the mechanics of combining the values of the series making up the composite, but rather the choice of items to include in the composite. In the first instance this involves a careful definition of the universe to be covered by the index. The purpose of the index must be clearly fixed in mind.

As the universe, once defined, generally consists of more series than it is practical to survey, a sample of the series to be covered must be taken. Because the universes are large and very heterogeneous in most instances, and because it is necessary, for comparability, to maintain the same values for a period of years, the samples used in index number construction are usually judgment samples. Great care is taken, by making extensive preliminary studies of the universe, to ensure the representative nature of the sample chosen.

Related to the problem of deciding what series to include is the problem of deciding how much weight each series should be given in the composite. An index of food prices might include the prices of both ground beef and pork chops, but how important should one be in relation to the other in the composite? The preliminary studies and surveys made to determine the choice of series to include in the composite will often supply the data for determining how much weight to give each series.

In addition to series and weights, the period of time to use as a base for the construction of the index is another consideration. It is desirable to choose a fairly recent period as a base because the immediate past is more readily recalled than the distant past and more useful comparisons can be made if the index has a recent base. It is also desirable to have as a base a time period during which conditions were fairly normal, so that comparisons and values of the index will not be distorted by an unduly high or low base value. In many cases it is desirable to use a period of years as a base in order to average to a norm. This may make comparisons more difficult, however, because it involves recalling what the entire base period was like.

Samples, weights, and bases are held constant over a period of years in order that comparability of index values may be maintained. All three, however, become out of date with the passage of time. Therefore, it is necessary to make extensive major revisions of composite indexes from time to time to make sure the sample series, the weights, and the base period are representative and useful.

BASIC CONSTRUCTION TECHNIQUES

Most composite index numbers today are constructed by one of three methods: (1) weighted relative of aggregates, (2) weighted arithmetic mean of relatives, and (3) unweighted geometric mean of relatives. The first two methods are more common than the third, for a weighted index is generally superior to an unweighted one. Nevertheless, the latter method is the best unweighted method, and is used where weights cannot be determined, as in historical studies, or where lack of time or money prevents their determination. All three methods will be illustrated in turn.

Weighted Relative of Aggregates

Table 19-1 gives data on retail dairy prices and annual consumption by a family of four, to be used in our illustrations.

Lowercase p is used as the symbol for price and lowercase q as the symbol for quantity. A subscript of 0 indicates the price or quantity of the base period, a sub-

Table 19-1 Retail dairy prices and consumption, 1977, 1978, and 1979

Dairy product	Unit of quotation	Annual con- sumption, 1977 (q_0)	Average price		
			1977 p_0	1978 p_1	1979 p_2
Milk	$\frac{1}{2}$ gal	400	$0.80	$0.82	$0.86
Butter	pound	25	1.50	1.65	1.50
Half and half	pint	100	0.50	0.54	0.58
Cheddar cheese	pound	50	1.80	1.89	1.71

script of 1, the price or quantity of the time period after the base period, and so on. We shall use the year 1977 as the base year in our illustrations.

The first retail dairy price index computed from the data in Table 19-1 is a weighted relative of aggregates. The necessary calculations are illustrated in Table 19-2.

Each column contains the results of multiplying the average price of each commodity in a given year by the annual consumption of each commodity in 1977. As one proceeds from year to year, only the prices change, while the quantities consumed which are being used as weights remain constant. This makes the index a true price index, for it changes only with changes in price. The quantity weights used were those of the base year, since these are the ones used in general practice. Any set of constant weights could be used and still give a price index, however. Base-year weights are generally used because they involve fewer problems of data collection.

The products in any column are then summed (aggregated) to find the total amount of money spent in each year. These aggregates are converted into indexes by dividing each year's aggregate through by the aggregate of the base year, 1977 ($497.50). The results are shown in the table. In symbols using base-year weights, our

Table 19-2 Weighted relative of aggregates index of retail dairy prices

Dairy product	1977 $p_0 q_0$	1978 $p_1 q_0$	1979 $p_2 q_0$
Milk	$320.00	$328.00	$344.00
Butter	37.50	41.25	37.50
Half and half	50.00	54.00	58.00
Cheddar cheese	90.00	94.50	85.50
Aggregate	$497.50	$517.75	$525.00
Index, %	100.0	104.1	105.5

index is

$$I_p = \frac{\Sigma p_n q_0}{\Sigma p_0 q_0}$$

The 1978 index of 104.1 shows that the price of 400 half-gallons of milk, 25 lb of butter, 100 pints of half and half, and 50 lb of cheese (the 1977 quantities consumed) was 4.1 percent higher then than the price of the same bill of goods in 1977. In 1979 the price of this same bill of goods was 5.5 percent higher than in 1977. In both cases, the index shows only the price changes in the fixed 1977 bill of goods. As suggested earlier, such a set of weights may become out of date and unrealistic with time and are generally reviewed, revised, and updated at periodic intervals. A set of constant weights must be used, however, to provide comparability from one time period to the next to ensure that changes in the index are price changes only.

Weighted Arithmetic Mean of Relatives

We shall now use our retail-dairy-price data of Table 19-1 to illustrate our second method of index number construction, the weighted arithmetic mean of relatives. The necessary calculations for this technique are illustrated in Table 19-3.

The first step in the construction of this index (and any other average-of-relatives index—see the geometric mean of relatives below) is the computation of the (price) relatives. This is done for each commodity in the index by dividing the base-year value (price) of that commodity into the values (prices) of the base and other years. This is, in effect, the construction of a simple index for each series that is to make up the composite index. It is one advantage of this general method that it provides individual simple indexes for each series, as well as the composite index for all series. The relatives for our retail-dairy-price data appear in the first three columns of Table 19-3.

Table 19-3 Weighted arithmetic mean of relatives index of retail dairy prices

Dairy product	Price relative			Value weight $p_0 q_0$	Weighted relative		
	1977 $100\dfrac{p_0}{p_0}$	1978 $100\dfrac{p_1}{p_0}$	1979 $100\dfrac{p_2}{p_0}$		1977 $p_0 q_0 \times 100\dfrac{p_0}{p_0}$	1978 $p_0 q_0 \times 100\dfrac{p_1}{p_0}$	1979 $p_0 q_0 \times 100\dfrac{p_2}{p_0}$
Milk	100.0	102.5	107.5	$320.00	32,000	32,800	34,400
Butter	100.0	110.0	100.0	37.50	3,750	4,125	3,750
Half and half	100.0	108.0	116.0	50.00	5,000	5,400	5,800
Cheddar cheese	100.0	105.0	95.0	90.00	9,000	9,450	8,550
Total	...	...	...	$497.50	49,750	51,775	52,500
Index %	...	...	...		100.0	104.1	105.5

The fourth column of Table 19-3 gives the values (price times quantity) of the consumption of each product in the base year. These are to be used as weights. The next three columns contain the results of the weighting of each price relative in each year by its appropriate value weight. The weighted relatives for any year are then summed and divided by the sum of the weights ($497.50). The resulting quotients are the indexes shown.

Our formula for the weighted mean was

$$\text{wt } \overline{X} = \frac{\Sigma wX}{\Sigma w}$$

Here the values of X are the price relatives and w the weights of the base-year values, $p_0 q_0$. Our general formula for price index number construction, therefore, is

$$I_p = \frac{\Sigma \left(p_0 q_0 \times 100 \frac{p_n}{p_0} \right)}{\Sigma p_0 q_0}$$

An observant reader will notice that this reduces to become the same as our weighted relative of aggregates and that our numerical results are the same in both cases. The aggregate method is an easier method of constructing the composite index, but the relative method does have the advantage mentioned earlier of presenting both simple indexes and the composite. There are problems in the construction of quantity indexes where the aggregate method cannot be used. These problems involve combining series in different units which cannot be added together (aggregated). However, as relatives have no units, an average of relatives may be used.

Since the numerical results here are the same as previously, they may be interpreted in the same way.

Unweighted Geometric Mean of Relatives

Most index numbers constructed today employ one of the two methods just discussed. If, however, an unweighted index number must be constructed because adequate weights are unavailable or cannot be obtained economically, the best unweighted method is the unweighted geometric mean of relatives as it is free of bias (to be discussed below).

The geometric mean, like the arithmetic mean, is a calculated average; that is, it is defined operationally. The geometric mean G of a series of numbers, $X_1, X_2, X_3, \cdots, X_n$, is defined as

$$G = \sqrt[n]{X_1 \times X_2 \times X_3 \times \cdots \times X_n}$$

or the nth root of the product of n items. For calculation purposes a transformation into logarithms is useful. We may write

$$G = \text{antilog} \frac{\Sigma \log X}{n}$$

Table 19-4 Illustration of bias in unweighted arithmetic mean of relatives

Commodity	Price		Price relative	
	1977	1979	$100 \dfrac{p_{79}}{p_{77}}$	$100 \dfrac{p_{77}}{p_{79}}$
A	$0.50	$1.00	200	50
B	1.00	0.50	50	200
Total	...	...	250	250
Index (unweighted $\overline{X}$)	...	...	125	125

since a summation of logs is a multiplication process, and the averaging by n, the equivalent of extracting the nth root.

We need the geometric mean to average our relatives because an arithmetic mean will give a biased result. This can best be explained by an illustration. Table 19-4 shows that, if we compute an unweighted arithmetic mean of the price relatives for 1979, using 1977 as a base, we obtain a value of 125, indicating a price increase from 1977 to 1979. However, if we change the base to 1979 and compute an index for 1977 on 1979 as a base, we again obtain a value of 125, indicating higher prices in 1977 than in 1979. This contradicts our earlier answer, indicating higher prices in 1979 than in 1977. When averaging time ratios, the arithmetic mean is said to have an upward bias, since it gives results larger than they should be.[1] The geometric mean of the price relatives in Table 19-4 is the same in both cases:

$$G = \sqrt[2]{200 \times 50} = \sqrt[2]{50 \times 200} = \sqrt[2]{10,000} = 100$$

The index of 100 is unbiased. In general, the geometric mean has the property of giving an unbiased average of time ratios.

Table 19-5 repeats the price relatives from Table 19-3 and, in addition, contains the computations necessary for an unweighted geometric mean of the relatives. After the relatives have been computed, the next step is to take the logarithm of each relative. These logs are shown in the last three columns of the table. They are then totaled by years and averaged by dividing by the number of items. The antilogs of these averages are our price indexes shown in the last row of Table 19-5. In symbols, we have

$$I_p = \text{antilog} \dfrac{\sum \log \left(100 \dfrac{p_n}{p_0}\right)}{n}$$

The 1978 index of 106.3 percent indicates that prices rose an average of 6.3 percent between 1977 and 1978. The 1979 index of 104.3 indicates that retail dairy

---

[1] It was possible to use an airthmetic mean in our previous illustration of the weighted arithmetic mean of relatives since the base-year-value weights themselves have a downward bias that just offsets the upward bias of the arithmetic mean.

Table 19-5 Unweighted geometric mean of relatives index of retail dairy prices

Dairy product	Price relative			Log of price relative		
	1977 $100\dfrac{p_0}{p_0}$	1978 $100\dfrac{p_1}{p_0}$	1979 $100\dfrac{p_2}{p_0}$	1977 $\log\left(100\dfrac{p_0}{p_0}\right)$	1978 $\log\left(100\dfrac{p_1}{p_0}\right)$	1979 $\log\left(100\dfrac{p_2}{p_0}\right)$
Milk	100.0	102.5	107.5	2.0000	2.0107	2.0315
Butter	100.0	110.0	100.0	2.0000	2.0414	2.0000
Half and half	100.0	108.0	116.0	2.0000	2.0334	2.0645
Cheddar cheese	100.0	105.0	95.0	2.0000	2.0212	1.9777
Total	...	...	...	8.0000	8.1067	8.0737
Average	...	...	...	2.0000	2.0267	2.0184
Index %	...	...	...	100.0	106.3	104.3

prices rose an average of 4.3 percent between 1977 and 1979. In interpreting these averages, it should be remembered that they are unweighted.

LINK RELATIVE INDEX NUMBERS

The index numbers we have discussed so far have all had a single fixed time period as a base. For some purposes it is desirable to have an index number with a constantly changing base. Usually, the changing base is the immediately preceding time period. For example, the base for 1979 would be 1978, while that for 1978 would be 1977. The base for May would be April, while the base for April would be March. A variation of the latter would be to use May of a year ago as the base for this May. Index numbers of the former type with a fixed base are termed "chain indexes"; those of the latter type with a changing base are called "link relatives."

Table 19-6 illustrates a simple link relative for manufacturing employment. In interpreting the link relatives, it should be remembered that the comparison is with the preceding year only. For example, the 1973 link of 105.1 (the largest link) should not be misinterpreted as indicating that 1973 was a year of maximum employment. It does indicate that the largest single year-to-year change in the data took place between 1972 and 1973.

Many index numbers in use today, as, for example, the Consumer Price Index, are first computed as a link index and later converted to a chain index. Computation first as a link index allows for easier modification in those cases where a product must be replaced because it no longer exists or some weight change is felt necessary. Table 19-6 presents the results of the conversion of the link relatives into a chain index in the last column. The conversion is based on the relationship that the chain index for any period would equal the link for the same period times the chain of the preceding

**Table 19-6 Link relative and chain indexes of United States
manufacturing employment, 1968-1976**

Year	Employment, (thousands)	Link relative	Chain index (1972 = 100)
1968	19,781	...	103.6
1969	20,167	102.0	105.7
1970	19,349	95.9	101.4
1971	18,572	96.0	97.3
1972	19,090	102.8	100.0
1973	20,068	105.1	105.1
1974	20,046	99.9	105.0
1975	18,347	91.5	96.1
1976	18,956	103.3	99.3

Source: Monthly Labor Review.

period. Using L for link index and C for chain index, we have

$$C_n = L_n C_{n-1}$$

The first value for the chain is established automatically as 100.0 for the period chosen as the base. In our example, 1972 was chosen as the base period. The chain for 1973 is obtained by multiplying the 1973 link of 105.1 times the 1972 chain of 100.0 to obtain a value of 105.1. The chain for 1974 equals the 1974 link of 99.9 times the 1973 chain of 105.1, or 105.0. The process is continued to the end. To go backward from 1972 one need merely solve the general expression for the chain of the preceding period:

$$C_{n-1} = \frac{C_n}{L_n}$$

For example, the 1971 chain is obtained by dividing the 1972 link of 102.8 into the 1972 chain of 100.0, obtaining 97.3. This process is repeated to the end of the data.

SOME COMMON IMPORTANT INDEXES

In business today managers are much more apt to study already constructed index number series to aid in decision making than they are to construct index series of their own. For this reason we shall include here a brief discussion of three of the most basic and widely used index number series. All government series, they are the Wholesale Price Index and the Consumer Price Index of the Bureau of Labor Statistics, and the Monthly Index of Industrial Production of the Federal Reserve Board. We shall discuss each in turn.

Wholesale Price Index

The Wholesale Price Index, constructed by the U.S. Bureau of Labor Statistics, is the oldest price index in the United States. It originated in 1902 and has been extended backward to 1749. Currently it is published on a monthly basis, supplemented by an interim weekly index. The Bureau also publishes a Daily Index of Spot Market Prices, which, while related to the weekly and monthly indexes, is not strictly comparable to them.

The name of the Index is misleading, for historically it has been not an index of prices paid by wholesalers and jobbers but a more basic index of primary market prices. The primary market of any commodity is that involving its first commercial transaction.

However, the Bureau has recently come out with a new revision of the index based on the prices of finished goods only in order to eliminate the multiple-counting inherent in the old system, which priced the same goods as raw materials, semifinished, and finished product. This new version is in addition to the old version.

The coverage of the Index is very broad, ranging from raw materials to finished goods. A judgment sample of about 2,700 items covering 250 industries is used for the monthly index. Plans have been made to greatly expand the list to many more products and 500 industries by the mid-1980s, and to replace judgment sampling by scientific sampling. The interim weekly index is based on 200 commodities. The Daily Index is based on 22 commodities.

The method of calculating the Index is basically a weighted mean of relatives. (The Daily Index is an unweighted geometric mean of relatives.) Weights are derived from census data such as the Census of Manufacturers. Weights in current use reflect 1972 values of shipments. The year 1967 is used as a base. A link-chain procedure is employed in actual calculations.

The large sample allows for the breakdown of the total index into many sub-indexes. There are, for example, 15 major product groups, 88 subgroups, and 250 product classes. Additional indexes are presented for various stages of processing and for varying degrees of durability. The large number of breakdowns makes this Index a most useful one to business managers, allowing them to follow basic price trends in the economy and in their own fields of business.

Consumer Price Index

The Consumer Price Index of the Bureau of Labor Statistics first appeared in 1918, at which time it was extended back to 1913. Originally known as the Cost of Living Index, it has in fact always been a price index, being constructed with a fixed weighting pattern. A true "cost of living" index would be a value index in which both price and quantity change. As fixed weights do get out of date with time, the Index has been revised and updated several times since 1918. The Bureau introduced new weights in 1977 based on 1972-1973 survey data.

The Index, which is published monthly, has been an attempt to measure the changes in the prices of goods and services purchased by the families of urban wage earners and clerical workers, a group making up about 40 percent of the population. The "market basket" of weights used in constructing the index is based on surveys of actual expenditures of families of this type. About 400 items are priced in 56 urban areas. A wide range of goods and services is covered, including such things as food, apparel, rent, haircuts, doctor bills, bus fares, and gas bills. In addition to an all-item

United States index, subindexes are published for eight major groups, such as food, housing, and apparel, and for many subgroups. Similar all-item indexes and subindexes are published for the 25 largest cities.

Early in 1978, the Bureau will introduce a new version of the Index based on several thousand items priced in 85 cities. More important, the new index will be based on the buying habits of all metropolitan-area residents, a group making up about 80 percent of the population. This new index will be in addition to an expanded and updated version of the old index.

The method of index construction employed is a weighted mean of relatives. Link-chain procedures are again used in the actual calculations. The index currently has 1967 = 100 as a base.

The index has its widest use in the adjustment of wage rates and the evaluation of the real level of wages. It was first established in World War I for this purpose in the shipbuilding industry. Since World War II it has been increasingly used for wage-rate adjustments, through the use of escalator clauses in many wage contracts.

Industrial Production Index

The Industrial Production Index is issued monthly by the Federal Reserve Board. It is a quantity index showing changes in the physical volume of activities of manufacturing, mining, and utilities. Durable manufactures make up about 52 percent of the total index; nondurable manufactures, 36 percent; mining, 6 percent; and utilities, 6 percent.

The Index is based on over 200 series and uses data in terms of actual physical output such as tons, yards, or board-feet, wherever possible. When physical output data are not available, e.g., as in shipbuilding, where the time to produce one ship is much longer than a month, a series such as man-hours expended or materials consumed is used instead. Actual construction of the Index is by means of a weighted mean of relatives. Weights are based on value added as shown by the Census of Manufactures. The Index currently has 1967 = 100 as its base. Breakdowns are published for the four major categories of the Index. In addition, they are provided for 25 major industrial groups and 175 subgroups.

The industries covered in this Index account for over a third of the national income. The Index is widely used, therefore, as an indicator of the general state of the economy. It will tell us whether production is increasing or decreasing and, through its numerous subgroupings, where the changes are taking place.

USES OF INDEX NUMBERS

Purchasing Power

The reciprocal of a price index may be used to show the purchasing power of the dollar relative to the type of goods whose prices were measured by the index. This purchasing power itself will be relative to the base period on which the index is constructed.

In May 1977, the all-item Consumer Price Index was 180.6 on the 1967 base. The purchasing power of the 1967 consumer dollar in May 1977, therefore, was 100.0/ 180.6, or $0.553. If another price index had been used (e.g., the Wholesale Price Index), it would have shown the purchasing power of a kind of dollar other than that of the consumer.

Deflation

Another use of index numbers is the division of a dollar-value time series by an appropriate price index number series in order that one may see the amount of the change in the series that was physical in character, i.e., the result of changes in quantities. For example, a retail-sales series could be divided by a retail-price index to determine how much of an increase in the former series resulted from an increase in the volume of goods sold.

A similar computation is the division of a monetary wage series by the Consumer Price Index to determine "real wages."

Escalators

Index numbers are used in the operation of "escalator clauses" in various contracts. The Consumer Price Index is used as an escalator in many wage contracts, wages being adjusted up or down automatically with movements up or down in the Index. The Wholesale Price Index, or some component of it, may be used as an escalator for adjusting prices at the time of delivery in long-term business contracts.

Studying Business Conditions

Index numbers may be studied as indicators of general business conditions. Such study, along with the study of other indicators, is a preliminary stage in business forecasting and planning.

The Wholesale Price Index and its components are studied by a business to follow basic price movements and plan the company's price policies in light of this analysis. The company can compare its own price movements with those of the Index. The Index of Industrial Production and its components are studied to follow changes in the physical volumes of production, to make comparisons, and to plan accordingly. Many other special indexes are studied carefully by those operating in the fields to which they are applicable.

STUDY GUIDE

Concepts Worth Remembering

Define:

1. Index number: simple and composite
2. Price indexes
3. Quantity indexes
4. Value indexes

5. Chain index
6. Link index
7. Geometric mean
8. Weighted relative of aggregates
9. Weighted arithmetic mean of relatives
10. Unweighted geometric mean of relatives

Self-Test

Multiple-choice questions. Circle the letters of the statements which correctly complete the questions. There may be from one to four correct answers.

1 Index numbers may be classified as:
   (a) Simple, composite, or mixed indexes.
   (b) Price, quantity, or value indexes.
   (c) Link or chain indexes.
   (d) Aggregate or averages of relatives indexes.

2 Index numbers:
   (a) Usually use judgment samples.
   (b) Usually use changing weights.
   (c) Must have a period of years as a base.
   (d) Need to be revised every 10 years.

3 The weighted relative of aggregates method of constructing a price index:
   (a) Shows changes in individual series prices as well as giving a composite index.
   (b) Keeps weights constant in order to show price changes only.
   (c) Generally uses current year weights.
   (d) Shows changes in the price of a fixed bill of goods.

4 The weighted arithmetic mean of relatives method of constructing an index:
   (a) Shows changes in individual series prices as well as giving a composite index when used to construct a price index
   (b) Uses base-year quantities as weights when used to construct a price index.
   (c) Gives the same results as the weighted relative of aggregates when used to construct a price index if equivalent weights are used.
   (d) Can be used to construct quantity indexes in problems where a weighted relative of aggregates cannot be used.

5 The unweighted geometric mean of relatives method of constructing an index:
   (a) Uses a geometric mean because an unweighted arithmetic mean of relatives gives a biased result.
   (b) Is the best unweighted method.
   (c) Is used when weights are unavailable or cannot be obtained economically.
   (d) Uses logarithms in its calculations.

6 Link relative indexes:
   (a) Have a fixed base.
   (b) Are the first step in the calculation of many government indexes, e.g., the Consumer Price Index.
   (c) Show prices at a peak for the largest link value.
   (d) Show price changes only from the previous time period.

7 The Wholesale Price Index is:
   (a) Constructed by the U.S. Bureau of Labor Statistics.

(b) An index of jobber or "wholesale" prices.

(c) Published monthly.

(d) Calculated as an unweighted geometric mean of relatives.

8 The Consumer Price Index:

(a) Is constructed by the Federal Reserve Board.

(b) Is a cost of living index.

(c) Employs a weighted mean of relatives and link-chain procedures in its calculation.

(d) Was first put out during World War I.

9 The Industrial Production Index:

(a) Is constructed by the Federal Reserve Board.

(b) Is a quantity index.

(c) Employs a weighted mean of relatives in its calculation.

(d) Uses value added data as weights.

10 Index numbers are used:

(a) In the form of complements to show purchasing power.

(b) To deflate a series by multiplying through by the index values.

(c) In the operation of "escalator clauses" in various contracts.

(d) As indicators of general business conditions.

Questions to Think About

1. Explain the difference between a simple and a composite index number. What is the use of each type?

2. Explain the differences among price, quantity, and value indexes. Give an example of each type.

3. Discuss the sampling problem of index number construction.

4. List the three commonly used methods of constructing index numbers. What are the advantages and disadvantages of each method?

5. Explain and illustrate why the geometric mean is used in the calculating of an unweighted average of relatives.

6. Distinguish between a link and a chain index number.

7. List the three major government index numbers discussed in this chapter. Give a brief description of each.

8. List and explain the uses to which index numbers are put.

Problems

1

Dairy products: prices and production in the United States, 1970, 1972, 1974, 1976

Dairy product	Wholesale price per pound				Production, millions of lb			
	1970	1972	1974	1976	1970	1972	1974	1976
Butter	$0.704	$0.696	$0.674	$0.944	1,137	1,102	962	979
American cheese	0.649	0.714	0.973	1.161	1,431	1,644	2,930	2,062
Fluid milk	0.057	0.061	0.083	0.097	117,436	120,278	115,416	120,356
Nonfat dry milk	0.263	0.331	0.586	0.635	1,448	1,224	1,020	962

Source: Survey of Current Business.

(*a*) Construct a dairy products price index for all four years on 1970 as a base using the weighted relative of aggregates method and 1970 weights.

(*b*) Repeat (*a*) with 1976 weights.

(*c*) Construct a dairy products price index for all four years on 1970 as a base using the weighted mean of relatives method and 1970 weights.

(*d*) Repeat (*c*) with 1976 weights.

(*e*) How would one interpret the various index values computed in (*a*) through (*d*)?

(*f*) Construct a dairy products price index for all four years on 1970 as a base using the unweighted geometric mean of relatives method. What advantages and disadvantages does this method have in comparison with those used above?

2

Grain prices and production in the United States, 1970, 1972, 1974, 1976

Grain	Wholesale Price per bushel				Production, millions of bushels			
	1970	1972	1974	1976	1970	1972	1974	1976
Barley	$1.13	$1.23	$3.40	$3.06	410	424	304	372
Corn	1.33	1.26	3.14	2.56	4,110	5,553	4,651	6,216
Oats	0.72	0.85	1.66	1.74	909	692	614	546
Rice†	0.08	0.10	0.25	0.14	8,290	8,540	11,240	11,560
Rye	1.15	1.07	2.99	2.92	39	29	19	15
Wheat	1.79	1.87	5.53	3.87	1,378	1,545	1,796	2,142

†Rice prices are per pound and production is millions of pounds.
Source: Survey of Current Business.

(*a*) Construct a grain price index for all four years on 1970 as a base using the weighted relative of aggregates method and 1970 weights.

(*b*) Repeat (*a*) with 1976 weights.

(*c*) Construct a grain price index for all four years on 1970 as a base using the weighted mean of relatives method and 1970 weights.

(*d*) Repeat (*c*) with 1976 weights.

(*e*) How would one interpret the various indexes computed in (*a*) through (*d*)?

(*f*) Construct a grain price index for all four years on 1970 as a base using the unweighted geometric mean of relatives method. What advantages and disadvantages does this method have in comparison with those used above?

3

Nonferrous metal prices and production in the United States, 1970, 1972, 1974, 1976

Nonferrous metal	Price per pound				Production, 1,000's of short tons			
	1970	1972	1974	1976	1970	1972	1974	1976
Aluminum	$0.287	$0.264	$0.341	$0.445	3,976	4,122	4,903	4,251
Copper	0.583	0.512	0.773	0.696	1,720	1,665	1,597	1,611
Lead	0.156	0.150	0.275	0.231	572	619	664	610
Zinc	0.153	0.178	0.359	0.370	534	478	500	484

Source: Survey of Current Business.

(a) Construct a nonferrous metals price index for all four years on 1970 as a base, using the weighted relative of aggregates method and 1970 weights.

(b) Repeat (a) with 1976 weights.

(c) Construct a nonferrous metals price index for all four years on 1970 as a base using the weighted mean of relatives method and 1970 weights.

(d) Repeat (c) with 1976 weights.

(e) How would one interpret the various indexes computed in (a) through (d)?

(f) Construct a nonferrous metals price index for all four years on 1970 as a base using the unweighted geometric mean of relatives method. What advantages and disadvantages does this method have in comparison with those used above?

9

Capital expenditures for roadway and structures by class 1 railroads in the United States, 1965-1976

Year	Millions
1965	$327
1966	399
1967	374
1968	368
1969	421
1970	358
1971	314
1972	368
1973	449
1974	527
1975	486
1976	549

Source: Yearbook of Railroad Facts, 1977 Edition, p. 56.

(a) Construct a link relative index for the data above.

(b) Convert your link relative index into a chain index, using 1972 for a base.

(c) Interpret both of the index values you have computed for 1975.

Student Project

Design, collect the data for, and construct a price index of prices paid by students attending your college in obtaining their education.

Answers to Self-Test

1 (b), (c), (d); 2 (a); 3 (b), (d); 4 (a), (c), (d); 5 (a), (b), (c), (d); 6 (b), (d); 7 (a), (c); 8 (c), (d); 9 (a), (b), (c), (d); 10 (c), (d).

TWENTY
WHY STATISTICS? AN OVERALL REVIEW

We shall close our discussion by repeating our first chapter's opening question, "Why statistics?" We hope the intervening chapters have provided an ever-growing and more complete answer to that question.

Part I considered the problems of gathering and presenting numerical data. Chapter 2 introduced us to the general format of a statistical study and ways of classifying statistical data and attempted to highlight some of the major problems of collecting data. No business decision based on statistical analysis can be any sounder than the data collected for the analysis. Chapter 3 dealt with the ways of presenting statistical data in the form of tables and graphs.

Part II concentrated on the descriptive tools of analysis used for quantitative data. Chapter 4 dealt with organizing this type of data in tabular form and its presentation in graphic form, both of which constitute preliminary analysis for this type of data. In Chaps. 5 and 6 we studied the statistical measures which are used to summarize quantitative data. We learned to locate a set of data on the scale of values (averages) and to determine the width or interval of the scale the set occupied (measures of variability). Such descriptive measures provide the basic tools of statistical analysis.

In Part III we studied statistical inference—the ways of making sound decisions on the basis of limited information. Chapters 7 and 8 dealt with probability, the basic tool of all inferential methods. Chapter 9 covered the use of samples in collecting data. Sampling distributions were discussed in Chap. 10. Chapters 11 through 14 covered various sampling applications, starting with simple estimation, proceeding through hypothesis testing to modern statistical decision making, and ending with some special topics, including the analysis of variance and quality control.

Part IV (Chaps. 15 and 16) introduced the methods for making decisions about one set of data on the basis of information contained in related sets of data. These are the techniques of regression and correlation analysis.

Part V covered the problem of making decisions about the future based on the behavior of statistical data through time in the past. All decisions involve the future, since they are a current choice between alternative courses of action. However, in these chapters we studied the techniques of analyzing past data to aid in forecasting where that data might be in the future. Chapter 17 dealt with trend analysis, usually useful in long-term forecasting, while Chap. 18 covered cyclical and seasonal analysis, useful to intermediate and short-term forecasting. Chapter 19 presented index number methods used in analyzing general business conditions as a background for all forecasting.

The first chapter stated that statistics is a body of methods for obtaining and analyzing numerical data in order to make better decisions in an uncertain world. The chapters that followed showed how numerical data were obtained and analyzed as a basis for decision making. This, then, is the answer to "Why statistics?" Statistics provides the body of methods needed for sound decision making by management in our uncertain and numerically minded world.

GLOSSARY

A posterori (posterior) probabilities a form of conditional probability determined by the use of Bayes' theorem.

A priori (prior) probabilities probabilities based on advance knowledge of the behavior of the process in question.

α **risk** the probability assigned to a Type I error in a testing problem.

Acceptance region a portion of a sampling distribution which if containing the sample result would lead to the acceptance of the null hypothesis.

Acceptance sampling statistical quality control techniques used in determining if a completed lot meets specifications.

Action limit the value of the boundary between the acceptance and rejection regions, stated in the units of the original variables being used in testing.

Addition rule the rule used to determine with what probability one of several possible alternative events will occur. In its simplest form, $P(A \text{ or } B) = P(A) + P(B) - P(AB)$.

Alternative hypothesis the hypothesis that will be accepted if the null hypothesis is rejected.

Analysis the process of using statistical techniques to describe a set of statistical data and make inferences therefrom.

Analysis of variance a statistical technique to divide the total variance of a series of observations into component parts each of which is associated with a possible source of variation, and to assess the importance of the various sources.

Area (geographical) classification a qualitative classification using the geographical origin of the data as the basis for their classification.

Arithmetic mean a calculated average defined as the value of the sum of the numerical values of a series of items or numbers divided by the number of items or numbers.

Array a tabular presentation of quantitative data wherein the data are arranged in order of magnitude.

Average deviation see **mean deviation**

Averages (also termed measures of location, points of central tendency, or clustering points) point values used to locate and summarize the entire set of varying values making up a distribution.

β **risk** the probability of making a Type II error during hypothesis testing.

Bar chart a form of graph used for presenting kind data or chronological data.

Bayes' theorem a theorem used to compute posterior probabilities, generally as a revision of prior probabilities in light of experimental evidence.

Bayesian decision theory modern methods of statistical decision making using Bayes' theorem to revise probabilities.

Bell-shaped curve a frequency curve characterized by a single peak and trailing off in both directions from that peak.

Bias see **systematic error**

Binomial distribution the distribution over n independent trials of the probability of the number of occurrences of an event which may either occur or not occur with a constant probability on a single trial.

Calculated averages (means) averages defined in terms of some arithmetic operation which yields the answer.

Caption the column headings of a table.

Census a complete enumeration of a statistical universe (population).

Central limit theorem a theorem which states that the random sampling distribution of arithmetic means approaches a normal distribution as the size of sample increases regardless of the distribution of the population (universe) being sampled.

Chain index an index number with a single fixed period as a base.

Chart see **Graph**

Chi-square distribution a continuous probability distribution used in single-sample variance problems and various goodness of fit tests.

Chronological classification a classification of statistical data over time according to a set of consecutive actual historical dates—most commonly referred to as a "time series."

Class intervals the groupings used in the construction of frequency tables.

Classification the placing of statistical data into groups—a preliminary step in analyzing statistical data.

Cluster sample a variation of multistage sampling wherein all items in the final stage are used.

Clustering points see **Averages**

Coefficient of correlation the square root of the coefficient of determination. An alternative measure of the degree of correlation.

Coefficient of determination the measure of the relative closeness of the relationship in a correlation analysis.

Coefficient of regression the slope coefficient of a regression line. A summary measure of the pattern of the relationship.

Coefficient of variation the relative standard deviation computed by dividing the absolute standard deviation by its own arithmetic mean.

Collection the process of obtaining numerical data for a statistical investigation (study).

Column diagram a form of graph for presenting a frequency table.

Combinations the method of counting the number of possible outcomes in situations where order is immaterial and repetition of elements is not permitted.

Composite index number the combining of the information of a number of related time series into a new single series which attempts to show the general movement of the entire group.

Conditional probabilities probabilities whose value is dependent on the previous occurrence of another event.

Confidence intervals the statistical procedure for making universe estimates from sample data.

Constant seasonal a set of seasonal indexes that remain the same over a period of years.

Continuous probabilities probabilities in which the measurement of the occurrence of events is usually done using calculus to measure areas.

Continuous variable a variable having values at all points along its possible range of values. Usually obtained by measurement.

Control chart a chart of the measurements of some quality characteristic for consecutive samples over time. Used in process control.

Convenience sample a sample wherein items for the sample are selected by taking those which are most readily available.

Correlation analysis statistical techniques for studying the relative closeness of the relationship among several quantitatively classified variables.

Cost of uncertainty the expected long-run opportunity loss of the best decision.

Critical ratio the value of the test ratio in a testing procedure at the boundary between the acceptance and rejection regions.

Crude mode the simplest form of estimating the mode of a frequency distribution using the midpoint of the modal interval as the modal value.

Cycle a roughly repetitive wavelike movement in a time series with a duration greater than 1 year, generally averaging 3 to 5 years in length.

Cyclical relative a measure of the cyclical variation in a time series determined by dividing the actual data by a measure of trend.

Decision a choice among alternative courses of action.

Decision making under certainty a decision situation in which knowledge of the states of the world exists.

Decision making under uncertainty a decision situation in which the states of the world are not known in advance of the decision.

Degrees of freedom (df) the number of unrestricted opportunities for variation in a problem. The divisor for unbiased population variance estimates.

Dependent events events of a kind that the probability of a second event occurring is conditional on the occurrence of a first event.

Dependent (paired) samples samples chosen in such a way that the choice of an item for one sample automatically includes a corresponding or related item for the other sample.

Deviation measures of variability techniques which measure variability as the average amount by which the values of the set differ from their own average.

Discrete probabilities probabilities in which the measurement of the occurrence of events is done by counting.

Discrete variable a variable taking on values only at certain points along its possible range of values. Usually obtained by counting.

Dispersion (variability) the property of frequency curves concerned with the horizontal spread of a set of data. Measured as an interval.

Distance measures of variability measures which use the difference (interval) between two points as the measure of variability.

Editing the process of carefully checking returned questionnaries or schedules for obvious errors.

Empirical probabilities probabilities based on experimental evidence.

Expected monetary value (EMV) the anticipated long-run average gain of selecting a particular course of action (making a particular decision).

Expected net gain from sampling (ENGS) the difference between the expected value of sample information for a particular sample and the cost of that sample.

Expected opportunity loss (EOL) the anticipated long-run average opportunity loss of making a particular decision.

Expected value of certainty (EVC) the expected value of always making the correct decision.

Expected value of perfect information (EVPI) the difference between the expected value of certainty and the expected monetary value of the optimal decision. Also equal to the cost of uncertainty. The most management should be willing to pay for additional information before making a decision.

Expected value of sample information (EVSI) the expected reduction in the cost of uncertainty that a particular sample will produce.

F-distribution a continuous probability distribution used to compare two sample variances in testing to see if they represent the same universe.

Finite-universe correction (also finite population correction) common factor used to adjust standard error formulas when sampling from a finite universe (population).

Frame the means used to identify the items making up a statistical universe.

Frequency curve a smooth-curve representation of a conceptual or theoretical frequency distribution.

Frequency distribution see **Frequency table**

Frequency polygon a form of graph for presenting a frequency table.

Frequency table (distribution) a tabular presentation of quantitative data wherein the data are classified into intervals.

General-purpose table (reference table) a table arranged to allow for the easy looking up of material.

Geographic classification see **Area classification**

Geometric mean a calculated average defined as the nth root of the product of a set of n items.

Gompertz curve a growth curve used in trend analysis.

Graph (chart) a pictorial representation of numerical data.

Grouped data a set of data in the form of a frequency distribution.

Growth curves mathematical curves used to represent trends which have mathematical properties logically corresponding to the processes of economic growth.

Homoscedacticity the property of a set of variances which makes them all equal to each other.

Hypergeometric distribution the distribution which gives the probabilities of the number of occurrences of an event which may either occur or not occur on a single trial, but whose probability of occurrence on a single trial is conditional on what happened on other trials.

Independent events events of a kind such that the probability of a second event occurring is unaffected by the occurrence or nonoccurrence of a first event.

Independent (non-paired) samples samples chosen in such a way that the selection of an item for one sample in no way determines the selection of an item for the second sample.

Index number a relative (percentage) statement of relationship between two numbers usually of different time periods.

Infinite universe a statistical universe which is conceptually unbounded.

Insignificant difference a difference between the sample value and the hypothesized population value associated with the acceptance of the null hypothesis. A difference which quite probably could have been due to random sampling errors.

Irregular movements in a time series lacking a definite pattern.

Judgment (selective) sample a sample wherein items for the sample are deliberately chosen by an investigator who is usually an expert in the subject field of the study.

Kind classification a general qualitative classification based on any attribute of the data other than their geographical source.

Kurtosis the relative peakedness of a frequency curve.

Less than cumulative frequencies the number of frequencies less than the upper limit of any interval in question.

Level of significance the value assigned to the α risk in hypothesis testing.

Line graph a form of graph used for presenting chronological data.

Link relative index an index number with a changing base, usually the value of the preceding time period.

Logistic curve a growth curve used in trend analysis.

Lower-tailed test a one-tailed test with the rejection region in the lower tail of the sampling distribution.

Mail questionnaire the set of questions used when collecting primary data by using the U.S. Postal Service.

Mean (average) deviation the arithmetic mean of a set of absolute deviations which have been computed as the differences of the individual values from the median. A deviation measure of variability.

Means see **Calculated averages**

Measures of location see **Averages**

Median that value of a set of values which exceeds the values of no more than one-half of the items or is itself exceeded in value by no more than one-half of the items.

Method of least squares a technique used in fitting regression lines that has the mathematical property of making the sum of the squared deviations of the points from the regression line a minimum.

Method of selected points a technique used in fitting trend lines which forces the trend line to pass through certain predetermined (selected) points.

Mode the value in a set which occurs most often and around which the values of the other items tend to cluster.

Moving averages a set of averages over time obtained by dropping the first item in the set and replacing it by the next item in the series before calculating the next average.

Moving seasonal a set of seasonal indexes which exhibit a systematic change in timing or amplitude or both over a period of years.

Multiple choices the method of counting the number of possible outcomes in situations where order is important and repetition of elements is permitted.

Multiple regression and/or correlation regression and correlation analysis involving three or more variables.

Multiplication rule the rule used to determine with what probability several simultaneous or successive events will occur. In its simplest form, $P(AB) = P(A)P(B|A)$.

Multistage sample a type of probability sample using random selection through several steps (stages) to arrive at the final sample.

Mutually exclusive events events such that the occurrence of one event precludes the occurrence of an alternative or alternative events.

Nonnumeric classification see **Qualitative classification**

Nonsampling error either systematic or unsystematic error.

Normal curve the most useful of the continuous probability distributions. When plotted, it appears as a bell-shaped, symmetrical curve with tails approaching but not touching the horizontal axis.

Normal deviates standard scale values for a normal curve.

Null hypothesis a statement of belief with respect to a statistical universe which is so stated as to be testable in terms of random sampling procedures and errors. The hypothesis that is actually tested by a statistical testing procedure.

Numeric classification see **Quantitative classification**

Objective probabilities probability statements based on process knowledge or experimental evidence.

One-tailed (sided) test a statistical test of an hypothesis with the rejection region lying entirely in one tail of the sampling distribution being used for the test.

Open-end interval an interval which is not closed on one end, e.g., "$10,000 and over."

Operating characteristc (OC) curve a plot of the probabilities of accepting the null hypothesis against various alternative values of the parameter being tested.

Opportunity loss the difference between the payoff of the best act that could have been selected given a state of the world and the payoff of any other act for the same state of the world. Profit foregone due to failing to make the best decision.

Parabola (second-degree curve) a form of mathematical curve used to represent trends characterized by squared values of the independent variable. It is used in both natural-number and logarithmic forms.

Parameter a statistical measure for a universe or population.

Partial regression and/or correlation regression and correlation analysis of the relationship of two variables as part of a multiple analysis.

Payoff the gain or loss associated with a particular decision and a particular state of the world.

Permutations the method of counting the number of possible outcomes in situations where order is important but repetition of elements is not permitted.

Personal investigation the direct collection of primary data through the use of personal contact by ennumerators.

Point estimate an estimate in the form of a single value.

Points of central tendency see **Averages**

Poisson distribution if an event can occur at random over a large area or long period of time, the Poisson distribution gives the probabilities of the event occurring in a small area or short interval of time. Occurrences are defined; nonoccurrences are not.

Positionary averages averages defined by describing a specific place or location in the data.

Posterior analysis the analysis of a decision problem after sampling, using Bayes' theorem.

Posterior probabilities see **A posteriori probabilities.** Used to refer to the revised set of probabilities in a bayesian decision problem.

Power the complement of the β risk.

Power curve a plot of the probabilities of rejecting the null hypothesis against various alternative values of the parameter being tested.

Presentation the process of using tables, graphs, or words to present the results of a statistical analysis.

Price indexes index numbers which measure only the change in prices.

Primary data data collected for a particular study under the control and supervision of the person making that study.

Primary source a source of secondary data which was its own collection agency.

Prior analysis the analysis of a decision problem before sampling.

Prior probabilities see **A priori probabilities.** Also used to refer to the probabilities in a bayesian decision problem before their revision in light of sample evidence. May be either objective or subjective in nature.

Probability the formal tool for measuring and expressing numerically degrees of certainty or uncertainty.

Probability distribution a distribution given the probabilities of all possible outcomes for a set of mutually exclusive events.

Probability sample a sample wherein items for the sample are chosen by some form of chance (random) procedure. Each universe item must have a known chance of appearing in the sample.

Process control statistical quality control techniques which attempt to control the manufacturing process while it is operating, thereby preventing the production of poor-quality product.

Qualitative classification a point in time classification of statistical data wherein the data are classified according to some unmeasurable nonnumeric attribute of the data—also known as a nonnumeric classification—also further subdivided into kind and area (geographic) classifications.

Quantitative classification a point in time classification of statistical data wherein the data are classified according to the size or magnitude of their numerical values— also known as a numeric classification.

Quantity indexes index numbers which measure only the change in the physical volume of various activities.

Quantity of information weighting factor in continuous posterior analysis—the reciprocal of the appropriate variance.

Quartile deviation one-half the difference between the first and third quartiles. A distance measure of variability.

Quartiles points used to divide a distribution into four parts. The first quartile (Q_1) has no more than one-fourth of the values smaller and no more than three-fourths larger. The third quartile (Q_3) has no more than three-fourths smaller and no more than one-fourth larger.

Random digits a set of digits used to draw random samples. Tables of random digits are constructed so as to have no predictable patterns. Any digit has an equal chance (probability) with any other digit of appearing at any position in the table.

Random sample a sample chosen from the universe in such a way that all samples of the same size have an equal chance of being selected. For this type of sample, each universe item has an equal chance to appear in the sample.

Random selection the selection of items by a procedure which chooses items only by chance.

Range the difference between the highest value in a set of data and the lowest value of the set. A distance measure of variability.

Rank correlation a technique used to measure the relative closeness of the relationship between two sets of data which are in the form of rankings only.

Rate of acceleration a measure of the relative (percentage) change in the rate of change in the trend of a time series when the latter rate is not constant. A measure of the direction and degree of curvature of a trend line.

Rate of change a measure of the relative (percentage) growth in a time series as shown by the trend line.

Ratio to moving average method the most commonly used procedure for obtaining seasonal indexes.

Reference table see **General purpose table**

Regression analysis statistical techniques used for studying the pattern of the relationship and the absolute closeness of the relationship among several quantitatively classified variables.

Regression line the measure of the pattern of the relationship in a regression analysis.

Rejection region a portion of a sampling distribution which if containing the sample result would lead to the rejection of the null hypothesis.

Sample a scientifically selected subset of a statistical universe (population).

Sampling distribution a frequency distribution showing the frequency (probability) of all possible sample results for a specified sampling situation.

Sampling error the error of the difference that may exist between a sample result and the true universe result. Caused by the chance factors in sample selection.

Scatter diagram term used to describe the graphs drawn for a regression analysis.

Seasonal a repetitive fluctuating movement in a time series with a duration of 1 year.

Secondary data data available for use in a particular study but not originally collected for that study.

Secondary source a source of secondary data which was merely a compiling agency for already collected data.

Selective sample see **Judgment sample**

Semilogarithmic graph paper graph paper with an arithmetically ruled horizontal scale and a logarithmically ruled vertical scale. Used to study the relative (percentage) changes in a time series.

Sequential sample a type of probability sample wherein items are selected one at a time.

Significant difference a difference between the sample value and the hypothesized population value sufficient to lead to the rejection of the null hypothesis. A difference so great that it is improbable that it is due to random sampling errors.

Simple index number the conversion of the consecutive values of a single series into percentages of the value for some one time period chosen as a base.

Simple regression and/or correlation regression and correlation analysis involving only two variables.

Skewness the lack of symmetry in a frequency curve.

Special-purpose table a table designed to emphasize particular statistical information.

Standard deviation the quadratic mean of a set of deviations which have been computed as the differences of the individual values from the arithmetic mean. A deviation measure of variability.

Standard error of estimate the standard deviation of a regression analysis. A measure of the variability of the points around the regression line. Used as a measure of the absolute closeness of the relationship in a regression analysis.

Standard error of the arithmetic mean the standard deviation of a random sampling distribution of arithmetic means. A measure of sampling error.

Standard error of the difference the standard deviation of a random sampling distribution of the differences between values from independent samples. A measure of sampling error.

Standard error of the estimate of an individual Y the measure used to qualify estimates from a regression line. The measure allows for both sampling error and unexplained variability.

Standard error of the percentage the standard deviation of a random sampling distribution of percentages. A measure of sampling error.

State of control term used to describe the fact that a process is subject to chance variations only.

States of the world possible conditions (values) of the universe to be sampled.

Statistic a statistical measure for a sample.

Statistical description the process of and techniques for summarizing the essential characteristics of a limited set of data, usually a sample.

Statistical inference the process of and techniques for generalizing about a statistical universe on the basis of sample information.

Statistical quality control the control of the quality level of manufactured product by statistical techniques, particularly the use of samples.

Statistical universe (population) all items that might be surveyed in a particular statistical study if a complete enumeration were made.

Statistics (plural) a set of numbers.

Statistics (singular) a body of methods for obtaining and analyzing numerical data in order to make better decisions in an uncertain world.

Stratified random sample a type of probability sample. The universe is divided into relatively homogeneous subuniverses (strata) and a simple random sample is taken from each.

Stub the row headings of a table.

Sturges' rule a formula for estimating the approximate size of class interval to use in constructing a frequency table.

Subjective probabilities probability statements based on an individual's personal assessment of the likelihood that an event will occur.

Sum of squares the sum of the squared deviations from the arithmetic mean.

Systematic error (bias) a persistent one-directional error made during the collection process.

Systematic selection the selection of items by some regular pattern (e.g., every 10th item).

t **distribution** a continuous probability distribution used in problems involving an estimated standard error and a small sample.

Table an arrangement of numerical data in columns and rows.

Time series see **Chronological classification**

Trend the long-term underlying growth movement of a time series. Generally conceived of as being smooth, continuous, and irreversible in form.

Two-tailed (sided) test a statistical test of an hypothesis with the rejection region divided equally between both tails of the sampling distribution being used for the test.

Type I error the error in hypothesis testing of rejecting the null hypothesis when it is true.

Type II error the error in hypothesis testing of accepting the null hypothesis when it is false.

Ungrouped data a set of data not in the form of a frequency distribution.

Unsystematic error human and mechanical errors made during a survey which have no set pattern of occurrence.

Upper-tailed test a one-tailed test with the rejection region in the upper tail of the sampling distribution.

Value indexes index numbers which measure the change in the total value of related series whether the change results from a price change, a quantity change, or a combination of the two.

Variability see **Dispersion**

Variance the square of the standard deviation, itself used as a measure of variability in advanced statistics.

Weighted mean a special form of the arithmetic mean wherein the values of the items being averaged are weighted before averaging.

A

TABLE OF COMMON LOGS

N	0	1	2	3	4	5	6	7	8	9
1.0	0.0000	0.004321	0.008600	0.01284	0.01703	0.02119	0.02531	0.02938	0.03342	0.03743
1.1	0.04139	0.04532	0.04922	0.05308	0.05690	0.06070	0.06446	0.06819	0.07188	0.07555
1.2	0.07918	0.08279	0.08636	0.08991	0.09342	0.09691	0.1004	0.1038	0.1072	0.1106
1.3	0.1139	0.1173	0.1206	0.1239	0.1271	0.1303	0.1335	0.1367	0.1399	0.1430
1.4	0.1461	0.1492	0.1523	0.1553	0.1584	0.1614	0.1644	0.1673	0.1703	0.1732
1.5	0.1761	0.1790	0.1818	0.1847	0.1875	0.1903	0.1931	0.1959	0.1987	0.2014
1.6	0.2041	0.2068	0.2095	0.2122	0.2148	0.2175	0.2201	0.2227	0.2253	0.2279
1.7	0.2304	0.2330	0.2355	0.2380	0.2405	0.2430	0.2455	0.2480	0.2504	0.2529
1.8	0.2553	0.2577	0.2601	0.2625	0.2648	0.2672	0.2695	0.2718	0.2742	0.2765
1.9	0.2788	0.2810	0.2833	0.2856	0.2878	0.2900	0.2923	0.2945	0.2967	0.2989
2.0	0.3010	0.3032	0.3054	0.3075	0.3096	0.3118	0.3139	0.3160	0.3181	0.3201
2.1	0.3222	0.3243	0.3263	0.3284	0.3304	0.3324	0.3345	0.3365	0.3385	0.3404
2.2	0.3424	0.3444	0.3464	0.3483	0.3502	0.3522	0.3541	0.3560	0.3579	0.3598
2.3	0.3617	0.3636	0.3655	0.3674	0.3692	0.3711	0.3729	0.3747	0.3766	0.3784
2.4	0.3802	0.3820	0.3838	0.3856	0.3874	0.3892	0.3909	0.3927	0.3945	0.3962
2.5	0.3979	0.3997	0.4014	0.4031	0.4048	0.4065	0.4082	0.4099	0.4116	0.4133
2.6	0.4150	0.4166	0.4183	0.4200	0.4216	0.4232	0.4249	0.4265	0.4281	0.4298
2.7	0.4314	0.4330	0.4346	0.4362	0.4378	0.4393	0.4409	0.4425	0.4440	0.4456
2.8	0.4472	0.4487	0.4502	0.4518	0.4533	0.4548	0.4564	0.4579	0.4594	0.4609
2.9	0.4624	0.4639	0.4654	0.4669	0.4683	0.4698	0.4713	0.4728	0.4742	0.4757
3.0	0.4771	0.4786	0.4800	0.4814	0.4829	0.4843	0.4857	0.4871	0.4886	0.4900
3.1	0.4914	0.4928	0.4942	0.4955	0.4969	0.4983	0.4997	0.5011	0.5024	0.5038
3.2	0.5051	0.5065	0.5079	0.5092	0.5105	0.5119	0.5132	0.5145	0.5159	0.5172
3.3	0.5185	0.5198	0:5211	0.5224	0.5237	0.5250	0.5263	0.5276	0.5289	0.5302
3.4	0.5315	0.5328	0.5340	0.5353	0.5366	0.5378	0.5391	0.5403	0.5416	0.5428
3.5	0.5441	0.5453	0.5465	0.5478	0.5490	0.5502	0.5514	0.5527	0.5539	0.5551
3.6	0.5563	0.5575	0.5587	0.5599	0.5611	0.5623	0.5635	0.5647	0.5658	0.5670
3.7	0.5682	0.5694	0.5705	0.5717	0.5729	0.5740	0.5752	0.5763	0.5775	0.5786
3.8	0.5798	0.5809	0.5821	0.5832	0.5843	0.5855	0.5866	0.5877	0.5888	0.5899
3.9	0.5911	0.5922	0.5933	0.5944	0.5955	0.5966	0.5977	0.5988	0.5999	0.6010

N	0	1	2	3	4	5	6	7	8	9
4.0	0.6021	0.6031	0.6042	0.6053	0.6064	0.6075	0.6085	0.6096	0.6107	0.6117
4.1	0.6128	0.6138	0.6149	0.6160	0.6170	0.6180	0.6191	0.6201	0.6212	0.6222
4.2	0.6232	0.6243	0.6253	0.6263	0.6274	0.6284	0.6294	0.6304	0.6314	0.6325
4.3	0.6335	0.6345	0.6355	0.6365	0.6375	0.6385	0.6395	0.6405	0.6415	0.6425
4.4	0.6435	0.6444	0.6454	0.6464	0.6474	0.6484	0.6493	0.6503	0.6513	0.6522
4.5	0.6532	0.6542	0.6551	0.6561	0.6571	0.6580	0.6590	0.6599	0.6609	0.6618
4.6	0.6628	0.6637	0.6646	0.6656	0.6665	0.6675	0.6684	0.6693	0.6702	0.6712
4.7	0.6721	0.6730	0.6739	0.6749	0.6758	0.6767	0.6776	0.6785	0.6794	0.6803
4.8	0.6812	0.6821	0.6830	0.6839	0.6848	0.6857	0.6866	0.6875	0.6884	0.6893
4.9	0.6902	0.6911	0.6920	0.6928	0.6937	0.6946	0.6955	0.6964	0.6972	0.6981
5.0	0.6990	0.6998	0.7007	0.7016	0.7024	0.7033	0.7042	0.7050	0.7059	0.7067
5.1	0.7076	0.7084	0.7093	0.7101	0.7110	0.7118	0.7126	0.7135	0.7143	0.7152
5.2	0.7160	0.7168	0.7177	0.7185	0.7193	0.7202	0.7210	0.7218	0.7226	0.7235
5.3	0.7243	0.7251	0.7259	0.7267	0.7275	0.7284	0.7292	0.7300	0.7308	0.7316
5.4	0.7324	0.7332	0.7340	0.7348	0.7356	0.7364	0.7372	0.7380	0.7388	0.7396
5.5	0.7404	0.7412	0.7419	0.7427	0.7435	0.7443	0.7451	0.7459	0.7466	0.7474
5.6	0.7482	0.7490	0.7497	0.7505	0.7513	0.7520	0.7528	0.7536	0.7543	0.7551
5.7	0.7559	0.7566	0.7574	0.7582	0.7589	0.7597	0.7604	0.7612	0.7619	0.7627
5.8	0.7634	0.7642	0.7649	0.7657	0.7664	0.7672	0.7679	0.7686	0.7694	0.7701
5.9	0.7709	0.7716	0.7723	0.7731	0.7738	0.7745	0.7752	0.7760	0.7767	0.7774
6.0	0.7782	0.7789	0.7796	0.7803	0.7810	0.7818	0.7825	0.7832	0.7839	0.7846
6.1	0.7853	0.7860	0.7868	0.7875	0.7882	0.7889	0.7896	0.7903	0.7910	0.7917
6.2	0.7924	0.7931	0.7938	0.7945	0.7952	0.7959	0.7966	0.7973	0.7980	0.7987
6.3	0.7993	0.8000	0.8007	0.8014	0.8021	0.8028	0.8035	0.8041	0.8048	0.8055
6.4	0.8062	0.8069	0.8075	0.8082	0.8089	0.8096	0.8102	0.8109	0.8116	0.8122
6.5	0.8129	0.8136	0.8142	0.8149	0.8156	0.8162	0.8169	0.8176	0.8182	0.8189
6.6	0.8195	0.8202	0.8209	0.8215	0.8222	0.8228	0.8235	0.8241	0.8248	0.8254
6.7	0.8261	0.8267	0.8274	0.8280	0.8287	0.8293	0.8299	0.8306	0.8312	0.8319
6.8	0.8325	0.8331	0.8338	0.8344	0.8351	0.8357	0.8363	0.8370	0.8376	0.8382
6.9	0.8388	0.8395	0.8401	0.8407	0.8414	0.8420	0.8426	0.8432	0.8439	0.8445
7.0	0.8451	0.8457	0.8463	0.8470	0.8476	0.8482	0.8488	0.8494	0.8500	0.8506
7.1	0.8513	0.8519	0.8525	0.8531	0.8537	0.8543	0.8549	0.8555	0.8561	0.8567
7.2	0.8573	0.8579	0.8585	0.8591	0.8597	0.8603	0.8609	0.8615	0.8621	0.8627
7.3	0.8633	0.8639	0.8645	0.8651	0.8657	0.8663	0.8669	0.8675	0.8681	0.8686
7.4	0.8692	0.8698	0.8704	0.8710	0.8716	0.8722	0.8727	0.8733	0.8739	0.8745
7.5	0.8751	0.8756	0.8762	0.8768	0.8774	0.8779	0.8785	0.8791	0.8797	0.8802
7.6	0.8808	0.8814	0.8820	0.8825	0.8831	0.8837	0.8842	0.8848	0.8854	0.8859
7.7	0.8865	0.8871	0.8876	0.8882	0.8887	0.8893	0.8899	0.8904	0.8910	0.8915
7.8	0.8921	0.8927	0.8932	0.8938	0.8943	0.8949	0.8954	0.8960	0.8965	0.8971
7.9	0.8976	0.8982	0.8987	0.8993	0.8998	0.9004	0.9009	0.9015	0.9020	0.9025
8.0	0.9031	0.9036	0.9042	0.9047	0.9053	0.9058	0.9063	0.9069	0.9074	0.9079
8.1	0.9085	0.9090	0.9096	0.9101	0.9106	0.9112	0.9117	0.9122	0.9128	0.9133
8.2	0.9138	0.9143	0.9149	0.9154	0.9159	0.9165	0.9170	0.9175	0.9180	0.9186
8.3	0.9191	0.9196	0.9201	0.9206	0.9212	0.9217	0.9222	0.9227	0.9232	0.9238
8.4	0.9243	0.9248	0.9253	0.9258	0.9263	0.9269	0.9274	0.9279	0.9284	0.9289

N	0	1	2	3	4	5	6	7	8	9
8.5	0.9294	0.9299	0.9304	0.9309	0.9315	0.9320	0.9325	0.9330	0.9335	0.9340
8.6	0.9345	0.9350	0.9355	0.9360	0.9365	0.9370	0.9375	0.9380	0.9385	0.9390
8.7	0.9395	0.9400	0.9405	0.9410	0.9415	0.9420	0.9425	0.9430	0.9435	0.9440
8.8	0.9445	0.9450	0.9455	0.9460	0.9465	0.9469	0.9474	0.9479	0.9484	0.9489
8.9	0.9494	0.9499	0.9504	0.9509	0.9513	0.9518	0.9523	0.9528	0.9533	0.9538
9.0	0.9542	0.9547	0.9552	0.9557	0.9562	0.9566	0.9571	0.9576	0.9581	0.9586
9.1	0.9590	0.9595	0.9600	0.9605	0.9609	0.9614	0.9619	0.9624	0.9628	0.9633
9.2	0.9638	0.9643	0.9647	0.9652	0.9657	0.9661	0.9666	0.9671	0.9675	0.9680
9.3	0.9685	0.9689	0.9694	0.9699	0.9703	0.9708	0.9713	0.9717	0.9722	0.9727
9.4	0.9731	0.9736	0.9741	0.9745	0.9750	0.9754	0.9759	0.9763	0.9768	0.9773
9.5	0.9777	0.9782	0.9786	0.9791	0.9795	0.9800	0.9805	0.9809	0.9814	0.9818
9.6	0.9823	0.9827	0.9832	0.9836	0.9841	0.9845	0.9850	0.9854	0.9859	0.9863
9.7	0.9868	0.9872	0.9877	0.9881	0.9886	0.9890	0.9894	0.9899	0.9903	0.9908
9.8	0.9912	0.9917	0.9921	0.9926	0.9930	0.9934	0.9939	0.9943	0.9948	0.9952
9.9	0.9956	0.9961	0.9965	0.9969	0.9974	0.9978	0.9983	0.9987	0.9991	0.9996

AREAS (PERCENTAGES) UNDER THE NORMAL CURVE

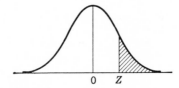

(Total area = 100 per cent)

Normal deviate (Z)	0.00	0.01	0.02	0.03	0.04	0.05	0.06	0.07	0.08	0.09
0.0	50.00	49.60	49.20	48.80	48.40	48.01	47.61	47.21	46.81	46.41
0.1	46.02	45.62	45.22	44.83	44.43	44.04	43.64	43.25	42.86	42.47
0.2	42.07	41.68	41.29	40.90	40.52	40.13	39.74	39.36	38.97	38.59
0.3	38.21	37.83	37.45	37.07	36.69	36.32	35.94	35.57	35.20	34.83
0.4	34.46	34.09	33.72	33.36	33.00	32.64	32.28	31.92	31.56	31.21
0.5	30.85	30.50	30.15	29.81	29.46	29.12	28.77	28.43	28.10	27.76
0.6	27.43	27.09	26.76	26.43	26.11	25.78	25.46	25.14	24.83	24.51
0.7	24.20	23.89	23.58	23.27	22.96	22.66	22.36	22.06	21.77	21.48
0.8	21.19	20.90	20.61	20.33	20.05	19.77	19.49	19.22	18.94	18.67
0.9	18.41	18.14	17.88	17.62	17.36	17.11	16.85	16.60	16.35	16.11
1.0	15.87	15.62	15.39	15.15	14.92	14.69	14.46	14.23	14.01	13.79
1.1	13.57	13.35	13.14	12.92	12.71	12.51	12.30	12.10	11.90	11.70
1.2	11.51	11.31	11.12	10.93	10.75	10.56	10.38	10.20	10.03	9.85
1.3	9.68	9.51	9.34	9.18	9.01	8.85	8.69	8.53	8.38	8.23
1.4	8.08	7.93	7.78	7.64	7.49	7.35	7.21	7.08	6.94	6.81
1.5	6.68	6.55	6.43	6.30	6.18	6.06	5.94	5.82	5.71	5.59
1.6	5.48	5.37	5.26	5.16	5.05	4.95	4.85	4.75	4.65	4.55
1.7	4.46	4.36	4.27	4.18	4.09	4.01	3.92	3.84	3.75	3.67
1.8	3.59	3.51	3.44	3.36	3.29	3.22	3.14	3.07	3.01	2.94
1.9	2.87	2.81	2.74	2.68	2.62	2.56	2.50	2.44	2.39	2.33

(Total area = 100 per cent)

Normal deviate (Z)	0.00	0.01	0.02	0.03	0.04	0.05	0.06	0.07	0.08	0.09
2.0	2.28	2.22	2.17	2.12	2.07	2.02	1.97	1.92	1.88	1.83
2.1	1.79	1.74	1.70	1.66	1.62	1.58	1.54	1.50	1.46	1.43
2.2	1.39	1.36	1.32	1.29	1.25	1.22	1.19	1.16	1.13	1.10
2.3	1.07	1.04	1.02	0.99	0.96	0.94	0.91	0.89	0.87	0.84
2.4	0.82	0.80	0.78	0.75	0.73	0.71	0.69	0.68	0.66	0.64
2.5	0.62	0.60	0.59	0.57	0.55	0.54	0.52	0.51	0.49	0.48
2.6	0.47	0.45	0.44	0.43	0.41	0.40	0.39	0.38	0.37	0.36
2.7	0.35	0.34	0.33	0.32	0.31	0.30	0.29	0.28	0.27	0.26
2.8	0.26	0.25	0.24	0.23	0.23	0.22	0.21	0.21	0.20	0.19
2.9	0.19	0.18	0.18	0.17	0.16	0.16	0.15	0.15	0.14	0.14
3.0	0.135	0.131	0.126	0.122	0.118	0.114	0.111	0.107	0.104	0.100
3.1	0.097	0.094	0.090	0.087	0.084	0.082	0.079	0.076	0.074	0.071
3.2	0.069	0.066	0.064	0.062	0.060	0.058	0.056	0.054	0.052	0.050
3.3	0.048	0.047	0.045	0.043	0.042	0.040	0.039	0.038	0.036	0.035
3.4	0.034	0.032	0.031	0.030	0.029	0.028	0.027	0.026	0.025	0.204
3.5	0.023	0.022	0.022	0.021	0.020	0.019	0.019	0.018	0.017	0.017
3.6	0.016	0.015	0.015	0.014	0.014	0.013	0.013	0.012	0.012	0.011
3.7	0.011	0.010	0.010	0.010	0.009	0.009	0.008	0.008	0.008	0.008
3.8	0.007	0.007	0.007	0.006	0.006	0.006	0.006	0.005	0.005	0.005
3.9	0.005	0.005	0.004	0.004	0.004	0.004	0.004	0.004	0.003	0.003
4.0	0.003									
4.5	0.0003									
5.0	0.00003									

$\mathbf{B}_2$

NORMAL DEVIATES

Single-tailed area, %	Two-tailed area, %	z
0.05	0.10	3.29
0.10	0.20	3.09
0.25	0.50	2.81
0.50	1.00	2.58
1.00	2.00	2.33
1.25	2.50	2.24
1.50	3.00	2.17
2.00	4.00	2.05
2.50	5.00	1.96
3.00	6.00	1.88
4.00	8.00	1.75
5.00	10.00	1.64
6.00	12.00	1.55
7.00	14.00	1.48
8.00	16.00	1.41
9.00	18.00	1.34
10.00	20.00	1.28
20.00	40.00	0.84
25.00	50.00	0.67
30.00	60.00	0.52
40.00	80.00	0.25
50.00	100.00	0.00

TABLE OF RANDOM DIGITS

1339	8429	1378	9206	9861
4089	4938	8754	4184	2676
7617	8133	1492	0699	0704
1152	6390	5466	2126	4818
6688	5584	4052	9340	3394
2862	9090	8125	0715	2307
3047	7782	6060	2127	4931
8119	0036	3732	6951	2143
6452	1727	4515	6062	2316
3923	6230	9285	7834	1325
3905	4419	6417	8143	2547
7273	4671	1785	0364	6855
2404	2859	8766	5372	2625
5171	2358	8233	1541	5732
8950	4045	8561	4747	9550
4616	6293	5627	8365	4955
0544	4978	2804	3270	0322
2608	3474	0968	7836	1526
4184	2658	8494	7939	1941
6147	0903	1256	6954	2444
6872	4085	2631	5756	1408
2233	5579	3492	2719	4708
5606	6259	2214	3719	5721
7866	4501	4674	2131	5320
7387	6180	4245	8830	1881
0046	4671	1803	2190	1279
9216	0848	5723	8087	6888
5773	3087	1880	9896	9585
8091	7263	3648	8492	7742
2046	6751	1903	2249	7237
1014	2425	5020	7043	1444
5867	2662	8873	6249	1237
4983	3334	6838	0742	4992
4235	7819	9790	8896	8584
6999	6991	6104	6587	5387
4150	9224	1655	7190	6277

4063	0394	9817	1580	9629
2612	3875	1466	8131	1318
3173	0544	4977	2719	4718
6621	8774	6224	8719	0706
1331	4441	8584	7006	7655
3177	0920	2930	5954	1440
5535	9085	7637	1439	5438
9280	7312	8582	6836	0522
2786	1476	9138	3020	5068
1930	4952	0181	8365	4951
0085	8614	0086	8747	3545
8127	0838	4728	7541	1726
4430	7499	7481	5622	7869
4870	1972	9221	1364	7849
2823	5131	8323	0643	5041
9161	5353	0661	6834	0319
2262	8510	9611	0812	2059
7999	7980	6048	0951	6136
9748	4637	8347	3127	5924
8384	6855	2383	0715	2299
2282	0510	1530	4590	3636
7316	8976	6664	3126	5810
6862	3130	6160	2199	2195
1795	1345	5892	5184	3668
0490	9497	9237	2956	8602
8821	0961	7068	3889	2872
0164	6611	7760	3859	9855
5394	4823	7190	6241	0424
2885	1472	8731	1910	2955
8514	9933	3259	9240	3323
5654	1080	9149	4107	4902
5181	3289	2276	9886	8568
5469	2435	6014	7452	2696
2394	1893	1239	5179	3161
9331	2537	6326	8943	3338
7155	2743	7149	2119	4101
4241	8386	7084	5582	3826
6463	2841	7006	7706	8388
7197	6983	5290	4367	1161
7318	9186	7811	8940	3021
5201	5326	7943	2300	2343
6720	8777	6562	2821	5002
5251	0416	2043	6379	4372
1669	8616	0260	6349	1330
4348	9253	4590	3606	4249
9165	5701	5906	6524	9004
9493	8837	2583	0979	8972
6208	7034	0498	0346	5026
7684	6168	3024	5500	5542

9798	9614	1037	4815	6395
5923	8246	2912	4167	0959
6934	0440	4524	6931	0110
1208	2071	9247	3982	2223
4618	6514	7957	3694	3173
0540	4643	9029	1943	6335
9849	4834	8337	2104	2583
0920	2962	9257	5052	0293
9627	2402	2664	9161	5340
9346	4028	6933	0307	1098
0952	6217	7939	1865	8443
2820	4842	9056	4710	5750
0824	3278	1160	7216	8894
8340	2402	2626	5259	1249
6243	0587	9328	2214	3692
2907	3709	4643	8956	4596
4209	5142	9444	3859	9836
3522	5763	2106	2799	2789
1722	3945	8506	9151	4328
7183	5564	2017	3790	2829
5782	3995	3515	5090	4167
0892	0112	1375	8927	1716
3388	2291	1471	8676	6352
1647	6407	7180	5212	6450
1542	5835	9375	6909	7885
6449	1449	6432	9643	4032
7243	1625	4225	6789	5765
2299	2238	6130	9222	1460
7491	6663	3022	5316	6991
6195	5774	3276	0947	5735
9286	7948	2767	9490	8565
5139	9058	4869	1820	3857
9628	2479	0458	6311	7486
6129	9088	7909	8839	2826
5517	7258	3096	2779	0754
6166	2865	9396	9006	9643
3953	9283	7682	5894	5368
2251	7389	6329	9319	1306
1936	5556	1214	2656	8330
1382	9660	5710	6780	4816
6466	3076	0693	0065	6639
0561	6678	4538	8387	7173
4542	8842	3119	5121-	7294
6786	5443	9813	1142	5377
3166	9856	5493	4824	7297
7058	2955	8535	2043	6429
9337	3116	4813	6174	3647
8378	6214	7703	8092	7327
0055	5624	8080	6171	3343

7744	2220	4319	6287	5072
2320	4379	2295	1815	3387
2158	7974	5382	3630	6664
3132	6380	4456	0106	0778
8618	0474	7892	7119	9103
9491	8629	1564	8044	2516
4125	6721	8849	3756	9390
8397	8124	0620	2629	5600
5680	3715	5252	0539	4523
6850	1867	8622	0861	7032
0281	8456	4103	4470	1503
1850	6857	2571	9740	3811
4930	7944	2401	2547	7330
0396	0093	9467	6266	2936
6625	9179	7146	1772	9004
9490	8577	6311	7439	1409
2367	9161	5337	9143	3525
6131	9307	0101	0259	6229
9157	4890	3976	1662	7894
7319	9285	7838	1726	4395
3993	3366	0062	6327	9109
0054	5510	6523	8840	2909
3877	1589	0595	0140	4171
1336	4981	3154	8601	8770
5807	6560	2575	0099	0080
8165	4700	4732	8009	8978
6784	5277	3001	3206	3836
7541	1665	8258	4064	0532
3809	4741	8875	6459	2440
6464	2878	0730	3766	0434
3880	1952	7196	6860	2890
1933	5338	9149	4115	5683
3999	3910	4964	1407	2187
0950	6044	0515	2111	3278
1164	7615	9179	7102	7331
0514	1998	1829	4754	0221
2376	0067	6840	0943	5322
7625	0198	0089	9044	3511
4636	8266	4949	9932	3161
9283	7646	2296	1981	0147
4942	9212	0505	1067	7846
2488	1341	5451	0565	7131
0296	9905	0508	1350	6378
4240	8282	6552	1796	1462
7696	7346	1958	7779	5757
1539	5471	2600	2674	0139
4143	8533	1854	7356	2983
1385	9906	0595	0199	0164
6638	0467	7198	7079	5057

0778	8589	7538	1371	8536
2179	0148	4989	3950	8977
6717	8519	0427	3190	2255
7768	4576	2227	4967	1744
6204	6695	6263	2656	8320
0403	0751	5912	7132	0358
6238	0119	2047	6769	3733
7085	5673	3043	7443	1819
3819	5789	4777	2529	5493
4815	6342	0622	2902	3128
5947	0707	1454	6936	0599
0591	9758	5648	0507	1283
9622	1872	9079	6990	6053
1415	2921	5121	7260	3285
1844	6283	4650	9691	8854
4285	2832	6041	0159	6134
9613	0942	5168	2039	6001
6202	6489	5407	6206	6830
9929	2847	7633	1034	4496
4167	0893	0221	2399	2374
9792	9000	9046	3676	1338
5178	3044	7482	5740	9764
6201	6399	6405	6965	3527
6236	9942	4190	3227	6001
6158	2046	6711	7901	8062
4342	8587	7345	1862	8085
6662	2940	6965	3484	1945
6494	5979	3946	8643	3016
4713	6080	4165	0714	2175
9694	9118	0995	0572	7795
7311	8468	5312	6591	5751
0940	5004	5491	4647	9420
1456	7102	7407	8115	9675
7233	0637	4434	7870	4892
4148	8984	7448	2286	0946
5574	3017	4824	7239	1211
2387	1113	2436	6104	6563
2961	9145	3660	9756	5377
3173	0488	9371	6569	3528
6396	6019	7944	2419	4391
3505	4111	5254	0681	8840
2877	0640	4675	2230	5251
0385	8980	7083	5440	9499
9405	0008	0853	6187	4958
0812	2097	1859	7846	2504
2981	1123	3478	1292	0512
1786	0461	6583	4899	4857
0603	0985	9549	4543	8913
0307	1071	8253	3599	3557

9273	6594	6068	2942	7162
3375	0929	3870	0946	5603
5989	4950	0034	3487	2257
7990	7033	0434	3940	7997
7752	3053	8447	3180	1199
1152	6385	4946	9581	7738
1563	7903	8307	9019	0988
9861	5984	4404	4869	1825
4420	6501	6613	8006	8624
1117	2829	5809	6804	7260
3325	5845	0367	7139	1108
1919	3922	6162	2386	1042
5276	2936	6568	3420	5438
9269	6261	2461	8615	0170
7274	4774	2216	3847	8615
0166	6848	1707	2491	1646
6320	8359	4311	5422	7639
1610	2682	0901	1014	2469
9412	0691	9852	5143	9510
0601	0762	7041	1184	9639
3552	8770	5841	0012	1229
4139	8090	7128	0001	0155
5738	9596	9277	7027	9794
9224	1664	8162	4465	1019
2971	0169	7160	3190	2206
2856	8486	7144	1576	9230
2252	7489	6490	5499	5465
2035	5555	1072	8334	1787
0579	8557	4266	0956	6571
3761	9870	6947	1739	5692
4954	0371	7490	6559	2525
5033	8433	1770	8791	7944
2375	9932	3161	9310	0325
2853	8242	2539	6490	5542
9843	4240	8279	6207	6972
4220	6299	6255	1836	5488
4359	0295	9844	4252	9466
6134	9603	9919	1829	4781
2921	5097	4855	0443	4807
5595	5153	0529	3469	0421
2531	5646	0314	1782	9996
9603	9951	5086	3756	9407
0187	8942	3220	5267	2031
5158	0995	0590	9690	8741
2890	1985	0573	7900	7913
9260	5287	4042	8271	5422
7641	1775	9373	6679	4642
8909	9826	2440	6499	6449
1438	5313	6619	8606	9218

1105	1611	2785	1374	8824
1283	9597	9313	0679	8641
2847	7644	2078	9896	9546
4174	1628	4454	9900	9912
1137	4923	7317	9065	5614
7112	8406	9042	3267	0029
2974	0450	5503	5881	4030
7098	6931	0076	7782	5993
5358	1224	3637	7344	1793
1130	4203	4558	0443	4804
5289	4244	8717	0454	5903
6210	7222	9487	8252	3462
9767	6512	7744	2211	3359
9336	2988	1863	8207	8968
5792	5026	7718	9615	1163
7509	8501	8686	7310	8320
0364	6788	5640	9666	6314
7730	0761	6955	2559	8519
0483	8797	8508	9364	5811
6997	6768	3672	0956	6565
3148	8052	3323	5709	6656
2312	3523	5836	9499	9458
5361	1555	7086	5701	5848
0673	8024	0447	5190	4199
4121	6304	6795	6340	0386
9081	7272	4505	5027	7786
6428	9301	9451	4626	7272
4537	8267	5009	6012	7220
9282	7545	2054	7559	3505
4039	8009	8961	5143	9501
9683	8035	1605	2139	6084
4589	3498	3360	9422	1629
4631	7773	5102	5366	2011
3185	1734	5206	5847	0605
1126	3757	9546	4240	8285
6828	9717	1499	1420	3427
6168	2989	1938	5761	1906
2519	4447	9238	3139	7096
6757	2468	9276	6929	9873
7256	2924	5425	8006	8612
9892	9193	8561	4744	9188
8041	2149	7059	3019	4975
2575	0166	6794	6206	6850
1872	9120	1140	5179	3186
1805	2385	0973	8315	9858
5750	0838	4668	1487	0243
4582	2852	8099	8071	5214
6676	4303	4642	8941	3147
7906	8566	5172	2474	9917

1648	6515	8064	4543	8898
8777	6526	9193	8524	0966
7668	4474	1933	5291	4496
4195	3734	7160	3221	5363
1734	5180	3249	8187	6942
1160	7188	6074	3565	0107
0847	5633	9012	0229	3234
6672	3890	2936	6556	2198
2008	2833	6221	8419	0373
7731	0838	4744	9194	8635
2215	3780	1878	9755	5359
1336	5034	8499	8479	6420
8469	5475	2982	1239	5192
4489	3477	1202	1411	2552
7771	4916	6533	9869	6873
4189	3166	9851	4990	4030
7119	9104	9531	2647	7400
7436	1103	1447	6216	7856
3515	5039	8975	6571	3774
1230	4286	2990	2089	1029
3957	9721	1867	8643	2995
2571	9717	1481	9609	0548
5446	0150	5206	5861	2063
8459	4395	3918	5776	3415
4983	3326	5992	5227	7979
5894	5319	7302	7590	6629
9566	6249	1225	3739	7741
1876	9491	8634	2051	7190
6197	5919	7904	8399	8350
3404	3909	4912	6159	2097
1874	9336	3031	6205	6806
7480	5575	3137	6914	8352
3598	3500	3605	4159	0109
1103	1488	0310	1316	2954
8370	5412	6626	9259	5260
1273	8647	3429	6365	2902
3188	2070	9094	8507	9257
4990	4054	9495	9061	5198
5054	0475	8008	8901	9101
9254	4707	5508	6404	6841
0966	7627	0370	7443	1792
1065	7608	8469	5394	4830
7925	0526	3179	1131	4330
7423	9756	5376	3031	6167
2932	6172	3435	6967	3716
5328	8150	3230	6315	7851
2985	1565	8138	1949	6948
1780	9792	9032	2246	6881
5086	3705	4287	3079	1027

3778	1680	9780	7824	0259
6233	9592	8884	7355	2953
8324	0816	2475	0049	4984
3427	6226	8928	1779	9726
2417	4199	4117	5921	8056
3669	0608	1419	3349	8347
3057	8828	1707	2440	6474
3957	9736	3357	9067	5814
7244	1705	2243	6606	7240
1293	0611	1741	5931	9128
1978	9828	2726	5419	7353
2675	0233	3573	0943	5289
4259	0199	0157	5879	3812
5104	5602	5852	1101	1297
1087	9817	1534	4986	3619
5581	3718	5578	3407	4153
9462	5681	3858	9740	3773
1104	1581	9751	4859	0855
6384	4793	4130	7141	1273
8675	6191	5370	2459	8404
8852	4151	9348	4189	3121
5292	4548	9437	3205	3800
3868	0757	6513	7884	6316
7956	3652	8951	4099	4043
8431	1610	2625	5226	7858
3668	0504	0912	2139	6134
9541	3709	4685	3215	4746
9426	2102	2320	4327	7071
4198	4056	9691	8851	3982
2232	5447	0174	7661	3855
9402	9649	4644	9134	2565
9084	7539	1476	9143	3486
2153	7490	6545	1064	7494
6983	5378	3225	5771	2964
9451	4578	2392	1641	5771
2930	5964	2421	4547	9289
8296	7912	9186	7865	4395
3923	6297	6063	2469	9462
5687	4494	3928	6736	0365
6964	3377	1153	6539	0481
8626	1322	3616	5254	0683
9051	4204	4690	3755	9347
4112	5398	5251	0419	2348
7185	5778	3674	1119	3060
9145	3721	5833	9231	2360
8367	5099	5105	5629	8620
0725	3290	2363	8690	7718
9595	9168	5982	4287	3028
5852	1107	1839	5796	5424

7871	4983	3307	4091	3282
1526	4170	1262	7549	2477
0193	9545	4079	2043	6383
4747	9481	7633	0949	5876
3562	9854	5298	5141	9331
2515	4039	7950	2996	2623
4979	2910	3964	0387	9126
1830	4843	9214	0690	9717
1442	5713	7076	4779	2769
9691	8895	8425	1031	4157
9953	5263	1636	5319	7258
3100	3193	2584	1019	2945
7510	8560	4643	9005	9594
9056	4739	8689	7654	3080
1114	2604	3097	2839	6777
4559	0532	3741	7936	1561
7766	4395	3998	3819	5807
6609	7571	4741	8865	5390
4464	0934	4345	8947	3685
2206	2858	8687	7441	1566
8210	9219	1140	5221	7409
8350	3391	2580	0664	7089
6002	6251	1382	9643	3980
2041	6172	3421	5534	8958
4841	9030	2071	9211	0398
0279	8200	8208	9051	4175
1728	4556	0207	0927	3663
0064	6474	3942	8215	9739
3661	9829	2789	1789	0776
8395	7996	7623	0026	2649
7642	1849	6819	8799	8735
2274	9764	6252	1484	9907
0669	7616	9296	8955	4541
8700	8780	6827	9589	8512
9743	4130	7220	9259	5194
4673	2043	6349	1341	5463
1865	8391	7591	6709	7694
7193	6552	1819	3740	7762
4033	7400	7408	8307	9042
3260	9309	0235	3786	2408
3248	8155	3673	1051	6236
9874	7312	8598	8479	6401
6511	7657	3385	1943	6277
4035	7563	3909	4819	6740
0820	2906	3544	7981	6165
2743	7060	3166	9806	0427
3177	0902	1150	6167	2900
2998	2805	3370	0440	4461
0580	8645	3202	3499	3483

1799	1797	1521	3721	5841
0030	3135	6702	6979	4912
6148	1035	4620	6649	1569
8528	1372	8649	3605	4188
3044	7521	9665	6224	8644
3072	0356	6043	0379	8311
9487	8253	3657	9446	4065
0664	7087	5884	4299	4281
2477	0233	3597	3315	4834
8302	8565	5171	2367	9099
9014	0460	6483	4831	7950
2987	1791	0906	1581	9763
6098	5933	9316	0994	0413
1720	3763	0088	8943	3274
0729	3654	9097	8804	9222
1499	1482	9717	1451	6632
9907	0621	2824	5261	1379
9326	1948	6793	6107	6837
0631	3836	7498	7365	3883
2199	2161	8315	9909	0890
9903	0298	0119	2116	3733
7119	9121	1285	9859	5789
4722	7006	7688	6514	7931

D

TABLE OF *t* VALUES

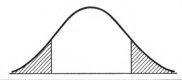

Degrees of freedom	Probability												
	0.9	0.8	0.7	0.6	0.5	0.4	0.3	0.2	0.1	0.05	0.02	0.01	0.001
1	0.158	0.325	0.510	0.727	1.000	1.376	1.963	3.078	6.314	12.706	31.821	63.657	636.619
2	0.142	0.289	0.445	0.617	0.816	1.061	1.386	1.886	2.920	4.303	6.965	9.925	31.598
3	0.137	0.277	0.424	0.584	0.765	0.978	1.250	1.638	2.353	3.182	4.541	5.841	12.924
4	0.134	0.271	0.414	0.569	0.741	0.941	1.190	1.533	2.132	2.776	3.747	4.604	8.610
5	0.132	0.267	0.408	0.559	0.727	0.920	1.156	1.476	2.015	2.571	3.365	4.032	6.869
6	0.131	0.265	0.404	0.553	0.718	0.906	1.134	1.440	1.943	2.447	3.143	3.707	5.959
7	0.130	0.263	0.402	0.549	0.711	0.896	1.119	1.415	1.895	2.365	2.998	3.499	5.408
8	0.130	0.262	0.399	0.546	0.706	0.889	1.108	1.397	1.860	2.306	2.896	3.355	5.041
9	0.129	0.261	0.398	0.543	0.703	0.883	1.100	1.383	1.833	2.262	2.821	3.250	4.781
10	0.129	0.260	0.397	0.542	0.700	0.879	1.093	1.372	1.812	2.228	2.764	3.169	4.587
11	0.129	0.260	0.396	0.540	0.697	0.876	1.088	1.363	1.796	2.201	2.718	3.106	4.437
12	0.128	0.259	0.395	0.539	0.695	0.873	1.083	1.356	1.782	2.179	2.681	3.055	4.318
13	0.128	0.259	0.394	0.538	0.694	0.870	1.079	1.350	1.771	2.160	2.650	3.012	4.221
14	0.128	0.258	0.393	0.537	0.692	0.868	1.076	1.345	1.761	2.145	2.624	2.977	4.140
15	0.128	0.258	0.393	0.536	0.691	0.866	1.074	1.341	1.753	2.131	2.602	2.947	4.073
16	0.128	0.258	0.392	0.535	0.690	0.865	1.071	1.337	1.746	2.120	2.583	2.921	4.015
17	0.128	0.257	0.392	0.534	0.689	0.863	1.069	1.333	1.740	2.110	2.567	2.898	3.965
18	0.127	0.257	0.392	0.534	0.688	0.862	1.067	1.330	1.734	2.101	2.552	2.878	3.922
19	0.127	0.257	0.391	0.533	0.688	0.861	1.066	1.328	1.729	2.093	2.539	2.861	3.883
20	0.127	0.257	0.391	0.533	0.687	0.860	1.064	1.325	1.725	2.086	2.528	2.845	3.850

Degrees of freedom	Probability												
	0.9	0.8	0.7	0.6	0.5	0.4	0.3	0.2	0.1	0.05	0.02	0.01	0.001
21	0.127	0.257	0.391	0.532	0.686	0.859	1.063	1.323	1.721	2.080	2.518	2.831	3.819
22	0.127	0.256	0.390	0.532	0.686	0.858	1.061	1.321	1.717	2.074	2.508	2.819	3.792
23	0.127	0.256	0.390	0.532	0.685	0.858	1.060	1.319	1.714	2.069	2.500	2.807	3.767
24	0.127	0.256	0.390	0.531	0.685	0.857	1.059	1.318	1.711	2.064	2.492	2.797	3.745
25	0.127	0.256	0.390	0.531	0.684	0.856	1.058	1.316	1.708	2.060	2.485	2.787	3.725
26	0.127	0.256	0.390	0.531	0.684	0.856	1.058	1.315	1.706	2.056	2.479	2.779	3.707
27	0.127	0.256	0.389	0.531	0.684	0.855	1.057	1.314	1.703	2.052	2.473	2.771	3.690
28	0.127	0.256	0.389	0.530	0.683	0.855	1.056	1.313	1.701	2.048	2.467	2.763	3.674
29	0.127	0.256	0.389	0.530	0.683	0.854	1.055	1.311	1.699	2.045	2.462	2.756	3.659
30	0.127	0.256	0.389	0.530	0.683	0.854	1.055	1.310	1.697	2.042	2.457	2.750	3.646
40	0.126	0.255	0.388	0.529	0.681	0.851	1.050	1.303	1.684	2.021	2.423	2.704	3.551
60	0.126	0.254	0.387	0.527	0.679	0.848	1.046	1.296	1.671	2.000	2.390	2.660	3.460
120	0.126	0.254	0.386	0.526	0.677	0.845	1.041	1.289	1.658	1.980	2.358	2.617	3.373
∞	0.126	0.253	0.385	0.524	0.674	0.842	1.036	1.282	1.645	1.960	2.326	2.576	3.291

Source: Appendix D is reprinted from Table III of Ronald A. Fisher and Frank Yates, *Statistical Tables for Biological, Agricultural, and Medical Research*, 5th ed., published by Oliver & Boyd Ltd., Edinburgh, 1957, by permission of the authors and publishers.

E

TABLE OF F VALUES

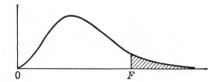

Upper 10% Points

df for denominator	df for numerator									
	1	2	3	4	5	6	8	12	24	∞
1	39.86	49.50	53.59	55.83	57.24	58.20	59.44	60.70	62.00	63.33
2	8.53	9.00	9.16	9.24	9.29	9.33	9.37	9.41	9.45	9.49
3	5.54	5.46	5.39	5.34	5.31	5.28	5.25	5.22	5.18	5.13
4	4.54	4.32	4.19	4.11	4.05	4.01	3.95	3.90	3.83	3.76
5	4.06	3.78	3.62	3.52	3.45	3.40	3.34	3.27	3.19	3.10
6	3.78	3.46	3.29	3.18	3.11	3.05	2.98	2.90	2.82	2.72
7	3.59	3.26	3.07	2.96	2.88	2.83	2.75	2.67	2.58	2.47
8	3.46	3.11	2.92	2.81	2.73	2.67	2.59	2.50	2.40	2.29
9	3.36	3.01	2.81	2.69	2.61	2.55	2.47	2.38	2.28	2.16
10	3.28	2.92	2.73	2.61	2.52	2.46	2.38	2.28	2.18	2.06
11	3.23	2.86	2.66	2.54	2.45	2.39	2.30	2.21	2.10	1.97
12	3.18	2.81	2.61	2.48	2.39	2.33	2.24	2.15	2.04	1.90
13	3.14	2.76	2.56	2.43	2.35	2.28	2.20	2.10	1.98	1.85
14	3.10	2.73	2.52	2.39	2.31	2.24	2.15	2.05	1.94	1.80
15	3.07	2.70	2.49	2.36	2.27	2.21	2.12	2.02	1.90	1.76
16	3.05	2.67	2.46	2.33	2.24	2.18	2.09	1.99	1.87	1.72
17	3.03	2.64	2.44	2.31	2.22	2.15	2.06	1.96	1.84	1.69
18	3.01	2.62	2.42	2.29	2.20	2.13	2.04	1.93	1.81	1.66
19	2.99	2.61	2.40	2.27	2.18	2.11	2.02	1.91	1.79	1.63
20	2.97	2.59	2.38	2.25	2.16	2.09	2.00	1.89	1.77	1.61

Upper 10% Points

df for denominator	df for numerator									
	1	2	3	4	5	6	8	12	24	∞
21	2.96	2.57	2.36	2.23	2.14	2.08	1.98	1.88	1.75	1.59
22	2.95	2.56	2.35	2.22	2.13	2.06	1.97	1.86	1.73	1.57
23	2.94	2.55	2.34	2.21	2.11	2.05	1.95	1.84	1.72	1.55
24	2.93	2.54	2.33	2.19	2.10	2.04	1.94	1.83	1.70	1.53
25	2.92	2.53	2.32	2.18	2.09	2.02	1.93	1.82	1.69	1.52
26	2.91	2.52	2.31	2.17	2.08	2.01	1.92	1.81	1.68	1.50
27	2.90	2.51	2.30	2.17	2.07	2.00	1.91	1.80	1.67	1.49
28	2.89	2.50	2.29	2.16	2.06	2.00	1.90	1.79	1.66	1.48
29	2.89	2.50	2.28	2.15	2.06	1.99	1.89	1.78	1.65	1.47
30	2.88	2.49	2.28	2.14	2.05	1.98	1.88	1.77	1.64	1.46
40	2.84	2.44	2.23	2.09	2.00	1.93	1.83	1.71	1.57	1.38
60	2.79	2.39	2.18	2.04	1.95	1.87	1.77	1.66	1.51	1.29
120	2.75	2.35	2.13	1.99	1.90	1.82	1.72	1.60	1.45	1.19
∞	2.71	2.30	2.08	1.94	1.85	1.77	1.67	1.55	1.38	1.00

Upper 5% Points

	1	2	3	4	5	6	8	12	24	∞
1	161.4	199.5	215.7	224.6	230.2	234.0	238.9	243.9	249.0	254.3
2	18.51	19.00	19.16	19.25	19.30	19.33	19.37	19.41	19.45	19.50
3	10.13	9.55	9.28	9.12	9.01	8.94	8.84	8.74	8.64	8.53
4	7.71	6.94	6.59	6.39	6.26	6.16	6.04	5.91	5.77	5.63
5	6.61	5.79	5.41	5.19	5.05	4.95	4.82	4.68	4.53	4.36
6	5.99	5.14	4.76	4.53	4.39	4.28	4.15	4.00	3.84	3.67
7	5.59	4.74	4.35	4.12	3.97	3.87	3.73	3.57	3.41	3.23
8	5.32	4.46	4.07	3.84	3.69	3.58	3.44	3.28	3.12	2.93
9	5.12	4.26	3.86	3.63	3.48	3.37	3.23	3.07	2.90	2.71
10	4.96	4.10	3.71	3.48	3.33	3.22	3.07	2.91	2.74	2.54
11	4.84	3.98	3.59	3.36	3.20	3.09	2.95	2.79	2.61	2.40
12	4.75	3.88	3.49	3.26	3.11	3.00	2.85	2.69	2.50	2.30
13	4.67	3.80	3.41	3.18	3.02	2.92	2.77	2.60	2.42	2.21
14	4.60	3.74	3.34	3.11	2.96	2.85	2.70	2.53	2.35	2.13
15	4.54	3.68	3.29	3.06	2.90	2.79	2.64	2.48	2.29	2.07
16	4.49	3.63	3.24	3.01	2.85	2.74	2.59	2.42	2.24	2.01
17	4.45	3.59	3.20	2.96	2.81	2.70	2.55	2.38	2.19	1.96
18	4.41	3.55	3.16	2.93	2.77	2.66	2.51	2.34	2.15	1.92
19	4.38	3.52	3.13	2.90	2.74	2.63	2.48	2.31	2.11	1.88
20	4.35	3.49	3.10	2.87	2.71	2.60	2.45	2.28	2.08	1.84
21	4.32	3.47	3.07	2.84	2.68	2.57	2.42	2.25	2.05	1.81
22	4.30	3.44	3.05	2.82	2.66	2.55	2.40	2.23	2.03	1.78
23	4.28	3.42	3.03	2.80	2.64	2.53	2.38	2.20	2.00	1.76
24	4.26	3.40	3.01	2.78	2.62	2.51	2.36	2.18	1.98	1.73
25	4.24	3.38	2.99	2.76	2.60	2.49	2.34	2.16	1.96	1.71

Upper 5% Points

df for denominator	df for numerator									
	1	2	3	4	5	6	8	12	24	∞
26	4.22	3.37	2.98	2.74	2.59	2.47	2.32	2.15	1.95	1.69
27	4.21	3.35	2.96	2.73	2.57	2.46	2.30	2.13	1.93	1.67
28	4.20	3.34	2.95	2.71	2.56	2.44	2.29	2.12	1.91	1.65
29	4.18	3.33	2.93	2.70	2.54	2.43	2.28	2.10	1.90	1.64
30	4.17	3.32	2.92	2.69	2.53	2.42	2.27	2.09	1.89	1.62
40	4.08	3.23	2.84	2.61	2.45	2.34	2.18	2.00	1.79	1.51
60	4.00	3.15	2.76	2.52	2.37	2.25	2.10	1.92	1.70	1.39
120	3.92	3.07	2.68	2.45	2.29	2.17	2.02	1.83	1.61	1.25
∞	3.84	2.99	2.60	2.37	2.21	2.09	1.94	1.75	1.52	1.00

Upper 1% Points

	1	2	3	4	5	6	8	12	24	∞
1	4052	4999	5403	5625	5764	5859	5981	6106	6234	6366
2	98.49	99.01	99.17	99.25	99.30	99.33	99.36	99.42	99.46	99.50
3	34.12	30.81	29.46	28.71	28.24	27.91	27.49	27.05	26.60	26.12
4	21.20	18.00	16.69	15.98	15.52	15.21	14.80	14.37	13.93	13.46
5	16.26	13.27	12.06	11.39	10.97	10.67	10.27	9.89	9.47	9.02
6	13.74	10.92	9.78	9.15	8.75	8.47	8.10	7.72	7.31	6.88
7	12.25	9.55	8.45	7.85	7.46	7.19	6.84	6.47	6.07	5.65
8	11.26	8.65	7.59	7.01	6.63	6.37	6.03	5.67	5.28	4.86
9	10.56	8.02	6.99	6.42	6.06	5.80	5.47	5.11	4.73	4.31
10	10.04	7.56	6.55	5.99	5.64	5.39	5.06	4.71	4.33	3.91
11	9.65	7.20	6.22	5.67	5.32	5.07	4.74	4.40	4.02	3.60
12	9.33	6.93	5.95	5.41	5.06	4.82	4.50	4.16	3.78	3.36
13	9.07	6.70	5.74	5.20	4.86	4.62	4.30	3.96	3.59	3.16
14	8.86	6.51	5.56	5.03	4.69	4.46	4.14	3.80	3.43	3.00
15	8.68	6.36	5.42	4.89	4.56	4.32	4.00	3.67	3.29	2.87
16	8.53	6.23	5.29	4.77	4.44	4.20	3.89	3.55	3.18	2.75
17	8.40	6.11	5.18	4.67	4.34	4.10	3.79	3.45	3.08	2.65
18	8.28	6.01	5.09	4.58	4.25	4.01	3.71	3.37	3.00	2.57
19	8.18	5.93	5.01	4.50	4.17	3.94	3.63	3.30	2.92	2.49
20	8.10	5.85	4.94	4.43	4.10	3.87	3.56	3.23	2.86	2.42
21	8.02	5.78	4.87	4.37	4.04	3.81	3.51	3.17	2.80	2.36
22	7.94	5.72	4.82	4.31	3.99	3.76	3.45	3.12	2.75	2.31
23	7.88	5.66	4.76	4.26	3.94	3.71	3.41	3.07	2.70	2.26
24	7.82	5.61	4.72	4.22	3.90	3.67	3.36	3.03	2.66	2.21
25	7.77	5.57	4.68	4.18	3.86	3.63	3.32	2.99	2.62	2.17

Upper 1% Points

df for denominator	*df* for numerator									
	1	2	3	4	5	6	8	12	24	∞
26	7.72	5.53	4.64	4.14	3.82	3.59	3.29	2.96	2.58	2.13
27	7.68	5.49	4.60	4.11	3.78	3.56	3.26	2.93	2.55	2.10
28	7.64	5.45	4.57	4.07	3.75	3.53	3.23	2.90	2.52	2.06
29	7.60	5.42	4.54	4.04	3.73	3.50	3.20	2.87	2.49	2.03
30	7.56	5.39	4.51	4.02	3.70	3.47	3.17	2.84	2.47	2 01
40	7.31	5.18	4.31	3.83	3.51	3.29	2.99	2.66	2.29	1.80
60	7.08	4.98	4.13	3.65	3.34	3.12	2.82	2.50	2.12	1.60
120	6.85	4.79	3.95	3.48	3.17	2.96	2.66	2.34	1.95	1.38
∞	6.64	4.60	3.78	3.32	3.02	2.80	2.51	2.18	1.79	1 00

Source: Appendix E is adapted from Table V of Ronald A. Fisher and Frank Yates, *Statistical Tables for Biological, Agricultural, and Medical Research*, 5th ed., Oliver and Boyd Ltd., Edinburgh, 1957, by permission of the authors and publishers.

F

PROPORTIONS OF AREA FOR THE χ^2 DISTRIBUTIONS

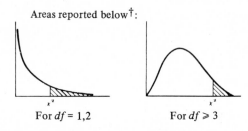

Areas reported below[†]:

For $df = 1,2$ For $df \geqslant 3$

df	Proportion of area										
	0.995	0.990	0.975	0.950	0.900	0.500	0.100	0.050	0.025	0.010	0.005
1	0.00004	0.00016	0.00098	0.00393	0.0158	0.455	2.71	3.84	5.02	6.63	7.88
2	0.0100	0.0201	0.0506	0.103	0.211	1.386	4.61	5.99	7.38	9.21	10.60
3	0.072	0.115	0.216	0.352	0.584	2.366	6.25	7.81	9.35	11.34	12.84
4	0.207	0.297	0.484	0.711	1.064	3.357	7.78	9.49	11.14	13.28	14.86
5	0.412	0.554	0.831	1.145	1.61	4.251	9.24	11.07	12.83	15.09	16.75
6	0.676	0.872	1.24	1.64	2.20	5.35	10.64	12.50	14.45	16.81	18.55
7	0.989	1.24	1.69	2.17	2.83	6.35	12.02	14.07	16.01	18.48	20.23
8	1.34	1.65	2.18	2.73	3.49	7.34	13.36	15.51	17.53	20.09	21.96
9	1.73	2.09	2.70	3.33	4.17	8.34	14.68	16.92	19.02	21.67	23.59
10	2.16	2.56	3.25	3.94	4.87	9.34	15.99	18.31	20.48	23.21	25.19
11	2.60	3.05	3.82	4.57	5.58	10.34	17.28	19.63	21.92	24.72	26.76
12	3.07	3.57	4.40	5.23	6.30	11.34	18.55	21.03	23.34	26.22	28.30
13	3.57	4.11	5.01	5.89	7.04	12.34	19.81	22.36	24.74	27.69	29.82
14	4.07	4.66	5.63	6.57	7.79	13.34	21.06	23.68	26.12	29.14	31.32
15	4.60	5.23	6.26	7.26	8.55	14.34	22.31	25.00	27.49	30.58	32.80
16	5.14	5.81	6.91	7.96	9.31	15.34	23.54	26.30	28.85	32.00	34.27
17	5.70	6.41	7.56	8.67	10.09	16.34	24.77	27.59	30.19	33.41	35.72
18	6.26	7.01	8.23	9.39	10.86	17.34	25.99	28.87	31.53	34.81	37.16
19	6.84	7.63	8.91	10.12	11.65	18.34	27.20	30.14	32.85	36.19	38.58
20	7.43	8.26	9.59	10.85	12.44	19.34	28.41	31.41	34.17	37.57	40.00
21	8.03	8.90	10.28	11.59	13.24	20.34	29.62	32.67	35.48	38.93	41.40
22	8.64	9.54	10.98	12.34	14.04	21.34	30.81	33.92	36.78	40.29	42.80
23	9.26	10.20	11.69	13.09	14.85	22.34	32.01	35.17	38.08	41.64	44.13
24	9.89	10.36	12.40	13.85	15.66	23.34	33.20	36.42	39.36	42.98	45.56
25	10.52	11.52	13.12	14.61	16.47	24.34	34.38	37.65	40.65	44.31	46.93

df	Proportion of area										
	0.995	0.990	0.975	0.950	0.900	0.500	0.100	0.050	0.025	0.010	0.005
26	11.16	12.20	13.84	15.38	17.29	25.34	35.56	38.89	41.92	45.64	48.29
27	11.81	12.83	14.57	16.15	18.11	26.34	36.74	40.11	43.19	46.96	49.64
28	12.46	13.56	15.31	16.93	18.94	27.34	37.92	41.34	44.46	38.28	50.99
29	13.12	14.26	16.05	17.71	19.77	28.34	39.09	42.56	45.72	49.59	52.34
30	13.79	14.95	16.79	18.49	20.60	29.34	40.26	43.77	46.98	50.89	53.67
40	20.71	22.16	24.43	26.51	29.05	39.34	51.80	55.76	59.34	63.69	66.77
50	27.99	29.71	32.36	34.76	37.69	49.33	63.17	67.50	71.42	76.15	79.49
60	35.53	37.43	40.48	43.19	46.46	59.33	74.40	79.08	83.30	83.38	91.95
70	43.28	45.44	48.76	51.74	55.33	69.33	85.53	90.53	95.02	100.4	104.22
80	57.17	53.54	51.17	60.39	64.28	79.33	98.58	101.9	106.6	112.3	116.32
90	59.20	61.75	65.65	69.13	73.29	89.33	107.6	113.1	118.1	124.1	123.3
100	67.33	70.06	74.22	77.93	82.36	99.33	113.5	124.3	129.6	135.3	140.2

†Example: For the shaded area to represent 0.05 of the total area of 1.0 under the density function, the value of χ^2 is 18.31 when df = 10.

Source: From Table IV of Fisher and Yates, *Statistical Tables for Biological, Agricultural and Medical Research*, 6th ed., 1974, published by Longman Group Ltd., London (previously published by Oliver & Boyd, Edinburgh), by permission of the authors and publishers.

G

BINOMIAL PROBABILITIES†

n	x	.01	.05	.10	.15	.20	.25	.30	.35	.40	.45	.50
1	0	.9900	.9500	.9000	.8500	.8000	.7500	.7000	.6500	.6000	.5500	.5000
	1	.0100	.0500	.1000	.1500	.2000	.2500	.3000	.3500	.4000	.4500	.5000
2	0	.9801	.9025	.8100	.7225	.6400	.5625	.4900	.4225	.3600	.3025	.2500
	1	.0198	.0950	.1800	.2550	.3200	.3750	.4200	.4550	.4800	.4950	.5000
	2	.0001	.0025	.0100	.0225	.0400	.0625	.0900	.1225	.1600	.2025	.2500
3	0	.9703	.8574	.7290	.6141	.5120	.4219	.3430	.2746	.2160	.1664	.1250
	1	.0294	.1354	.2430	.3251	.3840	.4219	.4410	.4436	.4320	.4084	.3750
	2	.0003	.0071	.0270	.0574	.0960	.1406	.1890	.2389	.2880	.3341	.3750
	3	.0000	.0001	.0010	.0034	.0080	.0156	.0270	.0429	.0640	.0911	.1250
4	0	.9606	.8145	.6561	.5220	.4096	.3164	.2401	.1785	.1296	.0915	.0625
	1	.0388	.1715	.2916	.3685	.4096	.4219	.4116	.3845	.3456	.2995	.2500
	2	.0006	.0135	.0486	.0975	.1536	.2109	.2646	.3105	.3456	.3675	.3750
	3	.0000	.0005	.0036	.0115	.0258	.0469	.0756	.1115	.1536	.2005	.2500
	4	.0000	.0000	.0001	.0005	.0016	.0039	.0081	.0150	.0256	.0410	.0625
5	0	.9510	.7738	.5905	.4437	.3277	.2373	.1681	.1160	.0778	.0503	.0312
	1	.0480	.2036	.3280	.3915	.4096	.3955	.3602	.3124	.2592	.2059	.1562
	2	.0010	.0214	.0729	.1382	.2048	.2637	.3087	.3364	.3456	.3369	.3125
	3	.0000	.0011	.0081	.0244	.0512	.0879	.1323	.1811	.2304	.2757	.3125
	4	.0000	.0000	.0004	.0022	.0064	.0146	.0284	.0488	.0768	.1128	.1562
	5	.0000	.0000	.0000	.0001	.0003	.0010	.0024	.0053	.0102	.0185	.0312
6	0	.9415	.7351	.5314	.3771	.2621	.1780	.1176	.0754	.0467	.0277	.0156
	1	.0571	.2321	.3543	.3993	.3932	.3560	.3025	.2437	.1866	.1359	.0938
	2	.0014	.0305	.0984	.1762	.2458	.2966	.3241	.3280	.3110	.2780	.2344
	3	.0000	.0021	.0146	.0415	.0819	.1318	.1852	.2355	.2765	.3032	.3125
	4	.0000	.0001	.0012	.0055	.0154	.0330	.0595	.0951	.1382	.1861	.2344
	5	.0000	.0000	.0001	.0004	.0015	.0044	.0102	.0205	.0369	.0609	.0938
	6	.0000	.0000	.0000	.0000	.0001	.0002	.0007	.0018	.0041	.0083	.0156
7	0	.9321	.6983	.4783	.3206	.2097	.1335	.0824	.0490	.0280	.0152	.0078
	1	.0659	.2573	.3720	.3960	.3670	.3115	.2471	.1848	.1306	.0872	.0547
	2	.0020	.0406	.1240	.2097	.2753	.3115	.3177	.2985	.2613	.2140	.1641
	3	.0000	.0036	.0230	.0617	.1147	.1730	.2269	.2679	.2903	.2918	.2734
	4	.0000	.0002	.0026	.0109	.0287	.0577	.0972	.1442	.1935	.2388	.2734
	5	.0000	.0000	.0002	.0012	.0043	.0115	.0250	.0466	.0774	.1172	.1641
	6	.0000	.0000	.0000	.0001	.0004	.0013	.0036	.0084	.0172	.0320	.0547
	7	.0000	.0000	.0000	.0000	.0000	.0001	.0002	.0006	.0016	.0037	.0078
8	0	.9227	.6634	.4305	.2725	.1678	.1002	.0576	.0319	.0168	.0084	.0039
	1	.0746	.2793	.3826	.3847	.3355	.2670	.1977	.1373	.0896	.0548	.0312

†Example: $P(X = 3 \mid n = 5, p = 0.30) = 0.1323$.

Source: Business Statistics (Schaum's Outline Series) by L. J. Kazmier. Copyright by McGraw-Hill, Inc. Used with permission of McGraw-Hill Book Company.

n	x	.01	.05	.10	.15	.20	.25	P .30	.35	.40	.45	.50
8	2	.0026	.0515	.1488	.2376	.2936	.3115	.2065	.2587	.2090	.1569	.1094
	3	.0001	.0054	.0331	.0839	.1468	.2076	.2541	.2786	.2787	.2568	.2188
	4	.0000	.0004	.0046	.0185	.0459	.0865	.1361	.1875	.2322	.2627	.2734
	5	.0000	.0000	.0004	.0026	.0092	.0231	.0467	.0808	.1239	.1719	.2188
	6	.0000	.0000	.0000	.0002	.0011	.0038	.0100	.0217	.0413	.0403	.1094
	7	.0000	.0000	.0000	.0000	.0001	.0004	.0012	.0033	.0079	.0164	.0312
	8	.0000	.0000	.0000	.0000	.0000	.0000	.0001	.0002	.0007	.0017	.0039
9	0	.9135	.6302	.3874	.2316	.1342	.0751	.0404	.0207	.0101	.0046	.0020
	1	.0830	.2985	.3874	.3679	.3020	.2253	.1556	.1004	.0605	.0339	.0176
	2	.0034	.0629	.1722	.2597	.3020	.3003	.2668	.2162	.1612	.1110	.0703
	3	.0001	.0077	.0446	.1069	.1762	.2336	.2668	.2716	.2508	.2119	.1641
	4	.0000	.0006	.0074	.0283	.0661	.1168	.1715	.2194	.2508	.2600	.2461
	5	.0000	.0000	.0008	.0050	.0165	.0389	.0735	.1181	.1672	.2128	.2461
	6	.0000	.0000	.0001	.0006	.0028	.0087	.0210	.0424	.0743	.1160	.1641
	7	.0000	.0000	.0000	.0000	.0003	.0012	.0039	.0098	.0212	.0407	.0703
	8	.0000	.0000	.0000	.0000	.0000	.0001	.0004	.0013	.0035	.0083	.0176
	9	.0000	.0000	.0000	.0000	.0000	.0000	.0000	.0001	.0003	.0008	.0020
10	0	.9044	.5987	.3487	.1969	.1074	.0563	.0282	.0135	.0060	.0025	.0010
	1	.0914	.3151	.3874	.3474	.2684	.1877	.1211	.0725	.0403	.0207	.0098
	2	.0042	.0746	.1937	.2759	.3020	.2816	.2335	.1757	.1209	.0763	.0439
	3	.0001	.0105	.0574	.1298	.2013	.2503	.2668	.2522	.2150	.1665	.1172
	4	.0000	.0010	.0112	.0401	.0881	.1460	.2001	.2377	.2508	.2384	.2051
	5	.0000	.0001	.0015	.0085	.0264	.0584	.1029	.1536	.2007	.2340	.2461
	6	.0000	.0000	.0001	.0012	.0055	.0162	.0368	.0689	.1115	.1596	.2051
	7	.0000	.0000	.0000	.0001	.0008	.0031	.0090	.0212	.0425	.0746	.1172
	8	.0000	.0000	.0000	.0000	.0001	.0004	.0014	.0043	.0106	.0229	.0439
	9	.0000	.0000	.0000	.0000	.0000	.0000	.0001	.0005	.0016	.0042	.0098
	10	.0000	.0000	.0000	.0000	.0000	.0000	.0000	.0000	.0001	.0003	.0010
11	0	.8953	.5688	.3138	.1673	.0859	.0422	.0198	.0088	.0036	.0014	.0005
	1	.0995	.3293	.3835	.3248	.2362	.1549	.0932	.0518	.0266	.0125	.0054
	2	.0050	.0867	.2131	.2866	.2953	.2581	.1998	.1395	.0887	.0513	.0269
	3	.0002	.0137	.0710	.1517	.2215	.2581	.2568	.2254	.1774	.1259	.0806
	4	.0000	.0010	.0112	.0401	.0881	.1460	.2001	.2377	.2508	.2384	.2051
	5	.0000	.0001	.0025	.0132	.0388	.0803	.1321	.1830	.2207	.2360	.2256
	6	.0000	.0000	.0003	.0023	.0097	.0268	.0566	.0985	.1471	.1931	.2256
	7	.0000	.0000	.0000	.0003	.0017	.0064	.0173	.0379	.0701	.1128	.1611
	8	.0000	.0000	.0000	.0000	.0002	.0011	.0037	.0102	.0234	.0462	.0806
	9	.0000	.0000	.0000	.0000	.0000	.0001	.0005	.0018	.0052	.0126	.0269
	10	.0000	.0000	.0000	.0000	.0000	.0000	.0000	.0002	.0007	.0021	.0054
	11	.0000	.0000	.0000	.0000	.0000	.0000	.0000	.0000	.0000	.0002	.0005
12	0	.8864	.5404	.2824	.1422	.0687	.0317	.0138	.0057	.0022	.0008	.0002
	1	.1074	.3413	.3766	.3012	.2062	.1267	.0712	.0368	.0174	.0075	.0029
	2	.0060	.0988	.2301	.2924	.2835	.2323	.1678	.1088	.0639	.0339	.0161
	3	.0002	.0173	.0852	.1720	.2362	.2581	.2397	.1954	.1419	.0923	.0537
	4	.0000	.0021	.0213	.0683	.1329	.1936	.2311	.2367	.2128	.1700	.1204
	5	.0000	.0002	.0038	.0193	.0532	.1032	.1585	.2039	.2270	.2225	.1934
	6	.0000	.0000	.0005	.0040	.0155	.0401	.0792	.1281	.1766	.2124	.2256
	7	.0000	.0000	.0000	.0006	.0033	.0115	.0291	.0591	.1009	.1489	.1934
	8	.0000	.0000	.0000	.0001	.0005	.0024	.0078	.0199	.0420	.0762	.1208
	9	.0000	.0000	.0000	.0000	.0001	.0004	.0015	.0048	.0125	.0277	.0537
	10	.0000	.0000	.0000	.0000	.0000	.0000	.0002	.0008	.0025	.0068	.0161
	11	.0000	.0000	.0000	.0000	.0000	.0000	.0000	.0001	.0003	.0010	.0029
	12	.0000	.0000	.0000	.0000	.0000	.0000	.0000	.0000	.0000	.0001	.0002
13	0	.8775	.5133	.2542	.1209	.0550	.0238	.0097	.0037	.0013	.0004	.0001
	1	.1152	.3512	.3672	.2774	.1787	.1029	.0540	.0259	.0113	.0045	.0016
	2	.0070	.1109	.2448	.2937	.2680	.2059	.1388	.0836	.0453	.0220	.0095
	3	.0003	.0214	.0997	.1900	.2457	.2517	.2181	.1651	.1107	.0660	.0349
	4	.0000	.0028	.0277	.0838	.1535	.2097	.2337	.2222	.1845	.1350	.0873

n	x	.01	.05	.10	.15	.20	.25	.30	.35	.40	.45	.50
13	5	.0000	.0003	.0055	.0266	.0691	.1258	.1803	.2154	.2214	.1989	.1571
	6	.0000	.0000	.0008	.0063	.0230	.0559	.1030	.1546	.1968	.2169	.2095
	7	.0000	.0000	.0001	.0011	.0058	.0186	.0442	.0833	.1312	.1775	.2095
	8	.0000	.0000	.0001	.0001	.0011	.0047	.0142	.0336	.0656	.1089	.1571
	9	.0000	.0000	.0000	.0000	.0001	.0009	.0034	.0101	.0243	.0495	.0873
	10	.0000	.0000	.0000	.0000	.0000	.0001	.0006	.0022	.0065	.0162	.0349
	11	.0000	.0000	.0000	.0000	.0000	.0000	.0001	.0003	.0012	.0036	.0095
	12	.0000	.0000	.0000	.0000	.0000	.0000	.0000	.0000	.0001	.0005	.0016
	13	.0000	.0000	.0000	.0000	.0000	.0000	.0000	.0000	.0000	.0000	.0001
14	0	.8687	.4877	.2288	.1028	.0440	.0178	.0068	.0024	.0008	.0002	.0001
	1	.1229	.3593	.3559	.2539	.1539	.0832	.0407	.0181	.0073	.0027	.0009
	2	.0081	.1229	.2570	.2912	.2501	.1802	.1134	.0634	.0317	.0141	.0056
	3	.0003	.0259	.1142	.2056	.2501	.2402	.1943	.1366	.0845	.0462	.0222
	4	.0000	.0037	.0349	.0998	.1720	.2202	.2290	.2022	.1549	.1040	.0611
	5	.0000	.0004	.0078	.0352	.0860	.1468	.1963	.2178	.2066	.1701	.1222
	6	.0000	.0000	.0013	.0093	.0322	.0734	.1262	.1759	.2066	.2088	.1833
	7	.0000	.0000	.0002	.0019	.0092	.0280	.0618	.1082	.1574	.1952	.2095
	8	.0000	.0000	.0000	.0003	.0020	.0082	.0232	.0510	.0918	.1398	.1833
	9	.0000	.0000	.0000	.0000	.0003	.0018	.0066	.0183	.0408	.0762	.1222
	10	.0000	.0000	.0000	.0000	.0000	.0003	.0014	.0049	.0136	.0312	.0611
	11	.0000	.0000	.0000	.0000	.0000	.0000	.0002	.0010	.0033	.0093	.0222
	12	.0000	.0000	.0000	.0000	.0000	.0000	.0000	.0001	.0005	.0019	.0056
	13	.0000	.0000	.0000	.0000	.0000	.0000	.0000	.0000	.0001	.0002	.0009
	14	.0000	.0000	.0000	.0000	.0000	.0000	.0000	.0000	.0000	.0000	.0001
15	0	.8601	.4633	.2059	.0874	.0352	.0134	.0047	.0016	.0005	.0001	.0000
	1	.1303	.3658	.3432	.2312	.1319	.0668	.0305	.0126	.0047	.0016	.0005
	2	.0092	.1348	.2669	.2856	.2309	.1559	.0916	.0476	.0219	.0090	.0032
	3	.0004	.0307	.1285	.2184	.2501	.2252	.1700	.1110	.0634	.0318	.0139
	4	.0000	.0049	.0428	.1156	.1876	.2252	.2186	.1792	.1268	.0780	.0417
	5	.0000	.4633	.2059	.0874	.0352	.0134	.0047	.0016	.0005	.0001	.0000
	6	.0000	.0000	.0019	.0132	.0430	.0917	.1472	.1906	.2066	.1914	.1527
	7	.0000	.0000	.0003	.0030	.0138	.0393	.0811	.1319	.1771	.2013	.1964
	8	.0000	.0000	.0000	.0005	.0035	.0131	.0348	.0710	.1181	.1647	.1964
	9	.0000	.0000	.0000	.0001	.0007	.0034	.0116	.0298	.0612	.1048	.1527
	10	.0000	.0000	.0000	.0000	.0001	.0007	.0030	.0096	.0245	.0515	.0916
	11	.0000	.0000	.0000	.0000	.0000	.0001	.0006	.0024	.0074	.0191	.0417
	12	.0000	.0000	.0000	.0000	.0000	.0000	.0001	.0004	.0016	.0052	.0139
	13	.0000	.0000	.0000	.0000	.0000	.0000	.0000	.0001	.0003	.0010	.0032
	14	.0000	.0000	.0000	.0000	.0000	.0000	.0000	.0000	.0000	.0001	.0005
	15	.0000	.0000	.0000	.0000	.0000	.0000	.0000	.0000	.0000	.0000	.0000
16	0	.8515	.4401	.1853	.0743	.0281	.0100	.0033	.0010	.0003	.0001	.0000
	1	.1376	.3706	.3294	.2097	.1126	.0535	.0228	.0087	.0030	.0009	.0002
	2	.0104	.1463	.2745	.2775	.2111	.1336	.0732	.0353	.0150	.0056	.0018
	3	.0005	.0359	.1423	.2285	.2463	.2079	.1465	.0888	.0468	.0215	.0085
	4	.0000	.0061	.0514	.1311	.2001	.2252	.2040	.1553	.1014	.0572	.0278
	5	.0000	.0008	.0137	.0555	.1201	.1802	.2099	.2008	.1623	.1123	.0667
	6	.0000	.0001	.0028	.0180	.0550	.1101	.1649	.1982	.1983	.1684	.1222
	7	.0000	.0000	.0004	.0045	.0197	.0524	.1010	.1524	.1889	.1969	.1746
	8	.0000	.0000	.0001	.0009	.0055	.0197	.0487	.0923	.1417	.1812	.1964
	9	.0000	.0000	.0000	.0001	.0012	.0058	.0185	.0442	.0840	.1318	.1746
	10	.0000	.0000	.0000	.0000	.0002	.0014	.0056	.0167	.0392	.0755	.1222
	11	.0000	.0000	.0000	.0000	.0000	.0002	.0013	.0049	.0142	.0337	.0667
	12	.0000	.0000	.0000	.0000	.0000	.0000	.0002	.0011	.0040	.0115	.0278
	13	.0000	.0000	.0000	.0000	.0000	.0000	.0000	.0002	.0008	.0029	.0085
	14	.0000	.0000	.0000	.0000	.0000	.0000	.0000	.0000	.0001	.0005	.0018
	15	.0000	.0000	.0000	.0000	.0000	.0000	.0000	.0000	.0000	.0001	.0002
	16	.0000	.0000	.0000	.0000	.0000	.0000	.0000	.0000	.0000	.0000	.0000

n	x	.01	.05	.10	.15	.20	.25	p .30	.35	.40	.45	.50
17	0	.8429	.4181	.1668	.0631	.0225	.0075	.0023	.0007	.0002	.0000	.0000
	1	.1447	.3741	.3150	.1893	.0957	.0426	.0169	.0060	.0019	.0005	.0001
	2	.0117	.1575	.2800	.2673	.1914	.1136	.0581	.0260	.0102	.0035	.0010
	3	.0006	.0415	.1556	.2359	.2393	.1893	.1245	.0701	.0341	.0144	.0052
	4	.0000	.0076	.0605	.1457	.2093	.2209	.1868	.1320	.0796	.0411	.0182
	5	.0000	.0010	.0175	.0668	.1361	.1914	.2081	.1849	.1379	.0875	.0472
	6	.0000	.0001	.0039	.0236	.0680	.1276	.1784	.1991	.1839	.1432	.0944
	7	.0000	.0000	.0007	.0065	.0267	.0668	.1201	.1685	.1927	.1841	.1484
	8	.0000	.0000	.0001	.0014	.0084	.0279	.0644	.1134	.1606	.1883	.1855
	9	.0000	.0000	.0000	.0003	.0021	.0093	.0276	.0611	.1070	.1540	.1855
	10	.0000	.0000	.0000	.0000	.0004	.0025	.0095	.0263	.0571	.1008	.1484
	11	.0000	.0000	.0000	.0000	.0001	.0005	.0026	.0090	.0242	.0525	.0944
	12	.0000	.0000	.0000	.0000	.0000	.0001	.0006	.0024	.0081	.0215	.0472
	13	.0000	.0000	.0000	.0000	.0000	.0000	.0001	.0005	.0021	.0068	.0182
	14	.0000	.0000	.0000	.0000	.0000	.0000	.0000	.0001	.0004	.0016	.0052
	15	.0000	.0000	.0000	.0000	.0000	.0000	.0000	.0000	.0001	.0003	.0010
	16	.0000	.0000	.0000	.0000	.0000	.0000	.0000	.0000	.0000	.0000	.0001
	17	.0000	.0000	.0000	.0000	.0000	.0000	.0000	.0000	.0000	.0000	.0000
18	0	.8345	.3972	.1501	.0536	.0180	.0056	.0016	.0004	.0001	.0003	.0010
	1	.1517	.3763	.3002	.1704	.0811	.0338	.0126	.0042	.0012	.0003	.0001
	2	.0130	.1683	.2835	.2556	.1723	.0958	.0458	.0190	.0069	.0022	.0006
	3	.0007	.0473	.1680	.2406	.2297	.1704	.1046	.0547	.0246	.0095	.0001
	4	.0000	.0093	.0700	.1592	.2153	.2130	.1681	.1104	.0614	.0291	.0117
	5	.0000	.0014	.0218	.0787	.1507	.1988	.2017	.1664	.1146	.0666	.0327
	6	.0000	.0002	.0052	.0301	.0816	.1436	.1873	.1941	.1655	.1181	.0708
	7	.0000	.0000	.0010	.0091	.0350	.0820	.1376	.1792	.1892	.1657	.1214
	8	.0000	.0000	.0002	.0022	.0120	.0376	.0811	.1327	.1734	.1864	.1669
	9	.0000	.0000	.0000	.0004	.0033	.0139	.0386	.0794	.1284	.1694	.1855
	10	.0000	.0000	.0000	.0001	.0008	.0042	.0149	.0385	.0771	.1248	.1669
	11	.0000	.0000	.0000	.0000	.0001	.0010	.0046	.0151	.0374	.0742	.1214
	12	.0000	.0000	.0000	.0000	.0000	.0002	.0012	.0047	.0145	.0354	.0708
	13	.0000	.0000	.0000	.0000	.0000	.0000	.0002	.0012	.0045	.0134	.0327
	14	.0000	.0000	.0000	.0000	.0000	.0000	.0000	.0002	.0011	.0039	.0117
	15	.0000	.0000	.0000	.0000	.0000	.0000	.0000	.0000	.0002	.0009	.0031
	16	.0000	.0000	.0000	.0000	.0000	.0000	.0000	.0000	.0000	.0001	.0006
	17	.0000	.0000	.0000	.0000	.0000	.0000	.0000	.0000	.0000	.0000	.0001
	18	.0000	.0000	.0000	.0000	.0000	.0000	.0000	.0000	.0000	.0000	.0000
19	0	.8262	.3774	.1351	.0456	.0144	.0042	.0011	.0003	.0001	.0000	.0000
	1	.1586	.3774	.2852	.1529	.0685	.0268	.0093	.0029	.0008	.0002	.0000
	2	.0144	.1787	.2852	.2428	.1540	.0803	.0358	.0138	.0046	.0013	.0003
	3	.0008	.0533	.1796	.2428	.2182	.1517	.0869	.0422	.0175	.0062	.0018
	4	.0000	.0112	.0798	.1714	.2182	.2023	.1491	.0909	.0467	.0203	.0074
	5	.0000	.0018	.0266	.0907	.1636	.2023	.1916	.1468	.0933	.0497	.0222
	6	.0000	.0002	.0069	.0374	.0955	.1574	.1916	.1844	.1451	.0949	.0518
	7	.0000	.0000	.0014	.0122	.0443	.0974	.1525	.1844	.1797	.1443	.0961
	8	.0000	.0000	.0002	.0032	.0166	.0487	.0981	.1489	.1797	.1771	.1442
	9	.0000	.0000	.0000	.0007	.0051	.0198	.0514	.0980	.1464	.1771	.1762
	10	.0000	.0000	.0000	.0001	.0013	.0066	.0220	.0528	.0976	.1449	.1762
	11	.0000	.0000	.0000	.0000	.0003	.0018	.0077	.0233	.0532	.0970	.1442
	12	.0000	.0000	.0000	.0000	.0000	.0004	.0022	.0083	.0237	.0529	.0961
	13	.0000	.0000	.0000	.0000	.0000	.0001	.0005	.0024	.0085	.0233	.0518
	14	.0000	.0000	.0000	.0000	.0000	.0000	.0001	.0006	.0024	.0082	.0222
	15	.0000	.0000	.0000	.0000	.0000	.0000	.0000	.0001	.0005	.0022	.0074
	16	.0000	.0000	.0000	.0000	.0000	.0000	.0000	.0000	.0001	.0005	.0018
	17	.0000	.0000	.0000	.0000	.0000	.0000	.0000	.0000	.0000	.0001	.0003
	18	.0000	.0000	.0000	.0000	.0000	.0000	.0000	.0000	.0000	.0000	.0000
	19	.0000	.0000	.0000	.0000	.0000	.0000	.0000	.0000	.0000	.0000	.0000

n	x	.01	.05	.10	.15	.20	.25	p .30	.35	.40	.45	.50
20	0	.8179	.3585	.1216	.0388	.0115	.0032	.0008	.0002	.0000	.0000	.0000
	1	.1652	.3774	.2702	.1368	.0576	.0211	.0068	.0020	.0005	.0001	.0000
	2	.0159	.1887	.2852	.2293	.1369	.0669	.0278	.0100	.0031	.0008	.0002
	3	.0010	.0596	.1901	.2428	.2054	.1339	.0718	.0323	.0123	.0040	.0011
	4	.0000	.0133	.0898	.1821	.2182	.1897	.1304	.0738	.0350	.0139	.0046
	5	.0000	.0022	.0319	.1028	.1746	.2023	.1789	.1272	.0746	.0365	.0148
	6	.0000	.0003	.0089	.0454	.1091	.1686	.1916	.1712	.1244	.0746	.0370
	7	.0000	.0000	.0020	.0160	.0545	.1124	.1643	.1844	.1659	.1221	.0739
	8	.0000	.0000	.0004	.0046	.0222	.0609	.1144	.1614	.1797	.1623	.1201
	9	.0000	.0000	.0001	.0011	.0074	.0271	.0654	.1158	.1597	.1771	.1602
	10	.0000	.0000	.0000	.0002	.0020	.0099	.0308	.0686	.1171	.1593	.1762
	11	.0000	.0000	.0000	.0000	.0005	.0030	.0120	.0336	.0710	.1185	.1602
	12	.0000	.0000	.0000	.0000	.0001	.0008	.0039	.0136	.0355	.0727	.1201
	13	.0000	.0000	.0000	.0000	.0000	.0002	.0010	.0045	.0146	.0366	.0739
	14	.0000	.0000	.0000	.0000	.0000	.0000	.0002	.0012	.0049	.0150	.0370
	15	.0000	.0000	.0000	.0000	.0000	.0000	.0000	.0003	.0013	.0049	.0148
	16	.0000	.0000	.0000	.0000	.0000	.0000	.0000	.0000	.0003	.0013	.0046
	17	.0000	.0000	.0000	.0000	.0000	.0000	.0000	.0000	.0000	.0002	.0011
	18	.0000	.0000	.0000	.0000	.0000	.0000	.0000	.0000	.0000	.0000	.0002
	19	.0000	.0000	.0000	.0000	.0000	.0000	.0000	.0000	.0000	.0000	.0000
	20	.0000	.0000	.0000	.0000	.0000	.0000	.0000	.0000	.0000	.0000	.0000
25	0	.7778	.2774	.0718	.0172	.0038	.0008	.0001	.0000	.0000	.0000	.0000
	1	.1964	.3650	.1994	.0759	.0236	.0063	.0014	.0003	.0000	.0000	.0000
	2	.0238	.2305	.2659	.1607	.0708	.0251	.0074	.0018	.0004	.0001	.0000
	3	.0018	.0930	.2265	.2174	.1358	.0641	.0243	.0076	.0019	.0004	.0001
	4	.0001	.0269	.1384	.2110	.1867	.1175	.0572	.0224	.0071	.0018	.0004
25	5	.0000	.0060	.0646	.1564	.1960	.1645	.1030	.0506	.0199	.0063	.0016
	6	.0000	.0010	.0239	.0920	.1633	.1828	.1472	.0908	.0442	.0172	.0053
	7	.0000	.0001	.0072	.0441	.1108	.1654	.1712	.1327	.0800	.0381	.0143
	8	.0000	.0000	.0018	.0175	.0623	.1241	.1651	.1607	.1200	.0701	.0322
	9	.0000	.0000	.0004	.0058	.0294	.0781	.1336	.1635	.1511	.1084	.0609
	10	.0000	.0000	.0000	.0016	.0118	.0417	.0916	.1409	.1612	.1419	.0974
	11	.0000	.0000	.0000	.0004	.0040	.0189	.0536	.1034	.1465	.1583	.1328
	12	.0000	.0000	.0000	.0000	.0012	.0074	.0268	.0650	.1140	.1511	.1550
	13	.0000	.0000	.0000	.0000	.0003	.0025	.0115	.0350	.0760	.1236	.1550
	14	.0000	.0000	.0000	.0000	.0000	.0007	.0042	.0161	.0434	.0867	.1328
	15	.0000	.0000	.0000	.0000	.0000	.0002	.0013	.0064	.0212	.0520	.0974
	16	.0000	.0000	.0000	.0000	.0000	.0000	.0004	.0021	.0088	.0266	.0609
	17	.0000	.0000	.0000	.0000	.0000	.0000	.0001	.0006	.0031	.0115	.0322
	18	.0000	.0000	.0000	.0000	.0000	.0000	.0000	.0001	.0009	.0042	.0143
	19	.0000	.0000	.0000	.0000	.0000	.0000	.0000	.0000	.0002	.0013	.0053
	20	.0000	.0000	.0000	.0000	.0000	.0000	.0000	.0000	.0000	.0001	.0016
	21	.0000	.0000	.0000	.0000	.0000	.0000	.0000	.0000	.0000	.0000	.0004
	22	.0000	.0000	.0000	.0000	.0000	.0000	.0000	.0000	.0000	.0000	.0001
30	0	.7397	.2146	.0424	.0076	.0012	.0002	.0000	.0000	.0000	.0000	.0000
	1	.2242	.3389	.1413	.0404	.0093	.0018	.0003	.0000	.0000	.0000	.0000
	2	.0328	.2586	.2277	.1034	.0337	.0086	.0018	.0003	.0000	.0000	.0000
	3	.0031	.1270	.2361	.1703	.0785	.0269	.0072	.0015	.0003	.0000	.0000
	4	.0002	.0451	.1771	.2028	.1325	.0604	.0208	.0056	.0012	.0002	.0000
	5	.0000	.0124	.1023	.1861	.1723	.1047	.0464	.0157	.0041	.0008	.0001
	6	.0000	.0027	.0474	.1368	.1795	.1455	.0829	.0353	.0115	.0029	.0006
	7	.0000	.0005	.0180	.0828	.1538	.1662	.1219	.0652	.0263	.0081	.0019
	8	.0000	.0001	.0058	.0420	.1106	.1593	.1501	.1009	.0505	.0191	.0055
	9	.0000	.0000	.0016	.0181	.0676	.1298	.1573	.1328	.0823	.0382	.0133
	10	.0000	.0000	.0004	.0067	.0355	.0909	.1416	.1502	.1152	.0656	.0280
	11	.0000	.0000	.0001	.0022	.0161	.0551	.1103	.1471	.1396	.0976	.0509

n	x	.01	.05	.10	.15	.20	.25	p .30	.35	.40	.45	.50
30	12	.0000	.0000	.0000	.0006	.0064	.0291	.0749	.1254	.1474	.1265	.0806
	13	.0000	.0000	.0000	.0001	.0022	.0134	.0444	.0935	.1360	.1433	.1115
	14	.0000	.0000	.0000	.0000	.0007	.0054	.0231	.0611	.1101	.1424	.1354
	15	.0000	.0000	.0000	.0000	.0002	.0019	.0106	.0351	.0783	.1242	.1445
	16	.0000	.0000	.0000	.0000	.0000	.0006	.0042	.0177	.0489	.0953	.1354
	17	.0000	.0000	.0000	.0000	.0000	.0002	.0015	.0079	.0269	.0642	.1115
	18	.0000	.0000	.0000	.0000	.0000	.0000	.0005	.0031	.0129	.0379	.0806
	19	.0000	.0000	.0000	.0000	.0000	.0000	.0001	.0010	.0054	.0196	.0509
	20	.0000	.0000	.0000	.0000	.0000	.0000	.0000	.0003	.0020	.0088	.0280
	21	.0000	.0000	.0000	.0000	.0000	.0000	.0000	.0001	.0006	.0034	.0133
	22	.0000	.0000	.0000	.0000	.0000	.0000	.0000	.0000	.0002	.0012	.0055
	23	.0000	.0000	.0000	.0000	.0000	.0000	.0000	.0000	.0000	.0003	.0019
	24	.0000	.0000	.0000	.0000	.0000	.0000	.0000	.0000	.0000	.0001	.0006
	25	.0000	.0000	.0000	.0000	.0000	.0000	.0000	.0000	.0000	.0000	.0001

n	x	.01	.05	.10	.15	.20	.25	p .30	.35	.40	.45	.50
50	0	.6050	.0769	.0052	.0003	.0000	.0000	.0000	.0000	.0000	.0000	.0000
	1	.3056	.2025	.0286	.0026	.0002	.0000	.0000	.0000	.0000	.0000	.0000
	2	.0756	.2611	.0779	.0113	.0011	.0001	.0000	.0000	.0000	.0000	.0000
	3	.0122	.2199	.1386	.0318	.0044	.0004	.0002	.0000	.0000	.0000	.0000
	4	.0015	.1360	.1809	.0661	.0128	.0016	.0002	.0000	.0000	.0000	.0000
	5	.0001	.0658	.1849	.1073	.0295	.0049	.0005	.0001	.0000	.0000	.0000
	6	.0000	.0260	.1541	.1419	.0554	.0124	.0018	.0001	.0000	.0000	.0000
	7		.0086	.1077	.1575	.0870	.0259	.0048	.0006	.0001	.0000	.0000
	8		.0024	.0642	.1493	.1169	.0463	.0110	.0017	.0001	.0000	.0000
	9		.0006	.0334	.1230	.1364	.0721	.0219	.0042	.0006	.0001	.0000
	10		.0002	.0151	.0890	.1399	.0985	.0387	.0093	.0014	.0002	.0000
	11		.0000	.0062	.0571	.1271	.1194	.0601	.0182	.0035	.0004	.0000
	12			.0022	.0327	.1032	.1294	.0839	.0319	.0076	.0012	.0002
	13			.0007	.0169	.0755	.1260	.1050	.0502	.0147	.0027	.0003
	14			.0002	.0079	.0499	.1111	.1189	.0715	.0260	.0059	.0008
	15			.0001	.0034	.0299	.0888	.1224	.0923	.0415	.0116	.0020
	16			.0000	.0012	.0164	.0648	.1147	.1088	.0606	.0207	.0044
	17				.0005	.0081	.0432	.0983	.1171	.0808	.0338	.0087
	18				.0001	.0038	.0264	.0772	.1156	.0987	.0508	.0161
	19				.0001	.0016	.0148	.0558	.1048	.1109	.0701	.0270
	20				.0000	.0006	.0076	.0370	.0875	.1145	.0888	.0418
	21					.0002	.0037	.0227	.0674	.1091	.1038	.0598
	22					.0001	.0016	.0128	.0477	.0959	.1119	.0788
	23					.0000	.0006	.0067	.0314	.0778	.1115	.0960
	24						.0003	.0032	.0189	.0584	.1026	.1080
	25						.0001	.0015	.0107	.0405	.0874	.1122
	26						.0000	.0006	.0055	.0259	.0687	.1080
	27							.0002	.0026	.0154	.0499	.0960
	28							.0001	.0012	.0084	.0336	.0788
	29							.0000	.0004	.0042	.0209	.0598
	30								.0002	.0020	.0119	.0418
	31								.0001	.0009	.0063	.0270
	32								.0000	.0003	.0031	.0161
	33									.0001	.0013	.0087
	34									.0001	.0006	.0044
	35									.0000	.0002	.0020
	36										.0001	.0008
	37										.0000	.0003
	38											.0002
	39											.0000

H

POISSON PROBABILITIES†

X	0.1	0.2	0.3	0.4	*m* 0.5	0.6	0.7	0.8	0.9	1.0
0	.9048	.8187	.7408	.6703	.6065	.5488	.4966	.4493	.4066	.3679
1	.0905	.1637	.2222	.2681	.3033	.3293	.3476	.3595	.3659	.3679
2	.0045	.0164	.0333	.0536	.0758	.0988	.1217	.1438	.1647	.1839
3	.0002	.0011	.0033	.0072	.0126	.0198	.0284	.0383	.0494	.0613
4	.0000	.0001	.0002	.0007	.0016	.0030	.0050	.0077	.0111	.0153
5	.0000	.0000	.0000	.0001	.0002	.0004	.0007	.0012	.0020	.0031
6	.0000	.0000	.0000	.0000	.0000	.0000	.0001	.0002	.0003	.0005
7	.0000	.0000	.0000	.0000	.0000	.0000	.0000	.0000	.0000	.0001

X	1.1	1.2	1.3	1.4	*m* 1.5	1.6	1.7	1.8	1.9	2.0
0	.3329	.3012	.2725	.2466	.2231	.2019	.1827	.1653	.1496	.1353
1	.3662	.3614	.3543	.3452	.3347	.3230	.3106	.2975	.2842	.2707
2	.2014	.2169	.2303	.2417	.2510	.2584	.2640	.2678	.2700	.2707
3	.0738	.0867	.0998	.1128	.1255	.1378	.1496	.1607	.1710	.1804
4	.0203	.0260	.0324	.0395	.0471	.0551	.0636	.0723	.0812	.0902
5	.0045	.0062	.0084	.0111	.0141	.0176	.0216	.0260	.0309	.0361
6	.0008	.0012	.0018	.0026	.0035	.0047	.0061	.0078	.0098	.0120
7	.0001	.0002	.0003	.0005	.0008	.0011	.0015	.0020	.0027	.0034
8	.0000	.0000	.0001	.0001	.0001	.0002	.0003	.0005	.0006	.0009
9	.0000	.0000	.0000	.0000	.0000	.0000	.0001	.0001	.0001	.0002

†Example: $P(X = 5 | m = 2.5) = 0.0668$.

Source: Business Statistics (Schaum's Outline Series) by L. J. Kazmier. Copyright by McGraw-Hill, Inc. Used with permission of McGraw-Hill Book Company.

X	2.1	2.2	2.3	2.4	*m* 2.5	2.6	2.7	2.8	2.9	3.0
0	.1225	.1108	.1003	.0907	.0821	.0743	.0672	.0608	.0550	.0498
1	.2572	.2438	.2306	.2177	.2052	.1931	.1815	.1703	.1396	.1494
2	.2700	.2681	.2652	.2613	.2565	.2510	.2450	.2384	.2314	.2240
3	.1890	.1966	.2033	.2090	.2138	.2176	.2205	.2225	.2237	.2240
4	.0992	.1082	.1169	.1254	.1336	.1414	.1488	.1557	.1622	.1680
5	.0417	.0476	.0538	.0602	.0668	.0735	.0804	.0872	.0940	.1008
6	.0146	.0174	.0206	.0241	.0278	.0319	.0362	.0407	.0455	.0504
7	.0044	.0055	.0068	.0083	.0099	.0118	.0139	.0163	.0188	.0216
8	.0011	.0015	.0019	.0025	.0031	.0038	.0047	.0057	.0068	.0081
9	.0003	.0004	.0005	.0007	.0009	.0011	.0014	.0018	.0022	.0027
10	.0001	.0001	.0001	.0002	.0002	.0003	.0004	.0005	.0006	.0008
11	.0000	.0000	.0000	.0000	.0000	.0001	.0001	.0001	.0002	.0002
12	.0000	.0000	.0000	.0000	.0000	.0000	.0000	.0000	.0000	.0001

X	3.1	3.2	3.3	3.4	*m* 3.5	3.6	3.7	3.8	3.9	4.0
0	.0450	.0408	.0369	.0334	.0302	.0273	.0247	.0224	.0202	.0183
1	.1397	.1304	.1217	.1135	.1057	.0984	.0915	.0850	.0789	.0733
2	.2165	.2087	.2008	.1929	.1850	.1771	.1692	.1615	.1539	.1465
3	.2237	.2226	.2209	.2186	.2158	.2125	.2087	.2046	.2001	.1954
4	.1734	.1781	.1823	.1858	.1888	.1912	.1931	.1944	.1951	.1954
5	.1075	.1140	.1203	.1264	.1322	.1377	.1429	.1477	.1522	.1563
6	.0555	.0608	.0662	.0716	.0771	.0826	.0881	.0936	.0989	.1042
7	.0246	.0278	.0312	.0348	.0385	.0425	.0466	.0508	.0551	.0595
8	.0095	.0111	.0129	.0148	.0169	.0191	.0215	.0241	.0269	.0298
9	.0033	.0040	.0047	.0056	.0066	.0076	.0089	.0102	.0116	.0132
10	.0010	.0013	.0016	.0019	.0023	.0028	.0033	.0039	.0045	.0053
11	.0003	.0004	.0005	.0006	.0007	.0009	.0011	.0013	.0016	.0019
12	.0001	.0001	.0001	.0002	.0002	.0003	.0003	.0004	.0005	.0006
13	.0000	.0000	.0000	.0000	.0001	.0001	.0001	.0001	.0002	.0002
14	.0000	.0000	.0000	.0000	.0000	.0000	.0000	.0000	.0000	.0001

X	4.1	4.2	4.3	4.4	*m* 4.5	4.6	4.7	4.8	4.9	5.0
0	.0166	.0150	.0136	.0123	.0111	.0101	.0091	.0082	.0074	.0067
1	.0679	.0630	.0583	.0540	.0500	.0462	.0427	.0395	.0365	.0337
2	.1393	.1323	.1254	.1188	.1125	.1063	.1005	.0948	.0894	.0842
3	.1904	.1852	.1798	.1743	.1687	.1631	.1574	.1517	.1460	.1404
4	.1951	.1944	.1933	.1917	.1898	.1875	.1849	.1820	.1789	.1755
5	.1600	.1633	.1662	.1687	.1708	.1725	.1738	.1747	.1753	.1755
6	.1093	.1143	.1191	.1237	.1281	.1323	.1362	.1398	.1432	.1462

					m					
X	4.1	4.2	4.3	4.4	4.5	4.6	4.7	4.8	4.9	5.0
7	.0640	.0686	.0732	.0778	.0824	.0869	.0914	.0959	.1002	.1044
8	.0328	.0360	.0393	.0428	.0463	.0500	.0537	.0575	.0614	.0653
9	.0150	.0168	.0188	.0209	.0232	.0255	.0280	.0307	.0334	.0363
10	.0061	.0071	.0081	.0092	.0104	.0118	.0132	.0147	.0164	.0181
11	.0023	.0027	.0032	.0037	.0043	.0049	.0056	.0064	.0073	.0082
12	.0008	.0009	.0011	.0014	.0016	.0019	.0022	.0026	.0030	.0034
13	.0002	.0003	.0004	.0005	.0006	.0007	.0008	.0009	.0011	.0013
14	.0001	.0001	.0001	.0001	.0002	.0002	.0003	.0003	.0004	.0005
15	.0000	.0000	.0000	.0000	.0001	.0001	.0001	.0001	.0001	.0002

					m					
X	5.1	5.2	5.3	5.4	5.5	5.6	5.7	5.8	5.9	6.0
0	.0061	.0055	.0050	.0045	.0041	.0037	.0033	.0030	.0027	.0025
1	.0311	.0287	.0265	.0244	.0225	.0207	.0191	.0176	.0162	.0149
2	.0793	.0746	.0701	.0659	.0618	.0580	.0544	.0509	.0477	.0446
3	.1348	.1293	.1239	.1185	.1133	.1082	.1033	.0985	.0938	.0892
4	.1719	.1681	.1641	.1600	.1558	.1515	.1472	.1428	.1383	.1339
5	.1753	.1748	.1740	.1728	.1714	.1697	.1678	.1656	.1632	.1606
6	.1490	.1515	.1537	.1555	.1571	.1584	.1594	.1601	.1605	.1606
7	.1086	.1125	.1163	.1200	.1234	.1267	.1298	.1326	.1353	.1377
8	.0692	.0731	.0771	.0810	.0849	.0887	.0925	.0962	.0998	.1033
9	.0392	.0423	.0454	.0486	.0519	.0552	.0586	.0620	.0654	.0688
10	.0200	.0220	.0241	.0262	.0285	.0309	.0334	.0359	.0386	.0413
11	.0093	.0104	.0116	.0129	.0143	.0157	.0173	.0190	.0207	.0225
12	.0039	.0045	.0051	.0058	.0065	.0073	.0082	.0092	.0102	.0113
13	.0015	.0018	.0021	.0024	.0028	.0032	.0036	.0041	.0046	.0052
14	.0006	.0007	.0008	.0009	.0011	.0013	.0015	.0017	.0019	.0022
15	.0002	.0002	.0003	.0003	.0004	.0005	.0006	.0007	.0008	.0009
16	.0001	.0001	.0001	.0001	.0001	.0002	.0002	.0002	.0003	.0003
17	.0000	.0000	.0000	.0000	.0000	.0001	.0001	.0001	.0001	.0001

					m					
X	6.1	6.2	6.3	6.4	6.5	6.6	6.7	6.8	6.9	7.0
0	.0022	.0020	.0018	.0017	.0015	.0014	.0012	.0011	.0010	.0009
1	.0137	.0126	.0116	.0106	.0098	.0090	.0082	.0076	.0070	.0064
2	.0417	.0390	.0364	.0340	.0318	.0296	.0276	.0258	.0240	.0223
3	.0848	.0806	.0765	.0726	.0688	.0652	.0617	.0584	.0552	.0521
4	.1294	.1249	.1205	.1162	.1118	.1076	.1034	.0992	.0952	.0912
5	.1579	.1549	.1519	.1487	.1454	.1420	.1385	.1349	.1314	.1277
6	.1605	.1601	.1595	.1586	.1575	.1562	.1546	.1529	.1511	.1490
7	.1399	.1418	.1435	.1450	.1462	.1472	.1480	.1486	.1489	.1490
8	.1066	.1099	.1130	.1160	.1188	.1215	.1240	.1263	.1284	.1304
9	.0723	.0757	.0791	.0825	.0858	.0891	.0923	.0954	.0985	.1014

X	6.1	6.2	6.3	6.4	*m* 6.5	6.6	6.7	6.8	6.9	7.0
10	.0441	.0469	.0498	.0528	.0558	.0558	.0618	.0649	.0679	.0710
11	.0245	.0265	.0285	.0307	.0330	.0353	.0377	.0401	.0426	.0452
12	.0124	.0137	.0150	.0164	.0179	.0194	.0210	.0227	.0245	.0264
13	.0058	.0065	.0073	.0081	.0089	.0098	.0108	.0119	.0130	.0142
14	.0025	.0029	.0033	.0037	.0041	.0046	.0052	.0058	.0064	.0071
15	.0010	.0012	.0014	.0016	.0018	.0020	.0023	.0026	.0029	.0033
16	.0004	.0005	.0005	.0006	.0007	.0008	.0010	.0011	.0013	.0014
17	.0001	.0002	.0002	.0002	.0003	.0003	.0004	.0004	.0005	.0006
18	.0000	.0001	.0001	.0001	.0001	.0001	.0001	.0002	.0002	.0002
19	.0000	.0000	.0000	.0000	.0000	.0000	.0000	.0001	.0001	.0001

X	7.1	7.2	7.3	7.4	*m* 7.5	7.6	7.7	7.8	7.9	8.0
0	.0008	.0007	.0007	.0006	.0006	.0005	.0005	.0004	.0004	.0003
1	.0059	.0054	.0049	.0045	.0041	.0038	.0035	.0032	.0029	.0027
2	.0208	.0194	.0180	.0167	.0156	.0145	.0134	.0125	.0116	.0107
3	.0492	.0464	.0438	.0413	.0389	.0366	.0345	.0324	.0305	.0286
4	.0874	.0836	.0799	.0764	.0729	.0696	.0663	.0632	.0602	.0573
5	.1241	.1204	.1167	.1130	.1094	.1057	.1021	.0986	.0951	.0916
6	.1468	.1445	.1420	.1394	.1367	.1339	.1311	.1282	.1252	.1221
7	.1489	.1486	.1481	.1474	.1465	.1454	.1442	.1428	.1413	.1396
8	.1321	.1337	.1351	.1363	.1373	.1382	.1388	.1392	.1395	.1396
9	.1042	.1070	.1096	.1121	.1144	.1167	.1187	.1207	.1224	.1241
10	.0740	.0770	.0800	.0829	.0858	.0887	.0914	.0941	.0967	.0993
11	.0478	.0504	.0531	.0558	.0585	.0613	.0640	.0667	.0695	.0722
12	.0283	.0303	.0323	.0344	.0366	.0388	.0411	.0434	.0457	.0481
13	.0154	.0168	.0181	.0196	.0211	.0227	.0243	.0260	.0278	.0296
14	.0078	.0086	.0095	.0104	.0113	.0123	.0134	.0145	.0157	.0169
15	.0037	.0041	.0046	.0051	.0057	.0062	.0069	.0075	.0083	.0090
16	.0016	.0019	.0021	.0024	.0026	.0030	.0033	.0037	.0041	.0045
17	.0007	.0008	.0009	.0010	.0012	.0013	.0015	.0017	.0019	.0021
18	.0003	.0003	.0004	.0004	.0005	.0006	.0006	.0007	.0008	.0009
19	.0001	.0001	.0001	.0002	.0002	.0002	.0003	.0003	.0003	.0004
20	.0000	.0000	.0001	.0001	.0001	.0001	.0001	.0001	.0001	.0002
21	.0000	.0000	.0000	.0000	.0000	.0000	.0000	.0000	.0001	.0001

X	8.1	8.2	8.3	8.4	*m* 8.5	8.6	8.7	8.8	8.9	9.0
0	.0003	.0003	.0002	.0002	.0002	.0002	.0002	.0002	.0001	.0001
1	.0025	.0023	.0021	.0019	.0017	.0016	.0014	.0013	.0012	.0011
2	.0100	.0092	.0086	.0079	.0074	.0068	.0063	.0058	.0054	.0050
3	.0269	.0252	.0237	.0222	.0208	.0195	.0183	.0171	.0160	.0150
4	.0544	.0517	.0491	.0466	.0443	.0420	.0398	.0377	.0357	.0337

					m					
X	8.1	8.2	8.3	8.4	8.5	8.6	8.7	8.8	8.9	9.0
5	.0882	.0849	.0816	.0784	.0752	.0722	.0692	.0663	.0635	.0607
6	.1191	.1160	.1128	.1097	.1066	.1034	.1003	.0972	.0941	.0911
7	.1378	.1358	.1338	.1317	.1294	.1271	.1247	.1222	.1197	.1171
8	.1395	.1392	.1388	.1382	.1375	.1366	.1356	.1344	.1332	.1318
9	.1256	.1269	.1280	.1290	.1299	.1306	.1311	.1315	.1317	.1318
10	.1017	.1040	.1063	.1084	.1104	.1123	.1140	.1157	.1172	.1186
11	.0749	.0776	.0802	.0828	.0853	.0878	.0902	.0925	.0948	.0970
12	.0505	.0530	.0555	.0579	.0604	.0629	.0654	.0679	.0703	.0728
13	.0315	.0334	.0354	.0374	.0395	.0416	.0438	.0459	.0481	.0504
14	.0182	.0196	.0210	.0225	.0240	.0256	.0272	.0289	.0306	.0324
15	.0098	.0107	.0116	.0126	.0136	.0147	.0158	.0169	.0182	.0194
16	.0050	.0055	.0060	.0066	.0072	.0079	.0086	.0093	.0101	.0109
17	.0024	.0026	.0029	.0033	.0036	.0040	.0044	.0048	.0053	.0058
18	.0011	.0012	.0014	.0015	.0017	.0019	.0021	.0024	.0026	.0029
19	.0005	.0005	.0006	.0007	.0008	.0009	.0010	.0011	.0012	.0014
20	.0002	.0002	.0002	.0003	.0003	.0004	.0004	.0005	.0005	.0006
21	.0001	.0001	.0001	.0001	.0001	.0002	.0002	.0002	.0002	.0003
22	.0000	.0000	.0000	.0000	.0001	.0001	.0001	.0001	.0001	.0001

					m					
X	9.1	9.2	9.3	9.4	9.5	9.6	9.7	9.8	9.9	10.0
0	.0001	.0001	.0001	.0001	.0001	.0001	.0001	.0001	.0001	.0000
1	.0010	.0009	.0009	.0008	.0007	.0007	.0006	.0005	.0005	.0005
2	.0046	.0043	.0040	.0037	.0034	.0031	.0029	.0027	.0025	.0023
3	.0140	.0131	.0123	.0115	.0107	.0100	.0093	.0087	.0081	.0076
4	.0319	.0302	.0285	.0269	.0254	.0240	.0226	.0213	.0201	.0189
5	.0581	.0555	.0530	.0506	.0483	.0460	.0439	.0418	.0398	.0378
6	.0881	.0851	.0822	.0793	.0764	.0736	.0709	.0682	.0656	.0631
7	.1145	.1118	.1091	.1064	.1037	.1010	.0982	.0955	.0928	.0901
8	.1302	.1286	.1269	.1251	.1232	.1212	.1191	.1170	.1148	.1126
9	.1317	.1315	.1311	.1306	.1300	.1293	.1284	.1274	.1263	.1251
10	.1198	.1210	.1219	.1228	.1235	.1241	.1245	.1249	.1250	.1251
11	.0991	.1012	.1031	.1049	.1067	.1083	.1098	.1112	.1125	.1137
12	.0752	.0776	.0779	.0822	.0844	.0866	.0888	.0908	.0928	.0948
13	.0526	.0549	.0572	.0594	.0617	.0640	.0662	.0685	.0707	.0729
14	.0342	.0361	.0380	.0399	.0419	.0439	.0459	.0479	.0500	.0521
15	.0208	.0221	.0235	.0250	.0265	.0281	.0297	.0313	.0330	.0347
16	.0118	.0127	.0137	.0147	.0157	.0168	.0180	.0192	.0204	.0217
17	.0063	.0069	.0075	.0081	.0088	.0095	.0103	.0111	.0119	.0128
18	.0032	.0035	.0039	.0042	.0046	.0051	.0055	.0060	.0065	.0071
19	.0015	.0017	.0019	.0021	.0023	.0026	.0028	.0031	.0034	.0037
20	.0007	.0008	.0009	.0010	.0011	.0012	.0014	.0015	.0017	.0019
21	.0003	.0003	.0004	.0004	.0005	.0006	.0006	.0007	.0008	.0009
22	.0001	.0001	.0002	.0002	.0002	.0002	.0003	.0003	.0004	.0004
23	.0000	.0001	.0001	.0001	.0001	.0001	.0001	.0001	.0002	.0002
24	.0000	.0000	.0000	.0000	.0000	.0000	.0000	.0001	.0001	.0001

UNIT NORMAL LOSS FUNCTION

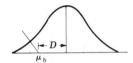

D	.00	.01	.02	.03	.04	.05	.06	.07	.08	.09
.0	.3989	.3940	.3890	.3841	.3793	.3744	.3697	.3649	.3602	.3556
.1	.3509	.3464	.3418	.3373	.3328	.3284	.3240	.3197	.3154	.3111
.2	.3069	.3027	.2986	.2944	.2904	.2863	.2824	.2784	.2745	.2706
.3	.2668	.2630	.2592	.2555	.2518	.2481	.2445	.2409	.2374	.2339
.4	.2304	.2270	.2236	.2203	.2169	.2137	.2104	.2072	.2040	.2009
.5	.1978	.1947	.1917	.1887	.1857	.1828	.1799	.1771	.1742	.1714
.6	.1687	.1659	.1633	.1606	.1580	.1554	.1528	.1503	.1478	.1453
.7	.1429	.1405	.1381	.1358	.1334	.1312	.1289	.1267	.1245	.1223
.8	.1202	.1181	.1160	.1140	.1120	.1100	.1080	.1061	.1042	.1023
.9	.1004	.09860	.09680	.09503	.09328	.09156	.08986	.08819	.08654	.08491
1.0	.08332	.08174	.08019	.07866	.07716	.07568	.07422	.07279	.07138	.06999
1.1	.06862	.06727	.06595	.06465	.06336	.06210	.06086	.05964	.05844	.05726
1.2	.05610	.05496	.05384	.05274	.05165	.05059	.04954	.04851	.04750	.04650
1.3	.04553	.04457	.04363	.04270	.04179	.04090	.04002	.03916	.03831	.03748
1.4	.03667	.03587	.03508	.03431	.03356	.03281	.03208	.03137	.03067	.02998
1.5	.02931	.02865	.02800	.02736	.02674	.02612	.02552	.02494	.02436	.02380
1.6	.02324	.02270	.02217	.02165	.02114	.02064	.02015	.01967	.01920	.01874
1.7	.01829	.01785	.01742	.01699	.01658	.01617	.01578	.01539	.01501	.01464
1.8	.01428	.01392	.01357	.01323	.01290	.01257	.01226	.01195	.01164	.01134
1.9	.01105	.01077	.01049	.01022	$.0^29957$ †	$.0^29698$	$.0^29445$	$.0^29198$	$.0^28957$	$.0^28721$
2.0	$.0^38491$	$.0^38266$	$.0^38046$	$.0^37832$	$.0^37623$	$.0^37418$	$.0^37219$	$.0^37024$	$.0^36835$	$.0^36649$
2.1	$.0^36468$	$.0^36292$	$.0^36120$	$.0^35952$	$.0^35788$	$.0^35628$	$.0^35472$	$.0^35320$	$.0^35172$	$.0^35028$
2.2	$.0^34887$	$.0^34750$	$.0^34616$	$.0^34486$	$.0^34358$	$.0^34235$	$.0^34114$	$.0^33996$	$.0^33882$	$.0^33770$
2.3	$.0^33662$	$.0^33556$	$.0^33453$	$.0^33352$	$.0^33255$	$.0^33159$	$.0^33067$	$.0^32977$	$.0^32889$	$.0^32804$
2.4	$.0^32720$	$.0^32640$	$.0^32561$	$.0^32484$	$.0^32410$	$.0^32337$	$.0^32267$	$.0^32199$	$.0^32132$	$.0^32067$
2.5	$.0^32004$	$.0^31943$	$.0^31883$	$.0^31826$	$.0^31769$	$.0^31715$	$.0^31662$	$.0^31610$	$.0^31560$	$.0^31511$
2.6	$.0^31464$	$.0^31418$	$.0^31373$	$.0^31330$	$.0^31288$	$.0^31247$	$.0^31207$	$.0^31169$	$.0^31132$	$.0^31095$
2.7	$.0^31060$	$.0^31026$	$.0^49928$	$.0^49607$	$.0^49295$	$.0^48992$	$.0^48699$	$.0^48414$	$.0^48138$	$.0^47870$
2.8	$.0^47611$	$.0^47359$	$.0^47115$	$.0^46879$	$.0^46650$	$.0^46428$	$.0^46213$	$.0^46004$	$.0^45802$	$.0^45606$
2.9	$.0^45417$	$.0^45233$	$.0^45055$	$.0^44883$	$.0^44716$	$.0^44555$	$.0^44398$	$.0^44247$	$.0^44101$	$.0^43959$
3.0	$.0^43822$	$.0^43689$	$.0^43560$	$.0^43436$	$.0^43316$	$.0^43199$	$.0^43087$	$.0^42978$	$.0^42873$	$.0^42771$
3.1	$.0^42673$	$.0^42577$	$.0^42485$	$.0^42396$	$.0^42311$	$.0^42227$	$.0^42147$	$.0^42070$	$.0^41995$	$.0^41922$
3.2	$.0^41852$	$.0^41785$	$.0^41720$	$.0^41657$	$.0^41596$	$.0^41537$	$.0^41480$	$.0^41426$	$.0^41373$	$.0^41322$
3.3	$.0^41273$	$.0^41225$	$.0^41179$	$.0^41135$	$.0^41093$	$.0^41051$	$.0^41012$	$.0^59734$	$.0^59365$	$.0^59009$
3.4	$.0^58666$	$.0^58335$	$.0^58016$	$.0^57709$	$.0^57413$	$.0^57127$	$.0^56852$	$.0^56587$	$.0^56331$	$.0^56085$
3.5	$.0^55848$	$.0^55620$	$.0^55400$	$.0^55188$	$.0^54984$	$.0^54788$	$.0^54599$	$.0^54417$	$.0^54242$	$.0^54073$
3.6	$.0^53911$	$.0^53755$	$.0^53605$	$.0^53460$	$.0^53321$	$.0^53188$	$.0^53059$	$.0^52935$	$.0^52816$	$.0^52702$
3.7	$.0^52592$	$.0^52486$	$.0^52385$	$.0^52287$	$.0^52193$	$.0^52103$	$.0^52016$	$.0^51933$	$.0^51853$	$.0^51776$
3.8	$.0^51702$	$.0^51632$	$.0^51563$	$.0^51498$	$.0^51435$	$.0^51375$	$.0^51317$	$.0^51262$	$.0^51208$	$.0^51157$
3.9	$.0^51108$	$.0^51061$	$.0^51016$	$.0^69723$	$.0^69307$	$.0^68908$	$.0^68525$	$.0^68158$	$.0^67806$	$.0^67469$

4.0	$.0^4 7145$	$.0^4 6835$	$.0^4 6538$	$.0^4 6253$	$.0^4 5980$	$.0^4 5718$	$.0^4 5468$	$.0^4 5227$	$.0^4 4997$	$.0^4 4777$
4.1	$.0^4 4566$	$.0^4 4364$	$.0^4 4170$	$.0^4 3985$	$.0^4 3807$	$.0^4 3637$	$.0^4 3475$	$.0^4 3319$	$.0^4 3170$	$.0^4 3027$
4.2	$.0^4 2891$	$.0^4 2760$	$.0^4 2635$	$.0^4 2516$	$.0^4 2402$	$.0^4 2292$	$.0^4 2188$	$.0^4 2088$	$.0^4 1992$	$.0^4 1901$
4.3	$.0^4 1814$	$.0^4 1730$	$.0^4 1650$	$.0^4 1574$	$.0^4 1501$	$.0^4 1431$	$.0^4 1365$	$.0^4 1301$	$.0^4 1241$	$.0^4 1183$
4.4	$.0^4 1127$	$.0^4 1074$	$.0^4 1024$	$.0^4 9756$	$.0^4 9296$	$.0^5 8857$	$.0^5 8437$	$.0^5 8037$	$.0^5 7655$	$.0^5 7290$
4.5	$.0^5 6942$	$.0^5 6610$	$.0^5 6294$	$.0^5 5992$	$.0^5 5704$	$.0^5 5429$	$.0^5 5167$	$.0^5 4917$	$.0^5 4679$	$.0^5 4452$
4.6	$.0^5 4236$	$.0^5 4029$	$.0^5 3833$	$.0^5 3645$	$.0^5 3467$	$.0^5 3297$	$.0^5 3135$	$.0^5 2981$	$.0^5 2834$	$.0^5 2694$
4.7	$.0^5 2560$	$.0^5 2433$	$.0^5 2313$	$.0^5 2197$	$.0^5 2088$	$.0^5 1984$	$.0^5 1884$	$.0^5 1790$	$.0^5 1700$	$.0^5 1615$
4.8	$.0^5 1533$	$.0^5 1456$	$.0^5 1382$	$.0^5 1312$	$.0^5 1246$	$.0^5 1182$	$.0^5 1122$	$.0^5 1065$	$.0^5 1011$	$.0^7 9588$
4.9	$.0^7 9096$	$.0^7 8629$	$.0^7 8185$	$.0^7 7763$	$.0^7 7362$	$.0^7 6982$	$.0^7 6620$	$.0^7 6276$	$.0^7 5950$	$.0^7 5640$

†The small numbers which appear as coefficients indicate the number of zeros immediately following the decimal point. For example, $.0^2 9957$ is the value .009957.

Source: Reproduced by permission of the copyright holders, The President and Fellows of Harvard College, from the Unit Normal Loss Integral table which appears as Table IV in *Introduction to Statistics for Business Decisions* by Robert Schlaifer, published by McGraw-Hill Book Company, New York, 1961.

INDEX